The Other Gujarat

The Other Gujarat

Takashi Shinoda

Popular Prakashan

Popular Prakashan Pvt. Ltd.
35-C, Madan Mohan Malaviya Marg,
Popular Press Bldg., Tardeo.
Mumbai - 400 034

First Published 2002

(3613)

ISBN 81-7154-874-1

PRINTED IN INDIA
By Jyoti Printery, 4/19, Milan Industrial Estate
Cotton Green, Mumbai-400 033
and Published by Ramdas Bhatkal for
Popular Prakashan Pvt. Ltd.
35-C, Pandit Madan Mohan Malaviya Marg,
Popular Press Bldg., Tardeo, Mumbai 400 034.

Contents

Part Two :
The Process of Polarization

Part Three :
Women's Issues

Preface

This book is the result of academic cooperation among researchers and social activists, who are interested in or associated with the social welfare of the weaker sections in Gujarat. Gujarat is a state of contrasts and contradictions. While good economic performance represents the brighter Gujarat, marginalization, segregation and invisibility of a large chunk of population, which has been left behind in the process of socio-economic development, represents its darker side.

The contrast has been historically moulded through class, caste and gender struggles. The book attempts to review Gujarat focusing on the weaker sections comprising of Scheduled Castes, Scheduled Tribes, Other Backward Classes and women.

We do not aim to emphasize only the backwardness of the weaker sections. Rather, we are more interested in highlighting the process of their social transformations, struggle for human rights and development, and identity issues. The merit of this book lies in this approach. The book also deals with the response of the upper castes toward the weaker sections, in order to analyse the nature of class structure in the state. We have thus tried to draw a comprehensive picture of the weaker sections in the society of Gujarat.

The book is in three parts. Part one deals with the mode of upward mobility among the backward classes as a socio-religious movement, struggle for social justice and unrest. Part two consists of papers highlighting the mode and process of class polarization and part three deals with issues of women who lag behind the mainstream of development. The intense struggle of the weaker sections, coupled with the various well meaning institutional reforms designed from time to time to empower their lot, does not seem to have improved their relative position vis-a-vis the upper strata. On the contrary, they seem to have been further marginalized in the course of the new economic policy. The Gujarat quake of January 2001 may accelerate this marginalization.

This book is not a direct outcome of the conference. Japanese researchers who had organized field surveys in Gujarat in the early 1990s took the initiative for its publication. Besides Junko Kiso, Tsuguo Nakasato and myself, Haruka Yanagisawa, Tokyo University, Pravin Visaria, Anil Gumber and BB Patel participated in the project, which was headed by Shinkichi Taniguchi, Hitotsubashi University, with the financial aid from the Ministry of Education, Japan. The joint project report entitled *Economic Change and Social Transformation in Modern and Contemporary South Asia,* was published by Hitotsubashi University in 1994, but it was for internal circulation only. For wider circulation of enlarged version, we invited new contributors through our network. In total, seventeen contributors responded. I am grateful to all of them.

I am deeply indebted to Achyut Yagnik, who suggested the main title of the book *The Other Gujarat.* This title is very compact and suggestive. One can catch the implications immediately. He has always been a source of inspiration for me. I am grateful to Anil Gumber who assisted me in editing the book at every stage. Without his cooperation, the book would not have been published. Also, my sincere thanks are due to Rakesh Basant, Indian Institute of Management, Ahmedabad and Sudarshan Iyengar, for their moral as well as practical support right from the outset. My stay in Ahmedabad has always been comfortable and exciting thanks to my friends. I have benefited enormously from Indira Hirway, Amita Shah, Jeemol Unni and Makrand Mehta.

Lastly, I have to mention two issues related to editorial arrangements. First is the name of caste, group or community. This is a very sensitive issue directly linked to their identity. Since this recognition is shared among contributors, I have not dared to unify the usage of these names. Second is related to the time gap between draft collection and publication. All the drafts reached me by 1998. But, it took many more years for publication. During this time gap, for example, the number of districts in Gujarat increased to twenty-five, and the provisional data of 2001 Census were released. We were not in a position to incorporate this new information in this book through it hardly affects our analysis. I would like to apologize to contributors and readers for the delay of this publication.

9-1-2002 **—Takashi Shinoda**

Introduction

Takashi Shinoda

1

Gujarat is one of the most successful states in India in terms of economic development. Its industrial structure is fairly diversified in commerce and manufacturing, resulting in a higher level of per capita income compared to other states in India. The share of urban population in Gujarat was 34.4 per cent in 1991 which is higher than India's average of 25.7 per cent. Gujarat also enjoys a relatively high literacy rate of 60.9 per cent against India's 52.1 per cent in 1991.

However, if we look at the lags and constraints hindering the much - needed progress of Gujarat, we come across a large number of people who are deprived of many welfare measures. As the Government of Gujarat itself admits, a large part of the area is backward, highly prone to droughts, floods, and scarcity of drinking water. Considerable regional variations are observed not only in the allocation of resources and production, but also in social, including educational indicators. Also, we notice that the benefits of economic growth have hardly percolated to the lower strata of society.

This book is the joint work of those sharing the view that the affluency of society is represented in the status of the weaker sections (WSs), who lag behind other mainstream communities/groups socially, economically, and politically, with common features such as marginalization, segregation, discrimination, neglect and invisibility. Out of many such segments of WSs which constitute the other Gujarat, we focus our attention on Scheduled Castes (SCs), Scheduled Tribes (STs), Other Backward Classes(OBCs), and women, taking into account their importance in population, political participation, degree of backwardness, and their role in regional integration.

The nature of backwardness among WSs has some similarity at the basic level, such as lack of resources and low level of income as economic indicators, and poor living environment and low level of education as social indicators. In the case of SCs there have to be added, the various forms of discrimination derived from untouchability. STs tend to be concentrated in backward areas, disadvantaged in social and economic terms. Unlike SCs and STs, OBCs have not benefited much from institutional reforms such as the reservation policy in Gujarat. They may also be considered to constitute a populous group which has not benefited from the economic growth. Women, particularly among the lower classes and in the backward areas, have suffered under the increasing pressure of marginalization in both economic and social life. Various aspects of the backwardness among WSs are examined, which provide us some clues to understand the mode and structure of the backwardness.

2

The term Gujarat is derived from the Gujjars who migrated from the north to the area under study in the medieval period. In the initial stage it meant the Gujjar Rashtra, the country where the Gujjars resided. However, with the formation and spread of the Gujarati language, the areas where Gujarati was intensively used was referred to as Gujarat.

Gujarat, already an important base for sea trade between the Arab world and South-East Asia before the arrival of the Portuguese in India, was one of the most commercialized regions in the Indian subcontinent. Diu and Surat prospered through the spice trade in the fifteenth and sixteenth centuries; Surat in particular was prized as a trading port by the Mughal Empire. In the sixteenth century, the Moguls seized Gujarat which then passed into the hands of the Marathas in the eighteenth century. The East India Company, which had achieved supremacy over the other European powers vying for a stake in India, concluded the Treaty of Bassein with the Maratha Gaekwad in 1803, thereby gaining a foothold in Gujarat. Until the middle of the nineteenth century the Company virtually ruled the entire area of Gujarat either directly or indirectly. Gujarat, which was part of the Bombay Presidency, consisted, for administrative purposes,

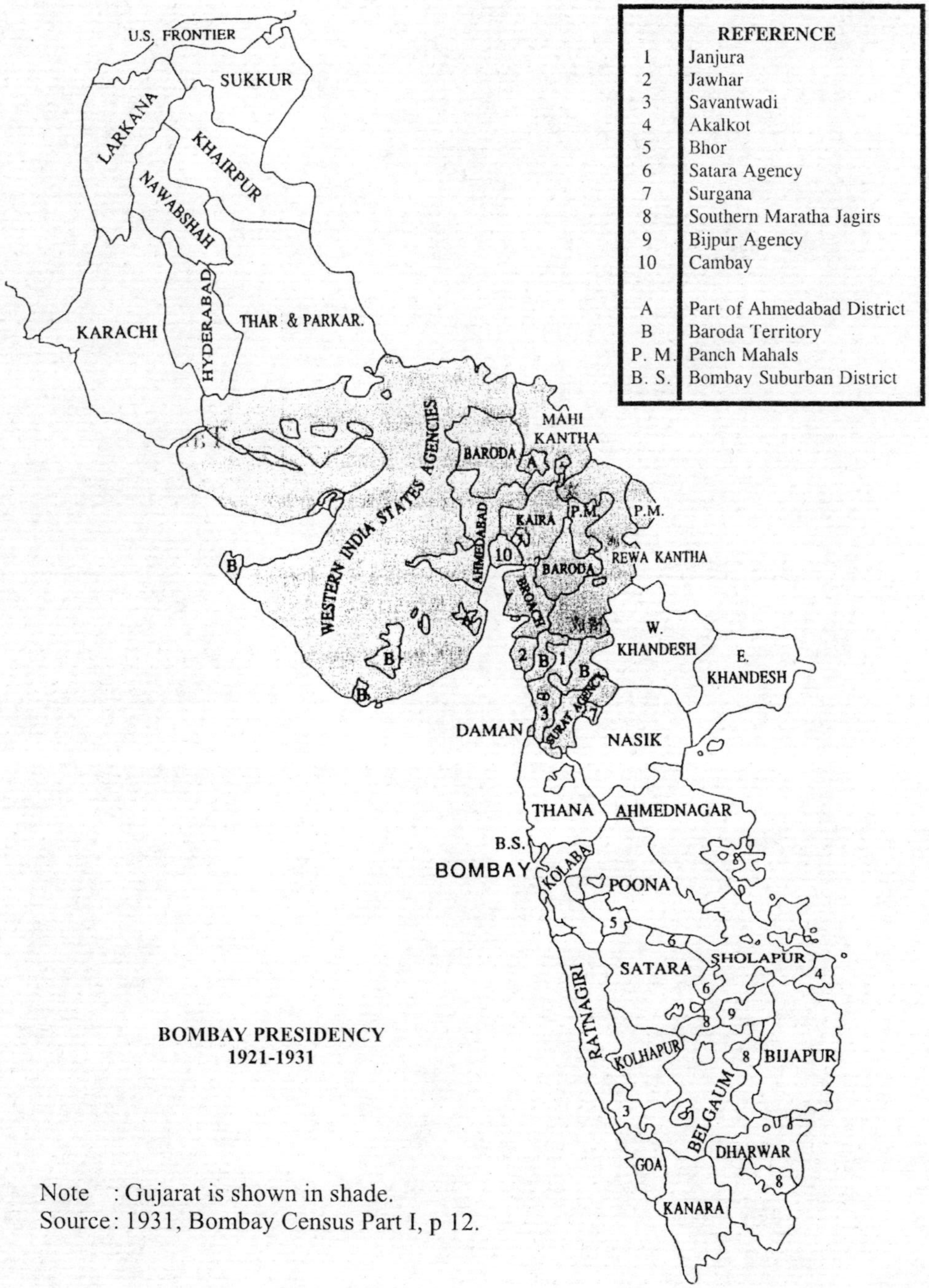

BOMBAY PRESIDENCY
1921-1931

Note : Gujarat is shown in shade.
Source: 1931, Bombay Census Part I, p 12.

of a British District, a State Agency, and a number of Princely States.

After Independence, these areas were integrated into the Indian Union in 1948. By the Indian Constitution of 1950, Saurashtra was classified as a 'B' state, Kutch as a 'C' state, while mainland Gujarat formed a part of the Bombay State in 1950. Following the setting up of the States Reorganization Commission of 1953, the Maha Gujarat Movement emerged in Gujarat for the formation of the Gujarat state with the inclusion of Bombay City and a part of the Thana district. The Movement could not fulfil its original purpose, and Saurashtra and Kutch were absorbed into the Bombay State in 1956 without separation on a linguistic basis. Finally, the Bombay state was bifurcated into Gujarat and Maharashtra in 1960; however, Bombay city remained with the latter.

Gujarat State consists of nineteen districts.[1] It may be divided into either two or five regions, based on common geographical and cultural factors. Gujarat can be divided into peninsular (Saurashtra and Kutch) and mainland Gujarat. The great Rann of Kutch stretches across the north part of Kutch. The peninsula has a curving coastline, which looks out onto the Gulf of Kutch, the Arabian Sea, and the Gulf of Khambhat (Cambay). It is connected to other regions by the harbours of Jamnagar, Porbandar, Bhavnagar, etc. Relatively free of Mughal and Maratha control, the region developed its own culture based on a large number of politically independent small and medium-sized kingdoms, collectively called Saurashtra. The mainland Gujarat itself is considerably different geographically from the peninsular region. In the east, a hilly area which runs north-south is the source of a number of rivers, which flow into the Gulf of Khambhat. The harbour towns of Khambhat, Bharuch and Surat played a very important role in the development of Gujarat. There are a number of inland cities, such as Ahmedabad and Vadodara, which greatly contributed to the regional growth in modern times. Though mainland Gujarat has far more variations than the peninsular region, it remains a well-defined area.

The five regions into which Gujarat is divided are Kutch (one district), Saurashtra (six districts), North Gujarat (three districts), Central Gujarat (five districts), and South Gujarat (four districts). North Gujarat is the most backward area of mainland Gujarat. Central Gujarat is the most developed area and is constituted of Ahmedabad, Kheda, and Vadodara districts, with a good balance of agriculture, industry and commerce. South Gujarat also has both agricultural and industrial bases. South Gujarat forms the granary of the state. The tribal population is concentrated in the eastern and southern part of the state and in those districts bordering Rajasthan, Madhya Pradesh and Maharashtra.

3

Here, we illustrate the salient features of castes in Gujarat,[2] based on the 1931 census. Out of the total 11.3 million population in Gujarat, Hindus shared 84.6 per cent, followed by Muslims (10.3 per cent), Jains (2.7 per cent), Christians (0.5 per cent) and Parsis (0.2 per cent) according to the 1931 Census. In the census, the Hindu population was classified into five groups; Advanced, Intermediate, Primitive, Other Backward, and Depressed Group, as shown in Table 1.

The advanced group was further divided into 'Brahmans: All Admissible Castes' and 'Other Advanced'. With the commencement of the census and classification of caste data, several petitions were submitted to the census office by caste organizations voicing concern about their own ranking or seeking a new ranking. Some of them sought to be considered as Brahmans. The census office made changes in the classification, if necessary. Hence the expression of 'Admissible'. Audich. Anavil, Moch and Nagar were populous castes among Gujarati Brahmans. They were spread over Gujarat, except the Anavil who were concentrated in south Gujarat. 'Other Advanced' consisted of Baniyas (Hindu Vaishnava) and upper class artisan castes. Populous Baniya castes were Shrimali, Porwad, and Lad, who mostly belonged to the Vallabhachari sect. Lohana and Soni were classified as 'Other Advanced'.

The intermediate group, most populous among the five groups, consisted of cultivator, nomad, and artisan castes. This group was understood to occupy the middle portion of the caste hierarchy, as the term itself suggested. However, the level of socio-economic development among the castes in this group was fairly high. Kanbi (Patidars), Rajput, Koli, etc. were the land owning castes belonging to this group. Ahirs and Bharwads were nomads, and artisan castes were Darji, Waland, Kumbhar, Lohar, Sutar, and Teli. Koli, nomadic castes, and some of artisan castes in this group formed the populous segments of OBCs, while Patidars emerged as the core of the upper caste alliance which has shaped the politics of Gujarat since the 1980s.

Table 1 : Hindu Population by Major Groups Across Regions of Gujarat, 1931

Region	Group						Total
	Advanced		Inter-mediate	Primitive	Backward	Depressed	
	Brahman	Other					
British District	123	89	1,686	369	90	210	2,567
	(4.8)	(3.5)	(65.6)	(14.4)	(3.5)	(8.2)	(100.0)
Princely State Agency	50	30	894	500	36	84	1,594
	(3.2)	(1.9)	(57.0)	(31.4)	(2.2)	(5.3)	(100.0)
Western State Agency	214	202	2,324	15	174	318	3,247
	(6.6)	(6.2)	(71.6)	(0.4)	(5.4)	(9.8)	(100.0)
Baroda State	124	87	1,373	312	53	203	2,152
	(5.8)	(4.0)	(63.8)	(14.5)	(2.5)	(9.4)	(100.0)
All Gujarat	511	408	6,277	1,196	353	815	9,560
	(5.4)	(4.3)	(65.8)	(12.5)	(3.7)	(8.5)	(100.0)
	[4.5]	[3.6]	[55.3]	[10.5]	[3.1]	[7.2]	[84.6]
Bombay Presidency	915	1,127	13,500	1,940	958	2,099	20,539
	(4.5)	(5.5)	(65.7)	(9.4)	(4.7)	(10.2)	(100.0)
	[3.5]	[4.3]	[51.4]	[7.4]	[3.6]	[8.0]	[78.2]

Notes :

1. The unit of population is one thousand.
2. Figures in parentheses refer to row percentages.
3. Figures in square brackets refer to percentages of total population including non-Hindu population.

Source :

Census of India 1931, Vol.8 Bombay Presidency,
Part 2, Vol.10 Western India States Agency, Part 2,
and Vol.19 Baroda, Parts 1 and 2, Bombay: 1931, 1933.

Table 2 : Religion/Caste Specific Population by Regions of Gujarat, 1931

Present Status	Religion/Caste Group	British District	Princely State Agency	Western State Agency	Baroda State	All Gujarat	
Advanced	Brahmans	123,426	50,167	211,184	123,714	511,491 (4.5)	(23.9)
	Lohanas	10,119	1,086	160,102	13,570	125,297 (1.1)	
	Sonis	15,513	3,880	32,628	12,145	64,163 (0.6)	
	Baniyas	62,784	25,433	62,909	11,486	192,612 (1.7)	
	Patidars	255,896	118,878	631,081	169,989	1,475,844 (13.1)	
	Jains	41,076	15,040	203,625	18,408	308,153 (2.7)	
	Parsis	14,359	1,352	871	7,127	23,709 (0.2)	
Intermediate	Rajputs	174,452	67,325	227,187	94,805	563,719 (5.0)	(38.6)
	Kolis	822,127	500,368	181,285	135,087	2,239,067 (19.8)	
	Artisan Castes	155,710	71,446	320,841	140,054	687,751 (6.1)	
	Other Intermediate	213,930	117,951	305,677	162,505	860,063 (7.7)	

Table 2 : (Continued)

Present Status	Religion/Caste Group	British District	Princely State Agency	Western State Agency	Baroda State	All Gujarat	
Backward	Nomadic Castes	63,560	19,052	298,264	70,915	451,791 (4.0)	(26.2)
	Backward Group	90,461	35,620	173,514	53,301	352,296 (3.1)	
	Depressed Group	210,147	63,916	318,223	203,043	815,326 (7.2)	
	Primitive/Tribes	485,363	525,936	15,572	357,071	1,383,922 (12.2)	
Others	Muslims	365,386	10,886	515,569	182,630	1,164,471 (10.3)	(11.3)
	Christians	42,596	3,351	1,396	7,262	54,605 (0.5)	
	Other Religious Groups	1,057	146	5,667	19,895	26,705 (0.2)	
	Total	**3,147,992**	**1,710,736**	**3,999,259**	**2,443,007**	**11,300,985 (100.0)**	**(100.0)**

Notes : 1. Caste grouping of 1931 Census is reorganized to adjust to the present status in consideration of socio-economic and political strength.

2. Figures in parentheses refer to vertical percentages.

Source : Same as in Table 1.

The term primitive group, used in the 1931 census, connoted Hindunized tribes. However, the demarcation between the lower Hindu castes and the primitive group was not clear, and the criterion of Hindunization was obscure. As a result, counting faced confusion. Major components of this group were Bhil, Chodhra, Dhodia, Dubla, Nakda and Talavia. The Bhils, most populous in this group, were regarded as most backward. The Dodias, the second populous, ranked high together with the Chodhras and the Naikda. This group largely corresponds to the social groups among the STs scheduled after Independence.

The other backward group consisting of Vaghri, Bairagi, Charan, Mochi, Khavas, Vanjari, etc., shared 3.1 per cent of all Gujarat population in 1931. The census office placed this group in between the intermediate group and the depressed group. Most of the castes in this group have been included in the list of OBCs in Gujarat.

The term depressed classes was first used by the British authorities in the late 1920s with the same meaning as "untouchables". This group consisted of such castes as Vankar, Chamar, Bhangi, Meghval and Garoda, etc. Vankar comprises more than half the population of this group, followed by Chamar and Bhangi. This group corresponds to SCs.

Table 2 gives the distribution of religion and caste population by region in Gujarat according to the 1931 Census. We have to put some reservations in assuming the present percentage share of caste population in Gujarat, based on the 1931 Census, because of some problems in classification and counting in the census. Also, demographic and other factors often work to change the size and even the entity of the castes. Yet, even with these factors in mind, we do get some idea about the strength of caste and caste group/alliances in comtemporary Gujarat.

4

Institutional reforms, particularly after Independence, played a very significant role in shaping the present social transformation. Most relevant institutional reforms, which have caused a lot of changes in the status of WSs, are the reservation policy, electoral system, land reforms, Panchayati Raj and poverty alleviation programmes such as the Twenty Point Programme.

The reservation policy was initiated during British rule; however, its development and implementation were realized by the proclamation of the Indian Constitution in 1950. The constitution drafted under the strong influence of Dr.B.R.Ambedkar, assured reserved seats to the historically discriminated groups in Parliament, higher educational institutions and government jobs. Out of the three categories of these groups manifested in the constitution, the government of India prepared a schedule for two categories and allotted 16 per cent of seats for SCs and 8 per cent for STs, while the Gujarat government allotted 7 per cent for SCs and 14 per cent for STs in proportion to their population in Gujarat.

Regarding the reservation for OBCs in Gujarat, the first commission formed in 1972, was chaired by A.N.Baxi, to fix the beneficiary group and to determine the contents of benefits. The Baxi Commission report, submitted in 1976, identified beneficiaries on the basis of caste. It identified 82 castes, and proposed 10 per cent reservation for colleges. Soon after the implementation of this policy, medical students started an anti-reservation agitation in 1980, demanding the abolition of reservation for OBCs. The agitation was suspended in April 1981, and the state government appointed a second commission chaired by C.V.Rane to evaluate the OBCs list of the first commission. The Rane Commision report of 1983 adopted income and occupation as criteria for the identification of beneficiaries, with an enhanced reservation of 28 per cent. The then chief minister, M.Solanki, announced just before the state assembly election of 1985 that 28 per cent reservation would be applied for the Baxi castes, which triggered fierce agitations and communal riots. The proposal has been put on hold.

Thus, the reservation policy for OBCs is very conservative in the light of the population of the lower classes in need of effective institutional measures. The total reserved seats, 31 per cent only, is smaller among major states. Yet, the policy as a whole has been working as one of the most important factors to shake the traditional caste class structure, in addition to achieving a greater politcal participation of these groups.

The institutionalization of universal suffrage assured WSs a new opportunity for active political participation. Today, the influence of a particular community over the number of voters is more important than the forwardness or backwardness of that community. The institutionalization of universal suffrage promoted a reorganization of leadership among backward communities and paved the way for political development of the populous communities.

A series of land reforms have also shaken the rural hierarchy to some extent. The land reforms initiated by the state government, though criticized as a law full of loopholes, certainly promoted land distribution among the lower classes.

The introduction of the Panchayati Raj in 1960, a major reform in rural administration after Independence, assured some segments of WSs participation in a three-tier system of local government; Village Panchayat, Taluka Panchayat, and Zilla (District) Panchayat. The Panchayati Raj institutions have been further empowered with the 73rd amendment of the Indian Constitution in 1992. Accordingly, Gujarat state revised its Panchayat Act in 1993. So far, the Panchayati Raj institutions have been handled by dominant castes, however, it is likely that the Panchayati Raj would encourage WSs more participation and power in the long run.

The Twenty Point programme, which was the centre of the campaign to eradicate poverty (*Garibi Hatao*), was instituted by Indira Gandhi (1917-1984) in 1975. This programme, which focused on WSs, was part of a policy to strengthen the support base of the Congress(I). The Programme revised in 1982 remains at the centre of the five-year plans of Gujarat.

5

In this process of social transformation both class-based and caste-based organizations developed. Caste associations were formed to uplift their social status by mobilizing their own resources for education and other social programmes. These associations also became a deciding factor in local, state, and parliament elections. Furthermore, caste federations with several castes of different social status emerged as a new force in the political arena. These organizations were active in forming political alliances with other backward communities to win the elections. This type of political alliance became very common after Independence.

A series of land reforms, though not thoroughgoing, have weakened the economic base of the traditional landlord class, particularly of the Rajputs, they have been soft toward the other upper castes. To cope with this new situation, the Rajputs, incorporating the populous

Kolis into their fold, formed the Gujarat Kshatriya Sabha in 1948, using the Kshatriyas as a flagship. This was a direct response to the introduction of universal suffrage. Because of the success of the strategy, SCs and the other lower classes also accelerated moves to identify themselves with the Kshatriyas.

The formation of the Kshatriya Sabha saw the beginning, in the post-Independence period, of alliances among the different castes. The WSs have developed political alliances for elections, using the advantage of their size of population. This alliance has been extended to Muslims, as is seen in the KHAM alliance, consisting of the Kshatriyas, Harijans, Adivasis, and Muslims. The KHAM alliance swept the state assembly election of 1980, and the Solanki government ruled Gujarat until 1985.

Already in the 1960s the political situation had become tense because of the rivalry between the Kshatriyas and the Patidars. From the middle of the 1970s to 1985, rivalry between the WSs' alliances and the upper caste alliances (Patidars, Baniyas, Brahmans) has occupied a central stage in politics. Apart from the elections, the clash between the two alliances took such a violent form as was seen during 1980 and 1985 anti-reservation agitations. Even before the resignation of the Chief Minister Madhav Singh Solanki, the KHAM alliance was on its way to collapse mainly because of internal factors. The growth of middle classes was a crucial factor to have promoted both polarization within own caste and tribe, and differentiation with other castes and/or social groups. In short, rivalry within WSs came to the forefront, which adversely affected the alliances.

There are considerable differences in the level of development among the various groups constituting the backward classes. Differences in social and economic conditions between SCs and STs are particularly conspicuous. Furthermore, there is a large difference in the educational and occupational structure among SCs and STs. According to the classification of the 1981 census, SCs are divided into thirty groups of which the most advanced are the Vankars and the Chamars, while among the forty groups of STs, the most advanced are the Dodiyas and the Chaudhris. The gap in the level of development between the advanced and backward groups among SCs and STs has been widening in recent years. They have benefited the most through reservation. As a result, underdeveloped groups openly insist on the removal of advanced groups from the schedule.

The advanced groups among SCs and STs began to recognize

that new commitment besides utilization of institutional reforms would be inevitable for their further development. Also, the anti-reservation agitations gave a shock to the SCs.

In response to these, the modern elite among the advanced SCs and STs have taken the initiative in networking their elite fellows, making their own media/journal, and forming class-based organizations in addition to caste associations. In this regard, the activities of the Vankar elites attract our attention. They started their monthly journal *Samaj Mitra* in 1987 (the *dalit* journal got a new momentum in the 1980s in Gujarat), and formed the Scheduled Castes Chamber of Commerce and Industry in Ahmedabad in 1993, jointly with the participants from the Chamar. The formation of the SC Chamber indicates their increasing power and aspiration. The Gujarat Vankar Sewa Samaj was formed in 1997 as a federal body to network regional Vankar Samaj in Gujarat. In 1997, a matrimonial directory was prepared for wider selection. Thus, their strategy for socio-economic development has not been much different from that of the Savarna elite.

However, the Vankar elite represents only a very minor segment of WSs. Majority of WSs particularly, women among the SCs, STs and OBCs, and those residing in backward regions, are badly affected by the imbalanced development of Gujarat. They are facing a crisis of further polarization and marginalization.

6

In this book, we have tried to trace how WSs have struggled for their human rights and development, and which type of new identity they are looking for besides examining various aspects of backwardness among WSs to understand the mode and structure of their backwardness. Also, in our effort to locate the position of the WSs in the social and political structure of Gujarat, we highlighted the response from the upper castes toward the WSs in the form of anti-reservation agitation and communal riots. Thus, we aim at presenting the overall picture of the WSs with due consideration to their dynamism and constraints, in the structural changes in Gujarat.

This book is divided into three parts based on the different types of social groups addressed by individual papers. Part one consists of papers analysing the status of backward classes, i.e. SCs, STs and OBCs. Part two includes papers dealing with the process of polarization and its effect on WSs in urban and rural Gujarat, while the papers depicting the situation on women constitute Part Three.

In Part One, we have highlighted the mode of upward mobility among the backward classes in the form of socio-religious movement, struggle for social justice, and unrest. Also, it is traced how the backward classes have been coping with the legal, institutional and economic development of Gujarat.

Self-identity and strategy for social development among *dalits* in Gujarat is quite different from their counterparts in Maharashtra, which has remained the centre of the dalit movement in India. Makrand Mehta, in his paper 'The Dalit Temple Entry Movements in Maharashtra and Gujarat 1930-48', examines the qualitative difference of the *dalit* movement between the two states by analysing the *dalit* temple entry movements, and attributes it to the nature of leadership generated by Gandhi and Ambedkar. He argues that the movement in Maharashtra was more radical and militant since Ambedkar inherited his Maharashtrian tradition like Phule's non-brahmin movement, and a military tradition among the Mahars, his own caste, since Shivaji's times. In other words, it was the movement by and for the *dalits*. While in Gujarat, the temple entry movement was countered by the Gandhian workers when it was about to escalate to a massive mill strike. Mehta sees the basic contradiction in the Gandhian propositions that encouraged the *dalits* for visiting the Hindu temples, but discouraged their Satyagrahas or legal action to achieve their temple entry. The annoyance of *dalits* in Gujarat has been partly rooted in their self-image which has been shattered under the strong influence of the Gandhian perceptions.

Social, religious and political movements among the *dalits* used to be tied up with their search for new identity, to escape from the stigma such as untouchability and to uplift their social position. Achyut Yagnik, in his paper 'Search for Dalit Self Identity in Gujarat', traces the variation of modes adopted by the *dalits* in their quest for self identity in the first half of this century. According to Yagnik, there are four distinct trends: (1) establishing caste organization and federation to institute a process of reform and seek higher social status by changing the caste name, (2) conversion (to Christianity), (3) transforming social movements into political ones (such as the movement for freedom), and (4) asserting self identity as *dalit*. The first three modes got momentum from the twenties, while the fourth started from the forties under the influence of Ambedkar. Yagnik points out that conversion to Christianity or Buddhism has never been attractive for the majority of *dalits* in Gujarat though conversion had some advantages, so the rest of the three modes remained as major ones for upward mobility.

After Independence the situation has changed drastically, and the upliftment of *dalits* has been seen largely as an administrative task and not as a part of social or political process. Actually the majority of *dalits* have been swept into the integrationist policy of the Congress which deployed caste based electoral politics. Though a segment of *dalits* benefited from institutional reforms such as reservation, they have hardly been united nor organized. Here, we observe a keen contrast with Patidars and Kolis who mobilized their own resources successfully to crystallize their 'Patel' and 'Kshtriya' identity. Yagnik sees this as the emergence of Savarna ideology.

Religious movement appeared as the most important mode for social development among the backward classes in Gujarat. However, unlike Patidars who could take the very powerful Swaminarayan sect, into their fold, the backward classes have faced much difficulty in developing themselves in this arena. N.R.Sheth in his paper 'A Spiritual Approach to Social Transformation', traces the impact of recent socio-religious movement known as *Swadhyaya* among the backward classes. *Swadhyaya* initiated by P.S.Athavale in the 1950s, aims at social transformation through action-based *bhakti*. The particular feature of *Swadhyaya* philosophy, according to Sheth, reflects in its belief that the individual can work as the most crucial variable in the action programme, and economic empowerment of the poor can be achieved without a direct attack on the affluence of the rich. The movement, which had a strong fold in Gujarat, has been supported by urban middle class *parivars* (followers) who regularly visit rural areas to set up study centres of self development, and to initiate creative community development. Since the seventies, special attention has been paid to the social transformation among a segment of disadvantaged groups such as the fisherfolk, Dungri Bhils, Vagharis and the *dalits*. However, '*Swadhyaya* could appeal to the relatively affluent and those among the non-affluent who can spare adequate time and energy on Swadhyaya work.'

Various institutional reforms constitute another important factor, which characterized the post-Independence development of the backward classes. Overall effects of institutional reforms for improving the position of the backward classes were considerable, though there were some constraints such as the under-utilization of reservation quota, and over-representation of beneficiaries from the upper strata of the targeted categories. At the same time, it is not deniable that a series of institutional reforms encouraged the backward classes to be more dependent on the state measures at the cost of strengthening their own associations. Takashi Shinoda, in his paper 'Legal, Institutional Development and Sweepers in Ahmedabad', focuses on the process and mechanism of how legal, institutional development has moulded the working and service conditions of sweepers over time, by the analysis of several awards set up for solving industrial disputes between sweepers and the municipality. In the case of sweepers, trade unions emerged as the major pressure group to solve their problems. However, the activities of trade unions were confined mainly to improve the service conditions of sweepers. Attention has hardly been paid to the issues related to their working conditions. His case study also shows that institutional reforms often lead the targeted group to dependency, stagnancy and retrenchment, unless the group had keen aspirations for mobilizing their own resources for the common goals of socio-economic and political development.

Adivasis outnumber the *dalits* in Gujarat. Though the Adivasis do not have the stigma of untouchability, they have been looked down by caste Hindus and humilitated systematically by the state apparatus. Their livelihood has long been confined to agriculture and forest produce mainly because they have been concentrated in hilly zones. Their society has experienced rapid changes in the recent years due to the penetration of market economy, the introduction of various development programmes, and 'the anti-people forest policy', resulting in further marginalization. Ghanshyam Shah, in his paper 'Unrest among the Adivasis and their Struggles', analyses various contemporary tribal movements in Gujarat with a view to highlight the major issues that Adivasis have raised, and the nature of their struggles. He classifies major issues into three: land rights, minimum wages, and tribal identity and self-rule. Though most Adivasis are engaged in agriculture, their land rights are not properly protected by the Government. Rather, the Government's forest and land policy has actually alienated Adivasis from their rights towards land and forest produce. In response to this, agitations and struggles were organized by Adivasis themselves or supported by NGOs, however, the struggles could never encompass all sections of Adivasis in Gujarat, due to emergence of socio-economic differentiation among the tribes and among the strata though their interests are not essentially antagonistic. As for their struggles and strategies for development regarding tribal identity, Shah identifies three schools of thought and political action such as developmentalist, culturalist, and tribal self-rule political activist, and concludes that unlike the Dalit Ambedkar movement, there is no overarching tribal ideology for tribal– non-tribal relationship, socio-economic relationship for production and distribution, political institutions and paradigm for development.

The Sardar Sarovar Project is one of the major development programmes which has directly affected the life of Adivasis. It is estimated that 245 villages will be totally or partially submerged in three states including Gujarat, and a little more than 15,000 families or about 80,000 persons are likely to be displaced. The weakest point of the project has been the resettlement and rehabilitation of the displaced Adivasi population. The project attracted worldwide attention, leading to a fierce debate between developmentalist and culturalist or environmentalist regarding the assessment of the project. Sudarshan Iyengar, in his paper 'Resettlement and Rehabilitation in the Sardar Sarovar Project: A Review of Policy Reforms and Implementation', points out how both developmentalist (planners and administrators) and culturalist (Morse-Berger and Narmada Bachao Andolan) have been biased in their framework and data-base, and concludes that the prospects for the resettlement and rehabilitation appear rather bleak. His arguments are based upon his own experience working as a member of ARCH-Vahini, an NGO entrusted with the task of resettlement and rehabilitation of the affected population.

Seasonal out-migration is very common among Adivasis inhabiting hilly regions in Gujarat. This is a consequence of unbalanced resource endowment and development between regions. Seasonal migration has acquired momentum over the last two decades, partly because of the decrease in the size of operational holdings, productivity and cropping intensity in hilly regions, and partly because of the increase in the demand for labourers for transplanting and harvesting crops in plain Gujarat where canal irrigation prevailed. Anil Gumber, in his paper 'Rural Development and Seasonal Migration in Gujarat: Pattern, Determinants, and Consequence', analyses the magnitude and determinants of seasonal migration among households displaced by the construction of a major irrigation dam in Panchmahals. He has discovered that incidence of seasonal mobility is higher among households with larger family size, smaller size of holding, low level of irrigation, cropping intensity and productivity. Furthermore, Gumber reveals that most of the households are living below poverty line in spite of a significant portion of income earned through seasonal migration. Thus, the overall picture of displaced households is that of stagnation and marginalization. A measure for improving the situation, he thinks is to utilise the Interstate Migrant Workmen's Act and divert resources to rural backward areas through rural industrialization and rural development programmes.

In Part Two, we have highlighted the mode and process of class polarization in urban and rural Gujarat. Two papers deal with urban issues and the other three papers on rural issues.

Gujarat experienced fierce communal riots in the eighties, which directly affected the life of WSs, particularly Muslims and the Backward Classes. The causes of the riots are deeply rooted in the political and economic transformation of Gujarat, a state which has been one of the most endemic to communal riots in India. Sujata Patel, in her paper 'Urbanization, Development and Communalisation of Society in Gujarat', explores the roots and implications of the communal riots in the local (Ahmedabad city), regional (Gujarat State) and country levels, and their interconnections. She argues that the power structure of Gujarat, dominated by upper castes till the sixties, has been reconstituted by the mobilization of the Kshatriya block, followed by the challenge from the emerging land-owning classes such as the farmers of Saurashtra who benefited from the green revolution, and by the challenge from the *dalits*.

Unlike as in the centre, the Congress in Gujarat was in a position to be able to mobilize the lower sections without incorporating the upper castes since the latter moved towards the Congress(O) after the split of the Congress in 1969. This resulted in the formation of the KHAM government between 1980 and 1985, which provoked a fierce and ruthless counterattack by the upper classes in the form of communal riots. She argues that the growing communalised politics fuelled the discontent among urban dwellers emerging as a result of structural changes both in production and urban organization. According to her, the decline of cotton textile industries and retrenchment of mill workers, the growth of an anti-social group which made money by illegal activities and emerged as a king maker, the use of the religious card by major political parties to gain support from the upper classes, and the gradual process of change in space and community identity, are major factors which resulted in the outbreak of riots. The seriousness of the riots lies not only in the breakdown of the political parties' legitimacy, but also in the collapse of hegemonic ideology among the WSs. She concludes that what is needed is another ideology which can regroup the various sections of society, until then the communal ideology would continue to inherit.

The factory workers in the organized sector, sharing only three per cent of total workers in India in 1991, have been relatively well organized, legally protected, and better in terms of service and working conditions than their counterparts in the unorganized sector. It is known that the bulk of factory workers had been recruited from the WSs in the early stage of industrialization. Junko Kiso, in her paper 'Factory Workers and their Mobility in Ahmedabad City', examines the social background of factory workers, their recruitment process, and the real condition of their internal and external mobility, with the aim of evaluating whether the factory labour market is functioning as a base for the transformation of society. She selected six factories of three different industries (textiles, engineering and chemicals), and of two different sizes (large and small factories), and conducted interviews from sample workers of different categories (managerial and clerical, technical, production, and contract workers). She finds that each category of workers is positively associated with caste ranking and the level of education. Also, the methods for job access for higher categories have been relatively formalized, while for production workers these continue to be on informal basis. Among the latter category, the informal network based on religion, caste or blood relations predominates over the other methods of recruitment, which restricts the entry of the bulk of job seekers who lack any personal connections. She also finds that the changing of jobs is the major form to gain upward mobility among the sample workers as promotion has hardly been institutionalized. Some sixty per cent of the sample workers have sometimes changed their jobs, but with more frequencies among the workers of upper castes and of upper categories. Since WSs have been recruited mainly as the workers of lower categories with many restrictions on their further development, it can be concluded that the factory labour market has not been functioning as a base for the transformation of society so far.

In the course of political and economic transformation in Gujarat, the WSs had to struggle in search of their new identity. This process has been painful and the new identity is yet to be moulded. At the other end, there have been considerable changes over time in the self-image among the upper strata of Gujarat society. Their perceptions towards the WSs have also changed since it represents the other side of the same coin. Mario Rutten, in his paper 'Elite Attitude Towards the Poor: Patidar Entrepreneurs in Rural Central Gujarat', explores how the self-image of the rural Patidar elite and its attitude towards the rural poor has changed. Interestingly, its self-image and behaviour towards the poor has been much influenced both by the political development in Gujarat, particularly in Kheda, and by the development of the entrepreneurship. According to him, social distance between the rural elite and the rural poor has been widening due to changes in labour relations, educational background, and residential location. The elite intensively uses contractors for the employment of farm and non-farm workers, and thereby depends less on its own family labour. Instead it prefers to send its children to reputed educational institutions in towns. It builds its new houses away from the original site, sometimes in towns. This new life pattern accords with its orientation towards upper caste-class solidarity beyond the village. They are more interested in regional and national issues particularly after the Kshatriyas started controlling the village panchayats. Since higher education is a very significant matter of its concern, it reacted fiercely against the reservation issues for OBCs. The rural elite views itself as the backbone for rural progress and stability, and considers the WSs as being major obstacles to future economic development. Therefore, according to them the WSs should be disciplined and kept firmly under control. Rutten concludes that these callous views about the WSs are common among the emerging middle classes whether in rural or urban India.

Gujarat experienced tremendous changes in its economic structure both in rural and urban areas since 1960s. A wave of green revolution, urbanization and commercialization has changed the rural scene especially in those areas endowed with better natural resources and infrastructural facilities. Kheda is one such district in Gujarat. Tsuguo Nakasato, in his paper 'Differentiated Diversification of Occupation in a Multi-Caste Village', depicts the changes in occupational structure among the WSs in a Kheda village between 1961 and 1991, with special reference to the influences of population growth, market-oriented farming, urbanization, education, and the dominance of the Patidars. Thus, his paper is closely linked with that of Rutten's. His finding shows a keen contrast regarding occupational diversification between the rural elite and the poor. While occupational structure among SCs, STs and OBCs has hardly been diversified during the thirty years, the dominant Patidars, with a stable base in agriculture, have ventured to cities and even to foreign countries to expand their socio-economic ties beyond the village. He also explores the idea that the Patidars firmly control the local labour market and other related issues, keeping the rural poor along the paternalistic line.

The recent industrial development in Gujarat has triggered a process of transformation among rural artisans, who had once been an integral part of village economies. Their fate is much of our concern because the majority of artisans belong to specific caste groups classified either as SCs (weavers and leather workers) or OBCs (carpenters, blacksmiths and potters) in Gujarat. A section of rural women are also engaged in traditional industries as full time or part time workers. Amita Shah, in her paper 'Changing Pattern of Rural Artisans in Gujarat: Need for a Fresh Policy?', analyses the major characteristics of changes in the structure of rural industries in recent years, and examines its implications for industrial policy. She observes a certain pattern of upward shift among the different size-segments in the unorganized manufacturing sector, and suggests a bi-polar structure whereby at the lower end, the small segment (without any hired labour) is getting transformed into the middle segment (employing 1-5 workers) and at the upper end, the large segment (employing 6-9 workers) is merging with the organized sector. Despite the upward shift, she argues, a large proportion of artisan-based activities still takes place in the small segment and in rural areas. She sugests a policy measure to promote clustering of rural artisans/industries and help them overcome their constraints like access to information, technology and infrastructural facilities through collective dynamism.

In Part Three, we have highlighted the issues of women, who constitute nearly half the population, but have been lagging behind the mainstream of development due to various constraints encountered in every sphere of their lives. Out of the three papers in this part, two papers deal with the recent economic and social aspects of women, while the other paper examines the old, but very contemporary issue of widows.

Despite the economic development, the overall performance in social development is not satisfactory in Gujarat. This is particularly because the development took place mainly in the areas endowed with favourable natural resources and infrastructural facilities. Thus, the development has benefited mainly advanced areas and upper strata of population, bypassing the vast backward areas and WSs including women. Indira Hirway and Darshini Mahadevia, in their joint paper 'Measuring Women's Development in Gujarat: Some Conceptual Issues and Empirical Results', examine the position of women in Gujarat not only in the economic field but also in social, cultural, political and environmental spheres, with due consideration to intra-state and regional variations. For this purpose, they elaborated their own Women Development Measure as an alternative to Gender Development Index and Gender Empowerment Index developed by UNDP, on the grounds that UNDP measures do not talk of social and structural capabilities of the women, having a strong bias in favour of the North. Their exercise depicts that women's development in Gujarat is more constrained by poor environment and ecology, less safety against violence, and wide regional disparities pose serious limits to women's development. Their conclusion is very critical to the narrow character of the economic growth in Gujarat which has worked against the development of women.

Women in rural areas are engaged in various economic activities besides their routine household work, though there are considerable variations among the classes and regions to which they belong. They play a key role, particularly among the poor households, in their survival strategies to make ends meet. Their role and behaviour is of keen concern in evaluating their contributions in the society. Jeemol Unni, in her paper 'Employment Status of Women in Gujarat in a Drought vs Normal Year', examines the differences in the mode of their survival strategies focusing on the employment status of women, between a normal year and a drought year and between an irrigated tract and a semi-arid dry tract of Mehsana district. She observes two types of employment strategies among the poor households in distress situations, that is, more participation of women and children as the visible work force, and an increase in the number of economic activities per worker. Actually, a large proportion of women have participated in a subsidiary activity as compared to men, irrespective of drought or tract. Thus, the role of women is crucial in maintaining the level of household incomes. Of course, the impact of drought was felt more severely in the semi-arid tract, and as her conclusion shows, the developed tract provided better opportunities for work to both men and women, while the villagers in the semi-arid tract were affected by severe underemployment.

In the course of the social reform movement in the nineteenth century, some issues on women evoked national concern. Widow remarriage was one such issue. Nearly one and half centuries have passed since the social reformers raised this issue. But widows, irrespective of their religion, are still being kept under various types of social restrictions on remarriage, property rights, employment, mobility and lifestyle, though there have been some changes in the mode of restrictions over time. Widows constitute the most marginalized segment among women. Varsha Bhagat-Ganguly and Amrita Shodhan, in their joint paper 'Shifting Perspectives on Widows' Issues in Gujarat', analyse critically the shifts in perspectives on widows' issues and their consequences and impact on the life of widows since the nineteenth century, and discuss the nature of problems with which widows, particularly among the lower classes face in contemporary rural Gujarat. According to them, widow remarriage was urgent only among the upper castes, while many other castes permitted in their caste constitutions not only widow remarriage but also property rights of widows over the first husband's property. The Hindu Widows' Remarriage Act of 1856, enacted without considering the practice of lower castes, had adverse effects on them because it disallowed the widows to retain their first husband's property. Despite a series of institutional reforms and government schemes for women after Independence, the issues of widows remain largely ignored both by the Government and the reformers, leaving widows in a multi-dimensional dilemma. Under these circumstances, remarriage is no solution for widows. As their survey reveals, an overwhelming majority of widows in rural areas are against remarriage for fear of further marginalization.

Thus, the overall picture of the other Gujarat, as illustrated in this book, is one of contrast and contradiction, despite the remarkable progress of its economy in the recent years. The case of Gujarat suggests to us that the trickle-down theory simply cannot be applied to the state and the country in India, where there are many factors hindering the percolation of developmental benefits. We are confirmed in our opinion that development will bypass the backward regions and backward communities, unless certain concrete and sensible measures are taken by the Government and the people. Already seven years have passed since the introduction of the new economic policy of 1991. By now, the new policy has not shown any favourable impact on the development of WSs, partly due to its failure in safety net schemes to safeguard the life of WSs, as well as due to its harsh nature where it has narrowed the life basis of WSs by restricting miscellaneous customary rights such as on land and in forest products which WSs have enjoyed so far. Furthermore, the economic crisis of Asia which has encompassed most of the East and South-East Asian countries, is about to cast a dark shadow on India. For several years to come, there will not be much change in the macro situation. WSs will be forced to face a tougher time in a crisis of further marginalization.

Notes

1. As mentioned in the preface of this volume, the current number of districts in Gujarat is twenty-five.

2. Sections 3 and 4 are based on the following works.

Shinoda, Takashi. 'Religion and Caste Groups in Gujarat, India : An Analysis of the 1931 Census,' (in Japanese) *Bulletin of Daito Bunka university* (March 1994) : 201-232.

————. 'Castes and Occupations in Gujarat, India : An Analysis of the 1931 Census', (in Japanese) *Bulletin of Daito Bunka University* (March 1995) : 81-105.

————. 'Entrepreneurs and Castes in Gujarat, India : An Analysis of the Member List of the Gujarat Chamber of Commerce & Industry,' (in Japanese) *Bulletin of Daito Bunka University* (March 1996) : 47-79.

————. *Indono Seisonin Kasuto Kenkyu* (A Study on the Status of Sweepers in India). Tokyo : Shunjushya (in Japanese), 1995.

1

The Dalit Temple Entry Movements in Maharashtra and Gujarat, 1930-1948

Makrand Mehta

Perhaps the most enduring feature of Indian civilization is its capacity to reshape India without causing violent upheavals and conversions. The history of the Indian dissent and protest movements shows that the codes of religious and social conduct as propounded by theologians and religious seers met with challenges at different periods of time. The medieval bhakti saints coming from low castes protested against the brahminical ritual and its hierarchical social order. Although the protest was *emotional* in essence, its social content showed that the medieval *sufis* and *sants* were painfully aware that the existing social and religious norms were oppressive and should be replaced by more humane and liberal cultural norms. In modern times the Western impact enabled Indians to articulate the problems of Indian Society, particularly the problems of untouchability, with a broader and sharper perspective. Cultural issues got crystallized when in the twentieth century, individuals like Gandhi and Ambedkar organized people within their fold, for mass action. Holding different ideologies, these people fought for the right of the *dalits* to use water, roads, public transport and educational institutions. They also fought for their right to enter Hindu places of worship. Thus their approaches become a significant point of enquiry. Taking into account the actual in this paper, how these movements took place, how they grew, reached their zenith, and eventually declined. The focus is on the Satyagrahas which took place at Nasik (Kalaram temple, 1930) and Ahmedabad

(Swaminarayana temple, 1948). I have argued that the Maharashtra Satyagraha was more militant and radical than its Gujarat Counterpart. I have used terms like Harijan, *dalit*, *atishudra*, Untouchable and Bhangi for historical reasons.

The Kalaram Satyagraha was directly organized by Ambedkar. The Swaminarayana Satyagraha was organized by Gandhian grass root workers, local Congress leaders and the Majur Mahajan Sangh (Textile Labour Association). The TLA was founded by Mahatma Gandhi in 1920. In order to understand the distinct character of these movements for cultural freedom and social justice, it is necessary to understand the nature of leadership generated by Gandhi and Ambedkar.

Gandhi

Gandhi's ideological norms provide an insight into the scale and intensity of the Swaminarayana temple entry Satyagraha. In his autobiography, Gandhi mentions that not only is the concept of Satyagraha different in many respects from passive resistance but that it was he who developed and applied the philosophy of Satyagraha in South Africa.[1] He also gives reasons for his decision to settle down in Ahmedabad after he returned from South Africa in December 1914. This was because the indigenous business culture and the concomitant pragmatic and conciliatory values which Ahmedabad had evolved over the past few centuries conformed to his own way of thinking. Although a modern textile city, Ahmedabad had nurtured her traditional norms in the process of transformation. Gandhi wanted to utilise this business-like tradition in trying out his experiments and in generating new trends in the early years of his career in India.[2]

Gandhi was very different in aspirations and behaviour from his political and cultural predecessors like Ranade, Swami Vivekanand, Dayanand Saraswati, Gokhale and Tilak. He affected the rhythm of history, the very foundation of the middle class tradition, by his disruptive-innovative activities.[3] Taking a long-range civilizational view of Indian history Ravindra Kumar observes:

> The gulf between the middle and the subaltern classes was breached by Mohandas Karamchand Gandhi, a political actor of truly epic proportions, who is widely regarded as the most significant figure in the struggle for liberation within India, Gandhi rejected the ideology of liberalism as the possible basis of a broad based nationalism within India. Instead, he drew upon moral power of the renouncer within Indian Society; just as he also drew upon the availability, within the Indian tradition, of per suasion through truth and self-suffering as instruments of social action.[4]

But this was not all. Gandhi's genius lay in his ability to interpret and bring down scriptural idea and injunctions to the realm of personal and social morality. He would not accept any religious injuction unless it stood the acid test of morality and justice. It was his moral strength which enabled Gandhi to attack the very core of Hinduism, namely, untouchability. He declared that he would cease to be a Hindu the moment it was established that untouchability was an integral part of Hinduism. It is again significant that unlike Swami Dayanand, Gandhi drew his strength not from the *Vedas* (the elitist source), but from the populist literature-the *puranas* and *smritis, akhyanas,* mythology, and folk tales. At the same time he preached the ideal of *seva*. Probably the operative part of seva as manifested in the Satyagraha, *tragu,* and *risaamanu* techniques (temporary severing of relations with friends and goverment to emphasize one's grievance), was Gandhi's greatest contribution to the socio-cultural and political integration of India. The ultimate goal of Hinduism is personal salvation, not social service. Gandhi's concept of *seva* was thus an act of innovation. Its implementation was no less innovative.[5]

This together with Gandhi's ability to integrate various strands of his personality with the traditional cultural norms[6] and his identification with the teeming millions whom he called *daridranarayana* enabled him to bring together reformers of all categories under one common umbrella. He attracted the younger generation of Western-educated intellectuals like G.V. Mavalankar, Indulal Yagnik, Kanailal Munshi, Shankarlal Banker, Mithuben Petit, Ansuyaben Sarabhai, and Kishorlal Mashruwala to his fold. He also attracted a large number of people like Ravishankar Maharaj who relied on traditional norms to transform Indian society. To Gandhi class and *varna* were not a great inhibiting factor in the process of social integration. The Majur Mahajan Sangh was based on the principles of class collaboration.

Ambedkar

Ambedkar was an untouchable from a Maharashtra village. He inherited the Maharashtrian and caste tradition, which differed strikingly from the one which prevailed in Gujarat. For instance Jyotiba Phule (1827-90) launched a mass movement against the orthodox forces of Maharashtra. Belonging to the *mali* caste he gathered together a large number of *dalits, sudras,* peasants, and even the Kshatriyas under his organizational fold — the *satyashodhak samaj* founded by him in 1873. Phule's non-brahmin movement got strength from the *Bahujan Samaj* and this turned out as a cultural revolt against the *varna* system in general and untouchability in particular. Ambedkar was using the *satyashodhak samaj* metaphors and idioms when he made statements such as 'the Congress is dominated by the *shethjis* and *bhatijis*'.[7]

Ambedkar belonged to the Mahar caste. The Mahars are spread in almost every village of Maharashtra. Their traditional place in the village community was as *balutedar* or *watandar* a village servant whose duty was to the village and whose recompense (*baluta* or gift in kind, and *watan* or land) came from the village. The Mahar *balutedar's* duties included arbitrating in boundary disputes, acting as village watchmen, sweeping the village roads, calling landowners to pay land revenue, guarding the government treasury, and tracking thieves to the neighbouring villages. But this was not all. They also seemed to have had a military tradition at least since Shivaji's times. The Mahars had served Shivaji as guards in the hill forts and soldiers in the artillery.[8] Ambedkar was himself born (1891) in the military camp at Mhow near Indore in the present Madhya Pradesh. Probably basing his belief on the army experience of his ancestors and giving credit to the British military system, Ambedkar declared :

> Until the advent of the British, the untouchables were content to remain untouchables. It was a destiny preordained by the Hindu God and enforced by the Hindu state.... Fortunately or unfortunately, the East India Company needed soldiers for their army in India and it could find none but the untouchables.... In the army of the East Indian Company there prevailed the system of compulsory education for Indian soldiers and their children, both male and female. The education received by the untouchables in the army gave them a new vision and a new value. They became conscious that the low esteem in which they had been held was not an inescapable destiny but a stigma imposed on their personality by the cunning contrivances of the priest. They felt the shame of it as they never did before and were determined to get rid of it.[9]

This shows that Ambedkar breathed a tradition different from Gandhi. This together with his bitter experiences during the childhood and the formative years of his career and also his education in the United States and England sharpened his views on the Hindu religion, culture and civilization. He expressed his militancy by giving shocks to the nationalist struggle against the imperial rule. It is true that he did not have as many listeners as Gandhi had, but he certainly made his presence felt. The Mahan Satyagraha (1927), launched by him to assert the right of the untouchables to use public tanks and his burning of the *Manusmruti* (1927), are too well known to be mentioned in detail. This was followed by the Parvati temple Satyagraha in Pune.[10] My point is that unlike Gandhi, Ambedkar strongly belived that the root cause of untouchability was the caste and the *varna* system. Ambedkar may sometimes, have been obsessed with this, but he felt intensely that unless the caste and the *varna* hierarchy was abolished tooth and nail, mere provocations or adjustments here and there, based on the business-like, pragmatic considerations, would be of little or no avail.

Gandhi was a mighty person indeed, and it was difficult to challenge him. Ambedkar's response to Gandhi and the Gandhian cultural and political movements was thus an act of the tragic and challenging *no.* His Satyagraha technique was more militant in character. This leads us to understand the nature of the Kalaram temple Satyagraha.

2

The time and the place selected by Ambedkar showed that he wanted to draw the public attention to his Satyagraha. The Kalaram Satyagraha ran parallel with Gandhi's Civil Disobedience Movement. While Ambedkar's aim was social justice, Gandhi's plank was political freedom.

The Kalaram temple is situated in Nasik, about 150 k.m. from Bombay. Nasik is a city of temples and priests, and is revered by the Hindus as 'the Kashi of the South'. Its total population in 1901 was 21490 including 1300 families officiating as priests of the hereditary supporters (*yajman*) and the pilgrims. They were well off, 'living in large houses, able to save, and occasionally lending money'.[11] The Mahars who lived in Nasik swept streets, worked as watchmen, and did other odd jobs.

Nasik, a place of great antiquity, lies on both the sides of the river Godavari. The sanctity of the Godavari and the popular belief that Rama lived here with Sita and Lakshman for some time has attracted Hindu pilgrims to Nasik for many centuries. The sacred settlement of the Panchvati on the east bank of the river, the *sati ghat* (where the *sati* ceremony was performed), Rama kund, Lakshman bridge, Sita gupha (cave), Sunder Narayana temple, the Balaji and the Nilkantheshwar temples, and above all, the Vithoba temple, has captured the imagination of innumerable Hindu pilgrims.[12]

The most magnificent temple in Nasik is the Ramji or the Kalaram temple. It is supposed to stand on the spot where Rama lived during his fourteen-year exile. According to the inscription it was built in 1782 by Sardar Rangrao Odhekar at a cost of Rs. 23 lakh. *The Bombay Gazetteer* published in 1883 gives the following description of the Kalaram temple :

> The Ramji or the Kalaram temple is in the centre of a large space enclosed by arched cloisters. To the east of the main building is a handsome assembly hall, which with the simple and massive masonry of the temple make one of the handsomest modern buildings in Western India. At about 200 yards north-east of Ramji's temple is Sita Gumpha or Sita's cave, an underground shrine, and a few yards to the north are some old banyan trees which are believed to represent the five banians from which Panchvati took its name.... In the shrine in the West of the temple, on a beautifully carved platform, stand images of Ram, Lakshman, and Sita, of black stone about two feet high. The image of Ram has gold mustaches and golden gloves.[13]

Nasik and its temples have always been held in great reverence by the Hindus. Any attempt to destroy the Kalaram temple, the most precious of all would have invited disaster.

3

The Kalaram Satyagraha did not take place suddenly. Ambedkar and his associates had visualized it as a long term campaign. It would be wrong to think as Keer, Kuber, Kamble, and Shahare have suggested that this movement was restricted to the Mahars.[14] The Mahar activists were of course there. The Satyagraha had also the moral support of the rationalists who had founded the anti-priest craft league in January 1930. But the newspaper reports highlighting the day-today incidents, show beyond doubt that the demonstrators also included Chamars like Shivarkar, and P.N. Rajbhoj, and Bhangis like Shivram Pala. A striking feature of the Satyagraha was the presence of about 500 women demonstrators who were trained in gymnastics.[15] Their group photograph enclosed in this paper serves as fascinating visual aid.[16] Women were given special status in the *Mahila Satyagraha Samiti*, the other committees being the Social Equality League, *Prachar Samiti*, and *Samanya Samiti*. The leading *dalits* like Patitapavandas, Shivarkar, Chokhabuva, Bagul, Tulsiram Kale, and Shivram Pala had made contact with the rural folk before the Satyagraha took place.[17] We shall now briefly describe the main incidents of the Satyagraha.

Ambedkar reached Nasik on 2 March 1930, going straight to the Maharwada. According to the newpaper reports about 10,000 Mahars, Chamars, and Bhangis received him there. They organized a rally on the same day but when they reached near the Kalaram temple, they found that an armed force under the British police official, Gordon, was protecting the temple.[18]

The next day a large number of municipal scavengers, the Bhangis as they were called, struck work. This added a new dimension. The *Bombay Chronicle* notes on 12 March : 'The strike by the municipal scavengers has created the problem of health and hygiene'. The municipal notices on the Bhangis to return to work fell on deaf ears. *The Gujarat Mitra* published from Surat reported on 9 March :

> A great Satyagraha and that too in a sacred place of pilgrimage abounding orthodox brahmins has taken place. About 15000 untouchables have gathered together in Nasik. Mahar females led the procession in military form. God Kala Rama had to be locked up probably against the unexpressed wish of the of the deity. The police and the officers must have had an anxious day for orthodoxy. Orthodox brahmins were so incensed that Satan tempted them to stone the wicked Satyagrahis. We pity their lot.

The Satyagraha became more aggressive in April. This was because the police gave harsh treatment to the demonstrators, including physical violence. The Hindus of Nasik district went to the extent of expelling the children of the untouchables from schools, closing the roads to them and not allowing them even to buy articles of their daily needs from the local markets.[19] Although the Shankaracharya Dr. Kurtakoti made honest attempts to pacify the upper-caste Hindus, they did not listen to him. For instance the *Bombay Chronicle* 4 April 1930, flashed the news of under the heading : 'Untouchables Triumph' and stated : 'Nasik orthodoxy has been outwitted. Hundreds of untouchables rushed to the temple and proclaimed their presence inside it with the cries 'Satyagrahis Jay.'

The Satyagraha took a violent turn on 9 April. This was *Ramnavmi* day, and according to a well-established tradition, the day of the Chariot procession carrying the image of Rama. Fortunately enough, a compromise was arrived at between the caste Hindus and the untouchables, to pull the Chariot together. But before the untouchables could hold a rope in their hands, the caste Hindus pushed them back and ran away with the Chariot, through a narrow street which was carefully guarded by armed police. The *dalits*, however, included gymnasts. They broke the police cordon and in a moment, crowds of untouchables pursued the Chariot amidst showers of stones. They empowered the *Savarnas* and captured the equipment. This was naturally followed by a bitter fight between the Satyagrahis and the caste Hindus.[20] The pious Ramnavmi day of 9 April turned out to be a disadvantage to the untouchables.

This was followed by another significant incident. S.C. Odhekar, one of the trustees of the Kalaram temple and the descendant of Sardar Rangrao Odhekar, the founder of the temple, declared that it was the private property of his family and that the untouchables had no legal right to enter it without the permission of the trustees.[21] He even tried to bring a legal injunction against the Satyagraha. But the *dalit* masses did not pay any bid to it. On the contrary, they seized the temple, and according to *Kesri*, during the confrontation which followed, a Mahar woman slapped Raghunath Ganesh, the priest of the temple.[22] In a literary sense this was a symbol of the centuries - old frustration and anger of the *dalits* and the subalterns.

Mahatma Gandhi who had been guiding the civil disobedience movement was watching the Kalaram Satyagraha with mingled anxiety. He had remained calm and quiet, but now he broke silence, to declare in his *Young India* :

> Take the disgraceful Nasik Quarrel... It has been stated that I am sacrificing the interest of the untouchables for the sake of Swaraj without the removal of untouchability. But what I do feel is that without Swaraj there will be neither communal unity nor removal of untouchability. He who runs may see that it is to the interest of the ruling caste (British people) to keep up the divisions among us. That caste is no more interested in Hindus and Musalmans coming together than in the removal of untouchability... Now a word to the 'untouchables'. I have advised them and I repeat the advice that it is wholly unnecessary for them to seek to force entry into the orthodox temples even through the method of Satyagraha. It is the duty of the 'touchable' Hindus to secure for the 'untouchables' to offer Satyagraha when the time is ripe... If they realize the truth of the statements I have made, they will at least suspend the (Kalaram) Satyagraha pending the struggle even if the whole mass of them will not join it as some of them have already done.[23]

The Satyagrahis, however, did not listen to Gandhi's advice. They prolonged their agitation. For example, they held a mass rally on 15 March 1931. As the caste Hindus threw stones at it, the *dalits* responded in the same manner. The Satyagraha was resumed in January 1923 but the Government arrested Dadasahab Gaekwad, Amritrao Rankhambe and other leaders in April. The Campaign, thereafter, died down without solving the issue in any tangible way. But it was the longest and the largest ever Satyagraha in a celebrated place of pilgrimage.[24] It certainly created a sense of awareness among the urban and the rural *dalits* that the plank of cultural freedom and social equality was as much relevant as political freedom, and they must fight to achieve their objectives.

We shall now turn to the Swaminarayana temple entry Satyagraha. Although the Harijans lauched a movement in other places of Gujarat also, our focus will be on the Swaminarayana temple.

4

The Swaminarayana sect has become powerful today in terms of numerical strength and money. Having temples in Gujarat and also in the United States and the European Countries, the sect has a following of about three million persons. An American student is currently studying the performance of the students following this sect. Her hypothesis is that they fare better in schools and colleges than the rest of the Gujarati students.

The Swaminarayana sect which had 3.21 lakh followers in 1872, emerged in the early part of the nineteenth century as a splinter group of Vaishnavism. It was started in the early nineteenth century by Sahajanand Swami (1781-1830), a brahmin belonging to Chhapiya, a village very close to Ayodhya. He started performing miracles and brought his subjects to a state of trance. This attracted the rural folk in increasing numbers. But this was not all. Sahajanand was a charismatic teacher and leader and he used simple Hindi and Gujarati to communicate with the masses and popularised Krishna worship. As he pacified the unruly Bhils and Kolis and also fought against *sati* and female infanticide, he was respected by the British who were then establishing law and order in Saurashtra. Soon he came to be regarded as an incarnation of Krishna. Bishop Reginald Heber met him in 1825 with a view to converting him to Christianity. But he was disappointed when the Swami calmly told him that there had been many avatars of God in different lands, one to the Christians, another to the Mussulmans, another to the Hindoos in time past; (but) another *avatar* of Krishna had taken place in himself.[25]

In any case Sahajanand attracted a large number of followers including the *sudras* and the members of the 'criminal tribes' such as the Bhils and the Kolis inhabiting the urban and the rural areas of Gujarat. Trying to keep the caste system intact, he nevertheless, appealed to the people to love each other and to live in peace and harmony. There is a strong tradition of love, sympathy and even compassion in Hinduism. Sahajanand made sincere attempts to bring about harmony a sense of brotherhood — among his numerous followers including some Muslims. When, for instance, Heber discussed with him the issue of caste he replied that he did not regard the subject as of much importance, but that he wished not to give offence (to his clients); that people might eat separately or together in this world, but that above, 'Oopur', pointing to heaven, those distinctions would cease, where we should be all 'ek ekhee jat' (one like another)'.[26]

The Swaminarayana sect thus emerged as a powerful organization during Sahajanand Swami's lifetime and more so after his death. In keeping with the organizational tradition of the Hindus, the sect kept the untouchables at arms length. In this manner the sect won the sympathy of the high caste Hindus as well as the Sudras. His following began to grow in size.

The Kanbis who were resourceful peasants *(sudras)* joined the Swaminarayana sect during Sahajanand's lifetime. The Swami absorbed and sanskritized them. Previously they were looked down upon by Brahminical Hindus and the prestigious sects, but now they acquired acceptance within the Swaminarayana fold. The sect recognized them and castes of comparable status as *sat-sudras* who were distinguished from ordinary *sudras*.[27] In the twentieth century they emerged as commercial farmers and industrialists on a modest scale. Some of them acquired wealth in the African countries. The sanskritization process together with these worldly achievements enabled the Kanbis to emerge as Patidars.[28] They became the pillars of the Swaminarayana sect. But this was not all. I have pointed out elsewhere that these *sat-shudras*, particularly in the rural areas, thwarted the attempts of the Gandhian grass root workers like Parixitlal Majumundar to absorb the Harijans into mainstream Hinduism and also into the freedom struggle.[29] My argument here is that, why should this rapidly rising sect with definite 'religious' and worldly goals allow itself to be polluted? Why should it harm itself by absorbing the *atishudras* within its fold? It was not for nothing that Gandhi had criticized both it and the Vallabha sect for propagating the values which he thought were contrary to the true spirit of Vaishnavism. In his letter dated 25 July 1918, to Maganlal Gandhi, he had said :

> To be sure, I have felt in all seriousness that Swaminarayana and Vallabhacharya have robbed us of our manliness. It was all to the good, of course, that people gave up drinking, smoking, etc., this, however, is not an end in itself, it is only a means. The love taught by Swaminarayana and Vallabh is all sentimentalism. They have made an undesirable effect on Gujarat.[30]

. My point is that the mass support of the Swaminarayana sect gradually narrowed down more and more to the richer groups in the rural and the urban areas. The Bhils and the Kolis of the earlier period were relegated into the background giving way to the richer sections. The appeals of social leaders like Dr. Sumant Mehta and Thankkar Bapa to the Swaminarayana *sadhus* to uplift the Adivasis and spread literacy among them (like the Christian missionaries) fell on deaf ears.[31]

This was the background of the Harijan temple entry movement in Gujarat.

5

Gandhi and his grass root workers in Gujarat had done considerable spade work among the Harijans before the Bombay Government, under its chief minister B.G. Kher, passed the Harijan Temple Entry Act in 1947.[32] Apart from this, the Majur Mahajan Sangh (TLA) had also inculcated a sense of self-respect among the untouchable industrial workers of Ahmedabad. They had played an important part during the Civil Disobedience Movement and also in the Quit India Movement. In fact, a large number of leaders among the Harijans such as Muldas Vaishya, Madhavji Parmar, and Viraji Bhagat had taken up the Harijan cause along Gandhian principles. This was reflected in the activities of several organizations such as the Vankar Vidyarthi Ashram (1921) and the Maha Gujarat Dalit (Harijan) Samaj (1925).

In the 1940s Ahmedabad contained a population of 5.91 lakhs. There were 71 textile mills with a labour force of 1.30 lakh including 8829 female textile mill workers. About 33000 Vankars traditionally called Dheds worked in the spinning and the throstle departments.[33] According to the census conducted by the Ahmedabad Municipality in 1931-32, the population of the untouchables inhabiting the city was as follows : 23760 Vankars, 11229 Chamars, 4729 Bhangis, 1214 Shenvas, and 989 Gerodas. That makes a total population of as many as 41,921 untouchables.[34] The TLA with its total recorded unemembership of 51,485 controlled the labour force of Ahmedabad. Although Marxist leaders like Dinkar Mehta, Dhanvant Oza and Ranchhod Patel had organized the Ahmedabad Mill Mazdur Union in 1933, its numerical strength was not more than about 3000 workers.[35] Oza informed me that he had to struggle a lot to organize workers on Marxist lines. The TLA was a respectable Gandhian labour union and its influence prevailed among even the workers who had not formally become its members.[36] In any case Ahmedabad had emerged as a major urban textile centre with a heterogenous population, by the time the temple entry Satyagraha took place.

The Gujarat Satyagraha was in response to the Satyagraha and the 'fast unto the death' organized by Krishnadasji, head of the Vallabha sect in Bombay, against the attempts on the part of the untouchables to enter the Vithoba temple in Pandharpur. Gandhian constructive workers like Ravishankar Maharaj, Mamasaheb Phadaka, Parixitial Majumundar, and the Harijan leader Muldas Vaishya went to Dakor (Kheda district) and together with the local Congress leaders organized a Satyagraha on 12 January 1948. This created tension because of the thousands of the *Savarna* Satyagrahis guarding the famous Ranchhodraiji temple. This upset 800 untouchables, and their leader Ravishankar Maharaj declared that he would not leave the place until the Harijans were allowed to enter the temple. Ravishankar had been an Arya Samajist before he came into contact with Gandhi. During the freedom movement under Gandhi he had changed the hearts of a large number of outlaws and had turned them into peace-loving citizens. He was highly respected among the people of the Kheda district because of his constructive activities. But the *Savarna* Satyagrahis were not prepared to listen to him. The jeering crowd beat him and his co-workers with sticks and kicks. The Maharaj, therefore declared a fast unto death. This led the local leaders to look for solutions. They contacted the temple authorities and it was decided to allow untouchables into the temple. They entered the temple the next day, but soon after, the *pujaris* purified it with the Ganga water.[37] The Harijans and their leaders succeeded in a similar manner with respect to the Surat and the Nadiad temples.

The Ahmedabad Satyagraha took place on 14 January 1948 with two batches of demonstrators marching from Congress House towards the Sarangpur Vaishnavite temple and the Swaminarayan temple. To the utter joy and satisfaction of the Satyagrahis they found that the gates of Sarangpur temple had already been opened to welcome them. After chanting *Vaishnava Janto Tenere Kahiye* and also a few national songs inside the temple, the untouchables went back to their respective homes.

On the other hand, when they reached the Swaminarayana temple they discovered that the temple authorities had secretly obtained a court injunction for preventing the entry of the Harijans. They had pleaded that they were not Hindus but followers of an entirely different religion and hence the Harijan Temple Entry Act did not apply to the Swaminarayana sect. They hung up a board at the temple gates stating : "Not for all the Hindus. Entry restricted only to the *Satsangis*, followers of the Swaminarayana sect.' This put Manibhai Shah (Municipal President), Khandubhai Desai (General Secretary of the TLA), Muldas Vaishya (President, Maha Gujarat Dalit (Harijan) Samaj) and other leaders into a considerably embarrassing situation. Kishorlal Mashruwala, a Gandhian intellectual and a staunch follower of the Swaminarayana sect wrote articles in the *Harijan Bandhu* that it was a pity that his sect had forgotten the original tenets of Sahajanand Swami. He added that the sect had always stood for love, non-violence, universal brotherhood, and human equality and that the Harijans were the true brothers of the Hindus. They must by allowed to worship the Lord. But what he added was more significant, The author of *Samuli Kranti* (Total Revolution) admonished the Harijans for their 'malicious political ambition'. He added :

> Why should the Harijans go to the temples at all?
>
> It is true that under the act, those who prevent the entry of the untouchables into the temple can be legally sued. But the untouchables should neither launch a Satyagraha nor should they take resort to the law for their narrow political goals.[38]

But the untouchables sat in *dharna* and took a vow that they would not leave the place until they succeeded. The next day big crowds of about 25,000 Harijans from the city and the surrounding areas gathered together. To the utter surprise of the TLA leaders, the Vankar demonstrators declared a strike in the textile mills. This opened a new dimension to the Satyagraha. The TLA leaders were scared as the strike prolonged for more than a week. The municipal Bhangis also created a problem of public health as they refused to do their jobs until they were allowed entry into the temple.[39] In the meantime, Krishnadasji Maharaj who had launched a Satyagraha at Pandharpur against the untouchables, visited Dakor and Vadtal and after contacting the *acharyas* of the temples there, came to Ahmedabad. Here he met Yagnapurushdasji, the *acharya* of the Swaminarayana temple. He, thus, mobilized the orthodox forces. In his public speech in Ahmedabad he declared that he would fight until death against the Harijan Temple Entry Act. He added :

> It is a sin to allow untouchables into the Hindu temples.... We are passing through a critical period. The internal invasion is from the untouchables and the external one is from the Muslims and Pakistan. I am not advising you to murder Muslims, but at least show them that we are now awakened and united.[40]

The Swaminarayana temple thus witnessed two Satyagrahas, one from outside the premises and the other from within. About 250 *sadhus* and *sants* undertook a fast. This was the situation when one of the untouchables informed Mahatma Gandhi about the grim situation and requested him to give justice to the untouchable Satyagrahis. Worn out in mind and body with the communal situation in the country, the old leader still preferred to reply. Three days before he was assassinated, the Mahatma wrote back that there was no separate caste of untouchables since they were an integral part of the four or the eighteen *varnas*. He emphasized that the trustees of the Hindu temples were not the real masters. The Hindu temples must be thrown open to all, irrespective of caste or creed. But he warned him :

> Those who undertake the Satyagraha even for religious purposes are doing great disservice to the Hindu religion. The act of Satyagraha for the temple entry is irreligious and sinful. We should keep hundred miles away from it. Till the *Savarnas* themselves welcomed them into their temples, the untouchables should bring the Ganga river into their doors and take a spiritual bath inside their homes.[41]

But things had changed. The Harijans fasting near the temple had also declared a strike to pressurize the temple authorities as well as their own TLA and Congress leaders. During my interview with a number of Satyagrahis, they told me that this, in fact, was not a religious issue for them. This was basically the question of their civic rights and cultural freedom, and that they wanted to assert themselves to protect and preserve their dignity and honour as the common citizens of the country.[42]

Thus the Satyagraha took a dramatic turn with the religious and economic issues being mixed up. The mill owners started pressurizing the TLA, and the latter started advising the Satyagrahis not to link the 'spiritual' with 'worldly' matters. But the untouchables retorted that Gandhiji had himself launched Satyagrahas against British rule. "The present Satyagraha", they argued, "is based on the Gandhian method of peace and non-violence."[43] The Congress and the TLA leaders, therefore, tried to put pressure on *Acharya* Yagnapurushdas and the trustees of the Swaminarayana temple. But they remained adamant. Kishorlal Mashruwala failed to convince those who controlled the temple. He and like-minded nationalists and Swaminarayans had no leverage with the temple management.

The textile mill strike had already created a problem. But the situation worsened when the *Vankar* textile mill workers in Kadi and Kalol (north Gujarat) and also Petlad (Kheda district) declared a token strike to express sympathy with their untouchables brethren. The leaders of the TLA got a rude shock. They started suspecting the communist hand. They began to blame the communists and their Ahmedabad Mill Mazdur Union. For this suspicion, they were not to blame, for the Ahmedabad Mill Mazdur Union had organized several industrial strikes during 1932-34. It had also published a booklet *Majur Mahajanni Kalank Katha* (black story of the Majur Mahajan) in 1946.[44] But all the contemporary evidence and also my interviews with Dhanvant Oza and the *dalit* satyagrahis show that the communists were innocent : They had taken a narrow view of religious movement. In spite of this fact, the TLA and the Congress leaders made them their hit-targets and advised the demonstrators not to be carried away by the 'atheists and the opportunists.'

The situation got so tense that it led Sardar Vallabhbhai Patel, then the Home and the Deputy Prime Minister of India to rush to Ahmedabad on 22 January 1948. The visit of the Sardar created an electrifying effect. In his characteristic style he took every one to task. He scolded the TLA leaders for leading the workers' strike on a non-economic issue. He passed acid remarks against the Swaminarayana sect. He said : "The Swaminarayanis have imprisoned God. Dr. Ambedkar is a member of our cabinet. If he visits your temple, are you going to stop him? Do not force us to break open the gates of your temple. I advise the trustees to pressurize the *acharya* and the *sadhus*."[45] In another speech the Sardar admonished the Satyagrahis :

> Why have you linked the religious issue with the economic? Remember, the days of demonstrations and fasts are now over. We are not going to tolerate that. Those who still want to remain hungry, let them do so. This will remove excreta from their stomach and will purify them."[46] He ridiculed the Marxist leaders for plunging into the game of politics. He declared, "What have they got to do with religion? They consider religion as the opium of the poor, and yet they have imposed themselves as the Champion of the workers.[47]

The presence of the iron-man of India yielded the desired effect. But this was one sided. Whereas *Acharya* Yagnapurushdasji, and the Swaminarayana *sadhus* stuck to their guns, the Harijans suffering from guilt, bowed down. The striking Harijans like Narsimh Makwana, Keshavlal Sonara, and Jayantibhai Arya sipped the fruit juice lovingly offered by Ravishankar Maharaj. The *Sandesh* published from Ahmedabad, in its 24 January issue, flashed the news that the "Harijan Satyagrahis have been convinced, and returned to their work. The mills have started functioning."

This paper clearly shows two distinct perceptions of Ambedkar and Gandhi towards Indian culture in general and the problems of the *dalits* in particular. In his recent book, B. R. Nanda has quoted a foreign authority in order to explain Gandhi's attitude to caste and untouchability. According to him, Gandhi thought that "if untouchability goes, the caste system goes."[48] Ambedkar, on the other hand, believed that untouchability would not be abolished if the caste system remained. It must be said to the credit of the Mahatma that he tried his best to stretch the thread of the Hindu *varna* system in his attempts to remove untouchability. But elasticity has its own limits, beyond which the thread would break. The Harijan Temple Entry Satyagraha bore the imprints of the Gandhian methods. The Gandhian workers who launched Satyagraha got scared when the untouchables declared a mill strike which resulted in a loss of 5 million rupees by 18 January.[49]

This is one aspect of the Satyagraha. The second and an equally important aspect was the Gandhian propositions that 1. The Harijans must visit the Hindu temples, and, 2. They should neither resort to law nor force open their entry through Satyagrahas. When, for instance, one of his agitated Harijan followers asked him not to tempt them into the temples, he had replied that they would remain untouchables until they publicly entered the temple. "Their *Hindutva* will remain incomplete without temples", he emphasized.[50]

These propositions suffer from inherent dichotomy. To raise the expectations of the untouchables without allowing them the only alternative - Satyagraha - to achieve their goal was morally unjustifiable. Later on of course, the Bombay High Court and the Supreme Court gave a ruling against the Swaminarayana sect.[51] But, by the time the supreme court verdict came (14 January, 1966) the socio-economic milieu had changed considerably and the attitudes of the *dalits* towards temples had also changed considerably.

As compared to the Ahmedabad Satyagraha, its Nasik counter part was qualitatively different. It was organized by and for the *dalits*. It was more radical and militant in nature; there were street-fights. The *dalits* wanted to show that they possessed strong nerves. Their main plank was social justice. The Kalaram Temple Entry Satyagraha was centred around questions such as 'why would the Satyagrahas be confined' to political freedom merely and not be extended to the realm of cultural and religious freedom?', and 'political freedom for whom?'

Notes

1. M. K. Gandhi, *An Autobiography or the Story of My Experiments with Truth* (Ahmedabad, 1992): 266.

2. Makrand Mehta, *The Ahmedabad Cotton Textile Industry : Genesis and Growth* (Ahmedabad, 1982), Makrand Mehta, 'From Sahajanand to Gandhi : Role Perception, Methods and Social Integration', *Journal of the Maharaja Sayajirao University of Baroda*, 27, no.1, (1978-79): 57-73.

3. *Ibid.*

4. Ravinder Kumar, *The Emergence of Modern India : Retrospect and Prospect* (New Delhi, 1990): 28-29.

5. Makrand Mehta, 'The Leader and His Milieu : Gandhi and Ahmedabad, 1915-20,' *Indian Historical Review*, 12, nos. 1-2, (July 1985 - January 1986): 173-87.

6. *Ibid.*

7. For details see Gail Omvedt, *Cultural Revolt in Colonial Society : The Non-Brahman Movement in Western India 1873 to 1930.* (Bombay, 1976).

8. Eleanor Zelliot, 'Learning the Use of Political Means : The Mahars of Maharashtra,' In Rajni Kothari (ed.), *Caste and Politics in India* (New Delhi, 1970): 29-69.

9. B. R. Ambedkar, *What Congress and Gandhi Have Done to the Untouchables*, 2nd edn. (Bombay, 1946): 189.

10. For details see Dhananjay Keer, *Dr. Ambedkar : Life and Mission* (Bombay, 1962).

11. Bombay Government, Gazetteer of the Bombay Presidency 16 Nasik (Bombay, 1883): 475-76.

12. The Imperial Gazetteer of India, 28 (New Edition Today and Tomorrow Printers and Publishers, New Delhi, n. d.): 410-12.

13. Bombay Gazetteer, *op.cit.*, 464; 517.

14. Dhananjay Keer, *Dr. Ambedkar : Life and Mission* (Bombay, 1962); W. W. Kuber, *Dr. Ambedkar A Critical Study* (Delhi, 1979); J. R. Kamble, *Pursuit of Equality in Indian History* (Delhi, 1955), M. L. Shahare, *Dr. Bhimrao Ambedkar : His Life and Work* (New Delhi, 1986); Sunanda Patwardhan. *Change among India's Harijans - Maharashtra : A Case Study* (New Delhi, 1973).

15. *Loksatta*, A Marathi daily published from Nasik, 4-19 March 1930; *Bombay Chronicle*, (Source : Maharashtra State Archives, Bombay).

16. *Bombay Chronicle*, 6 March 1930 (M. S. A.).

17. *Ibid*, 5 April 1930.

18. *Bombay Chronicle*, 3 March 1930; 6 March 1930; *The Times of India*, 3 March 1930 to 8 March 1930.

19. Shahare, *op.cit.*, 37.

20. Keer, *op.cit.*, 138.

21. *Kesri*, 12 April 1930.

22. *Kesri*, 12 April 1930; 15 April 1930.

23. *Collected Works of Mahatma Gandhi*, 14, 504-05.

24. J. Michael Mahar (ed.), *The Untouchables in Contemporary India* (Arizona, 1972): 82-84; K. N. Kadam, *Dr. Babasaheb Ambedkar and the Significance of His Movement : A Chronology* (Bombay, 1988): 93-99.

25. Reginald Heber, *Narrative of a Journey Through the Upper Provinces of India From Calcutta to Bombay, 1824-25 with Notes Upon Ceylon*, 2 vols. Vol.2 (London, 1828): 148.

26. *Ibid.* 152-53.

27. Raymond B. Williams, *A New Face of Hinduism : The Swaminarayana Religion* (Cambridge, 1984): 46.

28. For details see David Pocock. *Kanbi and Patidar : A Study of the Patidar Community of Gujarat* (Oxford, 1972).

29. Makrand Mehta. 'Gujaratman Thayeli Harijan Kalyannin Pravruttio, 1850-1935 Mulyarknatmak Sarvaiyu' (The Harijan Welfare Activities in Gujarat : An Evaluative Balance Sheet), *Arthat*, Centre For Social Studies, Surat, 9, 2, April-June 1990, 21-45.

30. *The Collected Works of Mahatma Gandhi*, 14 (Delhi, 1965) : 504-05; also see Gujarati version

31. Sumant Mehta. 'Dangnan Jangalo Ane Ehilo' (The Dang Jangles and the Bhils), *Yugdharma*, 5, no. 3, 1925, 190-92.

32. Bombay Government. *Report on the Working of the Backward Class Department for the years 1947-48 to 1949-50* (Poona, 1952): 2-14.

33. Kapilrai Mehta. *Amdabad Sarvasangraha* (Ahmedabad, 1948).

34. Ahmedabad Municipality. *A Report on the Census of the Ahmedabad City* Conducted in 1932 in Gujarati (Ahmedabad, 1934): 2-15.

35. Dhanvant Oza, *Samyavadi Andolan : Gujarat* (Ahmedabad, 1988); Dinkar Mehta. *Parivartan : Atmakatha* (Ahmedabad, 1968); Also interviews with Dhanvant Oza.

36. Interviews with Dhanvant Oza and Narsimh Makwana.

37. *Sandesh*, Ahmedabad, 16-12-1948.

38. *Harijan Bandhu*, 14-11-1948: 316-317 and 28-1949: 1; *Sandesh*, 14-1-1948 to 20-1-1948, *Gujarat Samachar*, 17-1-1948

39. *Ibid.*

40. *Sandesh,* 16-1-1948; *Gujarat Samachar,* 19-1-1948.

41. *Harijan Bandhu,* 1-12-1948, 4; also are *Collected Works of Mahatma Gandhi,* 90, 499-500.

42. Interviews with Karsandas Sonara, Jayantibhai Arya, Narsinhabhai Makwana and Vijaykumar Gadhvi.

43. *Ibid.*

44. Dinkar Mehta, *Parivartan Atmakatha* (Ahmedabad, 1968); Dhanvant Oza, *Samajvadi Andolan* (Ahmedabad, 1988).

45. *Prajabandhu,* 25-1-1948; *Gujarat Mitra,* 26-1-1948.

46. *Ibid.*

47. *Ibid.*

48. B. R. Nanda. *Mahatma Gandhi : A Biography* (London: 1958).

49. *Prajabandhu,* 22-1-1948; *Sandesh,* 20-1-1948

50. *Harijan Bandhu,* 19-3-1933, 12-13.

51. The Bombay High Court ruled on 3-10-1958 that the Swaminarayana sect was an integral part of Hindu religion. It ordered the authorities of the Ahmedabad temple to allow untouchables in their temples. Acharya Devendraprasad and Yagnapurushdas, therefore, went to the Supreme Court. It confirmed the decision of the Bombay High Court.

References

Ambedkar, B. R. *What Congress and Gandhi Have Done to the Untouchables,* 2nd edn., Bombay: Thacker, 1946.

Gandhi, M. K. *An Autobiography or the Story of My Experiments with Truth.* Ahmedabad: Navajivan, 1992.

Government of India. *The Collected Works of Mahatma Gandhi.* New Delhi: The Publications Division.

Kadam, K. N. *Dr. Babasaheb Ambedkar and the Significance of His Movement: A Chronology.* Bombay: Popular Prakashan, 1988.

Keer, Dhananjay. *Dr. Ambedkar: Life and Mission.* Bombay: Popular Prakashan, 1962.

Kuber, W. N. *Dr. Ambedkar: A Critical Study,* Delhi: Peoples Publishing House, 1979.

Kumar, Ravinder. *The Emergence of Modern India: Retrospect and Prospect.* New Delhi: Manohar, 1990.

Mehta, Makrand. *The Ahmedabad Cotton Textile Industry: Genesis and Growth.* Ahmedabad: New Order Book Co., 1982.

Mehta, Makrand. 'From Sahajanand to Gandhi: Role Perception. Methods and Social Integration'. *Journal of the Maharaja Sayajirao University of Baroda 27, 1,* 1978-79.

Mehta, Makrand. 'The Leader and His Milieu: Gandhi and Ahmedabad. 1915-20', *Indian Historical Review, 12,* nos. 1-2, July 1985-January 1986.

Mehta, Makrand. 'Gujaratman Thayeli Harijan Kalyannin Pravruttio, 1850-1935 Mulyanknatmak Sarvaiyu' (The Harijan Welfare Activities in Gujarat : An Evaluative Balance Sheet). Arthat, Centre for Social Studies, Surat 9, Pt. 2, April-June 1990.

Nanda, B. R. *Mahatma Gandhi: A Biography.* London: G. Allen & Unwin, 1958.

Omvedt, Gail, *Cultural Revolt in Colonial Society: The Non-Brahman Movement in Western India* 1873 to 1930, Bombay: Scientific Socialist Education Trust, 1976.

Patwardhan, Sunanda. *Change among India's Harijans - Maharashtra: A Case Study.* New Delhi: Orient Longman, 1973.

Pocock, David. Kanbi and Patidar. *A Study of the Patidar Community of Gujarat.* Oxford: Clarendon Press,. 1972.

Williams, Raymond B. *A New Face of Hinduism: The Swaminarayana Religion.* Cambridge: Cambridge University Press, 1984.

2

Search for Dalit Self Identity in Gujarat

Achyut Yagnik

When you call me 'dher'
I am hurt
and wish to kick you in the belly
when you call me untouchable
I am offended
and wish to slap you on the face
when you call me 'Harijan'
I am humiliated
and wish to spit on your back
when you call me a member of Scheduled Caste
I am insulted
and wish to money at your
....
when you call me Neerav Patel
I suspect you called me convert
(a crow that dyed his feathers white
to be called a swan)
and wish to turn away my facc
when you don't call me anything
I am annoyed that you neglected me altogether
and wish to call you back to call me
....
Yes. It's all a mess since the beginning
like the tale of a seven-tailed mouse.

Neerav Patel

The poignancy of this poem by Neerav Patel, a well known *dalit* poet of Gujarat, captures the intensely painful search for self-identity amongst the *dalits* of Gujarat. The twentieth century has been a period of complex transitions for the *dalits* of Gujarat. Even as we approach the end to the century neither the intensity nor the complexity of this change appears to reach a point of repose.

Pain and suffering is integral to transition, but the extent of suffering that the *dalits* have undergone is far greater than that of any other marginal community. All attempts at change and reform have met with strong opposition.

The Path to Modernity

The path to modernity for the *dalits* has been tortuous. Neither the rapid urbanization nor industrialization has made their entry into the modern secter any easier. Nevertheless, change has taken place. According to the census of 1991, the percentage of literacy amongst the *dalits* of Gujarat is similar to the literary levels in other communities, though a wide gulf separates *dalits* from other communities in Secondary and Higher education.

A small section of the *dalit* community has been able to get benefit from the policy of reservation in educational and Governmental or Semi-Governmental institutions. Apart from their participation in the organized service sector, a small section has also shown enterprenurial abilities. As a result of those processes a small but articulate middle class has emerged amongst the *dalits*.

Till the 1980s, the *dalit* middle class believed that they had successfully entered the modern space and the transition for the rest of the community would be far less tortuous.[1] Believing this, certain sections had also snapped ties with their community. But, the anti-reservation agitation and the riots which accompanied it then brought the folly of their belief into sharp focus. In a desperate attempt to re-establish their ties with the community, some resorted to joining the Hindutva organization of the party, while some tried to provide modern leadership to their caste organizations. It must be mentioned at this juncture, that those members of the *dalit* middle class, who had continued to struggle for *dalit* self-identity following Ambedkar, did not face this predicament.

Towards the end of the twentieth century the *dalit* middle class faces the same predicament, which it had to contend with at the time of Independence. At the time of Independence, the educated *dalits* were faced with two choices. One was the Gandhian path where the choice was to integrate with the larger Hindu Society. The other was the path of struggle and agitation to assert *dalit* self-identity, as suggested by Ambedkar. The *dalit* community in Gujarat has adopted both these paths. But the integrationist policy took the form of Congress-led caste-based electoral politics. A majority of *dalits* became partners in this process, while a minority continued to struggle for the assertive self-identity.

The *dalits* of Gujarat are once again faced with the moment of departure. They can either opt to integrate with the Hindu social order through the politics of Hindutva or caste-based coalition politics of the Congress. The other path implies a continued struggle for an assertive self-identity. Mobilization on the basis of Marxist tradition has never been a viable mode of politics or social reform in Gujarat. One can assume without much difficulty that this path may not appear very attractive to the new generation of *dalits*.

One must emphasize the qualitative difference between the Gandhian integrationist approach and the approach of the Hindutva ideology and Congress politics. The Gandhian approach not only emphasizes the upliftment of *dalits* but also places equal emphasis on the change of heart of Savarna Hindus. The establishment of the 'Gujarat Harijan Sevak Sangh' in 1932 was an experiment in this direction. The Sevak Sangh desired to abolish untouchability in all forms, eradicate all forms of social and religious inequalities and establish an equal, non-violent social order. They called upon the Savarna Hindus to be active agents of change. Despite the committed efforts of individuals such as Shri Thakkarbapa, Shri Nanabhai Bhatt, Shri Motibhai Amin, Smt. Vidyaben Neelkantha, Anasuyaben Sarabhai, Smt. Shardaben Mehta and Shri. Parikshitlal Majumdar the Sevak Sangh did not meet with much success. Shri. Majumdar in a letter to Gandhi in 1937 confesses that 'Barring one or two exceptions, no temples or wells have been opened to the Harijans'. Responding to this Gandhi wrote in *Harijan Bandhu* that henceforth he would stay in Bhangi colonies during his travels.

This shows that the 'change of heart' was not an easy process and that for *dalits* following Gandhi's process of integration was equally difficult.

The post-Independence political processes have made this approach more difficult to actualize. The language of 'soul force' or of 'change of heart' has no space in the political discourse. The upliftment of *dalits* is seen largely as an administrative task and not a part of the social or political process. This stand is best exemplified by a statement of Shri Ramlal Parikh, the Chancellor of Gujarat Vidyapeeth. Commenting upon the continuing practice of making the disposal of human waste a task to be the carried out by members of the *dalit* community he said, 'This is an administrative task. We do not believe that it is our responsibility. I feel that our responsibility is to do constructive work.' (*TOI*, Ahmedabad. 5 Oct 1995). This shows the departure from the earlier principles by contemporary Gandhians.

Congress politics called upon the *dalits* to integrate themselves into the 'mainstream' of the new nation-state. Constitutionally, the mainstream was of secular polity. But under the Congress rule, the mainstream remained 'Sanatani Hinduism'.

Disillusioned with the Congress certain sections of the *dalits* joined hands with the newly-emerging forces of Hindutva, with their emphasis on integrationist policies. Even this call to join the mainstream is proving to be a delusion. During the BJP rule in the mid-nineties the actual number of atrocities on *dalits* went up in Gujarat.

Self-identity : The Politics of Naming

The Central question facing the *dalits* of Gujarat has been that of self-identity. The pain and anger of social stigma of deprivation and oppression is a part of this quest.

In their quest for self-identity, the *dalit* community of Gujarat has adopted mainfold paths. Gandhi tried to provide a new identity to this community by giving it a new name 'Harijan'. This not only meant 'children of God', but it resonated with the sounds of the medieval Bhakti tradition. But in less than two decades after Independence, educated sections from this community started rejecting this word and identity. It was increasingly replaced by the term *dalit*, suggesting oppression, deprivation and injustice. The search for assertive identity, following the teachings of Ambedkar played a major role in the acceptance of this term.

The terms *dalit* and *'dalit literature'* which originated in Maharashtra have become in the last twenty-five years signifiers of *dalit* pride and assertive self-identity. By the 1990s these terms acquired an impassioned edge, the Press Council of India had to give a directive to the newspapers to not use the term 'Harijan', instead to employ the word *dalit.* It is significant that the acceptance and the spread of the term *dalit* is far greater than what the term 'Harijan' could achieve even during Gandhi's own lifetime.

The term used by any community to identify itself or describe other communities is not a mere sign, which is value free, But this sign is constructed by the socio-political, economical and ideological structures within which it seeks to operate.

The Savarna response to the *dalits* during the nineteenth century was as ambivalent as it is today. On the one hand, it was marked by empathy and an attempt to understand the *dalit* communities, while on the other hand apathy and indifference dominated.

What is perhaps the earliest printed reference to the *dalits* in Gujarat occurs in the diary of Durgaram Mehta, in 1843.[2] In this entry Durgaram recognizes the pain of untouchability, tries to establish the principle of equality and significantly refers to the *dalit* as 'Mahetar' and not the widely prevalent 'shed'.

In 1851, Dalpatram Dayabhai in his prize winning. 'An Essay on Caste',[3] asserted that caste is not created by God, caste is determined not by birth but by occupation, and that there was historical proof on the this kind of sub-divisions of caste. He negated the widely prevalent Vedic belief that castes were created by God from different parts of the body of the Purusha as poetic fancy. It is also significant that Dalpatram alludes to the fact that *dalits* were deprived of knowledge by the Brahmins and their present state is largely due to this deprivation.

But the call for the equality of all human beings given by Durgaram is halted by Govardhanram Tripathi. Govardhanram who through his novel Saraswatichandra provided a powerful critique of British colonial presence, takes a stand on the issue of caste while speaking to the 'Social and Literary Association' in 1902. Govardhanram viewed the caste system as a practical arrangement governed by performance of duties by castes to each other. While taking such a position, he disregards the oppression and injustice done to the *dalits* through this system of mutual performance of duties.

Social Awakening Among Dalits

While Govardhanram was addressing the 'Social and Literary Association', the *dalit* community in Gujarat was stirring and attempting to break free from age-old shackles.

Makanji Kuber Makwana[4] who was born in Ahmedabad in 1849 was leading the movement for self-worth and self-identity amongst the educated sections of the *dalit* society. Makanji's father had initially settled in Surat and later moved to Bombay. At the age of fifteen, Makanji learnt painting form an English artist in Bombay and became a painter. He opened a painting unit of his own and amassed considerable wealth.

Makanji tried to establish that Dheds or Vankars were originally Mayavat Rajputs and should be recognised as Mahyavanshis. He in 1908 wrote 'Mayavat Rajputs Prakash' and in 1911 wrote 'Mahyavanshi Atle' and 'Mayavat Rajputoday arthat Mahyavanshi no Udai'.

With his initiative and effort, a 'Panch Sudharak Commitee' was formed in 1907-1908 to frame rules and regulations of the Mahyavanshi caste which later came into existence as Mahyavanshi Rajput Gnyatina Kayda.' Further he helped various castes councils in Bombay, Navsari, Parchhola, Chikhali, Umbargam, Daman, Bharuch, Baroda, Ahmedabad, Karachi, Johannesburg. Pretoria, Durban and the United Kingdom to frame rules and regulations for the caste. He anchored movement for claiming Kshatriya status. Even after his death in 1924, the movement continued. Largely due to its efforts, the word Mahyavansi was officially recognized by the Government. In 1939, the Government of Bombay declared that from then on the word 'shed' would be discontinued from all Government correspondence and instead, Mahyavanshi would be used.

Like the Vankars of Surat, the Khalpa caste in Surat was also agitating for a change of name from Khalpa to Rohit. During the fourth decade of this century, the leaders of the 'Surat Jeela (Rohit) Kshatriya Pracharak Committee' was active in changing the names from Khalpa to Rohit. In 1940, a meeting of this committee was held at Navsari under the Chairmanship of Purshottm L. Chauhan, a Member of the Legislative Assembly of the erstwhile Bombay State. The committee passed a resolution that their caste members was loyal to the Congress, but regretted that in spite of sending a memorandum to the Bombay Government to change their names from Khalpa to Rohit; from Dhed to Mahyavanshi, from Garuda to Guru and from Bhangi to Rishi; the Government had only recognized the name Mahyavanshi, whereas other castes were not allowed to change their names.

The 'Mahyavanshi' movement is a significant departure in the quest for *dalit* self-identity because it tried to give a new self-image to the community, and also tried to instal caste reforms and forge unity amongst various castes of the *dalit* community.

Under the influence of Gandhi, the movement acquired a qualitatively different dimension. This movement placed an equal responsibility on the Savarna communities and moved from 'upliftment of untouchables' to the complete eradication of untouchability.

Conversion

Parallel to the movement of acquiring a new self-image, another equally significant movement was taking place amongst the *dalits* of Gujarat. This was the movement of conversion to Christianity. During 1899-1900, Gujarat had witnessed the most acute famine in modern times. During this period, largely due to the compassionate service rendered by the Christian missionaries, the process of conversion to Christianity gained momentum.

A large number of *dalits* in Central Gujarat, and especially in Charotar chose to convert to Christianity. With this act of conversion, their entry into modern education was rapid and to an extent, easy. According to a survey conducted in 1926, amongst the Christian *dalits* of Nadiad Taluka, in less than three decades of conversion, education had spread widely amongst the neo-converts.[5]

Table 1

Total (above 12 years)	Hindu	Christian	Muslim
Total women and men	4299	3499	186
Educated women & men	341	583	17
Percentage of literate	7.9	16.7	9.1

This survey clearly shows that for the *dalits*, conversion to Christianity was clearly a mode of entering the modern world through education, and through that, the aspiration for self-respect and self-identity was reflected. Due to the conversion the spread of education was rapid, which also led to the emergence of an articulate middle class. But no significant upward social mobility was acquired in the caste hierarchy.

The predicament of the Christian *dalits* came to the foreground when Savarna groups burnt down their houses in Uttarsanda during the 1981 anti-reservation agitation. This showed that they had not escaped from the oppressive gaze of the Savarnas. During the last few years, there has been a country-wide movement to include the Christian *dalits* as beneficiaries of the reservation policy. In Gujarat not only the Sangh Parivar, but some *dalit* intellectuals have also opposed their inclusion as the beneficiaries of reservation policy.

Despite the apparent advantages that conversion to Christianity promised, only about 10% of *dalits* in Gujarat have converted to Christianity. This suggests that the majority of *dalits* in Gujarat have not found it attractive to adopt the path of conversion. Not only has conversion to Christianity been limited, but Dr. Ambedkar's call to convert to Buddhism and create a neo-Buddhist identity did not find any resonance amongst the *dalits* of Gujarat.

Four distinct trends emerge as we analyse the first five decades of the twentieth century. In their quest for self-identity the first mode adopted by the *dalits* was to organize their castes and establish federation with other *dalit* castes, to institute a process of reform within the caste and seek a higher social status by changing the caste name. The second mode was conversion, by means of adopting Christianity. The third path attempted to transform social movements into political ones. Though this process had started before Gandhi, during the movement for freedom, it gained significant momentum as a large number of *dalits* joined the struggle for freedom. The significant presence of *dalit* youths in the Dandi March is an indication of this process. The fourth process was to assert self-identity as *dalit*, for which the principle moving spirit was Ambedkar.

Social movements based on the first three paths had begun in the second and the third decade of this century, while the fourth decade saw the emergence of assertionist self-identity. Since conversion to Christianity was not a mode adopted by a large number of *dalits*, we can state that *dalits* in Gujarat have adopted the other three modes to acquire and establish self-image and identity.

Even amongst those sections of the *dalit* community which followed either Gandhi or Ambedkar, a desire for achieving higher social status through a process of sensitization has continued. In 1947, 'Shri Maha Gujarat Guru Brahmin Samaj' congregated at Nadiad and resolved to change their caste name from Garada to Guru Brahman. In 1954, 636 villages of the Chamar community gathered at Santram temple in Nadiad and resolved to institute caste reforms.

Thus, the process which started with the Vankar community in Surat in the early parts of this century has gone on till the middle of this century in various *dalit* groups. Due to paucity of archival material and studies, it is difficult to ascertain the exact nature of caste reforms, the process of institutionalizing caste committees and their impact. But it is not that *dalits* are an exception. Even in the Savarna community, the process of social reform has been anchored in caste reform.

Savarna Mobilization

One of the most significant sociological developments in the post-Independence period has been the emergence of Savarna ideology. During the sixth decade when a separate state of Gujarat came to be formed, two significant caste-based mobilizations were taking place. The Patidar community was coming out of its Kunbi status, forging alliances within the Patidar groups and was acquiring a consciousness as a 'Samasta Patidar' community. On the other hand, due to the efforts of organizations like the Kshatriya Mahasabha, lower Kshatriya communities like Koli and Thakor were striving to achieve Rajput status and forge a larger Kshatriya identity. The process of land reforms instituted by the Bombay and Saurashtra states also contributed to the crystallization of 'Patel' and 'Kshatriya' identity.

The Green Revolution helped the land-owning castes to emerge as dominant castes and acquire considerable economic prosperity. With newly-acquired economic prosperity and a sense of being one united community, both the Patidars and Rajput communities acquired political power. As against these Savarna mobilizations, the *dalit* community was neither united nor could forge strategic alliances with other communities. The politically successful alliance of the Patidars and Kshatriya inagurated in Gujarat.

After the Nav Nirman agitation of the mid-70s, the Congress to recapture power forged an alliance of Kshatriyas, Harijans, Adivasis and Muslims, popularly known as KHAM. The *dalit* community, included in this alliance as Harijans, became a crucial link in this alliance. For the first time a ruling coalition had no place for the Savarna communities like Brahmins, Baniyas and Patidars. To counter this process, a new Savarna identity came to be forged.

The process of rapid urbanization and industrialization also helped to cement the new Savarna identity. Brahmin and Vaishyas in

Gujarat had lost their ownership of land in the sixth decade, due to the process of land reforms. These communities had joined the emerging service sector while the Patidars, with the help of surplus capital from land were making rapid strides towards industrialization.

A collusion of interests had helped these communities to forge a larger Savarna identity. The success in the KHAM formation had challenged the political domination of these groups. This identity and the sensed political deprivation in the Savarna community erupted in the form of Anti-Reservation agitations in 1981 and 1985. Gujarat witnessed the worst forms of caste oppression and brutality during these agitations.

It is not insignificant that what the rest of the country saw in the form of 'Anti-Mandal Agitations' was witnessed by Gujarat at least a decade earlier in the form of an Anti-Reservation agitation.

But neither of these agitations led to the formation of larger identity amongst the backward KHAM communities. The reasons for this failure lie in the nature of the KHAM alliance and the policies of the Governments comprising KHAM leadership itself. Even after capturing more than 80% seats on the basis of KHAM in the 1980 Assembly elections, the Congress Government did not take any policy measures which helped the KHAM communities. The Government did not institute or encourage land reforms. The 'inter-changability' of observations amongst the *dalits* and Adivasis was abolished, thus precluding any possibility of these communities forging a permanent alliance beyond caste and community boundaries. On the other hand, the Government policies which favoured rapid industrialization benefited the Savarna communities.

From Savarna Identity to Hindutva[6]

The last fifteen years in Gujarat have witnessed the rapid transformation of Savarna identity into a larger 'Hindu' identity.

After the 1981 agitation the national leadership of the BJP became conscious of the growing anti-BJP feeling among *dalits*, and by the mid-1980s they had systematically started co-opting *dalit* and Adivasi communities. By 1986-87, they had some success with the urban *dalits* using the VHP's Hindutva-based programmes. The party's anti-reservation stance was also corrected, and after 1985, the ABVP started talking in favour of a reservation system for the *dalits* and the Adivasis. The following year, the VHP, in one of its Hindu Yuva

Sammelans, asked the youth to dedicate themselves to the abolition of untouchability. They were also asked to work for the all-round development of the 'economically and socially backward Hindu brothers'. All this paid dividends. In the 1986 communal riots in Ahmedabad, which broke out during the 'Rath Yatra' of Lord Jagannath, there was a widespread belief that the *dalits* and Muslims were killing each other.

By the mid-1980s the message of the VHP, that the idea of Savarna had to be supplanted by that of Hindutva as the binding cement for Hindus, had spread. Earlier the ultimate symbolic target of hate was the *dalit*; now it was the Muslim. At last the Gujarati middle class — spread out over large cities like Ahmedabad, Baroda and Surat and more than forty other large towns, and consisting mainly of Savarna, but also *dalit* and Adivasi Government servants, teachers and petty contractors had begun to find security within the ideology of Hindutva. Cut off from older cultural and social ties, the class had learnt to use the ideology as a ready cure for rootlessness and as a substitute for traditions. Hindutva had become for this class a new Purana to validate their pre-eminence.

Significantly, the ABVP, the student wing of the BJP, was the first organization to raise a banner of protest against reservations in post-graduate medical studies introduced by the Gujarat government in 1981. The ABVP not only initiated the agitation but also took it to the middle class localities of Ahmedabad. But by the middle of 1982 however, the BJP leadership had changed its strategy and dropped its anti-reservation stance. Instead, the BJP workers in Gujarat started developmental and relief work in tribal areas and by 1983 they had begun to win over the *dalits*. During the Ekatmata Yatras of 1983, the local BJP-VHP leadership systematically involved *dalit* leaders. Again, when communal riots broke out in Ahmedabad during 1986, at the time of the annual Rath Yatra of the local Jagannath temple, the *dalits* were repeatedly invited by the BJP and the VHP to join in the holy war to protect Hinduism. The detailed narratives of the local police and media on the violent clashes that took place in industrial Ahmedabad conveyed the impression that the *dalits* and Muslims were out for each other's blood. In the wake of the 1986 communal riots, a series of stabbing incidents took place; the police reports made sure that they all appeared to involve only Muslims and *dalits*.

The VHP planned three major 'pilgrimages' between 16 November and 16 December 1983, for the whole of India; the Gangajal or

Ekatmata Yatra from Haridwar in the foothills of the Himalayas to Rameshwaram in Tamil Nadu; the Ekatmata Yatra from Pashupatinath in Nepal to Kanyakumari; and the Ekatmata Yatra from Gangasagar in West Bengal to Somnath in Gujarat. Twenty-three subsidiary pilgrimages were planned for Gujarat. They were to originate from different places and merge with one of the main ones from Gangasagar to Somnath. Their aim was to rise above caste, sect and denominational differences and invoke the spirit of unity amongst the Hindus. Signatories to the appeal to join the Yatras included the ABVP, the RSS, the Arya Samaj, the Rotary Club, the Lions Club and also, more notably, the Jain Sampradaya, Vaishnava Parivar, Sikh Sampradaya, Buddha Sampradaya and Bhartiya Dalit Varga Sangh. In other words, an attempt was made to associate virtually all the non-Hindu communities with the yatras and thus to isolate the Muslims.

The Yatras used not merely the symbol of sacred Ganga water, but also that of sacrificial rituals and pilgrimages. The routes of the Yatras were so charted that they touched the maximum number of shrines and centres of pilgrimage. Advantage was also taken of the fact that these temples were identified for centuries with different sects belonging to the three main streams of Hindu tradition— Shaivism, Shaktism and Vaishnavism. They also often bore the signatures of Jainism, Buddhism and Sikhism. In this respect, the Gangajal Yatra contained all the main features of subsequent programmes of the same kind. For instance, the route and the form of Advani's Rath Yatra, the links with the symbols of religious traditions that have originated in the subcontinent, and the attempt to construct a Hindu nationality that would span the major and minor sects and the different castes- were all there.

Only after 1984 did the VHP begin to use Ram in its mass mobilization programmes. The first organized effort was the Ram-Janaki Dharma Yatra in 1987. It took place throughout Gujarat including the tribal areas. The stated aim was to transcend caste and sect differences in the worship of Lord Ramchandra and to affirm the unity of the Hindus.

The meaning of that unity became clear during the Yatra itself. Virpur is a small town at the junction of Kheda, Sabarkantha and Panchmahal districts of Gujarat. On the day the Ram-Janaki Dharma Yatra was to pass through it, the town witnessed violent clashes between the local Hindus and Muslims and, for the first time in Gujarat, the tribals of nearby villages rushed in to attack Muslim localities and burn down Muslim shops and houses.

The second effort was the Ramshila Pujan — worship of sanctified bricks meant for the projected Ram temple at Ayodhya. The VHP organized the Pujan in 1989. After Gandhi's Dandi March, which took place as a part of the Independence movement, the Pujan turned out to be by far the most impressive mobilizational effort in Gujarat. It was successful beyond the VHP's wildest dreams, as even villages with no more than fifty to a hundred houses participated in the worship. Apart from sacred bricks made from the soil of their own land, VHP offered vast sums of money. *dalit* slums of Ahmedabad and less accessible tribal villages in far-flung areas took enthusiastic part in the programme.

Today, in some parts of the country, a '*dalit*-Bahujan' identity and alliance is being formed. There are two choices before the *dalit* communities : one, either to support the 'Hindutva' thrust and hope to be integrated within the larger Hindu formations or the second, to play a pivotal role in consolidating the *dalit* Bahujan Samaj. Their choice will determine the nature of their quest for self-identity.

Dalit Discourse

Once again the *dalit* community is facing a moment of decision and departure, so that the process of creating a *dalit* discourse is also faced with choices. Since 1975 the process of literary self-articulation amongst the *dalit* has taken the form of a movement through *dalit* literature.

It is not possible to discuss in detail the paths that *dalit* literature has taken in Gujarat. A quest for self-identity and self-articulation has been the anchor and moving spirit of *dalit* literature. *dalit* literature was inaugurated with poetry, which continues to be its most powerful form of self-expression. Although, there has been some movement towards experimenting with other literary forms like the short story and novel, *dalit* literature in Gujarati is yet to produce any significant autobiographical account, though personal experience has informed the narrative structure and contents of novels and short stories. The significant absence of autobiography suggests that the individuated identity amongst *dalit* writers, activists and intellectual is yet to be formed.

The autobiographical form demands an awareness of not only the present but also of the past. A historical subjectivity gives rise only to feelings and emotions, but not to autobiographical narratives. Especially when the past is painful and heart-wrenching amnesia about it appears an easier option. Whatever the reasons, *dalit* literature which has acquired a distinct voice in poetry and novels, has not made any noticable contribution in writing autobiographies and historical narratives. If historical awareness has informed the quest for self-expression, the self-sense of the *dalit* community may possibly have acquired different nuances.

Although in recent years some noteworthy developments have taken place. Dr. Dalpat Shrimali's Harijan Sant and Lok Sahitya Kanthasth Thi Granthasth[7] and Dr. Nathabhai Gohil's Saurashtra Harija Bhakta Kavio[8] seek to usher in a new historical awareness by taking the orality of *dalit* expression seriously. The movement towards documenting and reflecting upon the folk and the oral literatures of the Dalit community has helped the *dalit* search for identity in taking significant stops. But this awareness needs to be taken much further, towards the development of *dalit* perspectives on sociology and socio-linguistics.

There is some movement towards a sociology of *dalit* communities as well. Dr. Maheshchandra Pandya's *Sabarkantha Na Garo*[9] and Mr. V. A. Parmar's *The Mahyavanshis : The Success Story of a Scheduled Caste* are two studies which suggest that *dalit* intellectuals want to understand their social formations through their own categories. This will certainly add a new dimension to their notions about the self and its relation to larger societal processes.

Dalit Movements

In the search for self-identity the note of protest movements and assertionist movements is very significant. Mere subjective expression of feelings and emotions without a desire or an attempt to achieve the self-identity proves counter-productive.

From the early decades of this century *dalit* communities have agitated to assert their self-identity. It is not as if that their participation in movements has been confined to only caste-based agitations. The *dalits* of Gujarat have participated also in larger social and political movements like the Maha Gujarat Andolan.

During the 70s and 80s *dalits* in Gujarat had participated in movements of land reforms. Unfortunately, the nature and impact of their participation has not been studied. But as the pressure on natural resources increases and economically-deprived sections get more and more alienated from land and other natural resources such movements on their part will acquire much greater importance. During the 80s, the *dalit* Panthers Movement helped the community re-establish and strengthen ties with the legacy of Dr. Ambedkar. The history of the *dalit* Panthers is yet to be studied, but certainly their impact has not been without significance, though, their role has remained largely confined to responding and reacting to instances of oppression and injustice to the members of *dalit* community.

But unlike as in Maharashtra, the movement has not yet acquired institutional dimensions. Despite these movements, it is the specific caste organizations which have anchored the *dalit* search for upward mobility and self-identity. Any community which has historically suffered systematic oppression and structural deprivation is bound to be inward looking, both for sustenance and identity. Until the modern process can provide the *dalit* community with the wherewithal to deal with structural deprivation, it would be unfair to expect that traditional organizations and resources like the caste organizations will disappear.

It should be mentioned that the recent leadership among *dalit* communities largely comprises individuals who belong to educated urban sections, and their aspirations both for themselves and their community are informed by aspirations of the urban middle class. At the same time, the participation of Savarna groups and individuals in *dalit* agitations and struggle for justice has been dwindling over the years.

Thus, the *dalit* quest for self-identity has taken various forms, with considerable overlap between the modes adopted. Whether it was the movement towards sanskritization or the movement of conversion to Christianity and New Buddhism, it has at every step met with Savarna resistance. Despite short-lived success in forging political alliance like KHAM, the benefits of governance have not reached large sections of the *dalit* communities. While there have been attempts to integrate *dalit* aspirations within larger rubrics like Hindutva; the *dalits* have also led movements to assert their separate identity. Their quest has not been expressed merely socially and politically but through modes of powerful self-expression such as Dalit literature.

To conclude, we can re-emphasize that it is only through powerful agitations, empowering organizational structures and self-aware expression of their discourse, that the *dalit* quest for self-identity can be meaningfully attained.

Acknowledgements

An earlier version of this essay was published in Gujarati as 'Dalit Asmita Ni Khoj' *Vaacha*. Yr. I, Vol. 2. 1997. Tridip Suhrud prepared the first draft of the English Version.

Notes

1. These excerpts are from 'Mess' by Neerav Patel, published in his collection entitled *Burning From Both the Ends, Dalit Panther's Poetry Series* no. 1, (Ahmedabad, 1980). The translation from the Gujarati original is the author's own.

2. Durgaram Mehta established the *Manav Dharma Sabha* in Surat in 1843. This was perhaps the first organization in modern times which sought to go beyond boundaries of caste. For more details see, page 34, *Mehtaji Durgaram Mancharam Charitra*, Malipatram Rupram Neelkantanth, 1879.

3. *Gnayti Nibandh*, Dalpatram Dayhabhai, 4th Edition, Gujarat Vernacular Society, (Ahmedabad, 1887).

4. This section is based on Y. A. Parmar, *The Mahyavanshi : The Success Story of a Scheduled Caste,* Mittal Publications (Delhi, 1987) : 90-94.

5. *Prasthan*, 1, (Ahmedabad, 1926): 47.

6. This section is based on Ashish Nandy, Shikha Trivedi, Shail Mayaram, Achyut Yagnik, *Creating a Nationality : The Ramjanmabhumi Movement and the Fear of the Self,* Oxford University Press, (Delhi, 1995) : 100-109.

7. Dalpatbhai Shrimali, *Harijan Sant ane Loksahitya,* Palanpur : Sri Gurudev Prakashan, 1989.

8. Nathabhai Gohil, *Saurashtrana Harijan Bhakta Kavio*, 1987.

9. Maheshchandra Pandya, *Sabarkantha Na Garo*, (Gandhinagar, Gujarat Sahitya Academy, 1984).

3

A Spiritual Approach to Social Transformation

N.R. Sheth

My main intention in this paper[1] is to analyse the social contribution of a socio-religious movement known as *Swadhyaya*. The term *Swadhyaya* here will refer to the overall institutional and organizational embodiment of the movement - the goals, structure, norms, systems and activities. The fraternity of people following the Swadhyaya way of life is known as Swadhyaya *Parivar* or simply, the *Parivar* (lit. extended family). A person committed to *Swadhyaya* way of life is described as a *swadhyayi*. I propose to present a brief account of the genesis and growth of *Swadhyaya* and the thrust of its activities and programmes. I will then describe how *Swadhyaya* has influenced the lives of people among some disadvantaged sections of society in Gujarat and offer some thoughts on the role of *Swadhyaya* in social transformation. My observations and conclusions should be regarded as tentative. I am aware of the inadequacy of information and understanding, on the basis of which I have constructed the following story and its lessons.[2] Since August 1991, I have observed or participated in a variety of *Swadhyaya* activities and programmes, met many people associated with it across its hierarchy, and exchanged views and interpretations with its followers, friends and observers. I have also gone through some published literature on the subject.[3] All of this exposure, however, can add up to only a small quantity of raw material for my effort as against the complex social reality of the movement.[4] My search for a better understanding of the many facets of *Swadhyaya* and its interface with the socio-economic environment of which it is an integral part should continue during the days ahead.

The Genesis

The vision of *Swadhyaya* emerged in the early 1950s in the mind of an extraordinary scholar of human civilization, philosophy and religion. His name is Pandurang Shastri Athavale. He is endearingly known as *Dada* (Marathi equivalent of elder brother) within the *Swadhyaya* universe. *Dada* was born in a Marathi-speaking Brahmin family of religious-spiritual scholars and teachers. Through his early twenties, as he followed his father's professional practice of delivering discourses on Indian religion and philosophy, he had taken in an enviably wide spectrum of the history of western and other civilizations offered generously by Bombay's public libraries. *Dada*'s conscience in its entirety was stirred at an early age by the multidimensional adverse effects of various forms of human greed, selfishness and consumerism on human dignity and welfare. He was equally perturbed by the social reality of poverty, deprivation, exploitation and hatred suffered by the weaker sections of the society. He was anguished by the fact that religion was largely reduced to ritualism and blind faith, and used to serve vested interests of powerful priests and politicians. His deep understanding of the Indian spiritual heritage had convinced him that religion had much to offer to society in dealing with perennial evils like greed, hatred, corruption, misery and social disrespect for the poor and weak. His holistic perspective on religion and society created an abiding urge in him to revive and promote the value of religion as a living institution in the service of contemporary society.

Dada placed the human being at the centre of all thought and action on social development. The term *swadhyaya* is conventionally used in its literal sense of self-learning. However, in the *Parivar* context it is extended to include self-development and enlightenment. In *Dada*'s reckoning, thinkers and reformers such as Freud, Marx and Gandhi had striven hard to restore human dignity, but their efforts had not yielded expected results. Freud and Marx made wrong assumptions about human nature and desires. Gandhi's unavoidable preoccupation with politics blocked his programmes for moral and social regeneration through which he wanted to reach the most deprived and exploited people. In this background, *Dada*'s action plan for human development implied creation of lasting bonds of unity and fraternity among people, to enable them to rise beyond the debilitating traits of selfishness, greed, arrogance and exploitation.

And who could be a more effective pathfinder in dealing with this agenda than Lord *Yogeshwara*, the supreme entity of the well-known cream of Indian scriptures, the Bhagavadgita? *Dada* focused on *bhakti* (devotion) as the most effective and relevant for meaningful social existence. *Yogeshwara* symbolized God, the creator of all humanity and all that exists. His most significant abode is the heart of every individual. This conviction led *Dada* to propose the belief in an indwelling God and universal brotherhood under His Fatherhood. *Bhakti* constitutes the essence of human life which should be lived as a constant expression of gratitude to Him. Human beings should build and strengthen relations among themselves on the basis of *asmita* (recognition of dignified existence) and *atmiyata* (oneness or solidarity among all). Indeed, all acts of love and solidarity are manifestations of *bhakti* and gratitude to God. The most effective form of *bhakti* is *krutibhakti* (action-oriented devotion) rather than blind faith or ritualism. *Bhakti* is projected as a social force for dealing with current social problems. When a person uses his knowledge or skill in the service of his brethren, he is supposed to perform *puja* (worship). He is therefore a *pujari* (lit. priest but, in the present context, worshipper) offering his efficiency in gratitude to the Lord. A person's contribution of manual labour in any community-oriented activity is recognized as *shrambhakti* (devotion through labour).

The principal elements of the scriptural wisdom churned out by *Dada* within his special socio-religious perspective were transmitted to his devout audiences in Bombay with the help of the inexhaustible stories and lessons in religious literature. *Dada*'s inimitable style and ability to combine scriptural tales with popular experience helped him to put across the most profound lessons in delightfully simple language. His graciously simple personality with a magnetic effect on people and his inexhaustible powerhouse of youthful energy induced in his followers an unusual sense of holy respect and devotion for him and his preachings.

Beginning of Action

Dada initially thought he would pursue his plans for self-development by influencing the minds of the younger generations with a suitable educational programme. He explored ideas to set up educational institutions to promote learning in terms of its relevance to his ideas of human dignity, equality, welfare and development. An institution called *Tatvagnyan Vidyapith* (University of Philosophy) was set up in Thane in 1956. This institution offers young graduate-level students a two year education in Indian and western religion, science, philosophy and humanities. However, he soon realized that involvement in conventional modes of education would mean dependence on Government and other agencies for financial support and management of bureaucratic systems with their well-known vulnerability and pitfalls. In his understanding, survival of a social programme on public funds and formal-legal authority structures was inherently opposed to the basic concepts of *Swadhyaya* such as self-development, human dignity and action-based *bhakti*. The institution at Thane continues to run the two-year educational programme and also provides shorter exposures to *swadhyayis* according to specific needs from time to time. Three other institutions in Gujarat set up by the *Parivar* cater to the educational needs of children of rural *swadhyayi* families to enable them to retain their rural moorings and contribute to propagation of the *Swadhyaya* message. All these institutions are managed entirely with financial, academic and administrative resources available within the *Parivar*. But the idea of propagation of *Swadhyaya* through formal education was abandoned.

Meanwhile, *Dada*'s conscience was greatly disturbed by the atheistic propaganda aggressively launched in the fifties by international socialism by free and wide distribution of literature against basic religious beliefs in rural areas. *Dada* shared his anguish with his nineteen prominent disciples. He inspired them to extend their religious learning beyond their own character and conduct. It was time their *Swadhyaya* experience was carried to villages to contain the effects of socialist propaganda against God and help the masses to understand the significance and value of active and reason-based religion. The disciples wondered how they, the Bombay-based upper-middle class professionals and businessmen, could reach the rural masses. *Dada* prescribed the following approach.

(1)Your main task should be to carry the *Swadhyaya* message to the last man in the village you visit. However, your trips will be a part of your own learning and development. Do not assume the role of preachers or social workers.

(2)The villagers have no experience of anyone visiting them without expecting anything in return. Hence they will not trust you easily. You may have to use infinite patience and ingenuity to convince people that you really do not expect anything in return for your visits. As a first step, you should take a pledge not to accept any material hospitality from your hosts barring plain water. You will bear all the costs of your visits.

(3) Your visits to villages and contact with the masses will be a continuing process and an integral part of your life and work. And yet, you will continue to do all your other work. You should normally dedicate two days in a month for 'Gods Work'.

Trips of Devotion

The guidelines energized the disciples. They launched their rural visits in some villages in the Kachchha-Saurashtra region of Gujarat. As the programme crystallized, it was given the title *bhaktipheri* (trip of devotion).

It was indeed tough for the visitors to gain acceptability from the villagers they visited. In many cases, they were insulted, threatened, humiliated or neglected by the people. However, they were determined to bear with all such treatment with love, patience and fortitude. They put up with all types of indifference, insult and aggression, often experiencing repeated fruitless travel between Bombay and Saurashtra. Gradually, the hosts were convinced about the totally unselfish and noble intentions of the visitors and responded with much love and gratitude. This initial trickle of love, faith and devotion soon became a stream of *Swadhyaya* with ever-increasing numbers of *Dada*'s disciples eager to make *bhaktipheri* an inseparable part of their life's mission and the masses of rural folk, ready to accept *Swadhyaya* as a way of life. Today the *Parivar* includes over two million people with over 50,000 study centres and 200,000 active *swadhyayis* in about 150,000 towns and villages in Gujarat, Maharashtra, Rajasthan, Madhya Pradesh, Uttar Pradesh, Andhra Pradesh and other states as well as countries outside India such as the USA, the UK and some places in Europe and the Middle East. Of these, nearly eighty per cent followers are in Gujarat and about ten per cent in Maharashtra.

Typically, a *bhaktipheri* visitor begins at a new place by conveying the essence of true religion with the help of anecdotes and interpretations from religious-spiritual literature and recitation of devotional songs and verses. For this purpose, they depend on the inexhaustible source of material based on *Dada*'s regular and occasional discourses documented in books, audio and video cassettes and a house magazine. In course of time, the host learns *trikal sandhya* which consists of ten verses of gratitude to God to be recited daily in three parts.

Centres of Self Development

When a reasonably large number of people in a place (around twenty) show sufficient commitment to *Swadhyaya*, a study centre (*swadhyaya kendra* is set up. The local *swadhyayis* meet for an hour on a fixed day every week, recite and learn new verses from scriptures, celebrate festivals and listen to *Dada*'s discourse. These weekly meetings enable the *swadhyayis* to meet socially, build new relations and strengthen existing relations of love. In course of time, special study centres for women (*mahila kendra*) are set up where women in a village or neighbourhood learn devotional hymns and scriptural knowledge. Later, exclusive study centres for children (*bal sanskar kendra*) are set up to induct children into *Swadhyaya*. An exclusive programme for young men entitled 'Divine Brain Trust' includes training in organization, leadership and social service as an integral part of religious and spiritual learning.

Impersonal Wealth

How would one deal with the ground-level economic problem of poverty and want without compromising the idea of human dignity in any manner? *Dada* brought in an innovative approach to this problem: production and distribution of collective wealth in a community, with full regard for equality and dignity of all human beings. The logic of collective wealth is anchored in the belief in God as the owner of all wealth. Wealth is generated and used in His name which makes it *apaurusheya* (impersonal). This concept of impersonal wealth was put into practice first in relation to the fisher community in Gujarat, as we shall see later. Subsequently, the concept was extended to launch a variety of socio-economic experiments in rural areas. One such experiment is called *yogeshwara krushi* (the Lord's farm) which involves cultivation of a plot of farmland by turns by *swadhyayis* in a local community. All inputs on this plot are contributed by the community as an offering to the Lord and the proceeds from its output are kept in a fund from which the poor are provided financial help as *prasada* (grace). Another experiment in this category is *vruksha mandir* (tree temple) which involves collective cultivation of a barren plot of land to grow economically and environmentally useful trees and orchards. In this case, the responsibility of cultivation is borne by a group of villages in the neighbourhood of the cultivated tree plot. When a village attains the status of a *swadhyayi* village (with nearly the whole population following *Swadhyaya* discipline), the people there are permitted to construct a *loknath amrutalayam* (the immortal abode of the people's Lord). It consists of a temple which is built entirely by the resources and labour contributed by the local community. The ritual worship of the images in the temple is performed in turn by the local people regardless of caste distinctions. All the offerings by the people are collected in a fund in the Lord's name and used in the interests of the poor people. At present, the *Parivar* has in its mix of programmes over 3225 farmplots dedicated to *yogeshwara krushi*, sixteen *vruksha mandirs* and ninety one *loknath amrutalayams*. Similar experiments have been launched in recent years with respect to the economic activities of diamond cutting, dairy-farming and vegetable-selling. An experimental mechanical workshop near Ahmedabad and a retail groceries shop in Junagadh have been set up and are being managed on the principle of impersonal wealth.

Circulation and Celebration

A remarkable feature of *Swadhyaya* work is constant circulation of activists - from *Dada* down to the workers at the taluka and village levels. *Dada* and his niece known as *Didi* (Marathi equivalent of sister, who shares with Dada the overall responsibility for the mission) undertake frequent trips to the various regions with a significant *Swadhyaya* following. They renew their contacts with local people, advise them on future activities and extension of the mission, and review on-going projects. Workers from the regions and sub-regions also visit Bombay to seek advice from *Dada* and *Didi* on various aspects of their work. A multi-storeyed building in central Bombay is used as *Swadhyaya* headquarters. This building houses various administrative units to manage accounts, publications, video and audio recording facilities, public relations, etc.

The active workers travel with incredible regularity and discipline. A large number of people including engineers, lawyers, teachers, doctors, businessmen, etc., living in Bombay have been making one, two, or at times more trips every month to remote places in Gujarat as a part of their *bhaktipheri* obligation. Similarly, people living in various urban centres of Gujarat and elsewhere periodically visit villages in various areas on *bhaktipheri* mission. Moreover, activists at the district and lower levels frequently attend meetings relating to routine work, new projects or special functions and ceremonies. Once in a year, *swadhyayis* from adjacent talukas in a district undertake a week-long goodwill visit to each other under a programme called *tirthayatra* (pilgrimage to holy shrines).

Several mammoth gatherings of *swadhyayis* have been held so far at different places; they have been attended by hundreds of thousands of people on each occasion. A pioneering gathering of this type was the *tirtharaj milan* (meeting at a premier holy place) at Allahabad for three days in March 1986. About 350,000 people from various parts of India and abroad participated in this meeting. Since then, several large gatherings have been held at various places. These are usually linked with *Dada*'s birthday which is observed as an occasion to dedicate oneself to the promotion of human dignity.

Creative Community Development

In recent years *Swadhyaya* has made a notable contribution to socio-economic development in the area of augmentation of water resources for human consumption and farm productivity. *Dada*'s close familiarity with the alarming problem of scarcity of water through his ever-growing contacts with people at all levels led him over a decade ago to recognize the need for replenishment of underground water. He inspired *swadhyayis* to devise methods of recharging of village wells by harvesting of rain water. He also advised people to minimize evaporation of water consumed by them by facilitating its flow underground. *Dada*'s concerns and ideas were accepted by a group of activists in the Junagadh area. They worked hard in collaboration with farm scientists and technical experts to evolve simple and inexpensive methods of recharging village wells and reservoirs. The process of recharging for the most part involved physical labour of digging and clearing soil. Capital investment was extremely low, limited to common pipes and filters.

The *Swadhyaya* activists developed proficiency in the methods of recharging by acquiring knowledge about the various types of reservoirs and their physical settings. They estimated the need of recharging about 80000 wells in the Saurashtra-Kutch region. By May 1994, about 23000 wells were already recharged. Manual labour for the project was provided in the usual *Swadhyaya* spirit by fellow *swadhyayis* who offered their energy in the form of *shrambhakti*.

Dignity for the Disadvantaged

An important aspect of the *Swadhyaya* mission to reach the ideals of human dignity, social equality fortified by divine fraternity and social justice, was to induct the destitute and the deprived of the society. In the seventies, *Dada*'s attention turned towards the fisherfolk along the coastal areas of Gujarat and Maharashtra. Subsequently, special efforts were launched to induct into *Swadhyaya* some tribal groups and sections of *Vaghari* (an ex-tribal community known for anti-social and criminal proclivities) and *dalit* (traditionally suffering from the scourge of untouchability and social degradation) communities. In this section, I present a brief and rather sketchy account of the process of social transformation generated by *Swadhyaya* among these four disadvantaged sections of population in Gujarat.

Fishing for Fraternity

The fisherfolk in Saurashtra and South Gujarat regions have traditionally lived in extreme poverty and squalor. The men are known for drunkenness, other vices and profanity of conduct within the family and the community. *Dada* spent a considerable time with them, understood their situation and kindled hope in their hearts by his message of universal brotherhood and human dignity. He gave them a dignified new name *Sagarputra* (child of the ocean-god). *Dada*'s efforts were supported by the *bhaktipheri* contacts by *swadhyayi* groups over long periods. The fisherfolk gradually learnt *trikal sandhya* and acquired the salient aspects of religious and spiritual knowledge. The *Swadhyaya* ethos guided them to change their personal and social behaviour. They gradually accepted upper-caste norms of cleanliness, decency, self-respect, respect for others, confidence and freedom from vices. As they began to internalize the belief in an indwelling God, it was fairly easy to get out of addiction, filth and indecency in His name.

Knowledge about acute poverty suffered by a large section of the fisherfolk stirred *Dada*'s mind. He looked for ways of meeting their needs without diluting the *Swadhyaya* goal of promotion of human dignity and equality. He invoked the concept of religion and worship as a social force. He persuaded them to agree that the contributions received as offerings to the deity in the community temple from the people, could be treated as the community's resource. It would be used to help people in need who would receive such help secretly and impersonally as *prasada* from God. It was also decided that the relatively better-provided fishermen would put aside a part of their earnings to contribute to a common fund in the Lord's name. This fund would be partly used to help the poor and starving brethren. The income generated by these contributions was managed carefully to raise enough money to buy a fishing boat on behalf of the community. The first such boat was bought in 1981. *Dada* suggested the name *matsyagandha* (a legendary fisherwoman) for the new acquisition. An innovative method of management of fishing was adopted on *Dada*'s advice. The motorised trawler was used for fishing everyday. However, the expedition was manned each day by a group of fishermen from the community on a rotating basis. The day's collections were credited to a common fund in the name of God. One-third of the total revenue was earmarked to be offered as *prasada* to the poor and destitute members of the community. The balance was sent to the *Swadhyaya* funds in Bombay for future use for the members of the community.

This was, after *bhaktipheri*, a major stride in the *Swadhyaya* movement. Work was exhilaratingly converted into worship. The worker on *matsyagandha* does not receive any compensation for his work. In fact, he takes his own food for the day on the expedition. He works on the expedition in the role of a *pujari.* He treats the boat as a temple.

The first *matsyagandha* experiment was eminently successful. It served to minimize the state of deprivation of the poorest fisherfolk families. It also contributed to a corpus of funds which continues to grow. This achievement inspired several such ventures in the coastal regions. Today, there are over thirty *matsyagandha* boats functioning to generate impersonal wealth. The fishing communities involved in these ventures have become economically better provided. Their children have begun to receive better formal education in addition to the religious and moral education they are offered through *Swadhyaya* children's centres. Many families have acquired symbols of modern living in terms of clothing, furniture, transport and entertainment instruments. During the last few years, the accumulated funds on *matsyagandha* account have been used to invest in transport trucks to generate further impersonal wealth or to help poor fisherfolk to engage in small scale trade and commerce. A total amount of Rs. 35,00,000/- was recently disbursed by *Dada* to young fishermen to enable them to launch a small business enterprise.

In one village, a Brahmin priest could not cope with the pressure of work to officiate at rituals and ceremonies. *Dada* inspired and trained a few fishermen to conduct the main rituals such as weddings. They were also sanctified by the sacred thread. These new priests filled the void created by unavailability of the traditional priest. But *Dada* asked the new fishermen priests to hand over their income from priestly work to the traditional Brahmin. The new priests would serve the social needs but not deprive the Brahmin of his traditional source of income. This humble episode carries a vital message in human dignity and social equality. A new socio-economic role was conferred upon people in the lower sections of social hierarchy without compromising the economic interest of those who were dependent on that role.

The Tribal Turnaround

Swadhyaya was introduced into the tribal community of the *Dungri Bhils* in the Vijaynagar taluka of the Sabarkantha district in Gujarat during 1983-84. Until then, the tribals had lived in abject poverty. They survived mainly on tiny bits of land and forest products. Many of them supplemented their income by boot-legging, petty theft and robberies. Men spent much of their time in drinking and gangsterism. The rural population in the region felt terrorized by the tribals and often suffered assaults from them. The rural population included a caste group called the *Kachchhi Patel* who were migrants from the Kachchh region and had acquired significant holdings of land in this region. Some leading members of this caste had taken to *Swadhyaya* before they left Kachchh. They served as a link for a group of Bombay *swadhyayis* who began *bhaktipheri* in the region especially aimed at the tribals. They began weekly trips to the region in three groups. The local people treated them with much indifference and hostility. However, they were not deterred by such experiences and continued to visit the villages and appeal to the local people to accept their message of love and brotherhood. Gradually, the tribals were persuaded to interact with the visitors. They realized that the strangers had no selfish design on the local people. They began to understand that they had been travelling from Bombay just to build a relation of love and brotherhood with the local people. The original fear and distrust disappeared. A tribal youth leader was invited by the visitors to spend a few days in Bombay. He met *Dada* and participated in a training programme. He pledged active involvement in spreading *Swadhyaya* among his people. In course of time, *Swadhyaya* study centres were established in various places and people learnt the elements of *Swadhyaya* discipline and also undertook *bhaktipheri.*

Swadhyaya changed the lives of the people in the region. *Dada* gave them a new name *Vanavasi* (forest dweller) as a mark of a new social identity. Those who spent a lot of time in drinking, petty robberies and idle gossip gave up such habits. They paid greater attention to work on their land or whatever else they did for livelihood. Their *swadhyaya* mentors in their neighbourhood and in Bombay introduced them to modern methods of farming which raised their incomes. On some occasions they were offered financial aid under government's rural development programme. They declined such help under the influence of the lessons they had learnt in self-dependence and human dignity. They would rather work hard, save money and achieve a better quality of life. Those who could barely sustain their families began to earn significant incomes to live decently. Their family life which was punctuated by frequent deprivations and discord became more harmonious, peaceful and happy. Women and children who were usually victims of the male earner's arrogance and wayward behaviour developed a sense of dignity and self-confidence. They learnt to sing religious hymns with admirable command over language and sing songs filled with *Swadhyaya* ideas and ideals. Children learnt to turn down offers of free gift.

Rama (not her real name) is a young housewife from a small peasant family in a tribal hamlet. I met her in July 1994 during a brief visit to her homestead. She responded to questions on her personal and social life with a quality of candour and confidence that would make any well-nurtured urban woman envious of her with her four-grade primary education. She said:

I was very young when I was married. My husband, like most other men in the village, was a liquor-addict. We were very poor in spite of about ten acres of land at our disposal. When my husband returned home from the farm, he immediately demanded food and often beat me cruelly.

She added: The ideas and activities of *Dada's* *Swadhyaya Parivar* arrived in our village some years ago. Since then, our family life has changed radically. We have learnt trikal sandhya and other Sanskrit hymns prescribed by *Swadhyaya.* We meet our village-folk and also regularly visit neighbouring villages on *bhaktipheri*. My husband works hard on the farm. We now take multiple crops. Our annual income is close to one lakh rupees. Our elder daughter is in the twelfth class. Our two daughters will not be married until they become adults.

Tribals generally live in dispersed settlements with each house located on the edge of a plot of farm land. This condition creates barriers in physical and social communication among the residents of a local community. *Dada* invented a remarkable method of reinforcing bonds among these people. A *ghar-mandir* (house temple) was established in each settlement. The temple consists of a set of divine images along with a minimum paraphernalia of items for worship and upkeep. This shrine moves from house to house in the settlement. Each family attends to the shrine and perform rituals of worship for a week and then transfers it to another household. The formal worship is held in the morning and evening every day. The other families are welcome to join in the chorus of devotion and gratitude.

This novel method of community worship had considerable social significance. When a householder has the responsibility of hosting a shrine in his house, he cannot indulge in any profane habit or behaviour. Hence, he abstains from such habits while he hosts God. Once he begins to abstain from bad habits, he realizes the monetary and social gains of temperance and good behaviour. *Swadhyaya* thus propels reform into one's personal and social behaviour.

The tribal population chronically suffers from ailments such as scabies (due to unclean habits) and tuberculosis (due to malnutrition). A group of *swadhyayi* medical practitioners and consultants began to visit tribal villages as a part of their *bhaktipheri* commitment. As a result of this experience, *Dada* realized the concrete value of continuing medical assistance for the tribal community. Accordingly, a dispensary was set up in a village in September 1994. A large number of *swadhyayi* doctors from the Sabarkantha region as well as far away places like Ahmedabad made commitments to serve this facility as *pujaris*. The community in and around the dispensary has access to modern medical treatment. Scabies and other sanitation-based ailments have been brought under control.

Dignifying the Dalit

The socio-economic plight of the *dalit* sections of society (scheduled castes, formerly treated as untouchables) was for long a matter of concern for *Dada*. He had admiration for reformers like Gandhi and Ambedkar in their efforts to raise the status and dignity of these groups. However, he was convinced that the political and communal dimensions of such reform movements would not allow for a social and psychological equation of love, respect and dignity between *dalits* and caste Hindus. During the latter years of the eighties, *swadhyayis* in Ahmedabad and other urban centres in Gujarat developed contacts with *dalit* groups in their areas. The response was encouraging. In 1990, about 500 *dalit* men and women were invited to a special congregation in Ahmedabad. Over 150 local families volunteered to provide local hospitality to the *dalit* guests. For this purpose, the *swadhyayi* hosts were asked to make sure that every member of a host household was ready to accept the unusual guests without any reservation whatsoever. *dalit* men and women spent two days in upper caste homes, sharing space and facilities as members of a family. *Swadhyaya* moved that day in a significant step towards abolition of one of the most obnoxious social barriers in Indian society - the curse of untouchability.

Dada was present during the special meeting in Ahmedabad. He explained to the *dalits* his ideas of human dignity and universal brotherhood. As a mark of recognition of their dignity, it was decided that the *dalits* would be known in the *parivar* as *bhavalakshi* (compassion-oriented). Since then, about 3000 *dalit* families have adopted *Swadhyaya* in Gujarat. Two-thirds of these *swadhyayis* are in Ahmedabad. They have adopted a new life-style to include the *Swadhyaya* norms of personal hygiene, temperance, love, fraternity, hard work, attendance in *Swadhyaya* meetings and celebrations and *bhaktipheri*. As in the case of other disadvantaged sections, the *dalit swadhyayis* have acquired a sense of dignity and confidence. A *dalit* was asked whether he still retained hatred towards the Brahmins. He replied, "I feel I am a Brahmin. There is no question of hatred towards anyone. *Swadhyaya* has dissolved all my hatred."

A young female *dalit* doctor and her doctor husband from the same community are prominent *Swadhyaya* activists. She offered a most touching view of the plight of ex-untouchables due to the treatment received by them from caste-Hindus:

While a street dog can roam from the corridors of a *dalit* house to the courtyard of a caste-Hindu, a *dalit* child is not allowed to follow that path. We have suffered extreme humiliation and torture for centuries. Leaders like Gandhiji and Ambedkar tried hard to remove the indignities and inequalities suffered by us. But they could not reach the minds and hearts of ordinary people. When *Swadhyaya* convened a mass meeting of *dalits* in Ahmedabad, it was an unbelievable breakthrough for us. We were invited to meet *Dada* within the premises of a temple. We received from *Dada* a clear message of genuine equality and fraternity with the higher castes. The message was transmitted to us with a clear understanding that *Swadhyaya* did not expect any political or financial benefit by spreading the message of spiritual and social equality.

Devi's Devotees

Activists in Ahmedabad and some other places have influenced several *Vaghari* clusters and persuaded the residents to accept the *Swadhyaya* way of life. The *Vaghari* community is notorious for criminal tendencies and unbecoming behaviour. The burden of earning bread is usually borne by women who practise petty itinerant trade in the streets. The men generally laze around and indulge in all types of vice. They spend much of their time in acts of petty violence, theft and gangsterism.

The influence of *Swadhyaya* has changed this profile of the community. In the *Parivar* parlance, the title *Vaghari* has been replaced by *Devipujak* (the devotees of the goddess). Women continue to slog as bread-earners by selling utensils, old clothes and sundry articles. But they have adopted many symbols of middle-class behaviour. They save money. They have acquired decent household goods and minor luxury articles. They have been able to wean their menfolk away from vice and perennial domestic quarrels and wife-baiting. Families in a neighbourhood which were conventionally at war with one another have begun to unite and cooperate. The boys here have stopped participating in gang wars and criminal acts. They have begun to help their families by earning or receiving formal education. They recite *trikal sandhya* and other verses of prayer in chaste Sanskrit. *Vaghari* families attend weekly discourses and participate in celebration of festivals. They also undertake regular rounds of *bhaktipheri* to spread the message of Yogeshwara and the thoughts of *Dada* which, they are sure, have pulled them out of an existence of deprivation and worthlessness.

Contribution to Social Transformation

What role can a mission such as *Swadhyaya* play in the process of social transformation in India? Where does it stand as an alternative approach to socio-economic development in developing countries?

An answer to this question would depend essentially on one's choice of the meaning of social transformation. Social scientists, philosophers, rulers, non-ruling elite and ordinary citizens tend to construct their own images of social reality on the basis of their experience and perceptions. These constructs of reality are judged by an observer in relation to an ideal state of reality or utopia guiding his inquiry. Social transformation is then measured, in varying degrees of objective clarity and accuracy, in terms of the magnitude and pace of change in attaining the chosen utopia. I have no intention of attempting an elaborate discussion of this subject. However, it is not out of place here to underscore the relativity of concepts, models and interventions in social transformation due to variations in people's equations of current reality and goals of transformation. This is why, for instance, poverty or hunger may not qualify as a significant factor in human development, for those of us who regard macro-level techno-economic progress as the primary goal of social transformation.

For the present purpose, it will be useful to side with those scholars and practitioners in social transformation whose utopia is based on the principles of social equality, justice, freedom and dignity enshrined in the Constitution of India.[5] These people are perturbed by the pervasive failure of Indian society to move significantly towards the cherished goals, since they were formally adopted in 1950. They also share misgivings about the capability of the state and its numerous agencies to lead the society on the right track with the structural reforms in its economic, political and social sub-systems as contemplated and practised over more than four decades since Independence. The gap between the desired social goals and reality, and the obstacles to making a satisfactory progress towards the goals constitute the problem of social development.

An expanding school of thought on this subject places India in the company of other nations in the so-called Third World (or the South), and assumes considerable similarity in their problems of social development.[6] This school emphasizes the cumulative evidence of failure to solve the problems of social development in the South of both the neo-classical and Marxist paradigms of economic and political reforms. Both these paradigms are based on a rational scientific approach to social living and progress, predominance of a centralized and monolithic mode of development and preponderance of the role of the state in management of the development process. These paradigms oriented to the western mode of social thinking and outlook, have left unresolved, critical problems like poverty, disease, illiteracy, degradation of natural resources and inequitable distribution of wealth. Hence, it is suggested that we should look for alternative modes of development that would be compatible with the conditions and needs of the Third World countries. The main elements of the alternative modes of development proposed by this school include (i) special concern for human welfare and quality of life; (ii) use of local knowledge, resources and values; (iii) participation of people at the grassroots level in organizing and managing their socio-economic affairs and (iv) decentralization of power to enable deprived and vulnerable sections of society to resolve the conditions of inequality.

Contemporary non-Government efforts in socio-economic development are usually built on the assumption that the problems of poverty, injustice, degradation, etc., emanate from the economic, social and political structure and are sustained by a legacy of ignorance and powerlessness among the weaker sections. Hence the main approach towards resolution of the problems involves alteration or modification in the current structure. For this purpose, the economic, social or political dominance of the affluent sections (the rich, the dominant castes, the political bosses, the male of the species, etc.), needs to be challenged. Social action is advocated for raising the economic, social and political resources and capabilities of the weaker sections (the poor, the depressed castes, minority communities, women, etc.). This process of social intervention, currently popularized with the title 'empowerment', includes mobilization of the weak to gain functional awareness of their situation and collective action to secure control over social resources (wealth, status, power) to improve their lot. This effort in conscientization and mobilization of the weaker sections is generally believed to involve an assumption of disharmony and conflict of interest between the affluent and the weak in a specific social context. An important part of the strategy of development is to enable the weak to acquire a countervailing power to gain a larger share in resources, opportunities and control over both. Such action programmes often involve discord, confrontation and conflict in dealing with the problems of exploitation and degradation.

Swadhyaya has adopted a different approach to empowerment of the weak. This approach recognizes the individual as the most crucial variable in the action programme for dealing with a social problem. Hence, transformation of the individual is the central concern in all *Swadhyaya* activities. A spontaneous expression often used by Dada to summarize his mission is 'I want to awaken the human being'. As Roy (1993), suggests, *Swadhyaya* implies emancipation of the human being from self-centred economism and seductive consumerism. The positive aspect of this emancipation is to lead an individual through a process of moral regeneration in which he internalizes the basic values, adopts and reflects them in concrete behaviour and attitudes and transmits them regularly to other persons as an agent of change.

Facets of Regeneration

The process of moral regeneration is a multi-dimensional intervention covering a wide spectrum of a *swadhyayi's* personal and social life. Let us briefly examine its main facets.

Swadhyaya emphasizes primarily a course of self-learning and self-development for a person who is inducted into it. In reality, the content and process of learning is meticulously planned at each stage. A person involved in *bhaktipheri* interacts with strangers and new members in prescribed stages, which include songs, anecdotes, Sanskrit verses and thoughts on society and religion. *Dada*'s discourses provide the mainspring for this learning and contain a wealth of knowledge, experience and ideas. The ideas cover relevant parts of the contributions of major thinkers ranging from Vedic scholars and Socrates to Marx, Gandhi, Einstein and others of their ilk. *Swadhyaya* has enabled and empowered ordinary men and women to understand the role of ideas in life and disseminate the ideas to others. This gives confidence, dignity and a new meaning to social existence. It is not rare to hear from the lower classes and tribal communities that *Swadhyaya* is effective in human development because it is based on the foundation of *bhakti* and ideas from scriptures. On numerous occasions I have been told by *swadhyayis* how their life and outlook changed, consequent to their exposure to *Dada*'s ideas.

Swadhyaya has given a lot of confidence to its followers in their personal and social conduct. *Swadhyayis* constantly exchange information and ideas among themselves. They also need to communicate with others during *bhaktipheri*, celebration of festivals and numerous other activities. They are aware that human dignity is one of the main pillars of *Swadhyaya*. Consequently, they acquire enough self-learning through human interaction along with straightforwardness, fearlessness and mutual respect.

Swadhyaya has inculcated a distinct sense of order and discipline among its followers. Go to any small or large gathering of *swadhyayis*. The first pleasant sight is where they remove their footwear. You will invariably see the pairs of shoes, etc. placed neatly in an order. They compulsively sit in neat rows. They always wait for their turn in all matters. The *Parivar* has developed enough strength of trained volunteers to regulate traffic, help people and maintain discipline and order in gatherings, however small or large. In fact, the *Parivar's* ability to cope with gatherings of several lakhs of people has become legendary. In places where *Swadhyaya* commands a significant following, the local non-*swadhyayi* population habitually develops trust in a *swadhyayi* for discipline, honesty and integrity.

Swadhyaya emphasizes cleanliness of mind and body. Hence people in the lower socio-economic strata with a pervasive culture of unclean habits in respect of the body, have adopted a code of personal hygiene and tidiness. They have also given up addiction to things such as tobacco and liquor. Interestingly, these changes in personal habits do not need to be prescribed or preached by *Dada* or anyone else. A *swadhyayi* adopts a new code of personal habits easily and quickly because he is fully convinced that the human body is the abode of God.

Any large function organized by the *Parivar* gives to any casual visitor, pleasant surprises in human creativity. During the last few years, I have seen festoons, banners, posters, pictures, badges, platforms, stages, etc., made with admirable aesthetic taste and talent with collective efforts by rural, tribal and other teams of men and women cutting across socio-economic hierarchy. The raw material for most decorative creations includes waste products such as broken glass, thermocole and cotton-waste.

Swadhyaya inculcates commitment to hard work. Work is regarded as a form of *bhakti*. A person who helps others or participates in collective efforts organized by the *Parivar* is expected to give his efficiency (skill, talent, knowledge) to the Lord in gratitude for being created by Him. A medical expert participating in a *Swadhyaya* clinic, an engineer contributing to plans for a *Swadhyaya* project, an accountant keeping accounts for a *Parivar* activity or project are all contributors to *shrambhakti*. It is not uncommon for *swadhyayis* to stand up to any odds to fulfill commitments to any individual or collective activity.

Swadhyaya brings together men and women from different strata in regular *bhaktipheri* meetings or special celebrations and collective projects. *Bhaktipheri* largely includes periodical visits by the urban middle class people to the abodes of underprivileged classes in rural and tribal areas. These visits offer an otherwise improbable opportunity to the visitors and the host family to interact with each other in a direct sharing of social space. Such interaction helps the privileged in the dissolution of personal and social ego which is one of the important elements of moral regeneration prescribed by *Dada*. This opportunity also facilitates an understanding among the rich upper castes about the realities of the socio-economic conditions of poorer and disadvantaged sections of rural population. Conversely, the poorer, lower-caste people get an exposure to the behaviour and attitudes of the more affluent sections of society. It would be greatly educative to find how such interaction moves the perspectives and conscience of the privileged and the underprivileged people towards one another.

We should take a special note of *Swadhyaya's* effective challenge to the centuries old view that untouchability in India is sanctioned by scriptures. The remarkable effect of this challenge on the interaction between high-caste Hindus and *dalits* is potentially a vital force in its contribution to social transformation. In the broader sense, the dissolution of collective egoism based on caste or class is an extremely important part of social education and transformation attempted by *Swadhyaya.*

Should we then recognize a *swadhyayi's* moral regeneration as a unique process towards a quality of life that any votary of social transformation in the present context could accept as a role model?

The various elements of the *Swadhyaya* quality of life are visible to an observer in any reasonably sustained contact with *swadhyayis* in various roles. A crucial aspect of this phenomenon is that a typical *swadhyayi* constantly reinforces his ideas and actions by a well-orchestrated belief that his task is essentially to follow *Dada*'s ideas and directives. These ideas and directives, in turn, are rooted in India's religious and spiritual heritage, which is sought to be resurrected to enrich and enliven modern society. These two factors - absolute faith in *Dada*'s leadership and its religious content - constitute extremely powerful sanctions for a *swadhyayi's* commitment to the new quality of life.

Any model of the quality of life presents a utopian image. The effect of the quality of life on a society would depend on the nature and degree of adherence to the model in the various facets of behaviour of the actors governed by it. In this sense, it is hard to say at present anything about conformity to the *Swadhyaya* way of life among the vast population of the *Parivar.* An important question in relation to social transformation is: in what way do the elements of *Swadhyaya* quality of life extend to comprehensively cover socio-economic behaviour of *swadhyayis?* As *Swadhyaya* constitutes a relatively small part of most *swadhyayis'* social living, the question raised here may have considerable significance. Such questions, however, are hard to answer. We need to know how a *swadhyayi* blends or connects the *swadhyaya* code of life with the complex socio-economic and political realities around him.

God as Social Role-Model

The *swadhyaya* programme of social transformation among the weaker sections of society follows from the postulate of indwelling God as a prime mover of all that exists. The main mission of God through his numerous incarnations has been to promote the well-being of society at large and protect the disadvantaged members from want and suffering. A *swadhyayi's* learning contains plenty of signals to lead him to adopt God's social role as a role model for his social activities. Accordingly, every individual should contribute to social reform by promoting common welfare and happiness. The special efforts to improve the socio-economic situation of the fisherfolk, *Vaghari, dalit* and tribal communities represent concrete action towards this objective. The socio-economic programmes such as *matsyagandha, amrutalayam* and *vrukshamandir* are unconventional and creative experiments in producing and distributing wealth with little, if any, interference by the forces of social control which dominate all other known systems of economic organization.

The spiritual idiom adopted in the concept of work and division of labour raises the motivation and commitment of every worker and gives him the much prized reward of self-fulfilment. This contributes to a rise in individual and collective productivity on the collective farm or fishing enterprise. It is also possible that the improved ethos of motivation and productivity would make people more motivated and productive in their individual and family enterprise. The economic value of emphasis on hard work and abstinence from liquor and other addictions also supplement the material gains for individuals, families and the community. However, the wider effects of *Swadhyaya* experiments on the motivation and productivity of the constituents are for the present only logical deductions which need to be empirically tested.

Swadhyaya seeks to deal with the problem of poverty partly through the creation of additional wealth by improved utilization of idle time and the distribution of the newly-created wealth in a manner which removes false pride in the giver and any feeling of embarassment or indignity in the receiver. Thus, modest attempts are made to contribute to the economic empowerment of the poor people without a direct attack on the affluence of the rich. A salutary social effect of this effort has been suggested by Ekins (1992), in the form of a new impulse and motivation for fostering care for the unfortunate. Also, the quality and degree of commitment of people to economic activity are raised by equating the role of a worker as a worshipper rather than as labourer, manager or owner of resources.

A major socio-economic value of *Swadhyaya* is its contribution to resolution of critical environmental issues. The *vruksha* mandir experiments constitute a direct participation in afforestation, as they are usually organized on barren lands which were for long written off as totally incapable of yielding farm produce. Apart from the immediate economic gains from these experiments, they also serve as models for social and economic innovation. The spiritual perspective guiding these experiments helps to build a harmonious and reverential relation between man and nature, as Ekins (1992) has commended.

Intellectual Assimilation of Faith

The unique approach of *Swadhyaya* to the task of forging and strengthening of social bonds helps to create a strong and immediate bond between the chief promoter and the last man, woman and child in villages and homesteads. The emphasis on regular weekly discourses and on *bhaktipheri* keeps the social bonds alive all the time. Further, the mandatory requirement for a *swadhyayi* to influence the thoughts and behaviour of others implies a ceaseless process of communication and contacts among *Parivar* members as well as *non-swadhyayis*. All social and political movements aim at ensuring participation of constituents at all levels, and also at constantly extending the base of membership. However, they make demands on the economic and social resources of members. Also, they often do not possess the crucial resource of deeply internalized and intellectually assimilated faith which *Swadhyaya* helps to inculcate across the length and width of its membership. Another distinguishing feature of *Swadhyaya* is its democratic approach to the relation between the mission and the individual members. A person is free to follow his cultural traditions and tastes, except when they wield socially damaging influences, as in the case of addictions and gambling.

It may be worthwhile to examine the role of *Swadhyaya* in social transformation at the level of local communities. Let us assume that the objective of status, wealth and power, promote an egalitarian spirit of human dignity in all respects and strive for an even distribution of knowledge, welfare and happiness among members of a population. We know how deeply Gandhi was committed to these objectives. His thoughts and actions against poverty, untouchability, ignorance and communalism were translated into a variety of programmes and institutions. Some of these (notably, adult education and rural industry) are still carried on with initiative and support from Government and non-Government organizations. Gandhi's faith in human goodness and altruism inspired Vinoba Bhave to attempt abolition of rural poverty through voluntary sacrifice by the rich. The effort proved almost futile. The rich proved to be far less generous, self-denying and honest than Gandhi and Vinoba had reckoned.

Modern non-Government organizations have adopted a variety of models and approaches in their programmes in social transformation. The exploitation and injustice suffered by the poor and disadvantaged sections are usually challenged in terms of democratic rights and the principles of equality and social justice. Equality and justice are sought to be achieved by collective action to generate pressures on the wielders of power or on Government machinery for legal and administrative intervention. During recent years, there has been a growing realization that social transformation can be more effective and sustainable if it is based on the specific cultural characteristics of the local population. However, the relationship between the rich and the poor, the exploiter and the exploited, the powerful and the powerless remains one of conflict or confrontation.

This is where *Swadhyaya* is different. Here, the idea of equality and fraternity of all human beings is built on the foundation of change. This foundation is reinforced by an unflinching faith in God as the father of all human beings. Human dignity and equality are built into the web of relationships which *Swadhyaya* constructs among people across all conventional social barriers. Control of greed, anger, intolerance and hatred is a part of the basic discipline. Self denial, giving and sharing are prescribed in small units and are common to everyone. They are also a continuous process. You do not just part with some material resource and forget a relationship. You give something all the time and strengthen the relationship. Building relations is most consequential.

Swadhyaya dreams of universalization of the process of building relations. This aspect is also acclaimed and adored by people across the world. *Swadhyaya* is engaged in spreading a unique quality of life. *Swadhyaya* implies that the new quality of life will lead to an economically more rewarding ethic-based work, greater productivity, thrift-oriented personal habits, availability of resources for the well-being and happiness of everyone. This new pattern of living is expected to bring the rich and poor together, remove the barriers of inequality and reinforce dignity. Dignity and equality are sought to be reinforced by shared knowledge of religious and spiritual heritage and its relevance for current social living in a global context.

Challenge of Change

The moral and social regeneration promoted by *Swadhyaya* is potentially capable of creating a collective force to propel the society towards human dignity and equality. It should however be remembered that the major political and economic forces in society are controlled by equations of power and wealth by conventional political institutions within the umbrella of the state and Government. *Swadhyaya* has chosen to avoid any participation in the political system as it regards power games as antithetical to its central objective. This exclusive approach would obviously restrict the scope and ability of *Swadhyaya* to deal with the problems of equality and dignity at the macro level. At the same time, involvement in the political process may easily invite the risk of collision with people and parties in power. It may also invite individuals and groups with an interest in power, to use the *Parivar's* achievements and clout to serve their vested interests. The net effect of political aloofness may consist of slow and uncertain progress towards the goal. "My aim", says *Dada*, "is not to change the world." "We should rejoice", says Rahnema (non-dated), "that there are such exceptional leaders and millions of followers."[7]

The *Swadhyaya* organization has so far been somewhat loose-ended, although in performance of tasks, there has been plenty of total commitment among all members which compensates for some organizational uncertainties. Decision-making has been largely based on the experience and judgement of *Dada* in whom divinity is imputed by the vast majority of *swadhyayis*. Reverence for him seems to play a major role in people's commitment to the *Swadhyaya* work and way of life. *Dada* is a continuous source of new ideas and innovative action plans. A major strength of *Swadhyaya* is that there are no long-term plans. Ideas originate according to a felt need in given situations. At the same time, the *Parivar* seems to have grown over-dependent on *Dada*'s guidance and leadership. Though yielding rich dividends in the current context, this may prove to be a handicap in the long run. This generates doubts and anxieties about the nature of problems to be faced by *Swadhyaya* in the absence of the chief designer and builder. *Dada* and most members of the *Parivar* do not foresee any major discontinuity in the years ahead in the absence of the leading light. A constitution has recently been prepared by *Dada* in consultation with senior *swadhyayis*. It is believed that this document contains guidelines to facilitate in course of time a smooth process of distribution of powers and responsibilities among people at various levels.

While *Dada*'s interpretation of spiritualism is based on the entire spectrum of spiritual wisdom through the history of world civilizations most of the beliefs and practices incorporated in *Swadhyaya* are drawn from ancient Indian scriptures which are closely linked with what is known as Hinduism. The movement has so far drawn a negligible proportion of non-Hindu populations in India and abroad. This fact raises questions such as whether *Swadhyaya* is essentially oriented to one particular religious faith in a secular society. This question is intellectually resolved by *Dada*'s conviction that *Swadhyaya* does not impose or prescribe any religious following and that participation in it is not incompatible with the beliefs and practices of any religion. A few non-Hindus are known to have adopted *Swadhyaya* while retaining their original faith. A group of Sikh intellectuals in Maharashtra have carried the *Swadhyaya* message to their co-religionists. *Dada* has been invited to several Christian congregations and earned much respect and love from eminent Christian missionaries. A major challenge faced by *Swadhyaya* is how to demonstrate and spread its central message of unity of God across the millions of fragments into which His children have shattered His *parivar*.

Swadhyaya, according to a casual observation, seems to have appealed to the relatively affluent and those among the non-affluent who can spare adequate time and energy on *Swadhyaya* work. It may have appealed to those who were spiritually inclined and could therefore take to *Swadhyaya* without much inner friction. On the other hand, it may have been embraced by those who had become too deviant in their social and personal conduct. The question is: does it attract extraordinary people in such disproportionate numbers? Among the poorer segments of the rural population, *Swadhyaya* perhaps attracts the upper economic crust. Some rural poor may have moved into the upper crust after embracing *Swadhyaya*. Thus, *Swadhyaya* may be socially selective. The question then is: is *Swadhyaya* likely to create new hierarchies and inequalities among specific social strata in villages? Would such an eventuality have new implications for human equality and dignity within rural communities?

There seems to be some ambivalence among the *Parivar* regarding socio-economic experiments. Projects such as *yogeshwara krushi* and *vruksha mandir* are usually presented to the outside world as experiments in generation and distribution of impersonal wealth for the well-being of a community as a whole, without compromising the need for adequate rewards for individual producers. On the other hand, it is often stressed that all such experiments are conducted with the main objective of strengthening the individual's commitment to *bhakti* and love and building new social bonds among strangers in a given neighbourhood. This leads to an apprehension that generation of impersonal wealth is projected by the *Parivar* as a desired objective, but in reality it is demonstrated merely as unreachable utopian dream.

I have in this concluding part brought out some long-term social consequences and issues involved in the *Swadhyaya* mode of social transformation. The relevant issues can be examined only in the light of adequate dependable information. Meanwhile, *Swadhyaya* beckons us on to a creative, blissful and sublime path to the utopia which most of us everywhere may covet. Keep moving, *Swadhyaya*. May the *Parivar* snowball.

Notes

1. An earlier version of this paper was presented in a seminar on social transformation organized by the Centre for Social Studies at Surat in December 1994. It was also brought out as a working paper by the Gujarat Institute of Development Research. I received valuable comments and suggestions from the participants at the Surat seminar and several other friends and colleagues. I am grateful to Professors Pravin Visaria and Vimal P. Shah for help and advice on drafts of the paper at various stages. I received most valued secretarial help from Vasanti V.A. and Sheela Devadas.

2. I first met *Dada* in August 1991 with an interest which was partly academic but had already grown beyond academics. Since then, I have continued to receive love, help and guidance from *Dada*, *Didi* and a large number of *swadhyayi* friends. In lieu of a detailed acknowledgement, I would simply like to record: Thank you for all those acts of kindness.

3. I am indebted to the scholars whose writings on *Swadhyaya* have both inspired and helped me in understanding its goals and activities.

4. My colleague, V.P. Shah and I are currently involved in a study of the social change generated by *Swadhyaya* in the Sabarkantha district of Gujarat. For the present, I crave your indulgence on observations and interpretations which may appear weak on validity or adequacy of information.

5. See, for instance, Kothari (1993).

6. For this part of the discussion, I have depended significantly on the recent contributions of Wignaraja (1993) and Ekins (1992).

7. '... it is particularly refreshing to find out that, despite the systematic and forceful colonization of minds by homo economicus ... there are still millions of people who refuse to be addicted by him..... It is also, perhaps a significant sign of the times to come, that in such a situation, a 'religious mind' like Dada invites the same millions' (Rahnema: non-dated: p.22)

References

Ekins, Paul. *New World Order: Grassroots Movements for Global Change.* London and New York: Routledge, 1992.

Kothari, Rajni. 'The Yawning Vacuum: A World Without Alternatives', *Economic and Political Weekly* (May 29, 1993): 1100-1107.

Rahnema, Majid, non-dated. *Swadhyaya: The Unknown, the Peaceful, the Silent Yet Singing Revolution of India* (Mimeo).

Roy, Ramashray, *Swadhyaya: Values and Message.* In Wignaraja 1993.

Srivastava, R.K. 'Swadhyaya Movement: Its Meaning and Message'. Paper presented at a seminar of the United Nations University, Rome, (September, 1986).

Wignaraja, Ponna. *New Social Movements in the South: Empowering the People.* New Delhi: Vistaar Publications, 1993.

4

Legal, Institutional Development and Sweepers in Ahmedabad

Takashi Shinoda

From 'invisible' to 'visible'

Sweepers have long been discriminated against in Indian society though their services have been essential for the maintenance of public health. They have been regarded as the lowest among the lower classes. In many parts of India, sweepers were not allowed to appear before the *Savarna* Hindus who believed that even the sight of the sweepers would pollute them. Thus, the sweepers were not only 'invisible' due to their low status but were also forced to be 'invisible' by various regulations which sometimes forced them to work during the night and in the early hours of morning to avoid any encounter with the *Savarna* Hindus. As such, it is not surprising that not much research work has been done on sweepers so far. Though there are a few good monographs (Malkani 1971; Pathak 1991; Shyamlal 1981, 1984, 1992; Sharma 1995), the most authentic data and information are provided by Government reports which investigated the service, working, and living conditions of the scavengers and sweepers.

The issues of sweepers attracted the attention of some reformers, such as the Arya Samaj and the Gandhians even before Independence. The Arya Samaj tried to influence the sweepers especially as it was a segment of the depressed classes which had many converts to other religions (Sharma 1985). It provided them with facilities for education besides encouraging the study of *Vedas*; however it did not incorporate any special agenda for the sweepers (Shyamlal 1992). On the other hand, some members of the Harijan Sevak Sangh committed themselves to the improvement of the working conditions of the scavengers (Agrawal 1934). They were inspired by M.K. Gandhi who practised self disposal of human excreta at his *ashram*. He blamed Hindu society for ill-treating the sweepers. He regarded the sweepers as mother, and the Hindu society as a baby considering the important role the sweepers played in caring for the society (Gandhi 1954). The Gandhians developed new type of latrines (Patel 1970) to reduce the workload of scavenging. It is also worth noting that the Government of the Central Provinces and Berar set up an enquiry committee on wages and working conditions of the sweepers (Thakkar 1939). However, the overall social effect of these measures was quite limited before Independence.

The actual improvement in the service and working conditions of sweepers took place only after Independence in the wake of the reform movements initiated by the Government and the Gandhians. Though some Gandhian organizations[1] played a very important role throughout these movements, the basic nature of this reform can be characterized as a top down reform. Guidelines for this reform were provided by various committees appointed by the central as well as the state Governments.

The Government of Saurashtra was quick in reviewing the conditions of scavengers (Saurashtra 1956); however, the report did not circulate beyond its territory. The first report of national importance was the Barve Committee Report (Bombay 1958b) submitted to the Government of Bombay. The report with a detailed analysis of the service, working and living conditions of scavengers evoked a keen interest among administrators and social activists all over India, though the analysis was confined to the Bombay state. Stimulated by the report, the central Government set up the Malkani Committee (India 1960) followed by the Pandya Committee (India 1969), the Basu Task Force (India 1990-91), and the National Scheme (India 1991-92). In the meantime, some other state Governments such as Haryana (Haryana 1972), and Karnataka (Karnataka 1976) also appointed enquiry committees on the service and working conditions of scavengers and sweepers. These reports also handled various aspects related to the socio-economic condition of the scavengers and sweepers.

As far as the central Government reports are concerned, the

main focus of the recommendations has clearly changed over time. In the initial stage, the working condition of scavengers constituted the central issue due to the prevalence of dry latrines (also called service latrines or receptacle latrines) and the common practice of transporting human excreta in a basket on the heads of scavengers. This malpractice was regarded as an insult to the dignity of the Indian society by Malkani (India 1960). Though both the Malkani and Pandya committees limited their final goals to abolish dry latrines, their recommendations were centred on the introduction of tools and equipment like wheel barrows, gloves and receptacles, as a measure to mitigate the hardship of scavenging, in view of the difficulty of abolishing dry latrines in a short time.

The reports also put stress on the importance of prohibiting the transportation of night soil on the seavenger's head and the construction of new dry latrines by law. This legal reform was supposed to cover all levels from the central legislature to the State Legislative Assembly and the local bodies. Prohibition of transporting night soil on the head was under the jurisdiction of the central legislature and was due for ratification by the State Legislative Assembly, while a ban on the construction of new dry latrines and/or the demolition of existing ones was mainly under the jurisdiction of local bodies. The relevant parts of the Provincial Municipal Corporation Act had to be modified so that the local bodies could enact effective bye-laws. Thus, legal development constituted one of the focal points in their recommendations.

In addition, the local bodies were expected to municipalize all the scavenging works within their territory, not only for improving public health but also for relieving the private scavengers from their unhealthy working conditions. Ironically, however, it was the private scavengers themselves who resisted such municipalization in fear of unemployment. In the process of municipalization, the local bodies used to absorb these private scavengers in their departments as permanent or temporary sweepers in addition to compensating the customary rights of scavengers in cash. Hence, it took a lot of time to municipalize scavenging works in many local bodies.

Another important incident was the launch of Bhangi Kasht Mukti Karyakram to mitigate the Bhangis hardship in the mid-sixties (Jairamdas 1969). The Harijan Sevak Sangh took the initiative in starting the scheme with the aim of abolishing any type of discrimination against 'Harijans' by 2 October 1969, the centenary of M.K.

Gandhi. The scheme was supported by the central Government and some state Governments, including Gujarat. In Gujarat, several state departments concerned, encouraged the local bodies, by frequent issue of circulars and resolutions, to limit the number of dry latrines by legal regulations and to absorb as many private scavengers as possible into their departments (Gujarat 1972). As such, local bodies were under tremendous pressure at the time of the centenary. Overall, the scheme was effective in attracting public interest and mitigating the hardship of scavengers, to some extent, in Gujarat, though it had a lot of limitations.

In the late seventies, public health became one of the most crucial issues in the world. In this connection, some world organizations such as the World Bank and the UNDP took a keen interest in improving public health in Gujarat. The Gujarat Government was also ready for launching the low-cost sanitation programme for spreading cheap substitute latrines with the financial assistance of the central Government. Accordingly, the Gujarat Panchayat and Municipal Laws were revised in 1980 and the Taluka Development Officer was empowered to construct proper latrine facilities at the expense of the house owners if they did not repair or construct their latrines within the time set by his/her order. Thus, the first low-cost sanitation programme started in 1984 with the financial assistance of the World Bank, UNDP and the central Government. Urban houses were the major target of the programme. The second low-cost sanitation programmes, launched for rural households in 1988, with the financial assistance of the World Bank, had the Safai Vidyalaya functioning as a nodal agency. As a result of the Bhangi Kasht Mukti Karyakram, and the first and the second low-cost sanitation programmes, the number of dry latrines decreased drastically in Gujarat by the first half of the nineties.

With the decrease in the number of dry latrines and with the process of municipalizing scavenging and sweeping work gaining momentum in Gujarat, most scavengers have been absorbed as sweepers in the local bodies. Nowadays, the majority of sanitation workers are road sweepers and the number of municipal scavengers are very few as far as the big cities are concerned, due to the spread of substitute latrines and the development of a sewerage system in these cities. Accordingly, the central issues have also shifted from the abolition of dry latrines to the improvement of service and working conditions of municipal sweepers and their rehabilitation.

As a part of my research work on the status of sweepers in India,

I undertook a socio-economic survey of the sweepers employed by the eight local bodies, including the Ahmedabad Municipal Corporation (AMC), in the Ahmedabad district in 1991. The survey was aimed at assessing the impact of the legal and institutional development on sweepers, besides tracing the occupational mobility of their households. As far as the AMC was concerned, I could collect some historical data from the AMC and the trade unions[2] to trace the changes in service, working and living conditions of sweepers over time. With full use of this data, this paper tries to analyse the impact of legal and institutional development on the service and working conditions of the AMC sweepers.[3] Though the analysis is confined to the AMC sweepers, the paper may have certain implications towards understanding the impact of legal and institutional development on sweepers employed by other municipal corporations in India.

Sweepers and Awards

The Industrial Dispute Act, 1947, defines the means for solving industrial disputes, such as conciliations, settlements and awards. The act, constituted of seven chapters, is designed to settle any industrial dispute regarding the employment or non-employment, the terms of employment, the conditions of labour between employers and employers, or between employers and workmen, or between workmen and workmen (India 1991b:12). Notably, the act is designed to cover most of the industrial disputes in private, Government, semi-Government and co-operative sectors. As the act defines, works committee, boards of conciliation, courts of inquiry, labour courts, tribunals, national tribunals, etc., are set up in accordance with the type and scale of industrial disputes.

Thus, even the industrial disputes in the local bodies are covered by the act. For example, personal and individual disputes which cannot be solved by conciliation are examined at labour courts or industrial courts. The disputes which are collective or related to the legal system itself are examined at tribunals. The state Government appoints arbitrators when both employers and employees agree to send the matter to tribunals. The arbitrator is obliged to grant his/her award within the period agreed upon by both parties. Award, the last means to solve industrial disputes in local bodies, has a legal power of compulsion though it does not consider the industrial disputes of the first and the second class staff because they are not categorized as workmen. The workmen, defined by the act, are the lower managerial staff, clerks and manual workers belonging to the third and the fourth class staff.

Ahmedabad, previously known as Karnavati, was found by Ahmad Shah I in 1411. It fell into the hands of the Mughals and the Marathas before the British occupied the city in 1825. Thereafter, the status of Ahmedabad changed several times. It was given the status of City Municipality in 1873, by the Bombay District Municipal Act (VI of 1873). Again, it was reorganized as a Borough Municipality in 1926. After Independence, it was given the status of Municipal Corporation in 1950, by the Bombay Municipal Corporation Act, 1949.

Since Independence, four individual arbitrators have been appointed for solving the industrial disputes in the AMC. Their awards have covered several essential problems of workmen, including their service, working, and living conditions. Thus, the awards dealt with issues related to employment, promotion, wages, holidays, labour days, labour hours, uniforms and housing. Most of these awards handled common problems among the third and the fourth class staff, while a few of them were related to a particular segment of workers such as the transportation workers and sweepers. Also, the AMC occasionally gave the arbitrators, the power of a one-man pay committee for the revision of wages related to all the employees, including the first and the second class staff. Though the recommendations of the one-man pay committee did not have legal force, they were generally accepted by both the parties. An analysis of these awards and recommendations would help us in tracing the changes in service, working, and living conditions of the sweepers employed by the AMC.

Shah Award (1948)

We know very little about the type of industrial disputes and the ways of solving the disputes prevalent before Independence. However, the major industrial disputes after Independence can be traced in the contents of awards which appeared in the gazettes. Just before Independence, the Government appointed H.V. Divatia, according to the Defence of India Rules, to solve the industrial disputes between *mukadams*, sweepers and the Ahmedabad Borough Municipality (ABM). After Independence, Divatia was soon replaced by Justice M.C. Shah though no reason was mentioned in the gazette. Shah was also entrusted with giving his award to the wage-related problems between the ABM and employees other than the sweepers. Accordingly, the first award was given by M.C. Shah in February 1948. The award was related to the following six demands of the sweepers:

The first demand was the revision of pay scales. The ABM had not changed the pay scale for sweepers since 1939 with the monthly wage remaining fixed at Rs.17 for males, Rs.15 for females and Rs.19 for *mukadams*. The fixed wage system was replaced by a new pay scale in 1945, i.e., Rs.17-0.5-22 for male sweepers, Rs.15-0.5-22 for female sweepers and Rs.19-1-25 for *mukadams*. The introduction of this pay scale was appreciated, though the minimum wage remained the same as before. So, the pay scale was upgraded in 1946. However, this revision did not satisfy the sweepers because the Bombay State had also revised the pay scale of their sweepers. Accordingly, the ABM sweepers demanded a further upgradation in their pay scale to the level of Rs.25-1-40 for both male and female sweepers and Rs.30-1-50 for *mukadams*. The arbitrator revised the pay scales to the level of Rs.25-1-30 for male sweepers and Rs.30-1-35 for *mukadams*, however, the pay scale for female sweepers was settled at Rs.23-1-30 on the ground that their contributions in sweeping work were relatively smaller than that of the male sweepers.

The second demand was to raise the temporary additional pay to the same level as enjoyed by the sweepers of the state Government. The arbitrator turned down this demand saying that the grain allowance, one of the original schemes of the ABM, and implemented since 1942, had been filling the gap.

The third demand was in regard to the payment of bonus - Rs.60 for the junior sweepers and Rs.120 for the senior sweepers per annum. This demand was also rejected because the arbitrator regarded the grain allowance as substituting fully for the bonus.

The fourth demand was a constant supply of uniforms to sweepers and umbrellas to *mukadams*. And, the fifth demand was to employ *harijan* cleaners as drivers. These cleaners had been recruited urgently for sweeping at the time of the sweepers' strikes in June 1946. The term, *harijan* cleaners, suggests that they belonged to 'Harijans' whose traditional occupation was not sweeping. The arbitrator again rejected these two demands saying that these demands had not been much emphasized by the trade unions.

The last demand was regarding the free supply of quarters or the payment of house rent allowance at the rate of Rs.10 per month for all the sweepers and *mukadams*. In all, 2703 sweepers and 65 *mukadams* were employed in August 1947. Assuming the number of sweepers' families to be 1600, the arbitrator pointed out that 360 families had been accommodated in the quarters with a nominal house rent of Rs.2 per month; 439 other families had benefited by the deduction of the sanitary cess. In addition, the ABM had a scheme to construct 772 new quarters. Thus, the arbitrator appreciated the efforts of the ABM and rejected the demand of the trade unions.

Jeejeebhoy Award (1958)

After the Shah award, industrial disputes on wages arose between the Ahmedabad Transportation Department and its labourers. Though both the parties reached an agreement in August 1956, the disputes broke out again. Accordingly, F. Jeejeebhoy, the President of the Labour Appellate Tribunal of India, was appointed to award his decision on these disputes as well as other unresolved disputes. He gave his award in February 1958, in which he dealt with the individual problems of sweepers and scavengers in addition to the general problems of workmen in all departments. Let us examine his individual award regarding sweepers and scavengers.

First, and perhaps the most important demand was to increase the number of permanent workers. The arbitrator, however, rejected this demand pointing out that the number of permanent workers had increased by 300 in 1957-58 while the work load had been decreasing due to the progress in the construction of paved roads. He also quoted the statement of the Commissioner that the AMB had a sufficient number of permanent sweepers.

The second demand was related to discrimination against the female sweepers. The trade unions accused the AMC of avoiding the employment of female sweepers and of settling their pay scales at a level lower than that of the male sweepers. The arbitrator accepted the demand and directed the AMC not to discriminate against female sweepers in terms of employment and payment. Accordingly, the pay scale of females was raised to the level of that of the males.

The third demand was regarding the Night Soil Department. The status of the department was casual. The trade unions demanded a permanent status and a quota seat for the permanent workers. The arbitrator argued that night soil work would decrease with the development of the sewer system, and also indicated that most of the department's casual workers had already been absorbed in other departments as permanent workers. Thus, this demand was rejected.

The fourth demand related to the reporting system. The AMC insisted that the workers should report four times a day before and after the morning and afternoon shifts at the main office for the convenience of the supervising workers, while the trade unions demanded that the reporting should be only twice a day at the labour sites. The arbitrator decided that reporting should be twice a day before each of the two shifts at the nearest muster station where tools and equipment were kept, taking into consideration the workers' convenience in commuting.

Other demands were regarding the promotion of workers of the Malaria Department and the provision of cycle allowance for some *mukadams* who were to accompany the inspectors for the supervision of the wide area. The arbitrator rejected the former and accepted the latter.

Jeejeebhoy's award for all workmen was also relevant for sweepers. The award was concerned with wages and the promotion of casual workers. As for wages, the arbitrator accepted the demand of a higher house rent allowance and the compensatory city allowance at the same level as adopted by the Bombay State. However, given the poor financial base of the AMC, the increase in pay scale was limited to Rs.5 only. Accordingly, the minimum wage for permanent sweepers showed a slight increase from Rs.70 to Rs.75 per month. Though the arbitrator encouraged the AMC to consider the promotion of casual sweepers, it was of a general nature without any compulsion. He did not touch the quota issue and rejected the demand of provident fund and various allowances for casual sweepers. However, the daily wage for casual sweepers was raised from Rs.2-8 to Rs.2-13 by the award.

Thakore Award (1976-80)

After the Jeejeebhoy award, disputes on wages emerged again in the early sixties. The focus of disputes was the revision of pay scales and allowances among workmen other than the sweepers and transportation workers. Accordingly, Indrajit G. Thakore, who had been appointed as an arbitrator, gave his award in March 1965. His award was very favourable for workmen. This is why disputes on wages never appeared again in the next ten years. In the meantime, however, the real wages had declined considerably due to inflation. Also, the central and state Governments, and the major private enterprises had revised the pay scales for their workers resulting in a considerable gap with the pay scales of the AMC. Thus, the revision of pay scales became inevitable and I.G. Thakore was again appointed as an arbitrator. He was also empowered to act as a one-man pay commission. His award and recommendations came during 1976-80. It covered sixteen demands of the sweepers, of which the major ones were as follows :

Labour Hours and Shifts

The prevailing labour hours for sweepers was eight with two shifts from 6 to 11 in the morning and from 3 to 6 in the afternoon. The trade unions complained that the sweepers were actually restrained for twelve hours a day assuming that the average time of one-way commuting was one hour. As a result, the sweepers could neither spare enough time to look after their family nor for their socio-cultural activities. The trade unions also reported that water was generally out of supply when they came back home. And, this is why, the trade unions strongly demanded a decrease in labour hours to seven with only one shift. The AMC rejected this demand on the ground that the cut in labour hours would necessitate an additional employment of sweepers, which the AMC could not afford due to its poor financial position. The AMC also pointed out that the cut in labour hours among sweepers would bring about inequality with other workmen because eight hours labour was common among manual workers in the AMC and was also prevalent in private enterprise, including the textile industry. After a careful examination of the relevant Government reports of Malkani, Bharve, Pandya and Vyas committees, the arbitrator confirmed that the recommended labour hours had never exceeded seven hours and that there had been no special recommendations on labour shifts in these reports. He ordered the AMC to finance a delegation represented by the trade union leaders to investige other municipal corporations like Delhi, Bombay, Pune and Nagpur. The investigation revealed that Bombay and Pune set labour hours at seven with two shifts, while Delhi and Nagpur applied seven and half hours with one shift. The arbitrator argued that eight hours labour was against the recommendations of the above reports and the customs of other municipal corporations, and that additional employment would not be necessary if each sweeper worked more efficiently. Thus, he awarded seven and half hours with a reservation that the labour hour should be seven only in the future. As for labour shifts, he rejected the demand on the ground that one shift would be impossible and impractical in the present setting of the AMC.

Nursing Centres

Female sweepers had to bring their infants to labour sites because of non-availability of nursing centres. The trade unions, therefore, demanded that the AMC run nursing centres at the muster stations. The AMC refused their demand on the ground that sweepers had not used the nursing centre set up in a hospital on an experimental basis, and stated that there was not enough space for a nursing centre in the muster station. The arbitrator awarded that the AMC should try setting up a nursing centre somewhere near the muster station, and not in a hospital far from the labour sites.

Medical Care Services

The trade unions revealed that municipal hospitals and dispensaries could hardly be utilised by the sweepers as they closed by the time the sweepers were released from their work. The trade unions also testified that sweepers had been discriminated against for using services at municipal hospitals. So, they demanded that health facilities should be improved and medical aid should also be extended to sweepers' children who constituted a high risk population for TB. The arbitrator instructed the AMC to open medical counters during a suitable time and at proper places for the sweepers. He encouraged the sweepers to file a case whenever they were discriminated against. However, the demand regarding sweepers' children was turned down on the ground that a particular section could not be favoured to maintain equality with other sections.

Promotion of *Umedwars*

These were the casual workers whose names were put on a waiting list. The trade unions demanded that an *umedwar* with more than one year work experience should be promoted to a permanent worker known as *kaymi*, while the AMC insisted that such promotions would be possible only against vacancies. The arbitrator regretted the fact that many *umedwars* had been constantly retained for several years. He took this fact as a proof that there had been constant and considerable work which exceeded the workload of a *kaymi*. Subsequently, he ordered the AMC to increase the number of *kaymis* in three phases taking into consideration the AMC's financial condition. He made three groups of *umedwars*, in the order of their registration numbers, out of those who had already worked for more than five years with more than 240 labour days in a year as on 1 January, 1978 and directed the AMC to promote the first group in April 1978, the second group in April 1979, and the third group in April 1980. He also suggested that this award was not confined to sweepers alone and that the qualification and conditions applied by him for promoting *umedwars* should be regarded as flexible.

Promotion of *Hangamis*

This category of casual workers were never registered in a waiting list of any kind. The sweeping of *chawls* (residential areas of the lower classes) was not under the jurisdiction of the AMC. However, if some *chawl* residents requested the AMC for sweeping with payment, the AMC sent *hangamis* to their localities on the basis of annual contract. The *hangamis*, occasionally recruited by the AMC, had been totally unprotected in terms of continuity of their work. The arbitrator, who could not find any reason to distinguish *hangamis* from other sweepers such as *umedwars* and *kaymis*, ordered the AMC to promote the qualified *hangamis* who had cleared the above-mentioned qualification (as stated in the fourth demand), to *kaymis* by setting an additional quota of *kaymis*.

Arrangement of Quarters

The trade unions complained that quarters were not allotted to about 1,000 of the 3,200 *kaymis*, and that the casual workers (nearly 600) were not considered for allotment. They criticized the AMC for suspending the additional construction of quarters. The arbitrator, referring to the AMC's timely initiatives shown in the past for constructing quarters for 'Harijans', ordered the AMC to prepare a new scheme of quarters, taking its financial condition into consideration. He specified that quarters should be constructed in the same ward where sweepers were working. He also referred to the necessity of financial support by the AMC in the form of subsidies and loans to encourage the private construction of houses by sweepers themselves.

Employment for Children

The workers demanded preference for their children for employment in the AMC, on the ground that it was very hard for them to take up any occupation other than sweeping. The arbitrator referred to the Jeejeebhoy award which introduced a compensatory employment system in case of death during the employees' services, but did not suggest any new policy in this regard. Instead, he just emphasized that the sweepers' children should fully utilise the quota reserved for the Scheduled Castes and Other Backward Classes, and that they should be employed by other departments, too.

Provision of Unclean Allowance

An allowance of Rs.10 per month was provided to 1,200 out of the 3,500 sweepers. The trade unions insisted that the allowance should be provided to all the sweepers since sweeping included the removal of animal dung and human excreta. The arbitrator, however, was of the opinion that the removal of animal dung had nothing to do with the allowance, which should be confined to those workers who worked in places where open defecation was prevalent.

Number of Holidays

The sweepers could enjoy one full holiday a week, but were forced to work a half day on national holidays. So, the trade unions insisted that the national holidays should be considered as full holidays. They further argued that if this was not accepted then as an alternative, wages for two days should be paid for a halfday's work on the national holidays. The arbitrator, after the examination of the Second and the Third Central Pay Commissions' reports and the Second Gujarat State Pay Commission's Report, came to the conclusion that the national holidays could not be full holidays for sweepers due to the 'public' nature of their work. Instead, he sanctioned an additional five days of holidays with pay for the sweepers. He instructed further, that all holidays of the central as well as the state Governments should be applied to the sweepers as half-holidays on the ground that the number of holidays in the AMC was smaller than in other municipal corporations.

Barot Award (1984-1992)

After the Thakore award, the trade unions again demanded a revision of wages, including pay scales on the ground that Thakore could not thoroughly examine the pay scales of all classes, and also because there had been a considerable rise in general prices. The AMC also agreed to settle the issue by award. Consequently, G.S. Barot was appointed as an arbitrator. Between 1984 and 1992, he gave his award mainly concerning the general revision of pay scales and allowances, as well as the revision of wages for those untouched by the Thakore award, in addition to the promotion scheme for workmen. There was no special award for sweepers, since their problems had been thoroughly examined in the Thakore award. However, the general revision of pay scales and allowances, and the introduction of the promotion scheme had much to do with their economic conditions. We, therefore, examine some of the important issues related to the income of the sweepers.

The revision of pay scales was the most crucial issue. Thakore tried to revise the pay scales to the same level as recommended by the Second Gujarat State Pay Commission, and Barot followed Thakore. While Barot was examining the issue, the report of the Third Gujarat State Pay Commission was submitted in June 1985. Also, the report of the Fourth Central Pay Commission appeared in December 1985. Soon after this, the Gujarat Government revised the pay scales of state Government servants incorporating the recommendations of the Fourth Central Pay Commission. Thus, the award of Barot, with the initial intention of following the State Pay Commission, subsequently accepted the recommendations of the Fourth Central Pay Commission for the revision of pay scales of the AMC workmen. Accordingly, the pay scale of sweepers was revised from 196-3-220-EB (Efficiency Bar)-3-232 to 750-12-870-EB-14-940. In the revised pay scale, it takes ten years to reach the wage of Rs.870, and another five years to reach the maximum wage of Rs.940. The most important improvement in this revision was a quantum jump in basic wages, which also contributed in improving the welfare of sweepers, including pension holders.

Barot examined about 30 kinds of allowances. Of these, interim relief, dearness and compensatory city allowances, which were common for all workmen, were revised according to the recommendations of the Gujarat State Pay Commission. In addition, some other allowances relevant for sweepers such as washing, *gandgi* (unclean), nightsoil, bad climate (unhealthy circumstances) and *silai* (stitching) were also raised in the light of inflation. The most complicated case was that of the revision of house rent allowance since house rent varied very much even among those who resided in the same type of AMC quarters, but had occupied these at different points of time. Some occupants paid no rent, while some others enjoyed the house rent allowance equal to 15 per cent of their basic pay in exchange for a nominal payment of house rent to the AMC. The arbitrator awarded a fixed house rent allowance of Rs.150 per month to sweepers who paid a fixed rent for their quarters and who resided in accommodation other than the AMC quarters, and no house rent allowance to those with no, or, nominal house rent.

Promotion constituted another focal issue in this award. There was no promotion system among the manual workers of the third and the fourth classes. They were put on the same job under the same pay scale. Therefore, the trade unions demanded the application of higher pay scales to them after certain years of service. Soon after the arbitrator started his examination on the issue, the state Government announced a promotion scheme for its workmen in February 1991. The scheme was designed to assure its workmen, whose maximum wage was less than Rs.3,500 per month, the first shift to a higher pay scale after service of 12 years, and the second shift after 24 years. Accordingly, the arbitrator gave his award to apply the scheme to the AMC workmen in May 1991. Soon after in July 1991, the state Government took further action in revising its promotion scheme so as to give the first promotion after 9 years, the second after 18 years and the third after 27 years. As soon as Barot awarded this new promotion scheme with four pay scales : 750-940, 775-1025, 800-1150 and 950-1400 for the AMC's workmen, the AMC filed a case in the High Court in 1992. At present, a single pay scale of 750-940 is applied to all sweepers.

As Thakore pointed out, the wages of the permanent sweepers were better than those of most of the manual workers. Further, it was very common among the sweeper's households to have two or more members employed by the AMC either as permanent or as casual sweepers. Thus, their household income was not necessarily insufficient for their socio-economic development provided they made optimum use of their income. Though the new promotion scheme is still pending, their income has increased further due to the revision of pay scale by Barot. However, unless these sweepers start investing their income towards promoting education and occupational diversification, they would be more bound down to doing sweepers jobs which have become more secure and attractive economically over time.

Employment Policy of the AMC

An examination of awards confirmed that demands of the trade unions were centred on the revision of pay scales and allowances, and the improvement of employment and service conditions. In particular, the enlargement of the quota of permanent sweepers and the improvement of their service conditions made focal issues for the benefit of the sweeping community. It would, therefore, be appropriate to trace here, the changes in the employment policies of the AMC and their impact on the community of sweepers.

Waiting List

The Pandya Committee Report of 1969 revealed that most of the local bodies used to recruit their permanent sweepers both through waiting lists and compensatory appointment (India 1969). It also pointed out that a few local bodies reported recruitment through labour exchange.

The AMC has been maintaining two types of waiting lists until around 1972, though the origin of these lists is unknown to us. Workers in acting status were put onto list A, while substitute workers, engaged as substitutes of permanent and acting status sweepers on their holidays and leave, were put onto list B. When any permanent vacancy was created by retirement, death or any other reason, a new permanent worker was recruited from list A, according to seniority, in terms of registration number and work period. Likewise, any vacancy among the workers in acting status was filled from list B according to seniority. Workers in acting status could enjoy similar service and working conditions as permanent workers, except for the benefits of provident fund and house construction loan. Workers in list B were casual workers called *'umedwars'* (candidate), whose daily wages were worked out by dividing the total monthly salary of the permanent sweeper (consisting of basic wage, dearness and compensatory city allowances) by 26, the number of maximum labour days (excluding

Sundays) in a month. *Umedwars* were not given any benefit other than the daily wage. Moreover, the AMC was overstaffed with *umedwars* due to its policy of coping with any labour shortage or irregularity caused by permanent and acting status sweepers. Since the daily demand for substitute workers underscored the number of *umedwars* to a considerable extent, their labour days varied considerably. The substitute works were given to *umedwars* according to seniority. So, those who had registered earlier could enjoy similar working days as permanent sweepers, while those with recent registration were left with none, or a few days of work in a month. Thus, there was a large variation in terms of labour days among *umedwars*. Another category of workers called *hangamis* were engaged in sweeping chawls on an annual contract or cleaning the road and sewage during the monsoon season on a monthly contract with the AMC. The minimum daily wage was applied to *hangamis*. Though it had often been revised, the amount was always lower than the daily wage of *umedwars*.

Both the lists, A and B were revised annually on the basis of the applications of the candidates. The AMC used to promote some candidates from list A to permanent positions, and from list B to list A, and a fresh recruitment to list B, until the early seventies. However, the AMC suddenly suspended the revision in 1973, on the ground that the number of candidates in each list was very large. The trade unions reacted quickly resulting in an agreement with the AMC to start again the fresh recruitment of candidates in a new list C. It was also agreed to maintain both the lists, A and B, without any additional recruitment. Casual workers in list C were also called *umedwars* and were put under the same service and working conditions as those of the workers in list B. However, with the creation of a new list, workers in list B had great advantage over the list C *umedwars* regarding promotion. Thakore, who gave his award regarding the problems of sweepers in January 1973, had to cope with this complicated situation. Thakore ordered the AMC to promote all the eligible candidates, who had a working experience of more than five years with the minimum annual labour days of 240 as on January 1, 1978, to permanent sweepers by 1980. The criterion was soon revised in June 1978, when the AMC decided to apply Barot's individual award on the daily rated workmen in the engineering department for the promotion of sweepers. Accordingly, the criterion was relaxed to more than five years work experience with the total working days of 900. Thus, the very strict criterion of annual labour days was replaced by the total labour days in favour of the sweepers. By these awards, most of the workers both in A and B lists were promoted to permanent workers by 1980. Since then, the AMC has been maintaining list C only.

Compensatory Appointment

Compensatory appointment is a system to recruit, on the grounds of compensation, a substitute from the family which had become economically poor due to disablement or death of a permanent worker during his/her service tenure. It is evident from the Pandya Committee Report that the system prevailed among the major local bodies all over India, in the late sixties (India 1967). Since the system has direct influence on the socio-economic mobility of sweepers, we shall examine how the system has been shaped in the AMC.

There was no rule on compensatory appointment before the Jeejeebhoy award of 1958. Jeejeebhoy dealt with the demand of trade unions that, in case of death of a permanent worker, his/her spouse or one of the other family members should be employed as a permanent worker on the grounds of compensation. After examining the issue of compensatory appointment, Jeejeebhoy ordered the AMC to employ a spouse or another family member as a permanent sweeper on a priority basis if the candidate had been residing together with the deceased sweeper and proved to be fit mentally and physically. He justified it on the ground that it was not easy for their community to take up a job other than sweeping and that the family would be forced to vacate their free rent quarters unless someone else from the family was employed by the AMC. However, since Jeejeebhoy did not clarify other conditions such as the maximum age of the deceased sweeper and the level of family income, the AMC decided to apply the system only to those surviving families who had lost all sources of income due to death of a permanent worker during his/her service tenure. The surviving family with no source of income was called "niradhar", while the beneficiary of the compensatory appointment was named "warasdar" or successor.

Compensatory appointment shaped by the Jeejeebhoy award was amended, for the first time in 1972. Both the AMC and the trade unions agreed to incorporate disablement during service in the conditions of compensatory appointment. Disability, a permanent unworkable condition due to illness or injury, was recognized with a certificate issued by the municipal hospital. Yet, the condition of *niradhar* continued to remain the same.

Meanwhile, the state Government revised, in reverse direction, the rules of its compassionate (so expressed, instead of compensatory) appointment which had been shaped in 1975. As a result of the revision effected in May 1977, beneficiaries were confined to the surviving families of manual workers of the third class and all workers of the fourth class who had died in service. The age of beneficiaries was also regulated in the light of the recruitment rules with some relaxation. The beneficiaries were expected to be employed within five years after the incident. The system was confined only to the surviving families whose income was less than Rs.400 per month; however, the income limit has been raised several times thereafter to adjust for inflation and, thus set at Rs.1000, in 1990. Overall, this revision of the state Government was aimed at tightening the rules for application of compassionate appointment, which also indirectly affected the AMC's policy of compensatory appointment.

During the period of the Thakore award, a lot of applications were submitted for compensatory appointment. And, most of the cases were settled in favour of the applicants thanks to a progressive atmosphere during the award. As Table 1 shows, as many as 150 *warasdars*, mostly the applicants during this award, were employed as permanent sweepers, each in 1981-82 and 1982-83. However, the number of recruited *warasdars* suddenly came down to nil in 1983-84 due to the introduction of AMC's employment cut policy, partly because of its acute financial crisis, and partly because of the set-back of the trade union movement caused by a split among them.

The Deputy Commissioner in charge of public sanitation, in his circular of March 1984, directed the departments concerned to apply compensatory appointment only to such cases where death or disability had occurred at least five years before the retirement age (60 years). The circular, aimed at curbing the number of applications for compensatory appointment, served the purpose by removing the high risk age group from consideration.

The trade unions became active again with their recovery from the set-back. Their agitation in 1986 against the AMC drew some concessions from the Commissioner, who in his circular of January 1987, directed the departments concerned, to relax the age limit up to 58 years. However, in the same circular, he also specified that the surviving family who could get financial support from the non-residential family members, or the surviving family whose widow got employed after remarriage, should not be considered as *niradhar*. This specification suggests that there were some such cases among the applicants. Thus, the standards of *niradhar* were tightened though the age limit was slightly relaxed. The overall effect of the circular was not much in favour of the trade unions, resulting only in a minor increase in the number of sanctions since 1986.

Table : 1 Number of Applications for Compensatory Appointment by Reason (1980/81 - 1991/92)

(No. of Applications/Sanctions)

Year	Applications by Reason				Sanction
	Decease	Disablement	Retirement	Total	
1980-81	1	0	0	1	N.A.
1981-82	1	0	1	2	153
1982-83	3	1	0	4	157
1983-84	21	14	1	36	0
1984-85	37	19	1	57	8
1985-86	13	3	8	24	7
1986-87	19	2	1	22	16
1987-88	10	4	3	17	27
1988-89	3	2	0	5	32
1989-90	5	1	0	6	39
1990-91	4	1	1	6	24
1991-92	N.A.	N.A.	N.A.	N.A.	35
Total	117	47	16	180	498

Notes : (1) Financial year of the AMC is from April 1

(2) The Figure of 1991-92 is based on the record upto August only

(3) All applications on the ground of retirement were rejected.

Source : The Ahmedabad Municipal Corporation

Another wave of agitation, in May 1991, led to an agreement between the AMC and the trade unions on the age limit, the range of *warasdar*, and the standards of *niradhar*. With this agreement, the age limit was further relaxed to $59^{1/2}$ years i.e., up to six months before retirement. Also, the range of *warasdar* was fixed for the first time with such specifications as sons, unmarried/divorced daughters, widows/widowers, sons' wives. Most important of all was the dissolution of *niradhar's* standards, by which any family member within the above range became eligible to be a permanent sweeper without any consideration of family income. This agreement was designed to be valid since January 1987. As a result, most of the cases of decease and disablement considered in the previous agreement were relieved, while older cases continued to be out of consideration. This new system of compensatory appointment could have serious effects on the socio-economic development of sweepers. The system, very favourable for the community of sweepers in terms of job security, could work as their new customary right, which could be inherited through generations. This system of entrenchment could tighten their ties further with sweeping, at the cost of diversification of their occupational structure, which is essential for their development. Another possible effect of the system was to raise the share of *warasdars* among permanent sweepers, in the long-run. This could hamper the promotion of sweepers from *umedwar* to *kaymi* since the total umber of permanent sweepers was fixed at a given time. It could also indirectly hamper the promotion from *hangami* to *umedwar*.

Conclusion

By the analysis of the awards, we can trace the changes in the pay scales of the sweepers of the ABM/AMC since the forties. After the introduction of pay scales in the ABM, in 1945, they have been revised several times so as to catch up with the level prevalent among the fourth class staff of the state Government. However, the gap of allowances between the AMC and the state Government workmen remained unadjusted even in the Thakore award. This was done by Barot who had been eager to adjust the AMC's wage system, including the allowances, to that of the state Government. Since the pay scales of the state Government were adjusted to that of the central Government during his term, the AMC's workmen could consequently enjoy the same pay scale as the central Government workmen.

Compensatory appointment was introduced by Jeejeebhoy in 1958. Initially, the system was applied to *niradhars*, only when their *kaymi* sweepers had deceased during their service. Disablement was added later, in 1972. The AMC, obliged to make a further compromise to enlarge the quota of permanent sweepers by the Thakore award in the late seventies, adopted a tough policy for recruiting permanent sweepers in the eighties. It promoted a small segment of *umedwars* from amongst those who had already cleared the eligibility for promotion. Also, strict standards and measures were applied to identify an eligible *waraslar* from among the *niradhars*. The trade unions reacted to the AMC's recruitment policy toward sweepers with strikes and enhanced court struggle. As a result, in May 1991, the AMC agreed with the trade unions to recruit all the eligible *umedwars* since January 1987 as workers on an acting status, assuring a promotion to *kaymis* after one year. Also, the standards of compensatory appointment have been relaxed to a considerable extent.

Another focal issue raised in the nineties is the introduction of upward shift of pay scales called 'promotion' among the AMC's workmen. Barot, through his award, decided to apply the state Government's revised promotion scheme of May 1991 to the AMC's workmen. The promotion scheme was designed to improve the wages of the workmen considerably. However, the AMC quickly reacted to his award and filed a case in the High Court in 1992. As the examination is, at present, in the stage of final hearing, a decision is likely to come soon.

After Independence, the socio-economic conditions of the AMC's sweepers have improved considerably in the wake of legal development for sweepers. Their pay scales have been revised several times and the compensatory appointment has also been introduced. In addition, the quota of permanent sweepers has been enlarged with the population growth and the expansion of area under the jurisdiction of the AMC. And, if the promotion scheme is implemented, the posts for the AMC's permanent sweepers will be much more attractive to their community.

Despite the overall improvement mentioned above, there are still some drawbacks regarding their working condition, socio-economic status and political upward mobility.

First, their working condition remains largely the same since the demands of the trade unions have been centred on more employment and more wages at the cost of the improvement of their working conditions. Rather we may say that they have been afraid of improving their working condition drastically because it could restrain or reduce the number of permanent sweepers through modernization or mechanization. As a result, though there were some improvements in terms of tools and equipment, sweepers basically face the same hazardous and unhygienic working conditions, which constitutes one of the major reasons for both high mortality and high incidence of disablement during their service.

Second, the introduction of compensatory appointment which assures employment to their surviving family may lead to entrenchment of the right of employment among those families who have already been employed by the AMC. Obviously, the waiting list will be abolished sooner or later because fresh recruitment has been suspended since 1986. Accordingly, employment through compensatory appointment becomes dominant in the nineties. It implies that sweepers already employed by the AMC tend to make full use of compensatory appointment as indicated by the fact that the number of retired sweepers is negligible in recent years. Thus, compensatory appointment emerges as a new customary right.

Though the AMC's permanent sweepers enjoy a far better institutional climate than their counterparts in medium or small local bodies and are said to be better off among manual workers in Ahmedabad, they still seem to be paralysed by disabilities which hamper their socio-economic development. Their major disabilities lie not in their material standards, but in the lack of a centripetal force in their organization or association. In the process of municipalizing sweeping and scavenging, the trade unions emerged as a major institution for the municipal sweepers. Though the trade unions were functional, their activities were confined to the improvement of service conditions. Furthermore, those who took the initiative in the trade union activities were not sweepers themselves, but leaders from other communities. Thus, sweepers, the largest segment of municipal workers, were regarded as a good object for mobilization by the trade union leaders. It is well known that caste associations played a vital role among those castes which had aspirations for mobilizing their own resources for the common goals of socio-economic and political development. The formation of a centripetal force makes up the core of these caste associations. As things stand now, there is not much scope for the AMC's sweepers to form effective caste associations. It is not easy for them to break away from their social as well as political isolation without launching some sort of a mass movement to overcome their internal weakness. The recent institutional development embodied in compensatory appointment, however, seems to push the AMC's sweepers in the reverse direction.

Notes

1. Representative Gandhian organizations in this regard are Harijan Sevak Sangh, Gandhi Smarak Nidhi, Safai Vidyalaya, Sulabh International and others.

2. Trade unions, as a major pressure group of sweepers, played a very significant role in shaping the service, working and living conditions of the sweepers through negotiations with the authorities concerned. The activities of the major trade unions in the AMC have covered various fields such as the increase of basic wages and allowances, introduction of compensatory appointment and relaxation of its conditions, the expansion of quota for permanent sweepers, constant supply of equipment, construction of the sweepers' quarters, etc. There were a lot of changes over time not only in the number of trade unions concerned but also in the type of their activities. Before the mid-seventies, it was only the Ahmedabad City Sweepers' Association (ACSA) that had worked for the AMC's sweepers. At present, the issues of sweepers are handled at least by five trade unions such as the Ahmedabad Municipal Nokar Mandal (AMNM), the Gujarat Municipal and Panchayat Kamdar Association (GMPKA), the Ahmedabad Municipal Kamdar Karamchari Union (AMKKU), All India Safai Mazdoor Congress (AISMC) and ACSA. In the mid-eighties, AMNM emerged as the largest and the most influential trade union for sweepers by absorbing a considerable number of *mukadams* and sweepers who left ACSA after a split caused by internal politics in 1983. As a strategy of expansion, AMNM made full use of the institutional organizations under its control such as the Ahmedabad Municipal Co-operative Bank and the Ahmedabad Municipal Servants' Consumers Co-operative Society. Also, legal struggles in court became common for solving the individual cases of sweepers, as indicated by the activities of AMNM and GMPKA. Thus, a change in hegemony among the trade unions was closely associated with the extent of their legal and institutional activities. The detail of this process of reorganization among the trade unions is analysed in Shinoda (1995).

3. The majority of the AMC's sweepers belong to the *Bhangis*. The 1981 census divides the Scheduled Castes in Gujarat into thirty groups, out of which the *Vankars* (traditionally weavers), the *Chamars* (tanners) and the Bhangis (sweepers and scavengers) constitute the three populous groups with their population shares in the total Scheduled Castes in Gujarat being 43.1 per cent, 27.2 per cent and 12.6 per cent, respectively. Notably, there is a considerable variation in the level of political, social and economic

development among the Scheduled Castes in Gujarat. The *Vankars* and the *Chamars* constitute an advanced group, while the *Bhangis* remain one of the most backward groups.

References

Agarwal, P.L. *Report of the Committee appointed by the Cawnpore Harijan Sevak Sangh to make a survey of the Social and Religious Disabilities, Working Conditions, and the Standard of Living of the Harijans of Cawnpore.* Kanpur : Harijan Sevak Sangh, 1934.

Ahmedabad. (compiled by the Ahmedabad Municipal Corporation). 'Award and Recommendations of Shri Indrajit G. Thakore, Arbitrator & One Man Pay Commission for Revision of Wage Scales, etc., Part IV', 1978a.

————. (compiled by the Ahmedabad Municipal Corporation). 'Adjudication between the Ahmedabad Municipal Corporation and the Workmen Employed under it in the Matter of Permanency of Daily Rated Workmen of the Engineering Department before Shri G.S. Barot', 1978b.

————. (compiled by the Ahmedabad Municipal Corporation). 'Award Part III of Shri G.S. Barot', 1987.

————. (compiled by the Ahmedabad Municipal Corporation). 'Award Part IX of Shri G.S. Barot', 1989.

————. (compiled by the Ahmedabad Municipal Corporation). 'Award Part XV of Shri G.S. Barot', 1991a.

————. 'The Formula of Settlement between the Ahmedabad Municipal Servants' Association and the Ahmedabad Municipal Corporation', 1991b.

Bhatt, Anil. *Caste, Class and Politics* : *An Empirical Profile of Social Stratification in Modern India.* Delhi : Manohar Publishers, 1975.

Bombay. 'Award in the Matter of the Industrial Disputes between the Ahmedabad Municipality and the Sweepers & Mukadams Employed under it before Mr. M.C. Shah'. Bombay: The Bombay Government Extra Ordinary Gazette, 26 February, 1948a.

————. 'Adjudication between the Ahmedabad Municipality & Its Workmen before Mr. M.C. Shah'. Bombay: The Bombay Government Extra Ordinary Gazette, 9 August, 1948b.

————. 'Arbitrator's Award between (1) Ahmedabad Municipal Corporation of the City of Ahmedabad and (2) the Ahmedabad Transport Service, and their Employees before Shri F. Jeejeebhoy.' Bombay: The Bombay Government Extra Ordinary Gazette, 6 March, 1958a.

————. *Report of the Scavengers' Living Conditions Enquiry Committee,* Bombay : Government of Bombay, 1958b.

Campbell, J.M. (ed.). *Hindu Castes and Tribes of Gujarat*, 2 Vols. Gurgaon: Vintage Books, 1988.

Census of India 1961. *Gujarat, Tables on Scheduled Castes and Scheduled Tribes.* New Delhi: 1964.

————. *Gujarat, The Shenvas : A Scheduled Castes of Gujarat*, New Delhi: 1972.

Desai, I.P. *Untouchability in Rural Gujarat*. Bombay: Popular Prakashan, 1976.

Enthoven, R.E. *The Tribes and Castes of Bombay*, 3 vols. Delhi: Cosmo Publications, 1975.

Galanter, Marc. *Competing Equalities : Law and the Backward Classes in India*. Delhi: Oxford University Press, 1984.

Gandhi, M.K. *The Removal of Untouchability*. Ahmedabad: Navjivan Publishing House, 1954.

Gillion, K.L. *Ahmedabad: A Study in Indian Urban History*. Berkeley and Los Angeles : University of California Press, 1968.

Gujarat. *Bhangi Kasht Mukti Karyakram*. Ahmedabad: Department of Social Welfare, 1972.

Haryana. *Report of the Commission Appointed to Enquire into the Living Conditions of the Safai Mazdoors Employed by Local Bodies and the Private Scavengers Working in the Haryana State*. Haryana: Local Government Department, 1972.

Hazari. *I Was An Outcaste: The Autobiography of an 'Untouchable' in India*. New Delhi: The Hindustan Times, 1957.

India. *Report of the Scavenging Conditions Enquiry Committee*. New Delhi: Ministry of Home Affairs, 1960.

————. *Report of the Committee to Study the Working and Service Conditions of Sweepers and Scavengers*. Delhi: National Commission on Labour, 1969.

————. *Report of the Task Force for Tackling the Problems of Scavengers and Suggesting Measures to Abolish Scavenging with Particular Emphasis on Their Rehabilitation*. New Delhi: Planning Commission, 1990-91.

————. *National Scheme of Liberation and Rehabilitation of Scavengers and Their Dependents*. New Delhi: Ministry of Welfare, 1991-92.

————. *Status of Rural Sanitation Programme in States and UTs*. New Delhi: Ministry of Rural Development, 1992a.

————. *The Industrial Disputes Act, 1947*. Lucknow: Eastern Book Company, 1992b.

Issacs, H.R. *India's Ex-untouchables*. Bombay: Asia Publishing House, 1974.

Jairamdas, J. *Bhangi Kasht Mukti and Bhangi Mukti*. New Delhi: National Committee for Gandhi Centenary, 1969.

Karnataka. *Report of the Committee on Improvement of Living and Working Conditions of Sweepers and Scavengers.* Government of Karnataka, 1976.

Kothari, V.N. *A Study of Economic Profiles of the Scheduled Castes in Gujarat.* Baroda: M.S. University, 1976.

Malkani, N.R. *Clean People and An Unclean Country.* Delhi: Harijan Sevak Sangh, 1971.

National Sanitation Improvement Foundation. *Organising Voluntary Action for Promotion of Low Cost Sanitation in Gujarat.* New Delhi: Consortium of Rural Technology, 1991.

Patel, B.B. 'Report on the Implementation of Minimum Wages for Sweepers in Village Panchayats in Saurashtra.' Ahmedabad: Gandhi Labour Institute, 1990.

Patel, Ishwarbhai. *Safai-Marg Darshika* (A Guide Book on Sanitation). Delhi: Harijan Sevak Sangh, 1970.

Pathak, Bindeshwar. *Road to Freedom: A Sociological Study on the Abolition of Scavenging in India.* Delhi: Motilal Banarsidass Publishers, 1991.

Rajput, K.C. 'Award. Judgement, Pay Commission Report & Important Circulars by Shri G.S. Barot.' Ahmedabad: The Gujarat Municipal & Panchayat Kamdar Association, 1992.

Randeria, Shalini. *'The Politics of Representation and Exchange among Untouchable Castes in Western India* (Gujarat)'. Unpublished Ph.D. thesis, Freien Universtat Berlin, 1992.

Raval, R.L. *Socio-Religious Reform Movements in Gujarat during the Nineteenth Century.* New Delhi: Ess Ess Publications, 1987.

Saurashtra, *Saurashtra Safai Kamdaro Angeni Rivyu Samitino (Vyas Samiti) Aheval.* Government of Saurashtra (in Gujarati), 1956.

Shah, Ghanshyam. *Caste Association and Political Process in Gujarat: A Study of Gujarat Kshatriya Sabha.* Bombay: Popular Prakashan, 1975a.

———. *Politics of Scheduled Castes and Tribes: Adivasi and Harijan Leaders of Gujarat.* Bombay: Vora & Co. Publishers, 1975b.

———. 'Caste Sentiments, Class Formation and Dominance in Gujarat' in F.R. Frankel and M.S.A. Rao (eds.), *Dominance and State Power in Modern India,* vol.2, 59-114. Delhi: Oxford University Press, 1990.

Sharma, Rama. *Bhangi Scavengers in Indian Society: Marginality, Identity and Politicization of the Community.* New Delhi: M.D. Publications, 1995.

Sharma, S.K. *Social Movements and Social Change: A Study of Arya Samaj and Untouchables in Punjab.* Delhi: B.R. Publishing Co., 1985.

Shinoda, Takashi. 'Socio-Economic Conditions of Sweepers Employed by Local Bodies in Ahmedabad District, India', in S. Taniguchi, H.Yanagisawa, T.Shinoda and F.Oshikawa (eds.), *Economic Changes and Social Transformation in Modern and Contemporary South Asia,* 241-69. Tokyo: Hitotsubashi University, 1994.

———. *Indono Seisonin Kasuto Kenkyu* (A Study on the Status of Sweepers in India). Tokyo: Shunjusya (in Japanese), 1995.

Shyamlal. *Caste and Political Mobilization: The Bhangis.* Jaipur: Panchsheel Prakashan, 1981.

———. *The Bhangis in Transitions.* New Delhi: Inter-India Publications, 1984.

———. *The Bhangi: A Sweeper Caste its Socio-Economic Portraits with Special Reference to Jodhpur City.* Bombay: Popular Prakashan, 1992.

Sinha, B.D., P.S.K. Menon and A.K. Ghosh. *Restoration of Human Dignity: Impact of Development Programmes on Scavengers.* New Delhi: Arnold Publishers, 1994.

Sinha, B.D. and A.K. Ghosh. *Evaluation of Low Cost Sanitation: Liberation, Training & Rehabilitation of Scavengers.* New Delhi: Arnold Publishers, 1990.

———. *Sanitation and Environment: Evaluation of Low Cost Sanitation in Gujarat.* New Delhi: Arnold Publishers, 1994.

Thakkar, A. V. *Report: Committee to Examine the Wages, etc. of Sweepers in Municipal and Notified Areas in the Central Provinces and Berar.* Nagpur: Local Self Government (CP and Berar), 1939.

5

Unrest Among the Adivasis and their Struggles

Ghanshyam Shah

Unrest among the Adivasis of Gujarat who constitute 15 per cent of the population is widespread. Their resources for livelihood are depleting very fast. And whatever is available is extensively owned, controlled and monitored by the state and/or non-tribal entrepreneurs resulting into further marginalization of a large number of the Adivasis. On the other hand, alternative avenues for survival, not to speak of better life chances, have not developed. As a result, confrontation of the Adivasis with the state and dominant strata of non-tribals is increasing; manifesting itself in day-to-day resistance, localized spontaneous protest and violent militant struggle.

At present, there is no one tribal movement in Gujarat which encompasses all sections of Adivasi society. Tribal society is not homogeneous. Like non-tribal society, it has undergone changes, thanks to the penetration of market economy, competitive polity and modern administrative system. The striking feature of the change is: emergence of socio-economic differentiations among the tribals, influencing their life style, value system and aspirations. As a consequence, perception and priorities of the issues faced by 'the tribal society' vary from strata to strata of the Adivasis. Priorities of relatively well - off middle class Adivasis are different from those of the forest workers. The former is more agitated over the issues of reservation in Government jobs and political offices, whereas the latter feel more provoked on the issue of wages for survival. Their interests are not essentially antagonistic, and more important, they do not perceive them as such.

But they do not join hands for a common fight. At the same time, traditional boundaries among the various tribes have weakened vis-a-vis the non-tribals, as the Adivasis irrespective of the strata, suffer from more or less the same treatment and prejudices of the non-Adivasis. This facilitates in constructing a bridge, though not solidarity among the various tribals. A sense of 'oneness' as Adivasis, cutting across not only tribes and economic strata within Gujarat, but also outside Gujarat as Indian Adivasis, is developing. In fact, an international movement of `indigenous' peoples has also begun to influence at least the vocal section of Adivasis of Gujarat. The present paper is an endeavour to analyse various contemporary tribal movements in Gujarat with a view to highlight the major issues that they have raised; and the nature of their struggles. Due to limitation of space, and also as studies on such movements in pre-Independence India and in the fifties and sixties are already available (Shah and Patel 1994), we shall largely confine our discussion to the movements of the eighties and the nineties.

Tribal Society

The Scheduled Tribes (ST), also called the Adivasis or indigenous people, constitute 8 per cent of India's population. According to the 1991 Census they are more than 67 million in number. There are more than seven hundred tribes. Some of the tribes such as the Gonds, the Bhils, the Santhals, the Oraons, etc., are spread over several states. Whereas several other tribes are confined to a block/taluka and even a few villages. Because of geo-political location, and historical legacy coupled with tribal, non-tribal relationships in cultural and political spheres, the Adivasis of the country may be divided into two categories: (a) Frontier tribes and (b) non-Frontier tribes. The former are those who inhabit the North-East Frontier States: Arunachal Pradesh, Nagaland, Meghalaya, Manipur, Tripura and Mizoram. These states form buffer zones between India and its neighbours and hence occupy a special position in the sphere of national politics. The non-Frontier tribes are spread over most of the states of the Indian Union, though they are concentrated in Gujarat, Maharashtra, Rajasthan, Madhya Pradesh, Andhra Pradesh, Orissa, Bihar, West Bengal and Himachal Pradesh. Most of the tribals of the Frontier States follow Christianity. Their relation with the caste Hindus of the plains has been limited and confined to the recent past. On the other hand, the tribals of the non-

Frontier States are largely influenced by Hinduism and their interaction with the non-tribal society dates back to several centuries. These differences are reflected in shaping socio-economic movements of the Frontier and Non-Frontier tribes.

Nearly one-tenth of the Adivasis in the country live in Gujarat. They are 6 million in number. Gujarat is one of the most developed states of India with a high degree of industrialization and commercial agriculture. Infrastructure facilities like roads and means of communication like transport, post-office and radio have reached every nook and corner of the state. The Market has penetrated all parts of the region. The development, however, has been lopsided. The Government of Gujarat has identified 56 out of 184 talukas as 'most backward' talukas. Of these, 32 are tribal talukas. They are backward in terms of economic activities, infrastructure facilities and quality of life.

Adivasis in Gujarat are concentrated in the eastern belt beginning from Sabarkantha in the north and Dangs in the south. Among all the districts of the state the highest concentration of tribal population is found in the Dangs (ninety-four per cent) in south Gujarat. It is a small district. Other tribal districts are: Valsad, Bharuch and Surat in South Gujarat having 55, 45 and 36 per cent tribal population, respectively. The Panchmahals in the eastern part of the state has 47 per cent tribal population. The other districts with a tribal population are Vadodara in Central Gujarat having 27 per cent, and Sabarkantha in North Gujarat having 18 per cent Adivasi population. Within these districts, the Adivasi population is concentrated in certain talukas (see Map).

The Adivasis of Gujarat are divided into several tribes. Many of them particularly the large tribes are divided into several endogamous groups. For instance, the Chaudharis are divided into four endogamous groups: Nana, Mota, Valavala and Bharutias. Some of them are further divided into Varjelas, those who have renounced worldly concerns and follow many of the rituals of the caste Hindus; and the Sarjelas destined to suffer and be exploited (Shah 1984). The major tribes in Gujarat are the Bhils, Dhodiya, Chaudhari, Gamit, Kokana, Pateliya, Varli, Dubala, and Kotwaliya. The Bhils constitute the single largest group and are spread from north to south. They are divided into several social groups and each of them has a different dialect and social life. The second largest group is that of the Dhodiyas found in Valsad and Surat districts. Unlike the other Adivasis, the Dubalas, now known as the Halpatis are tribals of the plain, who live with the

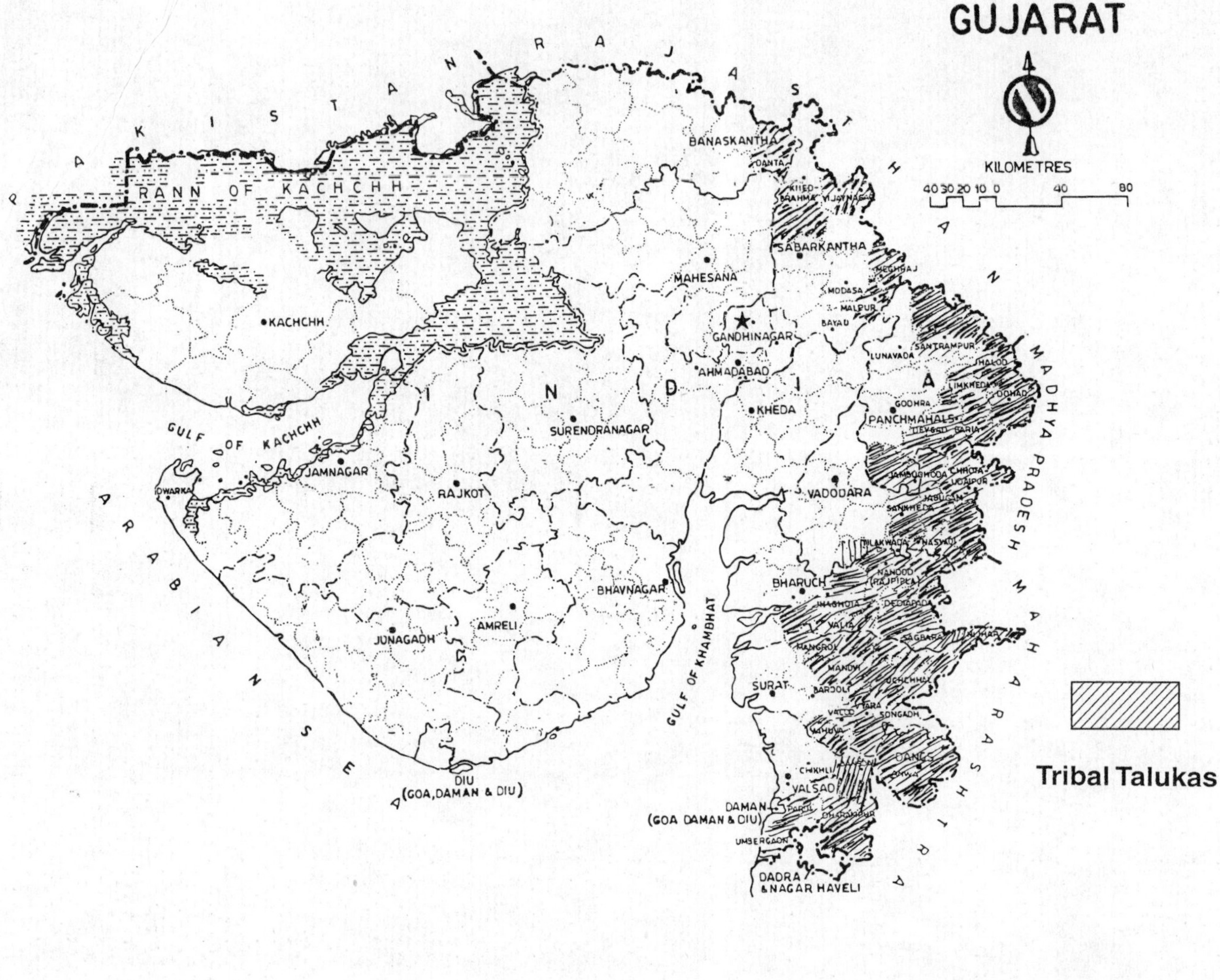
GUJARAT
KILOMETRES
40 30 20 10 0 40 80
Tribal Talukas
PAKISTAN
RAJASTHAN
MADHYA PRADESH
MAHARASHTRA
INDIA
ARABIAN SEA
RANN OF KACHCHH
GULF OF KACHCHH
GULF OF KHAMBHAT
KACHCHH
BANASKANTHA
DANTA
SABARKANTHA
MEGHRAJ
MODASA
MALPUR
BAYAD
MAHESANA
GANDHINAGAR
AHMADABAD
KHEDA
SANTRAMPUR
LUNAVADA
HALOD
LIMKHEDA
DOHAD
GODHRA
PANCHMAHALS
BARIA
JAMBUGHODA
CHHOTA UDAIPUR
JABUGAM
SANKHEDA
VADODARA
TILAKWADA
NASVADI
NANDOD (RAJPIPLA)
DEDIAPADA
BHARUCH
VALIA
SAGBARA
MANGROL
MANDVI
UCHCHHAL
SURAT
BARDOLI
SONGADH
DANGS
CHIKHLI
VALSAD
DAMAN (GOA DAMAN & DIU)
DHARAMPUR
UMBERGAON
DADRA & NAGAR HAVELI
SURENDRANAGAR
JAMNAGAR
DWARKA
RAJKOT
BHAVNAGAR
AMRELI
JUNAGADH
DIU (GOA, DAMAN & DIU)

caste Hindus and work as their agricultural labourers. In the past they were the Halis or bonded labourers. They are mainly found in Surat and Valsad districts. Dhodiyas and Chaudharies are relatively better off than others. They have taken advantage of the development programmes of the state.

This is also true in the sphere of education. Only 36 per cent of the Adivasis (excluding population 0 to 6 years) of Gujarat as against of 60 per cent of the state population are literate. And, literacy is not uniformly spread among all the tribal groups in all the districts. Most of the Dhodiya and the Chaudhari households of Surat and Valsad districts have availed the opportunities of education. But in the case of Halpatis and Kotawaliyas of the same districts, Nayakas of Vadodara district, the Bhils of the Dangs, the situation is quite grim. Most of them are illiterate. (Shah 1985).

More than ninety per cent of the Adivasis live in the country-side. Their settlement in urban areas has increased in the last three decades from 3 per cent to 8 per cent. A majority living in the urban areas work in the informal sector - in small factories, brick-kilns, road and building construction. Some work as hawkers. They are fragmented into small groups, unable to launch any struggle. They live a wretched life in slums. A tiny number of Adivasis consists of white collar employees, professionals like engineers, lawyers, medical practitioners and small entrepreneurs. A relatively stable monthly income and secure job make them a part of the larger middle class in their life style and value system. In the villages they do not mix freely with the rest of the Adivasis. They talk in terms of we (educated) and 'they' (the other Adivasis). At the same time, they are not integrated with the caste-Hindu middle class. They are kept at a distance by the latter in the work place as well as in the social sphere. A sense of being discriminated against in economic and political activities is widespread. They demand more white collar jobs, political offices and allocation of resources for tribal development. Pressure groups are formed within political parties and trade unions for a better deal for tribal members. They joined hands with the *dalit* (Scheduled Caste) middle class when the caste Hindu upper caste launched anti-reservation agitations in the eighties. They occasionally attend public meetings and sign on memoranda demanding more reservation for the ST and development programmes for the Adivasis. They are in the forefront among other Adivasis who articulate and reconstruct tribal identity. More about this later.

Struggle for Land Right

Agriculture is the main source of subsistence for the vast majority of the tribals in rural areas. According to the 1991 census, 88 per cent of the Adivasis are cultivators and/or agricultural labourers (Table 1). By now they are settled agriculturists. According to the survey carried out by the Centre for Social Studies in the late seventies, forty-six per cent of the tribal households are reported to be cultivators (Shah 1989). Their proportion has remained constant in the last decade. All the cultivator Adivasis do not necessarily have so - called legal ownership of land. Partly because there was no land survey in tribal areas, and partly, the tribals do not have any concept of individually - owned land. In the past, they used to cultivate land whereever it was available; they did not stick to one particular plot year after year.

Table 1: ST Main Workers by Economic Activities (1991)

	Particular	No.	%
1	Cultivators	1156516	48.88
2	Agri. Labourers	991967	39.36
3	Livestock, forest work, etc.	27197	1.07
4	Mining and quering	8097	0.32
5	House hold production	16294	0.64
6	Production other household	121885	4.84
7	Construction	27258	1.08
8	Industries and commerce	36398	1.45
9	Transport, warehousing & communication	33487	1.32
10	Other services	101765	4.03
	Total	**2520864**	**100.00**

Source: DISHA (1997).

Among the cultivators 16 per cent cultivate more than 4 hectares of land (Table 2). But all of them are not rich. They do not produce any marketable surplus. A tiny section consisting of those who have canal irrigation or own a diesel or electric pump is better off, and may be called middle or rich peasants. They cultivate cash crops and sell the surplus at competitive prices. They are no longer ignorant of price fluctuations in the market. An Adivasi who owned about 16 acres of land energized by a pumpset said, 'our village is on the road and connected with Unai, Buhari, Valod and Vyara (all taluka business centres). We inquire at all the places and sell at the place where we get the best price. We get a good price for groundnut at the Vyara Co-operative Ginning Factory. Baniyas (moneylenders cum traders) do not give such a good price; so we sell to the co-operative society.' (Shah 1989).

Table 2 : No. and Area of Holdings Operated by ST as per Agricultural Census 1990-91

	Particular	No.	%
1	Marginal (below - 1 ha.)	122635	31.73
2	Small (1.0 to 2.0 ha.)	104064	26.93
3	Semi-Medium (2.0 to 4.0 ha.)	95378	24.68
4	Medium (4.0 to 10.0 ha.)	57327	14.83
5	Large (10.0 and above ha.)	7057	1.83
	Total	**386461**	**100.00**

Source: DISHA (1997).

Such cultivators employ labourers during the harvest season. The members of their families work on their own farms but rarely work as wage-earners on others farms. Some of them grow more than one crop on their irrigated land and follow the model of caste- Hindu rich farmers. They no longer allow their female folk to work on the farm. Their women look after domestic work. Hiring of labourers has become a common practice. However the relationship between tribal labourers and their tribal masters is not the same as that of between tribal labourers and non- tribal employers. The non-tribal masters look down on tribal labourers, and treat them badly, whereas tribal cultivators rarely abuse tribal labourers on the ground of the latter being tribal. This is partly because both are socially related and share common customs and values. Moreover the rich tribal cultivator does not perform a merely supervisory role. In the recent past there have been signs of differences developing between the tribal employers and labourers. The former have begun to speak the language of non-tribal rich farmers. They abuse the labourers as being inefficient and lazy. Some of the prosperous cultivators have now started lending money to the poor and needy tribals at a high rate of interest. They purchase land from fellow tribals or become mortgagees of their land. According to one survey, 68 per cent of the tribal cultivators had mortgaged their land to other tribals (Masavi, n.d.).

A vast majority of the Adivasi cultivators, irrespective of the size of land ownership are poor. An Adivasi owning, say 25 acres or more land in the Panchmahals district or in the Songadh taluka of Surat district works as agricultural labourer during the lean season. This and other cultivators constitute a strata of poor farmers. They do not possess even a pair of bullocks. Their lands are barren, producing very little to sustain their family throughout the year. They work on their own as well as on others' farms, and during the harvest they help each other out, exchanging labour. During the off season, they join the force of labourers in forest and urban areas as 'unskilled' manual labourers.

Marginalization of the poor Adivasis has increased with the anti-people forest policy on the one hand and an increasing number of so - called development projects on the other, which alienates tribals from their land. Though by law the sale of land of tribals to non-tribals is prohibited, large tracts of land belonging to tribals have been acquired by the state. The Government acquired land from tribals for wild life sanctuaries, construction of dams and industrial complexes. Complete data on the land lost by the tribals under various projects is not available. However Table 3 which gives a picture of the extent of loss by the tribals in five irrigation projects is significant. In all the projects concerned, all or nearly all project - affected households losing land and habitats are tribals. The following data is under estimation. For instance, the data given in Table 3 regarding the tribals affected by the Sardar Sarovar Project (SSP) is only related to the Gujarat-villages submerged in water for the reservoir. It does not provide information about the tribals of Madhya Pradesh and Maharashtra and also who lost land in the construction of Kevadiya colony, the township built for the project. The Adivasis who have become oustees as their land was acquired by the state, protested against the state action. Some of them collectively launched a struggle against the policy of the state. The Adivasis affected by the SSP, launched struggles under the leadership of Chhatra Sangarsh Vahini, in the eighties for a better rehabilitation policy. And they succeeded in their demands. But the policy was not implemented in its spirit and later, which led to unrest among those oustees who suffered the most. For instance, the oustees of three villages were unhappy with the resettlement in new sites. They went on a hunger strike demanding better land than what they had received for resettlement. Having failed in their demands, some of them had gone back to their original villages (Oza 1997).

Table 3 : Displacement of Tribals in Gujarat due to Different Projects

Name of Project	Extent of submersion/displacement				
	Area (Hectares)	No. of villages	Total No. of families	Total No. of ST families	% of ST families
1 Sardar Sarovar	7470	19	1900	1880	99
2 Karjan	3677	28	2106	2106	100
3 Daman Ganga	7544	36	3149	2280	72
4 Kakrapara	1480	16	200	200	100
5 Jhagadia Lignite	80	1	30	30	100

Source: *Report of the Committee for Displaced Tribals due to Development Projects*, New Delhi: Ministry of Home Affairs, Government of India, 1984.

Besides this, there are a number of struggles of the Adivasis for land rights. These struggles do not have a uniform pattern of organization, strategies and leadership. The struggles in Bharuch, Dangs and Panchamahals provide evidences of three different types of movements.

Militant Struggle in Bharuch

Five talukas of Bharuch district - Valia, Dediyapada, Sagbara, Jhagadia and Nandod - have a predominantly Adivasi population. The tribals of the district have a long history of struggle against non-tribal landlords and British administration. The Adivasis of Valia and Dediyapada have remained in the forefront in the struggle. Valia is a taluka in Bharuch district, 73 per cent of its population is tribal, mainly Bhil-Vasava. The land of the Adivasis was usurped by non-tribal moneylenders cum landlords before Independence. Various land reforms of the post-Independent period did not confer land right to the tribals of the taluka. Hence, 80 per cent of the agricultural land of the taluka is continued to be owned by Rajputs, Patidars and Muslim landlords. Infact, the tribals cultivate their own land as tenants. Moreover, the landlords do not pay the stipulated minimum wages to the labourers. Under the leadership of the Kisan Sabha the tribals of the taluka struggled to get rights over the land. But the landlords having both economic and political power frustrated this movement. The landlords have also indulged into the business of forest contract, money-lending and smuggling of wood. They also occupy political position in Government, political parties and also in administration.

During the last two decades the Government acquired six thousand acres of land from the taluka to establish various industries. Consequently, the Adivasis working on these lands as tenants or labourers lost their source of livelihood. Most of them were not even employed in these industries on the pretext that they were unskilled. The Adivasis of the taluka often revolted against exploitation and humiliation. Several times they had gone on strike varying from a day to a week demanding minimum wages. Sometimes they destroyed the standing crop of landlords and also indulged in looting. The dominant group used all manner of means to curb the voice of the rebel tribals. Twelve leaders were murdered by the hired goondas of the police, and or, forest contractors - cum - landlords, or in so-called police encounters. One of the most important among them was Narsing Anup Vasava who mobilized the tribals by instilling in them, a sense of dignity. He strongly advocated that the Adivasis were rightful owners of both land and forest. Under his leadership there were a number of confrontations between the Adivasis and the landlords. Militancy of the Adivasis for their rights was projected by the dominant section and the media as 'dacoity'; and Valia was labelled the 'Chambal' of Gujarat. Narsing Vasava was killed by the police in 1981 while he was leading an agitation of the tribals to demand their rights over the forest. The elected leaders in the panchayat who voice the grievances of the tribals were either removed from office or harassed by false police cases. A number of cases of rape of tribal women by landlords and/or police have come to light. The police and other vested interests conspired to murder the Adivasi leader, Chhotubhai Vasava. In May 1993, a police troop of more than 130 policemen attacked Maljipura, the farm of Vasava. As Chhotubhai was away, the police terrorized the villagers and killed a close relative of Vasava. This incident created an uproar in the state. Several NGOs and social activists protested against the police terror. They demanded a judicial inquiry in to the episode. However, nothing happened to the culprits as they had the backing of the ruling party and the Chief Minister. Such terror has a long story. Bhanu Adhvaryu who belonged to the area and visited various villages during the early eighties observed that the terror of non-tribal land-grabbers and forest contractors with the support of police and forest department was responsible for violation of human rights of the tribals (Adhvaryu 1994). Augustine (1984) has described the horrifying stories of atrocities against the tribals of Valia.

The Adivasis of Dediyapada taluka have launched a struggle against the forest department on two issues. The Government has year-marked the area for a wild life sanctuary and acquired 4000 hectares of land. As a result not only have the tribals lost land for cultivation, but they are also not allowed to enter the area as it is designated as reserved forest. The tribals are harassed by the forest department. On the other hand, the private industry has been granted permission to cut down the forest at a nominal rate. Along with this, illegal cutting of forest with the connivance of the police department continues. The tribals have protested against illegal cutting of the forest and demanded their right to cultivate the land as they were doing in the past. The voluntary group, Action Research in Community Health & Development (ARCH) provides leadership to the people. Several demonstrations have been organized and ARCH has submitted a number of memoranda to the Government demanding an inquiry into the illegal cutting of the forest and provide legitimate rights to the tribals for their livelihood. The Government instead of taking action against the criminals, harass the activists and the tribals by filing false cases of looting and arson against them.

The struggles in Bharuch district led by Chhotubhai Vasava and ARCH Vahini differ in leadership and approach. The former is led by the local Adivasis themselves and have a continuity from the past. Whereas, the leadership of the latter, so far, is with non-tribals. The former tries to extend the movement to the tribals of other areas and raises the issue as we shall see in the section on tribal identity. Whereas the latter does not harp on the issue of tribal identity; it aims at linking the movement with non-tribals as well as tribals placed in similar situations. The former is militant and does not mind using violent means as and when necessary. The latter is non-violent but militant, and follows legal and other constitutional mechanism to attain its objectives.

Struggles in Dangs Led by CPI (ML)

Among the Adivasis of Gujarat, the Dangis are relatively late in becoming settled agriculturists. Till Independence, they were living more or less in isolation from the non-tribal society.

Traditionally, the Dangis considered the whole forest as their own. They never faced restriction on their movement and the use of forest products to meet their needs. Every year they were moving from one place to another in search of livelihood, and cultivating land wherever it was available. But it is no longer so. The Adivasis have been prohibited from entering the reserved forest. And, increasingly they have lost land for agriculture. In 1960 the Government classified the forest of Dangs into three categories: reserved forest, protected forest and unclassified forest. The area under each category has not remained constant. In fact, the area under unclassified forest which the tribals could use for cultivation, has actually declined. For instance, in 1961 under the Surat Circle, 6013 square km. forest land was divided into 2977 sq. km. as reserved forest, 818 as protected forest and 2218 sq. km. as unclassified forest. In 1979 the unclassified forest declined from 2218 sq. km. to merely 621 sq. km., whereas the area under the reserved forest has increased from 2977 sq. km. to 4318 sq. km. Hence, the area for cultivation for the Dangis has considerably declined. And, whenever they do cultivate any land, the forest department removes their crop and penalizes the cultivators.

In 1970, the Government ordered the transfer of 56, 214 hectares land for agriculture. But in reality, only 15,617 hectares of land was allocated to 17,638 Adivasi cultivators for agricultural purposes. Thus on an average each cultivator received less than one hectare of land for cultivation. According to the survey in 1968-69, from 79,409 hectares of land cultivated by the Adivasis, the forest department acquired 21,154 hectares land using all kinds of means, for forest plantation. According to the official record only 30 per cent of the Adivasi households have been registered as legal cultivators. Thus not only has the land for cultivation and dwellings declined, but the number of landless Adivasis has increased every year.

As the Adivasis lost land to the forest department and experienced harassment, sporadic confrontation between the Adivasis and forest or revenue department increased. Their demands were not paid any attention by any authority. In 1977, the Dangis organized a struggle. They submitted a memorandum to the Collector and made twelve demands. Their demands *inter alia* included: (a) Resurvey of the district and allocation of land to the Adivasis; (b) Ownership of trees to the cultivator Adivasis where the trees are located in the land possessed by them, and (c) Closing down of the nurseries and plantations made by the forest department on the land cultivated by the tribals. Several demonstrations, meetings and processions were organized to press their demands. The police and forest departments used all methods to diffuse the struggle of the Adivasis. These demands remained unresolved.

With the support of the leaders of CPI (ML), the Dangis formed the *Bhumihin Kisan Hakka Sangarsh Samiti* (BKSS) in the late eighties. The Samiti organized various struggles - demonstrations, rallies, dharana, meetings etc. - against the forest departments, demanding land for cultivation. This resulted in frequent confrontation. In several villages the Adivasis collectively took away 'forest' land and started cultivation. The Government removed their crops and arrested the cultivators and filed cases against them. An Adivasis of Mahal village said, 'when we demand land they do not give and when we take land they shoot us. How do we survive?' Besides repeating the demands of 1977, the BKSS demanded: (1) all those Adivasis from 110 old villages were forced by the forest department to evacuate, and that they should be allowed to settle in their old villages.(2) The Adivasis have not been given land as per the 1970 survey. Once again the survey of land and cultivators be carried out, and all those who were earlier cultivating land should be given possession of their land. All the landless households should be given at least 5 acres of land for self-cultivation. (3) The Adivasis should be given ownership rights of the trees grown on the land cultivated by them.

The Government did not heed the demands of the Adivasis. Instead, the leaders of the Samiti and other Adivasis were harassed by the authorities. They were arrested and false cases were filed in the court against them. The police had beaten a number of workers of the Samiti to terrorize them. Several Adivasis were killed in police firing. They are being humiliated day in and day out by officers at various levels. The main leaders of the struggle were arrested, and all measures were used to crush the movement. Though the organized struggle under the leadership of the BKSS is diffused, unrest continues.

Struggle in the Panchmahals

A similar struggle for the land rights and wages for the labourers emerged in the Panchmahal district in the late eighties. As deforestation increazed, and land for agriculture is rain fed, a majority of the Adivasis (nearly 63 per cent) of the district migrate seasonally in search of employment. Like the Dangis the Adivasis of the Panchamahals are frequently harassed by the forest department when they cultivate 'forest' land. DISHA (Developing Initiatives for Social and Human Action), a NGO, formed by Madhusudan Mistry in 1985 intervened and organized Adivasis. Mistry began his political activity as a trade unionist with the Majur Mahajan, Textile Labour Union in Ahmedabad. He then joined OXFAM and supported small grassroot groups. The purpose of DISHA was to work as a supportive core group for a network of grassroots people's organizations. It aims at empowering the poor to fight exploitation and alter relationship in their favour at the local level; and to influence the allocation of resources in order to improve their economic and social condition. In order to attain such objectives, mass base organizations are important. DISHA has so far formed twenty activist groups which include both informal groups and cooperatives as well as trade unions of agricultural labourers and forest workers.

DISHA formed the *Jamin Hit Suraksha Samiti,* Land Rights Protection Committee (LRPC) in 1987. The organization came into existence when several tribals were beaten, threatened and harassed by the local forest officers who wanted to do plantation work on the land cultivated by the tribals. The LRPC organized number of meetings at taluka and district headquarters demanding: 1. No plantation activity should be carried out on the land that was being tilled; 2. No fines should be levied without receipts; 3. No one should be subjected to violence or harassment; 4. Forest land being tilled should be converted to revenue (legally cultivable) land. Besides direct action of organizing demonstrations and meetings, DISHA used institutional mechanisms and media to bring political pressure on the Government. Some pro-poor Congress leaders supported the struggles launched by DISHA and worked as a link between the organization and the policy makers. In 1989 the Government agreed that the forest department should not tamper with those lands which were being cultivated prior to 1980.

Following this, DISHA carried out a survey and prepared a list of cultivators who were (a) without any cultivable land, (b)cultivating both forest as well as forest land; (c) those with proof of cultivating forest land in the three consecutive years of 1965, 1966 and 1967 (as they were informed that in such cases, land titles would be awarded immediately) and (d) those farmers cultivating forest land between 1967 and 1980. The information was then submitted to the Government for action. But nothing happened. Harassment of the tribal cultivators continued. In 1990, EKLAVYA, an offshoot of DISHA the umbrella organization of all the groups involved in struggles for land rights in Gujarat, organized a rally at Gandhinagar, the state capital in which one thousand tribal cultivators of forest land, mainly from Panchamahals and Sabarkantha participated. The rally demanded : (1) Transfer the forest land to the forest dwellers who have been tilling it for ten years or more, and (2) cancel the license of holding weapons so far provided to forest guards and other officers of the forest department; curtail their unlimited power to arrest forest dwellers on unbailable warrants. Again similar rally was organized in 1992 in Ahmedabad. The struggle continued.

In February 1994, a massive rally was planned at Ahmedabad. However, four days before the proposed rally, the Chief Minister invited the representatives of DISHA and LRPC for negotiation. A written agreement between the Government and EKLAVYA was prepared to the effect, that:

1. From now on, no tree plantation would be done by the Forest Department on land under cultivation prior to 1980;

2. No fine would be collected on such land;

3.The state Government would make a representation to the Union Government to get the forest land released;

4. As soon as the State Government received permission from the Union government, it would begin to give land titles/letters of ownership to the tribals (Poonam 1996).

As no step was taken by the Government to translate this agreement into action, the EKLAVYA again organized a rally in August in Ahmedabad for reiterating its demands. This was on the eve of the state assembly elections. The Chief Minister reiterated the Government's assurances and promised that no tribal would be displaced from the land he was cultivating.

Following this, a land title distribution function was organized in which the Government gave land titles to 80 tribals as a gesture of fulfilment of the promise. Table 4 shows the recipients of land titles by district as announced by the forest minister.

Table 4: Proposed Distribution of Land-titles to the Adivasis

District	No of Villages	No of farmers eligible for titles	Cultivated land (in hectares)
Banaskantha	92	1744	10284.39
Sabarkantha	198	3059	2526.49
Panchmahals	518	21034	20652.00
Vadodara	232	8265	8343.00
Kheda	25	1092	980.00
Bharuch	313	5110	6294.00
Surat	80	511	1733.00
Valsad	311	20968	8418.00
Dangs	39	167	117.06
Total	**1808**	**61950**	**51347.94**

Source: Poonam (1996).

But once again the Government was going at a very slow pace. Most of the eligible tribals have not yet received the title letters. The struggle continues.

Struggle For Minimum Wages

Landless labourers or those owning less than one acre of land are at the bottom of the hierarchy and form 22 per cent of the tribal population. Their main source of livelihood is manual labour on farms owned by others. They have hardly anything to sell but their labour. In Adivasi villages, most of the cultivators with small landholdings do not employ labourers. Labourers do not get work on the farms round the year. During the lean season, some of them take up forest or road construction work. Some migrate to towns to get any kind of manual work. Occasionally they starve or eat certain roots to mitigate their hunger.

The poor tribals collect minor forest products which they use for themselves and also sell in the market. They also manage to obtain employment for plantation and cutting wood. The forest labour co-operative societies which have formally eliminated contractors obtain a contract from the Government for cutting wood. However, these co-operative societies which came into existence in the fifties have been closed down by the Government in the mid-eighties with a view to ban forest cutting. The poor Adivasis who used to get employment for four to five months in a year have lost their major source of livelihood, and now forced to find an alternative source of employment. They migrate in search of work. Similarly the poor cultivators and landless labourers also migrate during the off season. They work in sugar cane farms, tobacco farms, brick factories, road construction and other sectors of casual labour. Jan Breman observes, 'They travel around the villages in small groups seeking work, returning again to their home bases after a span of time varying from a few weeks to a whole season. This relatively short distance facilitates such movement back and forth, and consequently many make the journey several times a year' (1985: 192). Their work conditions in sugarcane farms, tobacco factories, brick-kilns and other places are wretched.

One of the avenues of livehood for the Adivasis, is collection of forest product for their own consumption and sale. In the past they were using wood and bamboo for construction of their houses, making baskets and other material for sale. Now, whenever they use them, they are harassed by the forest and the police department. For instance, the Adivasis get a limited number of bamboos for their use and for making baskets for sale. For that they have to pay Rs. 1.50 per bamboo. On the other hand, paper factories pay only 7 paise per bamboo (Rs. 7 per ton). The Adivasis demand for more bamboos and at a cheaper rate. This was one of the demands of the BKSS in Dangs and ARCH Vahini in Bharuch district.

The DISHA has organized a struggle of the forest workers. Gujarat Van Majdur Mandal, that is Gujarat Forest Produce Gatherers and Forest Workers Union was formed by DISHA in the mid-eighties. The union mobilized forest workers through meetings, rallies, conferences and demonstration for demanding minimum wages. Besides these activities, pressures were brought on the policy makers through letters, memoranda and legal measures. The forest department has now began to pay the stipulated minimum wages. The organization is now demanding revision in the minimum wages from Rs. 15 to Rs. 46

per day for eight hours work. The labourers working for the forest department are demanding permanency in their jobs so that they get benefits like holidays, pension, medical help, etc.

Another issue that the DISHA has undertaken is wages for *tendu* leaf workers. *Tendu* (Thuniki) leaf is used for wrapping tobacco in indigenous beedi-making process. *tendu* trees are found in large numbers in the forest of Panchmahals. The Adivasis collect *tendu* leaf and give it to the forest department which then sells it to beedi traders. This work provides employment to Adivasis for two months or so. Earlier they were directly selling to the traders. The National Commission on Agriculture observed that: 'It is experience of all states that the nationalization (of *Tendu* Leaf Trade) not only brought extra revenue to the states, but also ensured payment of reasonable minimum wages to the collectors'. However, the Adivasis of Gujarat did not get 'reasonable minimum wages' for their work. DISHA took up their issue and mobilized the tribals involved in the collection of *tendu* leaf. Demonstration and rallies were organized demanding minimum wages. In 1991, the Forest Development Corporation raised plucking rate of *tendu* leaf from Rs.11 to Rs.20 for 100 bundles. Next year one rupee was raised, making it Rs. 21. The union is now demanding Rs.35 for hundred bundles. And recently (February 1997) the Government has conceded this demand.

Assertion for Tribal Identity and Self-Rule

Caste Hindu social institutions and rituals penetrated far and wide in tribal society. Most of the Adivasis call themselves Hindus and follow several principles of pollution and purity such as hierarchical order among themselves and restrictions on inter-dining and intermarriage. Caste Hindu Gods like Rama and Krishna have also become their legendary figures for worship. Several tribes follow the path of sanskritization. Notwithstanding this, they have a distinct cultural identity different from caste Hindus in general and dominant castes in particular, living on the plains. Distinctiveness is expressed in their dialect, cultural ethos and value system. The caste Hindu invariably look down upon the Adivasis as 'backward' and 'inferior'. And the elite, the intelligentsia, policy makers and bureaucrats, as a whole believe that the tribals have to move on the path of development, adopted by the 'mainstream', that is caste Hindus. For them, Adivasi means tribe, that is a stage in human evolution in the Darwinian sense. More important, Adivasis believe themselves to be separate from the caste Hindus. A sense of 'we' and 'they' among the Adivasis and caste Hindus is conspicuous. A sense of being different becomes strong among the Adivasis when they perceive that they experience - real or imaginary - injustice, and a feeling of being discriminated against. It is manifested in their day-to-day life situation, though relatively well articulated and expressed by educated middle-class Adivasis and their political leaders as distinct from the rest. However, articulation of being separate and a sense of injustice, and particularly ways to mitigate injustice differ. Broadly speaking there are three schools of thought and political action for strengthening tribal identity and tribal rule. They are (i) developmentalist or modernist, (ii) culturalist, and (iii) tribal self-rule political activist. The developmentalist school is the largest among all, believing in assimilation with the mainstream social institutions and following the path of 'progress' - capitalist growth and liberal social democracy - charted out by the dominant strata of society. The champions of this school have grievances particularly with those non-Adivasis who are holding position and power in various institutions. They compete with the elite of the dominant classes. In the process, factions within organizations consisting of Adivasis are formed who assert the rights of Adivasis. They work as pressure groups as well as active actors in electoral politics.

On the other hand, the culturalist school is an ardent believer of distinct separate identity of tribals as Adivasis, i.e. aboriginals, original natives. According to them the Adivasis have nothing in common with the non-tribals. They refuse to recognize the state and other political institutions as legitimate organizations to rule over them. These institutions and laws are alien. An early proponent of this school is *Sati-pati-panth* led by Kesari Singh. This group launched a militant struggle regarding the land issue in the fifties. It gave a call to Adivasis to drive out non-Adivasis who were exploiters and land-grabbers. The followers of the *Panth* boycotted elections and other institutions. They refused to pay revenue (Shah 1975). The *Panth* has now become a religious sect emphasizing the tribal way of life and belief. Its followers, though, attend the rituals of the *Panth* but do not keep away from educational and economic institutions run by the state. The influence of the *Panth* has its ups and downs, which increase when incidents of atrocities against Adivasis arise, and issues like land and forest rights become acute. The *Panth* does not organize collective action against the dominant classes or the state. Though its activities at present are largely confined to rituals, it provides a breeding ground for the groups advocating tribal autonomy and self-rule. Another group broadly following a similar approach emphasizing the cultural dimension of the Adivasi has emerged in the last five years. It is called *Adivasi Ekta Parishad*, i.e. a platform for unity among the Adivasis. The members of the Parishad belong to various non-Government activist groups and political parties. It believes that Nature is God and strives for protection of the Environment. Cultural distinctiveness which includes collective right over land as against individual ownership, tribal control over the forest and harmonious relationships between Adivasi and nature are emphasized by the *Parishad*. One of the leaders of the *Parishad* said:

> They (non-Adivasi leaders) want us to be Eklavyas of Mahabharat. Their sole purpose is to loot us and to subjugate us... History has not given any place to our heroes who also fought for the country's freedom. Socially we are ridiculed, economically we are suppressed and enslaved. We are made to lose our pride, self-respect and identity... Despite this humiliating past everything is not lost yet. We in our day to day life still preserve those human qualities which can rekindle our pride, identity and self-respect. We have to assert our presence, make it felt. We have to highlight the human values in our culture. The state is hostile to us. They want to usurp our identity as Adivasis.... (Quoted by Pinto 1997).

The proponents of this school do not, at this stage, believe in political programmes within or outside electoral politics. Stress is on rejuvenation of tribal consciousness and separate identity. Some of them believe that the demand for land titles or higher wages encourages individual ownership and generates divisions among the Adivasis. Activities of the group are so far confined to conferences of tribals of western India. Some of the leaders are active supporters of the political agenda of the tribal self-rule politically active school.

The third school is politically active. It demands self-rule for the Adivasis. The stronghold of the group is in Bharuch district which has, as mentioned earlier, a long history of militant tribal struggle on different issues. Chhotubhai Vasava is its leader. He formed the *Gujarat Adijati Vikas Paksh* (GAVP) on the eve of the 1995 state assembly elections. The party contested 14 assembly seats particularly in south Gujarat. Though it won only one seat, the party gave impressive performance against the Congress and the BJP. Later, the party captured Jhagadia and Valia taluka panchayats. Its political base is confined to Bharuch district in general and two talukas - Jhagadia and Valia - in particular. But its political appeal is widespread. The GAVP mobilized Adivasis of Gujarat and neighbouring states on the issue of Tribal Autonomous Councils for the Adivasis of western India covering Rajasthan, Madhya Pradesh, Maharashtra and Gujarat. Among the several demands that the GAVP made, the important ones which are related to tribal identity and autonomous rule are:

1. Protect tribal culture, identity and self-respect.
2. Introduce autonomy and self governance in tribal area;
3. Give total rights to Adivasis over forest, land and water;
4. Give ownership rights to tribals over forest land.

Besides this, the party made a number of demands for extension of development programmes such as establishment of educational institutions both for primary and higher learning, connecting the tribal belt with broad gauge railway lines, providing more employment to tribals, etc. While making such demands, it comes closer to the Developmentalist school accepting integration of the tribals with the mainstream though it differs in emphasis on the path of development. It is more militant than the Developmentalist school and advocates direct collective action to attain the rights of the Adivasis over land and forest.

The proponents of all the schools raise the issues of tribal identity, injustice against Adivasi and Adivasis rights over forest, land and water. They talk in idioms of 'we-Adivasis', and 'they non-Adivasis' as dominant and exploiter class. Among themselves they differ in their approach to tribal development and political action. However, unlike the Dalit Ambedkar movement, there is no overarching tribal ideology for tribal non-tribal relationship, socio-economic relationship for production and distribution, political institutions or paradigms for development. The talk of cultural distinctiveness, self-identity and autonomous rule have emotional appeal but the proponents often vacillate from the isolationist position of being distinct and separate, to integrationalist positions following the developmentalist approach. They do not sustain collective mobilization for a long time, as the tribal society is no longer the same as that in the nineteenth century.

Overview

There is a widespread disquiet among the Adivasis of western India. Their traditional resources are depleted and alternative avenues have not opened up. A large section of the Adivasis are becoming marginalized — becoming poor peasants, landless labourers in agriculture, forest and informal sector of urban economy. Minimum wages, rights over forest produce and land for agriculture are the major issues on which they fight. There is no Adivasi struggle in Gujarat mobilising all strata of Adivasi Society. Besides localized spontaneous struggles for protection of the forest, minimum wages and use of the forest produce; and also against tyranny of the police, forest officers and forest contractors, there are number of organized struggles on the issue of land, minimum wages, the right of tribals over forest and allocation of resources for tribal development. Some of them also raise the issue of tribal identity and self-rule.

References

Adhavaryu, Bhanu. *Rudra Vina no Jankar* (ed.). Chandu Maheriya (Gujarati). Ahmedabad: Gujarat Khet Vikas Parishad, 1994.

Augustine, P.A. *Supression of Valia Tribals: A Case of Human Rights Violation*. Delhi: Indian Social Institute, 1984.

Breman, Jan. *Of Peasants, Migrants and Paupers: Rural Labour Circulation and Capitalist Production in Western India*. Delhi: Oxford University Press, 1985.

Desai, I.P. *Understanding Slogan of Adivasi Swayat Raj in South Gujarat* (Mimeo.). Surat: Centre for Social Studies, 1971.

_____. 'Vedchhi Movement', in *History of Rural Development in Modern India*. I.P. Desai and Banwarilal Chaudhary. Delhi: Impex India, 1977.

DISHA. *Tribals in Gujarat*. Ahmedabad: DISHA, 1997.

Hardiman, David. *The Coming of Devi: Adivasi Assertion In Western India*. Delhi: Oxford University Press, 1997.

Joshi, Satyakam. *Politics of Tribal Autonomy: A Case of South Gujarat Tribals* (Mimeo.). Surat: Centre for Social Studies, 1996.

Krishnan, Poonam. *A Case Study of the Land Rights Protection Committee of Disha* (Mimeo.). Delhi: Oxfarm America, 1996.

Masavi, Mustadi. n.d. *Problems of Land Alienation among Tribals of Gujarat*. Ahmedabad: Tribal Research and Training Institute.

Oza, Nandini. 'Marginalisation, Protests and Political Action (A Case Study of the Tribals of the Villages in Gujarat Affected by the Sardar Sarovar Project)', a paper presented in seminar on *Tribals of Western India: Issues of Development and Marginalisation*. Surat: Centre for Social Studies, 1997.

Pinto, Stanny. 'Tribalism and Politics of Identity among the Tribals of South Gujarat', a paper presented in seminar on *Tribals of Western India: Issues of Development and Marginalisation*. Surat: Centre for Social Studies,1997.

Shah, Ghanshyam. *Politics of Scheduled Castes and Tribes*. Bombay: Vora and Company, 1975.

_____. *Economic Differentiations and Tribal Identity*. Delhi: Ajanta Publications, 1984.

_____. 'A Profile of Education among the Scheduled Tribes in Gujarat', in *Tribal Education in Gujarat*. Centre for Social Studies. Delhi: Ajanta Publications, 1985.

_____. 'Tribal Issues: Problems and Perspectives', in *Tribal Transformation in India.* 2, Buddhadeb Chaudhaury (ed.). New Delhi: Inter-India Publications, 1992.

_____. 'Ethnicity and Politics: A Study of Scheduled Tribes in Gujarat'. *The Journal of Social Science*, 2, 1 (January-March, 1989).

_____. (with Arjun Patel). *Tribal Movements in India* (Mimeo.). Surat: Centre for Social Studies, 1994.

6

Resettlement and Rehabilitation in the Sardar Sarovar Project : A Review of Policy Reforms and Implementation

Sudarshan Iyengar

1

The Sardar Sarovar Project (SSP), a multi-purpose project on the river Narmada in Western India, is undoubtedly one of the most controversial development projects in the world. Like many other development projects in India and in other developing countries, the weakest plank of the project has been the resettlement and rehabilitation (R & R) of the involuntarily displaced population, a large section of which is tribal. It is by now well-known that development-induced displacement is disruptive. Although planners and administrators have been slow in learning this, social scientists have been well aware of how development projects can make certain sections of the population worse off. In fact, according to Cernea, historically, social scientists have been much better at recording development tragedies than preventing them (Cernea 1991: 188). The planners and administrators even when aware of the tragedies it may cause, feel that the family getting displaced makes a sacrifice for the sake of the community (Varma 1985: i).

The case of the SSP with respect to the R & R has been further worsened because there has been a controversy over a number of other issues. It has been argued, for instance, that the project is economically non-viable (Paranjpye 1990). Similarly, issues have been raised with regard to SSP's environmental impacts and sustainability (Alvares & Billorey 1988; Kalpavriksh 1988; Morse-Berger 1992; Paranjpye 1990). There is by now a fairly strong international lobby which agrees with Alvares and Billorey's view that the SSP is a planned environmental disaster. Yet at another level there have been arguments about the relevance and correctness of imposing a non-tribal (mainstream society) concept of development on the tribals, who according to a few activists and concerned citizens have their own philosophy of life within which the mainstream concept of development doesn't fit. According to this school of thought, the mainstream society should not interfere with the traditional tribal societies and their modes of production. Even Morse-Berger seem to endorse what they call 'tribal culture economy'. This thesis has also been formulated and then propounded by the Narmada Bachao Andolan (NBA), an organization consisted of social activists and some tribals of the Narmada Valley. In fact, the NBA has challenged the conventional concept of development and has taken a stand that the conventional development is in fact destruction (Patkar 1988). Since, the SSP affects a large number of tribals, it is being argued that the tribals are being forced to accept a tragic future on account of an intrinsically non-viable and socially and environmentally perilous project.

The case for the R&R in the SSP is thus extremely vulnerable. Perhaps, it is this type of lobbying at the national and the international level that prompts many academicians to believe that the SSP is a planned destruction and that it has elements of a great and horrible act of deceit towards the tribals in the valley (Krishna Kumar 1996).

However, the entire controversy over the SSP in general and the R&R efforts in particular, deserve a more close and objective assessment than what has been attempted by most. Many important things have happened for the first time in the history of R&R in India. Compared to an uninspiring history of the R&R in the country until the recent past, significant policy reforms have been achieved in the case of the R&R policies of the SSP. Similarly, the implementation in the initial phase of the post-policy reform period has been moving in the right direction. It would indeed be relevant and important to understand the processes and events that took place in the R&R of the SSP since 1980 when the implementation of the dam project began in earnest. It would also be useful to know what plagues the implementation now. This paper is an attempt to review the policy reforms in R&R in the SSP, the implementation of the new policy, status of the R&R and the issues that are relevant for future. Rest of the paper is divided into three sections. In section two, historical evolution of the current R&R policy for the SSP is traced. In section three, implementation of the new policy is reviewed. This is done for two time periods, 1988 to 1993 and 1993 to 1997. In the fourth and final section, problems and prospects in R&R for the SSP are discussed. The paper has not discussed the post 1997 developments.

2

For a sound R&R effort in any involuntary displacement project, the formulation of the policy, its content, operational strategies and the execution and monitoring have to be sound. Cernea has described these steps to explain the process followed by the World Bank in arriving at the normative content and the operational guidelines on R&R, (Cernea 1991: 198). To begin with, the formulation of an R&R policy has to be sociologically informed. In this context, we shall now examine the evolution of the R&R policy for the SSP.

The Basic Provisions for the R&R

The river Narmada is an inter-state river. It originates in Madhya Pradesh and traverses a total distance of 1312 km before it merges with the sea in the Bay of Khambat on the west coast. For most part, it traverses between the mountain ranges of Vindyachal in the North and the Satpuda in the south. It is one of the oldest and sacred rivers (Paranjpye 1991; Verghese 1994; Varma 1985). Because of its peculiarly narrow path, the 214 km long SSP reservoir would submerge lands in Gujarat, Maharashtra and in Madhya Pradesh.

Two major riparian states Gujarat and Madhya Pradesh disputed over the extent of use of water. A number of meetings and committees could not resolve the issue and hence according to the provision of the Indian Constitution a Tribunal was set up in 1969 (For a brief and interesting historical account refer to Verghese 1994: 120-133). Obviously, the decision regarding the rehabilitation of the population affected by the projects also rested with the Tribunal. The Narmada Water Dispute Tribunal (NWDT), as it came to be known, gave its final report in 1978. (For major decisions and salient features of the SSP see Annexure I).

The NWDT ordered the Government of Gujarat to bear the total cost of rehabilitation in all the three states of Gujarat, Maharashtra and Madhya Pradesh. It made a basic provision for the allotment of a minimum of two ha. of irrigable agricultural land to each landholding family losing 25 per cent or more of agricultural land. 'Family' included husband, wife, minor children and other dependents on the head of the family. Further, every major son (18 years or above) was treated as a separate family (Report of NWDT Vol. II: 126-129). This basic provision itself was path-breaking in the history of R&R in India. In most of the projects, the persons losing land were given cash compensation which hardly enabled the affected persons to buy alternate land or any other equally productive asset. A large number of studies have documented this and the consequent impoverishment of the displaced population. (Alexander et al. 1991; Dalua 1993; Fernandes and Thukral 1989; Gumber 1998; Goldsmith and Hildyard 1984; Jayaratne 1990; Mahapatra 1990; Muthayya and Mathur 1974; Reddy et al. 1989; Reddy 1992; Sudarsen and Kalam 1990; Thukral 1992).

Although the provision of a minimum of two ha. of irrigable agricultural land was made to compensate for the loss of land, the NWDT provision had a serious lacuna. Firstly, it failed to take into account the characteristics of the tribal settlements and the economy where a large number of families do not own but only operate land for production. This land may belong to the forest department and/or, be government waste land. The NWDT thus continued to take a legalistic view of the situation which has its basis in the revenue administration system conceived and operationalized under the British regime. The land laws under the British totally ignored the community ownership and individual operations of land in the forest area by the tribal communities. Describing this Patel says, 'the fact of future displacement of these people by development projects nearly brought out to the surface a serious and embarrassing problem of unacknowledged tribal right to have access to the resources of livelihood in their ancestral land'. (ARCH 1988a: 3; Patel 1994: 1). Secondly, the NWDT provision also ignored female headed households, widows, single-woman families and the landless (Thukral 1989: 59).

Obviously, the NWDT Award provision for the tribals in the Valley was sociologically ill-informed. However, this was not all. The three state governments were not in a mood to even abide by the NWDT provisions. There were signs of retrogression.

Activists Group ARCH-Vahini Enters the Fray

With the declaration of the NWDT Award in 1978, the Government of Gujarat began the project work as well as the process of rehabilitation. It issued a Government Resolution (GR) in June 1979. In this GR, it made a crucial change which killed the spirit of the NWDT provision almost completely. The entitlement of a minimum of two ha. of irrigated land to 'each land owning family' was changed to 'each land holding'. In the tribal areas, both for cultural and historical reasons and also due to the laxity in the revenue administration, most of the land holdings are joint. A joint holding may, therefore, be operated by two, three or more independently living families. On the strength of this GR, the Government offered a minimum of two ha. of its waste land which was located more than 100 km. away from the native villages, to each holding and not to each family. The tribals living in the first five affected villages refused the Government offer. The government responded by taking a stand that those who rejected the offer were free to buy land on their own from the cash compensations that were paid for the land acquired. The 1979 GR, in the process of implementation, violated the spirit of NWDT Award completely. (ARCH 1988a: 2-4).

Armed with its 1979 GR, the Government was ready to ride roughshod over the poor, helpless and unorganized tribals, when in 1980 a group of activists engaged in health and development work among tribals and belonging to ARCH-Vahini, started frequenting the submerging villages. The panic-stricken and desperate tribals were reluctant to hear and do what the fresh-faced students advised them. Even the ARCH-Vahini activists were new to this game. They knew nothing or very little about land laws, NWDT Award, World Bank guidelines of 1980 etc. Had they known the complications, they would have probably given up (Patel 1994: 3). The tribals would have continued to tolerate them as sympathetic observers, but for a case in which the Government retracted on a written promise it had made in the process of implementing the 1979 GR based policy. This was towards the end of 1983. Till then the ARCH-Vahini was content with monitoring the implementation of the totally watered-down policy of the Gujarat Government. The silly slip by the Government led to a case of 'promissory estoppel' which was taken to the court. The tribals saw a ray of hope. They quickly organized themselves and the Government stood exposed.

The World Bank and the International Non-Government Organizations (NGOs)

In August 1983, ARCH-Vahini wrote a detailed letter describing and quantifying the dependence of tribals on forest land for agricultural production and hence their survival. The objective was to lobby the World Bank in favour of tribals. The Bank, till then, knew nothing about the problem of encroachers in the submergence zone because the Government had never supplied the information to the Bank. Since the Government treated the tribals cultivating forest and government waste land as 'illegal encroachers', it did not deem it fit to consider the encroachers as project-affected persons eligible for alternative agricultural land. Hence, it never found the necessity to report this aspect to the Bank. Although the Bank's initial response to the ARCH-Vahini's letter was cautious, it did get disturbed over the information on encroachers (ARCH 1988a: 6). This has been mentioned later in 1992 in the report of the Independent Review Mission (IRM) which was appointed by the then World Bank President Barbar Conable and was headed by Bradford Morse (Morse and Berger 1992: 48).

Simultaneously, the Development Policy Advisor of Oxfam, a British NGO was also kept informed. They in turn launched an international campaign for the rights of the tribals in the submergence zone of the SSP in India. The international NGOs upon learning of the Bank's involvement in the project, lobbied and created pressure on it directly as well as through their country Executive Directors. Besides OXFAM, the other major supporter in UK was Survival International, an NGO that fights for the rights of the indigenous communities world over.

The World Bank too was learning quickly about the lapses it had made in the past on the R&R front in the projects it had financed all over the world. In February 1980, it released an operational manual for R&R for the Bank-financed projects. Further, in 1982, another operational manual was prepared for tribal people. However, the Bank did not have any assessment of the ground reality with respect to submergence and resettlement. It was the August 1983 letter of ARCH-Vahini which provided critical information about the ground reality in the Narmada Valley. Perhaps, it was against this backdrop that Professor Thayer Scudder from California Institute of Technology, an international expert on R&R, was sent to India on a special Mission in November 1983 to assess the R&R situation in the SSP. The

Independent Review Mission, however, probably held the correct view that sending Scudder was an afterthought and the Bank had already completed the appraisal of the project and had totally missed out on the R&R. We shall come back to this issue a little later. Scudder's visit was instrumental in the Bank gaining an understanding that the NWDT provision for R&R would fail to cover a large number of tribal families who survived on Government and forest land. The Bank also realized that with the implementation of the then existing policy, it would not be able to ensure the application of the overarching principle of the Bank with respect to R&R. According to the principle, the involuntarily-displaced population should at least regain the standard of living which they enjoyed prior to displacement, after resettlement.

In his November 1983 report, Scudder had made two important recommendations. One was regarding agricultural land entitlement for the encroachers and landless families and the second was regarding release of denuded forest land for cultivation if the tribals so desired. His November 1983 mission was followed by another visit in September 1984 to assess developments with regard to his earlier recommendations. He met the ARCH-Vahini activists in which he was appraised of the ground reality and was provided all the facts and details he needed (Patel 1984: 6). Armed with this data on the ground reality and the performance of the Government of Gujarat on the R&R, the World Bank entered into the megotiations on the Loan Agreement (LA) with the Government of India and the three party states.

The May 1985 Loan Agreement

In May 1985, the World Bank entered into a Loan Agreement with the Government of India and the three states Gujarat, Maharashtra and Madhya Pradesh. Besides the techno-economic aspects of the project, the R&R conditions were also negotiated. Professor Scudder was the chief negotiator. He built upon the foundation of the NWDT Award and secured land entitlement for the encroachers and the landless in the submergence villages in the Valley. The Government of India also agreed to release the forest land if demanded by the displaced tribal population. This concession was a significant achievement because it was only in 1980, that the Forest Conservation Act was passed which forbade any use or transfer of forest land for any other purpose without the prior permission of the Ministry of Environment and Forests (MOEF), which also was created afresh in 1980. The MOEF was all for promptly and enthusiastically implementing the Act. The Gujarat Government was asked to seek environmental clearance from the Ministry because the SSP would submerge around 13,000 ha. of forest land. It may be mentioned here that the MOEF did not give clearance to the project until 1987. In this context, the Bank's achievement in the LA was highly significant. Another most important provision in the LA was that the displaced families were given the right to choose the agricultural land.

Evolution of the R&R Policy in Gujarat through Government Resolutions (GRs)

With the signing of the Loan Agreement with the Bank, the Government of India and the three state Governments were bound by certain commitments towards the tribals in the valley. The Government of Gujarat responded by issuing a new GR on May 30, 1985. It should be mentioned here that when the Government of Gujarat was negotiating the Loan Agreement with the Bank in 1985, it was also arguing a case in the Supreme Court and in its affidavits, it continued to accuse the tribals dependent on forest and government land as thieves, law-breakers and encroachers (ARCH 1988a: 6). However, after signing the Loan Agreement, the Gujarat Government was compelled to recognize the right of the encroachers. The GR however did not specify which land would be allotted to the encroachers. The Government waste land far away from the submergence villages was not acceptable to the affected tribals. The struggle thus continued.

In another GR of November 1, 1985 the Government made provision for a minimum of two ha. of land to each family connected with the land holding and not to each holding. This was also an improvement. The Government also offered choice to the tribal families in selecting the Government land. Three options were granted. However, if the families failed to select any, they had to buy land on their own. The family could then buy land only equivalent to its original land holding. A further concession was granted here. The difference between the market price of the land purchased and the cash compensation for the land was to be given as an ex gratia payment. This was a qualitative improvement over the NWDT Award which had stipulated that the cost of land in excess of compensation was to be initially borne by the Government and passed on subsequently as interest free

loan to the displaced families. However, the GR still violated the spirit of the LA which gave an entitlement of a minimum of two ha. to each family and of the family's own choice. In fact, by introducing the condition of three options, the Government, in effect, intended to bring back the same old 1979 policy. The affected families or the project affected persons (PAPs), as they came to be known later, refused to accept this new GR and the struggle continued.

In April 1987, The World Bank Mission found that the Government of Gujarat had not complied with the provisions made in the LA. The Mission members visited the interior-most villages and declared in the presence of the Government officials that all encroacher and landless families were entitled to a minimum of 2 ha. of land of their choice. To this, the Gujarat Government initially responded by saying that it did not care for the World Bank Loan and that it was not possible to give land entitlement to the encroachers and their major sons. Displaced tribal families' future hung in the balance for some time. The World Bank continued with its tough stance. Finally, the Government of Gujarat yielded but not before trying yet another angle to wriggle out of this commitment.

During the 1987 World Bank Mission visit, the Government maintained that there was not enough private land which could be offered to the displaced families. However, in the wrap up meeting, a member of the Bank Mission produced a long list of private owners who had shown willingness to sell land. This list was supplied to the Bank by the members of ARCH-Vahini. The government had no answer (Patel et al. 1991: 331).

The suspense ended in late December 1987 when the Government of Gujarat released three small GRs dated December 4, 14 and 17. The first one granted land of choice to each eligible land-owning family. It also granted as ex-gratia the difference between the cost of land purchased and the compensation. This was an improvement over the NWDT provision in which the difference in the cost was to be treated as an interest-free loan to the displaced family, to be repaid in 20 yearly installments.

The second GR replaced the November 30, 1985 GR for encroachers. The GR clearly recognized the entitlement of encroachers and their major sons and provided for two ha. of land of choice to each family and the grant of ex gratia to meet the cost of private agricultural land.

The third GR extended the same provision to the landless families. Thus, by December 1987, the Gujarat government had announced what has now come to be known as the most liberal RR policy package in India and perhaps in Asia. The provisions certainly conformed to the overarching principle of the World Bank's 1980 policy guidelines for projects involving involuntary displacement. By the provision of a minimum of two ha. of irrigable land of choice to each affected family, it became feasible to ensure at least the restoration of the standard of living enjoyed prior to displacement. The Bank has decribed this process as an incremental strategy for policy reforms in R&R of the SSP.

Between the Loan Agreement in May 1985 and the final policy declaration in December 1987, the tribal population facing involuntary displacement in the villages of Maharashtra and Madhya Pradesh was also organized. There too, a protest movement surfaced in February 1986.* Earlier, in March 1984, when the ARCH-Vahini had organized a protest rally, some tribal families from the submergence villages in Maharashtra had joined. However, their total involvement in the protest movement took place only at the beginning of 1986 (Verghese 1984 and Parasuraman 1993). This protest movement decided to oppose the project itself in August 1988. Therefore, its direct contribution to the policy reforms in Maharashtra and Madhya Pradesh was low. We shall return to the discussion on the protest movement in other states a little later.

Critique of the Bank's Incremental Strategy

A major and scathing criticism on the World Bank's incremental strategy for policy reforms in the R&R of the SSP was advanced by the Independent Review Mission in 1992. Their major argument was that the Bank had failed to implement its own policies which it had evolved in 1980 for projects involving involuntary displacement and in 1982, for projects involving involuntary displacement of tribals. The report says:

> absence of human and environmental assessment ab initio creates the impression that the demands of engineering carry more weight in the bank than the needs of people to be affected...(Morse-Berger 1992: 355).

Similarly, attacking the incremental strategy the Report says:

> The record of resettlement and rehabilitation in India, which has been unsatisfactory in virtually every project with a large resettlement component, should reasonably have prompted the Bank to adopt a less flexible standard for resettlement and rehabilitation of project-affected people. In this context, the Bank's incremental strategy to obtain compli-

ance, made explicit in 1989 greatly undermines prospects for achieving successful resettlement and rehabilitation(Morse-Berger 1992: 351).

According to the World Bank's Operational Manual of February 1980 for R&R, the Bank has to necessarily carry out an appraisal of the R&R component in every Bank financed project. The basic requirement for this appraisal is the data and the plan of resettlement which is to be provided by the borrowing country. In the case of the SSP, there was neither data on the total number of people affected nor a plan for resettlement. Since the basic data was absent, the Bank couldn't have carried out any appraisal and it did not. If it did not carry out an appraisal it had failed in implementing its own policy. The omission of the process was more serious because the project affected population was tribal.

The IRM made yet another charge that the Bank failed to have any consultation with the people who were actually affected. Referring to the 1982 Operational Manual on tribal people, which says that the design of an appropriate tribal component depended upon detailed and contemporary knowledge of the peoples to be affected, the IRM held that it was essential for the project-appraising authority to discuss in detail with those to be implanted. The report further says:

> In 1985, the basis for designing, implementing and assessing the overarching principle of at minimum retaining oustee's standard of living simply was not in place. The numbers of people to be affected were not known; the range of possible impacts had never been detailed, the effects of canal had been ignored; the social organization of the peoples to be displaced was little understood in Gujarat, and not at all elsewhere. There was virtually no sociology with which to formulate a policy that might achieve the Bank's long term objectives. Nor had there been any consultation with those at risk in virtue of which 'adequate participation' could be said to be taking place. There were no benchmark data with which to assess success or failure. The resettlement and rehabilitation component of the Sardar Sarovar Projects had never adequately been appraised (Morse-Berger 1992: 50).

Although it may be true that the World Bank did not appraise the R&R component of the SSP when it carried out the techno-economic appraisals of the project before 1983, it appointed Professor Thayer Scudder as a consultant and he visited India in November 1983. The World Bank has considered this visit as an R&R appraisal visit in the 1985 Staff Appraisal Report (Patel 1993: 4). Scudder also visited India again in September 1984 when he met the ARCH-Vahini team and discussed the field situation. This was over and above the written material and data supplied to him on the field reality and situation assessment. Prior to meeting Scudder, the ARCH-Vahini had written a long letter detailing the field situation and furnishing quantitative data as evidence to the World Bank in August 1983. Since then all review missions from the Bank made it a point to meet and discuss the field reality, people's minds and the Government's response with ARCH-Vahini and the tribal leaders in Gujarat. Hence, the IRM's contention that the R&R part of the project was never appraised and the affected people were never consulted does not seem to hold.

The IRM was also selective in quoting out of Scudder's report of November 1983 (Patel 1993: 4). It has mentioned only the lack of adequate information and data, inadequate institutional framework, NWDT Award's shortcomings and the state Governments' lack of commitment in honouring the NWDT Award. It has missed out totally on the information and data which Scudder received, the analysis he did and the recommendations he made. As stated earlier, he was also a key person in negotiating the R&R component in the Loan Agreement.

In the context of policy reforms, it would have been more pertinent if the IRM had examined, which it could have very easily, whether Scudder had studied the R&R problems in the SSP during his November 1983 visit and whether he studied them within the frame of the Bank's Policy of February 1980. In the absence of any uniform policy across the states, it was obvious that the Bank would start with the NWDT Award. Scudder, did appraise it but realized that the NWDT Award was inadequate. On the basis of the discussion with field NGOs and the Government and the data he gathered, he recommended crucial changes. The state Governments were forced to comply.

It appears that in its enthusiasm to fail the World Bank in its test, the IRM overlooked many important achievements of the local-international NGOs network and the Bank (Patel 1995:4). These achievements, which pressurized the Government of India and the state Governments to comply incrementally, did indeed promise to fulfil the overarching principle with respect to the standard of living of the World Bank's February 1980 guidelines. Further, by ensuring the clause of the land of choice and the commitment of the Government of India on behalf of the Ministry of Environment and Forest for the release of denuded forest land (if the tribals demanded it), the reformed R&R policy package of the SSP also conformed to the Banks 1982 Operational Manual on Tribals.

Activists both in the country and outside and even scholars have been rather impatient in examining the process and sifting evidence. For instance, Parsuraman (1993) starts by saying that the period covering early nineteen eighties was full of confusion. Both the government and the people were confused. However, in the early eighties, Government was out to short-change tribals as described earlier and people were simply stunned because of the shock and lack of proper and adequate information. There was no question of any confusion.

Parasuraman also seems to have misunderstood the sequence of events when he writes, "it was only after the completion of negotiations with the GOI for a loan, that the World Bank realized that R&R aspects had not been appraised at all. Thus, Dr. Scudder, an expert on resettlement issues was deputed by the Bank to analyse the situation ..." (Parasuraman 1993: 9). We have already shown that the Bank negotiated the Loan Agreement in late 1984 and it was finally signed in May 1985 whereas Scudder's first visit was in November 1983 and it was followed by a second visit in September 1984. It may also be recalled that Scudder was the main negotiator for the R&R in the Loan Agreement.

The IRM has harped only on the non-availability of data without which no plan regarding R&R could be formulated in the SSP. It seems to have overemphasized this aspect to prove that the Bank failed to do its homework. In the process, it has overlooked what has been achieved. The state Governments which were unwilling to implement even the NWDT Award and the Ministry of Environment and Forests, Government of India, which had taken a rigid stand over the issue of the release of denuded forest land for the resettlement of tribals, were persuaded into going beyond the NWDT Award. This by itself was no mean achievement. It should be remembered that the World Bank could do it partly because of the tremendous pressure that was built up by the local-international NGO network. Secondly, for those critics who think that the policy in all the three states should have been the one that was ultimately declared by the Government of Gujarat and that the World Bank failed in pushing these reforms through, it must be remembered that the Bank was dealing with the states of a federal union. Both Maharashtra and Madhya Pradesh had its own compulsions in not going as far as Gujarat could go and to which indeed it went. This aspect has been aptly described by Verghese. The caution exercised by Maharashtra and Madhya Pradesh may therefore be well understood. And, given states' rights in a federal polity: "there are limits beyond which they cannot be pushed. The World Bank tacitly recognizes this. The Independent Review did not and thought nothing of derogating from federal principles though both its members, Bradford Morse, an American, and Thomas Berger, a Canadian, come from federal countries. This is not to say that federal principles can ride roughshod over social justice. The NWDT, a Tribunal headed by a Supreme Court Judge, set out certain norms which are being observed" (Verghese 1994: 138).

And we know that all the three states have gone beyond the NWDT Award. The IRM's charge that the World Bank has not received compliance for its incremental strategy of policy reforms is thus untenable. Unfortunately, the IRM did not stop at that. It recommended the World Bank to 'Step Back', which caused ultimately more harm than good as we shall see in the discussion on implementation.

Policy Reforms in Maharashtra and Madhya Pradesh

R&R policy reforms in the case of Maharashtra and Madhya Pradesh need to be viewed in a somewhat different perspective. First of all, both the states have their state level policies for R&R. Secondly, both the states are still to harness all their major surface water resources. This is particularly true for Madhya Pradesh. Both the Governments have argued that the Gujarat state could be very liberal in its R&R package because the SSP is the last major multipurpose water project and hence the Government could afford to offer such a package. Thirdly, and more importantly, the activists led people's initiative for improving the R&R package which began in early 1986, very soon abandoned the cause of reforms in the R&R policy and implementation and directed all its efforts to oppose the project.

The tribals in both the states had almost the same set of problems as their counterparts in Gujarat. The 'encroacher farmers' did not have any land titles despite their occupation on lands for a number of years. The application of the NWDT Award would have proved relevant only for a handful of families and a large majority would not have been entitled for any compensation. Thus, the need for reforms and improvements over the NWDT Award was equally acute in Maharashtra and Madhya Pradesh.

Between 1986 and end of 1987 the Maharashtra and the Madhya Pradesh organizations had a similar charter of demands as that of the organizations in Gujarat. In the case of Maharashtra, the tribals also had a clear choice about the resettlement area. They wanted to settle in the denuded forest area that was relatively nearer to their native lands, and more importantly, had similar setting and environment. The Narmada Dharangrast Samiti (NDS), Dhule, the organization of tribals in Maharashtra put up a charter of thirty-eight demands, one of which was the allotment of denuded forest land for their rehabilitation. Even in Madhya Pradesh the tribals were looking for good alternative agricultural land and had shown clear choice for an improved policy of R&R (Patel 1994 and 1995). It may be worth recalling at this point that by the time tribals were mobilized and organized in Maharashtra and Madhya Pradesh in early 1986, the World Bank was already in total picture. The NGOs in Gujarat had already detailed the ground situation to the Bank in August 1983 and the pressure from international NGOs had begun.

Scudder had visited India twice and had made important provisions in the loan agreement that was signed in May 1985. The organization in Maharashtra in fact, invoked the provision made in the Loan Agreement when the Ministry of Environment and Forest, Government of India, declined to release the forest land that the Maharashtra tribals were demanding. Bruce Rich of the Environmental Defence Fund of the U.S. termed the MOEF's denial as a breach of agreement (Loan Agreement) at a U.S. Congressional hearing on the Narmada Projects (ARCH 1991; Verghese 1994: 149). Thus, between 1985 and 1988, a case for an urgent need to reform the R&R policy in the SSP was built up at the grassroots, local, national and international levels. Apparently, none of the organizations and the tribals in any of the three states indicated signs to oppose the project itself.

Interestingly, Parasuraman has built up a case which reads as though the decision to oppose the dam was the result of the frustrations experienced by the tribals and activists in the Valley during 1985-88 period. He refers to this period as 'Period of Tension' between people and the Government. The first case he mentions under this section is that of MOEF's denial to give environmental clearance to the project. This would have caused tension between the Government of Gujarat and the MOEF and not between the people and the government. He then refers to the lack of information and access to it to the tribals facing submergence. This is true and it is acknowledged by all those who were either working in or visiting the submergence area.

He then writes about the involvement of activists and their efforts to organize tribals in Maharashtra. These activists, according to him, pressurized the state government to provide and strengthen the basic facilities and social services like health and education. They also mobilized the youth among tribals to raise demands for better R&R.

He then says that with the activists on their side, the tribals submitted specific demands to the Government. These demands included right to information on all aspects of the dam, implementation of the NWDT Awards in all the three states, compensation for encroachers, a comprehensive blueprint of the R&R plan, right to exercise the choice for resettling in Gujarat or their own state, whichever they preferred, and the extension of the R&R package to the people affected by colony, canal, sanctuary and compensatory afforestation programme (Parasuraman 1993: 10-16).

Nowhere is any mention made about the intention of opposing the project. However, he then says that between 1985 and 1988, the Maharashtra and Madhya Pradesh Governments did not make any changes in the policy. There were some changes in the policy in Gujarat. Availability of land became uncertain. And, evidence from the resettled villages pointed to increasing misery and prolonged deprivation. Consequently, people decided to oppose the dam.

Let me begin by saying that it is true that both Madhya Pradesh and Maharashtra did not make any changes in their policies during 1985-88. They were willing to go by the NWDT Award. Madhya Pradesh was slow because even the first submergence was five years away in 1985. Maharashtra had requested the Government of India for the release of forest land in Somaval - a village in Taloda taluka in Dhule district. It was the MOEF which did not budge and clear it for release. It was about this land that Bruce Rich of EDF had made representation in the U.S. congressional hearing. This was indeed a violation of the condition accepted in the Loan Agreement by the Government of India.

It is surprising that Parasuraman thinks that the policy changes in Gujarat were trivial. We have seen how vital and how improved were the changes in the policy in Gujarat. It was probably a problem of perception. The activists in the valley and the intellectuals in urban centres perceived the improved policy document as merely a piece of paper (Patel 1993: 9). These activists in all probability did not wait to consult the tribals and their perception, but went ahead to declare the impossibility of the R&R in the SSP.

The issue of non-availability of land was also hastily judged. In fact, in Gujarat the tribals had on their own identified more than 4000 ha. of private lands that were available for sale (ARCH 1988b). Finally, the evidence from the resettled villages which did not generate confidence, could have been because of the fact that the community was in transition. The displaced families lived and tried to manage production at both the places, in the submergence village as well as the relocation site. This went on for years. And when they finally settled in the relocation sites, their conditions did show improvement (Verghese 1994). Surprisingly, both studies, one showing increasing misery and the other showing improvement, at the same site were conducted by the Tata Institute of Social Studies, Bombay (TISS), with which Parasuraman has been closely involved.

The real reasons for opposing the dam by the organizations in Maharashtra and Madhya Pradesh lay somewhere else. It was a priori decided that rehabilitation was impossible and that the project was economically not viable and environmentally hazardous. The opposition to the dam became much more important for the activists and the intellectuals in the country than the vital breakthrough that was achieved in the R&R policy formulation by the activists - international NGOs - and World Bank combine. (ARCH, 1988b, 1991; Patel 1994, 1995; Verghese 1993: 159-166).

Despite the stand taken by the organizations in Maharashtra and Madhya Pradesh, the Government did introduce reforms in their respective policies mainly due to the pressure from the World Bank. The final policy packages in the three states differ marginally. The IRM has been critical about it and has expressed dissatisfaction about non-uniform provisions. However, the current provisions do take care of the encroachers and landless labour families and has the potential to help regain the standard of living. The organizations in Maharashtra and MP should have tried to pressurize the state Governments soon after the announcement of the reforms in policy in Gujarat in 1987. Probably, the states then would have been under pressure and yielded.

3

In this section, it is proposed to review the implementation of the reformed R&R policy in the SSP for two periods, 1988 to 1993 and 1993 to 1997. The IRM submitted its Report to the World Bank in June 1992 and in unequivocal terms recommended that the Bank step back and conduct a comprehensive review before renewing any assistance. This has been a watershed in implementation of the policy in all three states. Further, the set of issues which were raised prior to the IRM and after its submission of the Report, also differ and hence it may be worthwhile to review both these periods separately.

The most important aspect of any well-formulated programme is its implementation. Governments as such have had very low credibility in designing and implementing development programmes in general and pro-poor programmes in particular. When the activists in the Narmada valley and intellectuals in urban centres dubbed the well-reformed policy on the R&R of the SSP as a mere piece of paper, it was an expression of doubt on the capacity of the Government to implement the policy it was pressurized to formulate. As is stated earlier, the activists in the valley had decided to oppose the project itself soon after the reformed policy was announced by the Government of Gujarat. NGOs in Gujarat expected that the new wave of enthusiasm with the victory in Gujarat would energize the activities in the Valley to take the fight to Maharashtra and MP, for which both the group as well as the tribals of Gujarat were ready (ARCH 1988a). The activists, however, somersaulted and abandoned the cause altogether. This left the NGOs in a dilemma (ARCH 1988b; Patel 1994: 8). The tribals in the Gujarat villages expected continued support from the activists in getting the reformed policy properly implemented by the Government and hence, NGOs in Gujarat decided to collaborate with the Government to implement the reformed policy.

By and large, most of the other NGOs in Gujarat expressed satisfaction over the new policy and offered support. A small but critical group of activists and organizations, however, joined the group of activists in the Valley and elsewhere in the country to oppose the project on the basis of their challenge to the reigning concept of development. The combined forces of activists and organizations came to be known as the Narmada Bachao Andolan (NBA) which is led by Medha Patkar. The NBA has continued to oppose the dam and to be critical of the implementation of the reformed policy in all the three states.

Let us first begin with the involvement of the NGOs in implementation. The GO-NGO collaboration helped in evolving certain institutional mechanisms which eventually worked well for some time. I propose to concentrate on this aspect a little more in the analysis of the implementation.

Building up a Data Base

As stated earlier, the IRM had raised the issue of lack of data base and information while criticizing the World Bank for not conducting the R&R appraisal. What the IRM expected of the Bank was that the latter should have prepared an R&R plan on the basis of the detailed data supplied by the project authority of the borrowing country. According to the IRM, this was a principle which the Bank itself had established, out of its learning from lending for development projects involving involuntary displacement.

The World Bank could not have extracted the requisite data from the states because of two reasons. First, until the reforms in the policy were announced, the Governments were either thinking of giving cash compensation to the land owners or allotting some Government waste land to them on the holding basis. This type of conventional resettlement practice would have required data on land-holding families. This information was available from the revenue records. The second type of information that the Government could have supplied was on houses and house owners since acquisition notices would have to be issued. The state Governments could not have supplied any other data. It is altogether a different story that the Governments didn't have updated data even on these two aspects.

Secondly, unless the normative content of the policy was not operationalized, i.e. unless the categories to whom the land entitlement applied, was not decided at the policy level, the exact number of families entitled to agricultural lands couldn't have been known. Thus, the IRM expected the data which couldn't have been generated before the policy decision.

At the time of implementation, therefore, the first task to be performed was to identify the persons who had land entitlement. Obviously this couldn't have been accomplished in one meeting. It was realized that the identification of eligible persons was going to be an ongoing process for some time until persons in all categories such as land owners, co-sharers, encroachers, landless labourers, the socially isolated and marooned, and the major sons, falling into all the above categories were identified. A committee was set up which came to be known as the List Committee. The Committee comprised of members from the Government department, and representatives from two voluntary organizations, ARCH-Vahini and Anand Niketan.

The main function of the Committee was to verify the claims of persons to be identified as project-affected persons and to ascertain their category. Unfortunately, the Government did not collect any baseline information about the families living in the submergence villages prior to issuing notifications. This made the verification work more difficult. However, the Centre for Social Studies (CSS), Surat, had, in 1981, conducted a census of all the 19 villages in Gujarat facing submergence. This household level data served as a benchmark. The second important source was the list prepared by the Gujarat NGOs while they organized the tribals. In addition, voters' lists, birth registrations, school-leaving certificates, which carry the date of birth, and ration cards etc., were also checked wherever available, to examine the claims. The Government of Gujarat had accepted giving land to major sons. There arose a need for fixing a cut-off date to decide whether a person was major or not, i.e. whether he was 18 or above. This date was 1 January 1987. While it is for an urban society to conduct their affairs according to the calendar, the rural and especially the tribal societies where the incentives to go to school are minimal, it was not possible to expect that the tribals would come up with exact birth dates or even birth-date records. It became necessary therefore to examine more than one kind of evidence to establish the domicile as well as the age of the person before confirming his eligibility.

It is important to emphasize that without the intimate knowledge of the affected population and without a deeper understanding of the tribal culture prevalent in the submergence villages, it would not have been possible for the List Committee to settle the claims. Further, it must also be emphasized that the job could be accomplished to the satisfaction of most of the tribal claimants largely because of the presence of the NGOs in the Committee as full members. The officials on their own and even with the formal people's representatives such as Members of Legislative Assembly (MLAs), Panchayat members, etc. would have found it extremely difficult, if not impossible, to settle all the claims to the satisfaction of the majority of the claimants.

A major issue that was raised with respect to the implementation of the reformed R&R policy relates to the total number of project-affected persons. And based on varied estimates, the opponents of the dam have formulated the thesis that the R&R in the SSP is impossible. The NBA has estimated the affected population in the following way. It has said that 1,50,000 tribals will be affected in 245 submergence villages; 1,70,000 farmers will be affected due to the canal network; Shoolpaneshwar Sanctuary will displace 40,000 tribals; thousands of families will be displaced because of Catchment Area Treatment (CAT) and Compensatory Afforestation (CA); thousands of landless labourers will be displaced as a result of transfer of private lands to the tribals. (ARCH 1993d: 3). The IRM has used this argument of the number of affected persons to point out the World Bank's failure in conducting the R&R appraisal. The IRM estimates the total number to 40,000 families in 1992 and argues: "needless to say, the financial, organizational, logistical problems of resettling the original estimate of 6,603 families (figure given by the NWDT) are substantially increased when the number rises by six times to the current estimate of 40,000 families" (Morse and Berger 1992: 51).

While being no apologist for the Government, we must state that the NBA and IRM figures are exaggerated. The displacement is limited only to the reservoir and the canal. Due to the reservoir, 245 villages will be affected. But that does not mean that all the households and all the agricultural lands of the villages will be fully submerged. This fact has neither been fully appreciated by the critics of the project nor fully highlighted by the project authorities. Important points in this context are the following:

1. Estimated figures of displacement in the villages of Gujarat and Maharashtra respectively are 4,500 and 3,000 families. In MP, the official figure of families affected is 23,000 (excluding families being affected because of back water effect). This has been accepted by the IRM also. However, out of these, nearly 67 per cent families are not likely to be uprooted from their place of origin either because, only their houses are going under submergence, or they are losing less than 25 per cent of agricultural land, or both. In all these cases there is no dislocation. A maximum number of 7,600 families may be dislocated. Thus, in all, a little more than 15,000 families or about 75,000 to 80,000 persons are likely to be displaced.

2. In canals, the displacement is limited to small and marginal land holders on the first few km length of the main and the branch canals. The IRM has given an estimate according to which 1100 farmers lose their entire holding. If at all there is dislocation, it will be for these 1100 farmers and their families.

3. There is not going to be any displacement in the Shoolpaneshwar Sanctuary and in Catchment Area Treatment (CAT) and Compensatory Afforestation (CA). In fact, the MOEF has after great reluctance, agreed in August 1994 in principle to the Gujarat Government's proposal to regularize 60,000 hectares and has accorded approval to the first 18,000 hectares of cultivation by tribals which includes the plots being cultivated in the Shoolpaneshwar Sanctuary and the CAT and CA land. Hence, there is no question of displacing people from there areas.

Unlike the general belief that the Governments have been underestimating the number of persons/families displaced, the MP government appears to have overestimated the number of families that face displacement. And yet, the charges of underestimation continue even in 1996. Kothari while reviewing various estimates on the total number of displaced persons arrives at his own figure of 400,000 (Kothari 1996: 1479). Interestingly, he has tried to also enumerate amongst the displaced, those dependent on private lands that were allotted to tribals in the relocation sites, i.e. secondary displacement. The IRM's silence on this issue is a tacit acceptance that the secondary displacement was totally a non-issue.

Land Purchase Committee (LPC)

We have seen earlier that a majority of affected tribals wanted private agricultural land for resettlement. We have also seen that the Loan Agreement made the land of choice one of its conditions in the R&R policy. The anti-dam movement raised many doubts about the availability of private lands. It was also argued during the times when the new policy was announced by the Government of Gujarat that the tribals would have to wander in search of private land, incurring their own expenditure and risk to health. All this was not to happen. The Government again responded to the need of the time and formed a Land Purchase Committee. It was headed by a revenue official at least of the rank of an Additional Collector. Its members were Government officials, selected MLAs, Panchayat presidents of Vadodara and Bharuch districts and those taluka Panchayats from where land was to be purchased, Sarpanchs (village heads) from selected submergence villages and representatives from ARCH-Vahini and Anand Niketan. It is a different matter that in early 1993, ARCH tendered its resignation from the membership to protest against unacceptable compromises, which we shall discuss latter.

It would be worthwhile to describe in some detail the process of land purchase and selection by the tribals. Prior to the announcement of the new R&R policy, some tribals had already explored the possibility of available private lands. In fact, some of them were readying themselves for the fall-back position of accepting compensation and buying private land instead of accepting the unacceptable Government waste land. This exercise came in handy when it was decided to purchase private lands. Also the system, i.e. the Land Purchase Committee was already in place. Some tribals also had the knowledge of fertile agricultural land in the plains because they seasonally migrated to work on some of these farms. Thus, the tribals made exploratory visits to the areas and talked to owner farmers to learn their attitudes to selling. These exploratory trips also triggered off communication among farmers that the Government was willing to buy land. The farmers then made offers to the LPC.

At this stage, it must be understood why the farmers were willing to sell their land which either had irrigation facility, or was to get it from the Narmada canals once the project was commissioned. According to the land laws of Gujarat, until recently, only a farmer could buy agricultural land and that too he/she had to be living within eight km radius so that he could operate the land. These laws had virtually frozen the land market in the state. The economic growth and development in Gujarat suggests that the industry and service sectors have done well while agriculture has been experiencing ups and downs (Iyengar 1996). Obviously, some agriculturists would like to sell land and invest in other rewarding enterprises. Secondly, their children have been educated and they are not interested in agriculture. Thirdly, in the rural areas of Vadodara district, the scope for non-farm employment has increased, and as a result the agricultural labourers have taken to non-farm labour which is more paying and gives exposure to city/town life. Thus, there is a serious shortage of labour in the fertile plains in central Gujarat. Due to these reasons, many farmers wanted to dispose of their land if proper prices could be realized. The SSP project offered exactly this opportunity.

The LPC members considered the proposals, gathered opinion about the quality of land, verified the preference and choice of the displaced groups and then negotiated the prices with the farmers who offered land for sale. The LPC members also formed sub-committees to inspect the offered land before the LPC could negotiate prices. The NGOs helped the officials in ascertaining the willingness of displaced groups and also in controlling the price of the land offered. The NGOs at times had to persuade displaced tribals to look for alternate sites if the prices are very high. Until the end of 1992, by which time substantial purchases were made to resettle almost all Gujarat and Maharashtra tribals willing to settle in Gujarat, the average prices settled for unirrigated and irrigated land were Rs. 11,500 and Rs. 18,000 per hectare respectively.

The LPC functioned well between 1988 to 1992. In early 1993, the discipline in the LPC got diluted. The norms that were set by the conventions rather than the rules, began to be violated. This happened specifically, when the MP government pressurized the Gujarat Government to first buy land, prepare sites and then invite the displaced tribal and other groups to choose and select sites. There was also a pressure to buy land faster. On the sellers side, the farmers also realized that the demand was reasonably high and hence the inferior pieces may also be pushed for sale. The commitment and seriousness of purpose may also have been lost among various lower level officials. All this resulted in some sub-standard purchases of land in the post-1992 period. One of the NGO members stopped attending meetings, protested and then resigned. An innovative institutional arrangement that was built slowly, dismantled. The LPC is still in existence but not with much credibility. This has been one of the critical blows to the healthy practices in R&R which had begun in Gujarat.

Process of Land Allotment and Joint Inspection Committee

The Sardar Sarovar Punarvasvat Agency - the official body for implementation, hired private vehicles to pick up the tribal family heads from the submergence villages to inspect the agricultural lands in the plains. Special four-wheel vehicles were pushed into service for the villages which did not have motorable roads. Tribal heads were accompanied by the members of the NGO groups. The lands offered for sale were visited and inspected. When the tribal groups selected the land, they submitted an application showing their choice for a particular site. The government then issued orders. Two ha. plots were mapped and then were demarcated on the site. Once the plotting was done, the groups visited again. During this visit, uncultivable plots and the plots with problems were rejected and only the plots that were accepted by the tribals were allotted. During this entire process, the NGO workers were constantly present. These processes took a long time. Arrangements for overnight stay in government guest houses in the project colonies and for food were made. After the completion of joint visits, the groups were dropped back in their villages. This service was offered not once but as many times as the groups had to come out of their villages and visit the possible resettlement sites.

Despite the care and caution exercised, there were cases in which the first allotment of the land plot was not acceptable to a member of the resettling group. A joint inspection committee was formed to tackle all such cases. This committee comprised of officials and representatives of the NGOs. The members made joint visits, invited experts from state agriculture departments, if necessary, and took the decision to change the plots if they were found unfit for cultivation. Thus, the entire process of land allotment went on smoothly. The IRM, which has been highly critical of the World Bank, has expressed its satisfaction over the resettlement in Gujarat, while continuing to air its serious concern towards the rehabilitation which is a long-drawn-out process (Morse and Berger 1992: 129-133).

Resettlement Experience in Gujarat: Critics Apprehensions 1988-92

The major criticism has been that since private lands have been allotted, the displaced tribal population has been scattered. The other criticisms include, loss of cultural life and natural resources support, allotment of uncultivable, inferior and waterlogged agricultural land etc.

To answer some of this criticism, one may have to refer to the IRM Report which has categorically stated that the tribals have selected land of their choice and decided to form the groups which they wanted. The social reality which has also been accepted by Scudder is that the tribals in the Narmada Valley are not homogenous, monolithic communities. The NBA leader Ms. Patkar has also mentioned the heterogeneity among tribals within a village. Noted tribal's advocate B.D. Sharma (1987) and Joshi (1987 and 1991) also agree that the tribals are not homogenous groups. The World Bank Loan Agreement says that the tribal communities may be resettled as a village, hamlet or a group that is formed out of choice. The tribals have indeed exercised their choice freely (ARCH 1993c: 6). It is true that the families belonging to one village in the submergence area are now settled in more than one village and in that sense they are scattered. However, if one considers the distances involved in the hilly mountains between the hamlets of a single village and the fact that all that distance had to be traversed on foot, the present scatter may be termed as compact settlement. The plains also offer the road network and transportation vehicles including the state transport bus services. Women in number of sites reported that the frequency of their visits from resettlement sites to the maternal home and families has infact increased.

The dependence of tribals on natural resources including the forest has been disproportionately emphasized both by the activists and the social scientists, particularly in the case of the tribals in the Valley. Even the IRM report has quoted their expert's report, according to which there are hardly any forests. Hence, dependence on forest produce, fish etc. is in fact, marginal. It is interesting that both the arguments, one relating to the commercialization of forests leading to massive degradation by vested interests and the other relating to heavy dependence of tribals on forest, are made simultaneously. Even the IRM report is not free of this anomaly. Except for fuel wood and some seasonal fruits, flowers and leaves (used to roll Bidis - indigenous cigarettes) and occasionally some fish, hardly anything else is available to the tribal people in these forests. In fact, I was told by a number of tribals that the teak and other house-building wood had disappeared so fast during the last 30 years that they find it extremely difficult to get wood even for house repairs and construction.

With regard to the quality of land, I have already mentioned that the LPC as well as the Joint Inspection Committee were in place and working well till 1993. There has been an erosion in the quality of work in these institutionalized set-ups, which I shall discuss in the next section. Till 1993, the cases of allotment of bad quality land were very few and all attempts were made to change those plots. The system was in place.

A large majority of Gujarat and Maharashtra families had been allotted land by December 1993. The progress between 1993 and 1996 has been slow. This time period coincides with the withdrawal of the Project from the World Bank. The review missions stopped coming. The pressure was off. No external agency was breathing over one's neck. The local resistance could at worse be ignored and at best be handled.

Implementation (1993-97)

Post - 1993 period does not seem to augur well for R&R in the SSP. The allotment of agricultural land and housing plots for most of the families in Gujarat was over. Families from Maharashtra were coming in large numbers and in both Maharashtra and MP the tribals had realized that their leaders were preoccupied with jubilation over the Morse-Berger verdict on the project, hence they had to act on their own if they wanted to get properly resettled. NGOs active in Gujarat were receiving feelers from villages of both the states. The stage was all set for the Gujarat Government to seize the initiative and get on with the job. But the administration couldn't respond and the post - 1993 R & R appear to have fallen into a quagmire, at least till this was written.

One of the Gujarat NGOs, ARCH-Vahini, which has actively collaborated has since the beginning of 1995 grown quite critical of the ways in which the Government administration in Gujarat is handling the resettlement of the displaced families largely from Maharashtra and MP. According to ARCH-Vahini, it appeared that the administration's main interest was in seeing that the affected families relocate themselves in new sites. Beyond that, it probably failed to perceive any responsibility. That proper and satisfactory relocation or resettlement is just the first step in the direction of proper rehabilitation is probably not known to the administration. This has been one of the major problems with the R&R in the post - 1993 period. More specifically, the following problems have been highlighted by ARCH-Vahini:

1. Drinking water facilities have generally been poor. The major source has been hand pumps. An ARCH-Vahini survey states that 200 hand pumps did not work at the time of survey. The quality of service rendered by another 150 hand pumps was found to be doubtful. Frequent breakdown of the pumps was the most common complaint.

2. From among those families which have been allotted agricultural land in consultation with ARCH-Vahini in the post - 1993 period, more than 400 families have been allotted plots which have one of the following problems: (a) the plots do not admeasure two ha., (b) Major parts of the plots are uncultivable, and (c) Plots have not been demarcated.

3. In all, about 500 families from MP have been allotted agricultural plots to which ARCH-Vahini workers were not a party. The problems were the following:

i. One site was in a village which has been the target of dacoits across the district border.

ii. Another site was in a village where the cattle-herder community is known to harass the cultivators, rendering cultivation impossible.

iii. Agriculture land was rendered uncultivable because of the unremovable roots of a grass weed locally known as Dabh.

iv. About 50 families had been shown good quality land but were subsequently allotted inferior quality of land.

4. The fourth set of problems relate to the quality and condition of the physical infrastructure in relocation sites. Approach roads, internal roads and drainage have not been laid down properly. It is reported by the resettlers that the quality of workmanship and the material used are sub-standard. In a number of cases the quality of roof tiles supplied was inferior. Despite repeated requests, these materials have not been changed.

5. Services of regular revenue administration have lagged behind, raising doubts about the intentions of the Government in providing the ownership title deeds of the allotted land to the relocated families.

The response of the administration and the Government is that they have initiated corrections and the complaints and shortcomings are being attended to. However, this has not convinced the ARCH-Vahini, and it has resigned from the membership of the executive committee of the autonomous rehabilitation agency known as Sardar Sarovar Punarvasvat Agency.

In the post - 1993 period, the MP government has taken a stiff stand against the work on the dam. It has taken the position that the resettlement efforts by the Government of Gujarat has not been satisfactory. Hence, further construction of the critical blocks of the dam was not being allowed. Presently, the matter is under review. The number of families allotted land between December 1993 and March 1996 has been much smaller. Only 1075 families have been allotted land, of which 828 tamilies are from MP. The pace of resettlement appears to have slowed down.

4

Problems and Prospects of R&R in SSP

The World's eye is upon the Sardar Sarovar Project. We have seen that the R&R programme of the project to begin with was as bad as it has been in any other development project involving involuntary displacement. We also saw that there were many land marks in the Project. For the first time, such a massive mobilization of the affected persons took place, and again, for the first time the struggle bore concrete results. For the first time, any state Government in the country announced and committed an R&R package which could be said to be fair and just to those who are to become involuntarily displaced. The setting up of a List Committee, the Land Purchase Committee, the GO-NGO collaboration and the process of the allotment of alternative agricultural land, etc., has happened for the first time. A combined effect of all these first time initiatives has been that the resettlement and relocation of the displaced population in the first phase, i.e. 1988-93 is by and large successful. This was also assessed and approved by the International Review Mission. However, problems seem to have once again plagued the R&R programme in the SSP.

Two sets of problems have affected the programme. The first set of problems is related to the Government's and the administration's understanding about resettlement and rehabilitation. Cernea has again recently drawn attention towards the processes involved in involuntary resettlement. He says:

'What is usually described as 'involuntary resettlement' consists of two distinct, yet closely related social processes: (a) displacement of people and (b) reconstruction of their livelihood; this reconstruction is sometimes called rehabilitation. Each has its own demands, risks, costs, logistics and socio-cultural and economic effects' (1996: 1516).

He adds, that in theory, the two processes are part of the same continuum, however, the second does not always follow the first. In the case of the SSP, it appears that the rehabilitation of the resettled population during 1988-93 is facing rough weather and the resettlement of the post - 1993 displaced families is plagued with problems. The Government and the administration is either not aware of or has decided to ignore the seriousness of both the problems. My own experience tells me that the officials at the various levels would hardly be able to appreciate these finer aspects of involuntary resettlement. Therefore, unless there are clear policy pronouncements and procedures for implementation, the implementors are going to mess up the R&R. Probably, inept handling of serious problems arising in the relocation sites with regard to reconstruction of living and livelihood, and the resettlement efforts in terms of allotment of land to the affected families from MP, has resulted in dissatisfaction among the displaced people. This, as a result, has prompted the otherwise effective and fruitful GO-NGO collaboration to break.

It appears that most of the persons in the Government and the administration feel that with the relocation of families from the submergence villages in Gujarat, the rehabilitation is complete. A majority of the affected families in Gujarat have got good quality land and a plot to build house, what more should the displaced families expect? The efforts required to set-up and organize the socio-economic life smoothly in the new sites, the efforts required to facilitate integration of the displaced population with the host communities, the efforts required to assess the requirement and the aspirations of the host communities, potential areas of conflict and co-operation between the host and the guest population, etc., are not being made in full earnest. Many of these aspects do not involve any monetary component, but they involve understanding and commitment on the part of Government officials. The officials seem to have failed to respond to the needs of the situation. The rehabilitation of the already resettled or relocated population appears to be in jeopardy.

The second set of problems relates to the role of the IRM, activists, and NGOs in and outside the country, in handling the SSP issue in general and the R&R issue in the SSP in particular. The Independent Review Mission came into existence because of the pressure placed by the national and international NGOs on the World Bank. One can raise a serious question as to whether it was required. Of course, even if one doesn't go into the rhetoric and say that the sovereignty of the nation was threatened by such international interventions, enough understanding existed within the country to seriously discuss the problems and look for solutions. The NBA never had a strong case against the SSP. This has been argued at length by ARCH-Vahini in its publications. However, once set-up, there shouldn't have been any argument against the setting up of the IRM. What is important is that the IRM did not remain objective in 'its search for truth' on both the major agenda items: resettlement and rehabilitation and the environmental impacts of the SSP. Again this has been argued at length by ARCH-Vahini in its publications (1992a, 1992b, 1992c, 1992d, 1992e, 1993a, 1993b, 1993c). The IRM by its advice to the World Bank to 'Step Back' from the project set such a process in motion that the reform processes, that were taking place in the project and in the system, got derailed. The World Bank, which was the main actor and the keel that could direct the ship was forced to leave. Both the national and the international NGOs celebrated this only to weaken the reform process that had just begun in a developing country.

The exit of the World Bank also weakened and further isolated the already isolated NGOs such as ARCH-Vahini, which had provided critical support to the Project and had collaborated in implementing the policy. It also eased the pressure on the Government. After we have seen how the policy reforms were won, it is probably clear by now that the Government could be better persuaded by the Bank and the combined strength of NGO network. Interestingly, what the NBA and its allies achieved by sending the World Bank packing was the rise in the chances of the failure of the R&R in the SSP which they have always predicted.

Had the IRM given a critical feed back and recommended continued but critical support to the SSP by the World Bank, the Bank Missions in conjunction with the sensitive NGOs such as ARCH-Vahini could have set into motion processes that would have ensured a decent resettlement of the rest of the Maharashtra and MP displaced families in Gujarat, as well as in their respective states, and it could have also designed a path to take the resettled population to a proper rehabilitation.

Now that it has not happened that way and both the resettlement and rehabilitation are at risk, and, an important and active NGO is getting out of the mainframe, the prospects for the R&R in the SSP appear rather bleak. Needless to say, it may still be better than it has been in a number of other dam projects in India because of the reformed policy on which the Governments cannot go back and also because some mechanisms have been in place and are likely to be there till the end; but the scope which the new experiment had is probably lost. I think that both the social activists in the country and the Governments are ready to throw the proverbial baby with the bath water.

Post-script : When this is going in press, a lot more has happened. A Grievance Redressal Authority (GRA) appointed by the Supreme Court has changed the scene. The Future holds some promise.

Annexure I

Salient Features of the Project
The Narmada Water Dispute Tribunal's (NWDT) Final Award

The NWDT, constituted in 1969, deliberated over the dispute between the four states Gujarat, Madhya Pradesh, Maharashtra and Rajasthan for 10 long years. In 1978, it gave its decision. The final order is contained in Chapter 22 of Volume II of the Report. The final order with regard to the period of operation of the order of apportionment says:

Our orders with regard to the equitable allocation in Clause III (Apportionment of the Utilisable Quantum of Narmada Waters) and IV (Order with regard to Excess Waters and Sharing of Distress) are made subject to review at any time after a period of 45 years from the date of the orders of the Tribunal: (Parentheses added) (Chapter XX Clause V: 123).

According to the final orders, allocation of water and dimensions of Dam etc. are as follows:

A. Allocation of Water Based on 75 per cent Dependability (in Million Acre Feet, (M.A.F.))

Madhya Pradesh	18.25 M.A.F.
Gujarat	9.00 M.A.F.
Maharashtra	0.25 M.A.F.
Rajasthan	0.50 M.A.F.
Total	**28.00 M.A.F.**

(An acre foot of water implies storage of 1 foot of water in one acre)

B. Height of the Dam Full Reservoir

Level (FRL)	455 feet / 138.68 m.
Maximum Water Level (MWL)	460 feet / 140.21 m.

C.	Full Supply Level (FSL) at the Regulator of the Main Canal	300 feet / 91.44 m.
D.	Power Allocation	
	Madhya Pradesh	57 per cent
	Maharashtra	27 per cent
	Gujarat	16 per cent

Salient Features of the Project

A. The Dam

1.	Type	Cement Concrete Gravity Type
2.	Length	1210 meters
3.	Maximum Height (from the deepest foundation	163 m.
4.	Height of the Top Level	146.5 m.
5.	Length of the Reservoir	214 km.
	Maximum width	16.9 km.
	Average width	1.77 km.
6.	Catchment of the River (up to dam site)	88,000 sq.kms.
7.	Live Storage of the Reservoir	4.73 MAF
8.	Spill ways	7 of 60' by 60' 23 of 60' by 55'

B. Main Canal

1.	FSL at Head Regulator	91.44 m.
2.	Length of the Main Canal up to the border of Rajasthan	460 km.
3.	Discharge at the Head	40,000 cubic feet per second
4.	Discharge at the Rajasthan border	2,500 cubic feet per second
5.	Bed width at the Head	73.1 m.
6.	Depth at full supply	7.6 m.

C. Distribution System

1. Branches — 42
2. Length of the network of canals — 66,000 km.
3. Annual irrigation — 1.8 million ha.

D. Electricity Generation

1. River Bed Power House (RBPH) — 1200 M.W.
2. Canal Head Power House (CHPH) — 250 M.W.

E. Submergence and Displacement

1. Submergence at Full Reservoir Level — 37,960 ha.
   a. Forest Area — 13,542 ha.
   b. Cultivable Area — 11,279 ha.
   c. Area under river bed and barren and uncultivable — 12,869 ha.

2. Nature of Submergence of Habitats
   1. Total number of villages affected — 245
      a. Number of villages facing total submergence — 3
      b. Number of villages facing partial submergence — 242
   2. Submergence by State and Type

State	Total submergence	Partial submergence	All
Gujarat	3	16	19
Maharashtra	-	33	33
Madhya Pradesh	-	193	193
All	3	242	245

In Madhya Pradesh, in 79 villages, more than 10 per cent of agricultural land will be submerged. In 89 villages, less than 10 per cent land will be submerged. In some villages out of these 89, only residential areas face submergence. In 25 villages, only government waste land will be submerged.

Annexure Notes :

*Majority of the 33,014 oustee families in Madhya Pradesh lose only houses and not land. Hence most of these oustees have to be resettled at their own villages and are not entitled to land. In our estimate only about 7,600 oustee families in Madhya Pradesh are entitled for land.

**The numbers include those who will be under the influence of backwater effect.

@ Figures are for December 1993.

Sources :

1. Patel Anil. 1994. *What do the Tribals Want in the Valley of Narmada?*
2. Agenda Notes of Sardar Sarovar Rehabilitation Agency 24.5.1996.

References

Alexander, K.C., Prasad, R.R. & Jahagirdar, M.P. *Tribals, Rehabilitation & Development.* Jaipur: Rawat Publications, 1991.

Alvares Claude and Billorey Ramesh. *Damming the Narmada: India's Greatest Planned Environmental Disaster.* Deharadun: Natraj Publishers, Also published by Penang, Malaysia: Third World Network, 1988.

ARCH-Vahini. *Displacement in Sardar Sarovar (Narmada) Project: A Gujarat Experience.* Mangrol, Rajpipla, April, 1988a.

_____ *Sardar Sarovar Oustees - Which Way to Go?: An Activists Dilemma.* Mangrol, Rajpipla, September, 1988b.

_____. ARCH-Vahini. 'Is R&R Impossible in SSP?: The Role of NBA (India), EDF (USA) and MOEF (India)'. *A Submission to Morse Mission.* Mangrol, Rajpipla, February, 1992a.

_____. *A Critique of Memorandum Submitted to the World Bank by the EDF and Other NGOs,* March 20, 1991. Mangrol, Rajpipla, September, 1992b.

_____. ARCH-Vahini, Letter to Mr. Lewis Preston, President, World Bank on Morse Report. Mangrol, Rajpipla, 1992c.

_____. Letter to David Jones, Associate Director, Oxfam U.K. on Morse Report. Mangrol, Rajpipla, September, 1992d.

_____. *The Independent Review: A Search for Truth?* Mangrol, Rajpipla, November, 1992e.

_____. *Morse-Berger Review of Sardar Sarovar Projects: A Counter View,* Mangrol, Rajpipla, January, 1993a.

_____. *The SSP Withdrawn From the World Bank: ARCH-Vahini's Views.* Mangrol, Rajpipla, April, 1993b.

_____. *The Sardar Sarovar Project: An Intellectual Fashion.* Mangrol, Rajpipla, July, 1993c.

_____. *Human Rights in the Sardar Sarovar Project: A Submission to Fact Finding Committee of PUCL.* Mangrol, Rajpipla, October, 1993d.

_____. *A Note on Number of PAPs in MP who are Entitled for Agricultural Land for Resettlement.* Mangrol, Rajpipla, March, 1994.

Asthana, Roli. 'Involuntary Experience: International experience.' *Economic and Political Weekly* 31, 24, 1996.

Amte, Baba. *Cry, The Beloved Narmada.* Amandwan: Maharogi Sewa Samiti, 1989.

Cernea, Michael, M. 'Involving Settlement: Social Research, Policy and Planning', in Cernea Michael M. (ed.), *Putting People First: Sociological Variables in Rural Development.* New York: Oxford University Press, second edition, 1991.

________. 'Public Policy Responses to Development-Induced Population Displacements' *Economic and Political Weekly* 31, 24, 1996.

Dabholkar, Dattprasad. *Mate Narmade* (in Marathi). Pune: Rajhans Pratishthan, 1990.

Dalua, A.K. *Environmental Impact of Large Reservoir Projects on Human Settlement.* New Delhi: Ashish Publishing House, 1993.

Escudero, C.R. *Involuntary Resettlement in Bank-Assisted Projects: An Introduction to Legal Issues.* Washington D.C: The World Bank, 1988.

Fernandez, A.P. 'No Dam is an Island', in Fernandez, A.P. (ed.), *Workshop on Rehabilitation of Persons Displaced by Development Projects: A Report.* Bangalore: Institute for Social and Economic Change and Myrada, 1990.

Fernandes, Walter and Thukral Ganguly Enakshi (eds.). *Development Displacement and Rehabilitation.* New Delhi: Indian Social Institute, 1989.

Gold Smith E. and Hildyard N. *Social and Environmental Effects of Large Dams*, San Francisco: Sierra Club Books, 1984.

Government of Gujarat. *No Canceling Tomorrow.* Gandhinagar: 1992.

Government of India. *The Report of the Narmada Water Dispute Tribunal with Its Decision.* 1 and 2, New Delhi: 1978.

Government of India. *Report of the Five Member Group Set up by the Ministry of Water Resources to Discuss Various Issues Relating to the Sardar Sarovar Project.* 1 and 2, 1992.

Goyal, Sangeeta. 'Economic Perspectives on Displacement.' *Economic and Political Weekly*, 31, 2, 1996.

Guggenheim, Scott. 'Development and Dynamics of Displacement', in Fernandez, A.P. (ed.) *Workshop on Rehabilitation of Displaced Persons by Development Projects: A Report.* Bangalore: Institute for Social and Economic Change and Myrada, 1990.

Gumber Anil. *Displaced by Development: Oustees of an Irrigation Project.* Rohtak: Spellbound Publications, 1998.

Gururaja Rao, A.V. 'Sardar Sarovar Project in Gujarat State: The Project and Rehabilitation Policy', in Fernandez, A.P. (ed.) *Workshop on Rehabilitation of Displaced Persons by Development Projects: A Report.* Bangalore: Institute for Social and Economic Change and Myrada, 1990.

Hakim, Roxanne. 'Vasava Identity in Transition: Some Theoretical Issues'. *Economic and Political Weekly* 31, 24, 1996.

Jayaratne, R.S. 'Involuntary Resettlement Consequent to the Construction of Three Large Dams and Reservoirs Under the Mahaweli Development Project, Sri Lanka', in Fernandez, A.P. (ed.). *Workshop on Rehabilitation of Displaced Persons by Development Projects: A Report.* Bangalore: Institute for Social and Economic Change and Myrada, 1990.

Iyengar, S. *Level and Pattern of Economic Growth in Gujarat, 1980-95*. Working Paper No. 72. Ahmedabad: Gujarat Institute of Development Research, 1996.

Joshi, Vidyut. *Submerging Villages - Problems and Prospects*. Delhi: Ajanta Publications, 1987.

_____. Joshi Vidyut. *Rehabilitation - A Promise to Keep* (A Case Study of SSP). Ahmedabad: The Tax Publications, 1991.

Kothari, Smitu. 'Whose Nation? Displaced as Victims of Development.' *Economic and Political Weekly*, 31, 24, 1996.

Kalpavriksha. *The Narmada Valley Project: A Critique*. New Delhi: Kalpavriksh, 1988.

Krishna Kumar. 'Narmada Debate: A Test of Modernity'. *The Indian Express*, July 11, 1996.

Mahapatra, L.K. 'Rehabilitation of Tribals Affected by Major Dams and Other Projects in Orissa'. Fernandez, A.P. (ed.) *Workshop on Rehabilitation of Displaced Persons by Development Projects: A Report.* Bangalore: Institute for Social and Economic Change and Myrada, 1990.

Morse, Bradford and Berger, Thomas. *Sardar Sarovar: Report of the Independent Review.* Ottawa, Resource Futures International (RFI) INC, Canada: 1992.

Muthayya, B.C. & Mathur, J.S. *Rehabilitation of Displaced Villagers.* Hyderabad: National Institute of Community Development, 1994.

Nagi Reddy, C.P. et. al. *Relocation and Resettlement Plan for Project Affected Persons Under Singoor Project*. Hyderabad: Centre for Economic and Social Studies, Begumpet, 1981.

Naik, P.J., Patil, Moradi, R.S. 'Reservoir Submergence and Rehabilitation in Six Villages in the Upper Krishna Project', in Fernandez, A.P. (ed.) *Workshop on Rehabilitation of Displaced Persons by Development Projects: A Report.* Bangalore: Institute for Social and Economic Change and Myrada, 1990.

NVDA. *The Bhil Track: A Study of Displaced Tribals*. Bhopal: Narmada Valley Development Authority, 1993.

Paranjpye, Vijay. *The Narmada Valley Project: A Holistic Evaluation of the Sardar Sarovar and Indira Sagar Dams*. New Delhi: INTACH, 1989.

Parasuraman, S. 'The Anti-Narmada Movement in India: Can the Resettlement and Rehabilitation Policy Gains be Translated into a National Policy'. *Working Papers.* The Hague: Institute of Social Studies, 1993.

_______. 'Outcomes for Displaced: Two Case Studies'. *Economic and Political Weekly* 31, 24, 1996.

Patel, Anil, et.al. 'Rehabilitation and Resettlement in Sardar Sarovar Project: Are the Critics Right?' *Social Action*. New Delhi: July-September, 1991.

_____. 'What do the Tribals Want in the Valley of Narmada?' Mangrol, Rajpipla. A Paper Presented in an International Conference on Indigenous People and Water Reservoir Development Projects. Montreal, Canada, April, 1994.

____. 'Reforms or Derailment Activists Dilemma Revisited', Mangrol, Rajpipla. A Paper Presented at Refugee Studies Programme (RSP) Conference on Development Induced Displacement and Improvement. Oxford, U.K. January, 1995.

Patkar, Medha. *Sardar Sarovar: Vikas Ki Vinash*, Dhule: Parisar, 1988.

_____. 'Sardar Sarovar Narmada: Open Letter to Sanat Mehta'. *The Economic Times*, September 28, 1989.

______. 'The Tragic Story of the Displaced: A Case Study of the Tribals Affected by Sardar Sarovar'. Fernandez, A.P. (ed.). *Workshop on Rehabilitation of Displaced Persons by Development Projects: A Report.* Bangalore: Institute for Social and Economic Change and Myrada, 1990.

Patkar, Medha. 'undated', 'Some Comments on Research Tools (Survey Schedule), prepared for Monitoring and Evaluation of R&R of Sardar Sarovar Oustees'. Dhule: Narmada Dharangrast Samiti.

Reddy, I.U.B. *Displacement and Rehabilitation*. New Delhi: Mittal Publications, 1992.

Scudder, Thayer. 'A Sociological Framework for the Analysis of New Land Settlements'. Cernea Michael, M. (ed.). *Putting People First: Sociological Variables in Rural Development.* New York. Oxford University Press, Second Edition, 1991.

Sinha, B.K. 'National Policy for Rehabilitation: Objectives and Principles'. *Economic and Political Weekly* 31, 24, 1996.

Sharma, B.D. 'A Letter Written to Naresh Chandra, Secretary Water Resources, Government of India', Commissioner of Scheduled Caste and Scheduled Tribes, New Delhi: Government of India, 1987.

Sudarsen, V. & Kalam M.A. (eds.). *The Uprooted Displacement Resettlement Development*. New Delhi: GIAN Publishing House, 1990.

Thukral Ganguli, Enakshi. 'Dams for Whose Development?'. Walter Fernandes and Enakshi Ganguli Thukral (eds.). *Development Displacement and Rehabilitation*. New Delhi: Indian Social Institute, 1989.

______. Thukral Ganguli, Enakshi. (ed.). *Big Dams, Displaced People: Rivers of Sorrow Rivers of Change*. New Delhi: Sage Publications, 1992.

TISS, *The Sardar Sarovar Project: Experiences with Resettlement and Rehabilitation*. Bombay: Tata Institute of Social Sciences, 1993.

Varma, S.C. *Human Settlement in Lower Narmada Basin.* Bhopal: Narmada Valley Development Authority, 1985.

Verghese, B.G. *Winning the Future: From Bhakra to Narmada, Tehri, Rajasthan Canal.* New Delhi: Konark Publishers Pvt. Ltd, 1994.

7

Rural Development and Seasonal Migration in Gujarat : Pattern, Determinants and Consequence

Anil Gumber

In recent years, seasonal mobility of landless and small peasant households has attracted the attention of researchers, resulting in well documented works. The incidence of seasonal mobility is higher among the tribal population inhabiting hilly regions. Several factors operating in these areas force the tribal people to migrate out seasonally, but regularly in search of employment. In effect, there is a considerable outflow of tribal migrants towards agriculturally-developed areas having canal irrigation facility thus, the phenomenon is mainly characterized as 'intra-rural mobility'. Such a seasonal migration pattern needs to be studied in the context of general development programmes as well as associated occupational mobility taking place in rural areas.

The following factors contributing to seasonal out-migration are noteworthy: An increase in population pressure on land, resulting in sub-division and fragmentation of holdings, leads to holdings becoming uneconomical. Low productivity of land without the possibility of any significant irrigation, reliance on an uncertain monsoon and a single seasonal crop, and non-availability of off-farm employment in the local area, strengthen the pressure to migrate. Finally, the pressure is very strong amongst small landholders whose emotional attachment to their land and environment prevents them from going out nently, on the other hand it induces them to move out in search of additional work during the slack season, as soon as various agricultural operations on their farms are over.

This paper highlights the general pattern of seasonal migration in Gujarat. It is followed by a case study of the magnitude and determinants of seasonal migration among households displaced by the construction of a major irrigation dam in Panchmahals district.

General Pattern of Seasonal Migration

The circular mobility of labourers is probably a consequence of unbalanced resource endowment in, and development of different regions. There is a net transfer of slack (unutilised) labour from backward areas to relatively developed areas as soon as the monsoon is over. An agriculturally developed area experiences a temporary spurt in the demand for labour at the time of sowing, transplanting, and harvesting. In some areas the demand is so high during peak seasons that it cannot be met solely by the local supply of labour; the area, therefore, attracts labourers from outside. The persistent gap between demand for, and supply of, labourers results in wage differentials across regions. The wage rate is higher in agriculturally developed areas receiving migrants, compared to that in relatively backward areas, which send migrants. For the same type of farm operations, the wage rate in an agriculturally developed area is often double than that prevailing in the sending (backward) area. Patel (1987), while analysing the data on seasonal out-migrants from a village in Surendranagar district in Gujarat, found, that by and large the mandays worked outside the village by migrant labourers formed about 50 to 85 per cent of their total work days and majority had worked outside the district. Further, the daily agricultural wage rate in the area to which these workers had migrated was higher than that in the district of origin by between 30 and 80 per cent. Thus, seasonal migration implies a higher wage rate as well as a larger number of days of employment for migrant workers. The gap between demand for and supply of labour affects both wage differentials and the duration of employment, and generates seasonal labour mobility between different regions.

Over a period of time, areas brought under canal irrigation have become the main centres of attraction for seasonal migrant workers. With the introduction of HYV technology, agricultural productivity has increased considerably; and has in turn, resulted in a heavy demand for agricultural labourers for harvesting crops sometimes twice or three times in a year.[1] Apart from harvesting, sometimes transplanting of paddy (which is a labour-intensive farm operation) also requires labourers from outside the region.[2] But the spurt in demand at the time of the crop harvest is much higher than for other farm operations.

Further, over a period of time, there is a gradual shift towards substitution of hired (migrant) labour for family labour. The new generation among households employing migrant labourers is better educated and has diversified their economic activities in or outside their villages. In effect, the regular inflow of seasonal migrants in these areas has facilitated the educated and young labour force to take up skilled and professional jobs outside the area and has encouraged the flow of permanent out-migration (for details see, Gumber and Visaria 1995).

Migrants also get casual employment in seasonally operated agro-based industries such as rice mills, sugar factories, etc., and in transportation of produce to and from these factories. Sometimes they perform other strenuous tasks in rural areas such as road construction, tree plantation, canal construction, etc. Elsewhere, it has been observed that some of the seasonal migrants had also worked in brick-kilns and salt-pans (Van der Veen 1979). However, a higher proportion of seasonal migrant labourers gets employed in crop harvesting operations rather than in other-rural based activities in the receiving region. Besides intra-rural seasonal migration, there is also seasonal rural-to-urban migration. After the monsoon, some labourers go directly to urban centres while others move first to agriculturally developed rural areas and then to towns, usually for construction activities.

There exist regional differences in the characteristics of seasonal migrants. Breman reports his experience in South Gujarat:

> Time and again in my daily round I came upon different categories of migrants: pastoral nomads from north Gujarat with their flocks; donkey drivers from the same area; 'navvies' from Saurashtra; road workers from Panchmahals; quarry workers from Bharuch district; and cane cutters from neighbouring Maharashtra State (Breman 1985:192).

A study in central Gujarat (Kheda district) also highlights the seasonal movement of three types of migrants who were engaged in different activities: agricultural labourers from Panchmahals district, bullock-cart owners from Ahmedabad district, and workers from Jalor district of Rajasthan to work in the rice mills. They flow in as soon as the paddy harvest season starts (Bhatt 1979).

In contrast to region and task-specific seasonal mobility, a very large proportion of seasonal migrants move to a contiguous area (a taluka or a district) for crop harvesting. In Surat district, majority of seasonal migrants came from the eastern talukas to the irrigated western talukas of the same district within a radius of up to 80 km. (Breman 1985:192). In the command area of the Ukai irrigation project in the same region, seasonal migrants came from Uchhal and Nirzar talukas affected by the same project. In Kheda district, majority of the seasonal in-migrants come from the adjoining Panchmahals district (Bhatt 1979; Gandhi and Shah 1978; Jayaraman 1979). This is confirmed by studies conducted in Panchmahals district to examine the nature of seasonal out-migration (Bureau of Economics and Statistics 1974; Gandhi and Shah 1978). Often, relatively short distances between the areas of origin and destination stimulates many short duration moves instead of a one long duration move. Depending on the distance, households select the members to be left behind to take care of the assets and sometimes also of the young children. The distance, in fact, influences both selectivity and duration of mobility of a household.

Salient Features of Seasonal Migration in Gujarat

Within Gujarat, seasonal in-and-out mobility of labourers has gathered momentum over the last two decades. For instance, in Matar taluka of Kheda district, the percentage of migrant labourers to total labourers increased from 2 to 14 between 1964-65 and 1974-75, and accounted for nearly 25 per cent of the wages paid to hired labour in 1974-75 (Shah *et al.* 1991:153). In Surat district, some 5,000 workers came for seasonal work from Maharashtra mainly for sugarcane cutting and crushing work (Patel 1987).

There is also evidence of seasonal out-migration, before Independence, mainly from Kheda and Panchmahals districts to Baroda and Broach districts during agricultural seasons particularly at the time of cotton picking, and from Kheda to Bhal tract of Ahmedabad at the time of the wheat and cotton harvesting (Desai 1948). After two decades of Independence, Kheda district was brought under Mahi canal irrigation, as a result of which the pattern of seasonal migration has been reversed. The region has become one of the important destinations for seasonal in-migrants from other districts.

The acceleration of migration over a period of time could be a result of imbalance between sending and receiveing regions. Such imbalance can be attributed to the following factors: (a) differentials in the population pressure on land; (b) growth of inequality between regions over time due to development of infrastructure, industry, and modernization of agriculture due to harnessing of the perennial rivers for irrigation and power; and (c) occurrence of frequent droughts and crop failures. Some of the studies highlight one or more of these factors to explain the seasonal mobility dynamics. The salient features of these studies on seasonal migration are presented in Table 1.

These studies have been carried out either in the sending or receiving areas or in both. Their review highlights the origins and destinations of seasonal mobility in Gujarat.

Firstly, there is seasonal out-migration from the tribal belt of Gujarat (bordering Rajasthan, Madhya Pradesh, and Maharashtra states). The areas covered by these studies have a heavy concentration of tribal population; some of these areas had even enumerated more than 90 per cent of scheduled tribe population in the 1981 census.

Secondly, seasonal mobility is intra-rural and is directed towards Kheda and Surat districts, having widespread canal irrigation in the command area of the Mahi and Tapi rivers, respectively. But the extent of irrigation is higher in Kheda than in Surat. While Surat experiences more of intra-district seasonal mobility, Kheda has more of inter-district seasonal migration from contiguous regions.

These studies have traced seasonal migrants either at their places of origin or at their destinations. Both approaches have advantages as well as disadvantages for understanding some of the socio-economic characteristics of migrants. In a study where a seasonal migrant is traced at the place of origin, information about the destination is often partial or not precise enough and the opposite is true when migrants are traced at destinations. Studies done at the destination can obtain more information about the living and working conditions of migrants by interviewing them and/or their employers, but unless full mobility history is recorded, the intermediate moves are generally overlooked. No study listed in Table 1 has tried to capture more than one move and might have missed the multiple activities of a migrant during the reference period in which he/she had remained away from home.

Table 1 : Selected Studies on Seasonal Mobility in Gujarat : A Summary

Source	Migration rate IM : In OM : Out	Coverage district	Sample size & survey period/ reference year	Aspects covered
1. Bhatt (1979)	IM:NA	2 villages in Kheda ownership of	90 employers with working, living and holdings above 5 acres	Origin, recruitment, health conditions
2. Breman (1985)	OM:in the range of 30 to 85 per cent of households	7 Villages of Valod and Uchhal talukas in Surat	60 households	Origin, magnitude and selectivity
	IM: 20 to 30 per cent of working population	Bardoli taluka in Surat	Anthropological approach	Duration, direction, recruitment, working conditions and daily life
3. Bureau of Economics and Statistics (1974)	OM: 93 per cent of households (Census); 86 per cent of households (sample)	3 villages of Dahod taluka in Panchmahals	Village Census, July-August, 1971 225 households, Aug. 1971 - July 1972	Occupation, income expenditure, selectivity assets, duration, destination, working days
4. Gandhi and Shah (1978)	OM: 63 per cent of households	2 villages each from Dahod, Devgadh Baria, Jhalod, Santrampur and Limkheda talukas in Panchmahals	Village Census, 222 households, November 1976	Selectivity, occupation direction, duration, indebtedness
	IM: 17 per cent of resident households	2 Villages each from Anand, Matar, Nadiad and Petlad talukas in Kheda	Village Census, 272 households, December 1976	Economic status of employers, origin, income-expenditure and saving

Table 1 : (Continued)

Source	Migration rate IM : In OM : Out	Coverage district	Sample size & survey period/ reference year	Aspects covered
5. Mehta (n.d.)	OM:10 per cent of households, 7 per cent of population	All 220 villages in the Dangs	Village Census, 2290 households, Sept.-Oct. 1982	Direction, duration, occupation and selectivity
	IM: NA	Bardoli,Mahuva and Chorasi (Chaltan) talukas in Surat and Valsad taluka in Valsad	120 migrant units of the Dangs origin, February 1983	Recruitment, working condition, income and saving
6. Jayaraman (1979)	OM:NA	The Mahi Command area in Kheda	100 migrant households of Panchmahals origin, July-Sep. 1978	Various determinants of seasonal mobility

Seasonal Mobility in the Study Region

The following analysis is based on an intensive study of the resettlement of households ousted by the construction of the Panam Irrigation Dam in Panchmahals district. For the allotment of new cultivable land at resettlement sites, the Government followed the following norm:

Area of land acquired	**Area of land to be allotted**
Up to 4 acres	Up to the extent of land acquired
4-12 acres	4 acres
12-15 acres	One-third of land acquired
15 acres and above	5 acres

On account of the Government's norm, majority of the land owners could not get the same size of holding as they had owned prior to submergence. As a result, many of them have experienced a considerable decline in the size of landholding after the submergence of their village sites. Though the rehabilitation process has levelled down the inequalities in land ownership in the affected area, it has affected the levels of living, particularly of those who have experienced a sizeable reduction in the size of landholding.

This study is based on primary data collected through a sample survey of the affected households as well as non-affected households remaining in the affected villages. To get a fair cross-section of affected households in the sample, all the 42 affected villages were arranged in descending order according to the proportion of submerged cultivable area in the village. In all 20 villages, where more than one-third of the cultivated area was submerged, were selected for the study. These 20 sample villages covered nearly 70 per cent of 2500 affected land account holders (*khatedars*) from all the 42 villages. For each of these villages, a list of *khatedars* was prepared on the basis of the land records up to 1971 (the year preceding dam construction). The landholders were distributed among three classes of holdings: up to 4 acres, 4 to 12 acres and more than 12 acres. We decided to interview randomly every fifth of the affected *khatedars* from each of the three size classes. Besides, all the affected landless families in the 20 villages were also interviewed. A sample of the non-affected households inhabiting the original villages, as a control group, were also interviewed. The survey covered 312 affected landowning households, 50 non-affected households, and 37 affected landless households. For their rehabilitation, 19 resettlement sites were created on forest land which were spread widely (the distance ranged between 5 and 100 km. from the reservoir) and differed in their physical environment.[3]

Our study of seasonal mobility among the affected and non-affected households is not primarily or exclusively focused on the subject. It is concerned with identifying the households which reported seasonal employment outside their villages. In effect, the seasonal migrants surveyed by us had gone out temporarily for work and had come back before, or at the onset of the monsoon. In our analysis, those reporting for seasonal employment outside their present village or rehabilitation site during the reference year (1984-85) have been classified as 'current seasonal migrants' and those who reported similar movements from their old villages before submergence have been classified as 'former seasonal migrants'. All seasonal migrants were asked detailed questions about their pattern of mobility.

Magnitude

About 41 per cent (128) of the 312 affected landed households sent out at least one member in search of employment during the reference year; out of 37 affected landless households, 17 (46 per cent) reported seasonal out-migration. Overall, nearly 42 per cent of the affected households (145 out of 349) have reported seasonal mobility. With respect to their past practices, only 9 per cent of the affected households reported seasonal migration. Thus, displacement seems to have considerably raised seasonal mobility among the affected households.

Of the former seasonal migrant households, about 30 per cent discontinued their seasonal movement after submergence (see Table 2). Some households had resorted to seasonal mobility after submergence but had discontinued the practice before the reference year. All of them have been resettled in the command area.

Over a period of time, seasonal mobility has evidently been on the rise among non-affected households as well. Like the affected households, only 8 per cent of them reported seasonal migration in the past but the percentage had increased to 30 at the time of survey. Moreover, none of them had given up seasonal migration and all the households that had reported mobility in the past had continued seasonal out-migration during the year preceding the survey.

Table 2 : Number and Proportion of Seasonal Migrants

	Affected						Non-affected	
	Landless		Landowners		All			
	No.	%	No.	%	No.	%	No.	%
Households :								
1984-85	17	45.9	128	41.0	145	41.5	15	30.0
Past	6	16.2	24	7.7	30	8.6	4	8.0
Common*	5	83.3	16	66.7	21	70.0	4	100.0
Workers :								
1984-85	49	43.0	298	36.2	347	37.0	32	29.1
	(20)		(74)		(94)		(6)	
Past	8	10.4	58	9.1	66	9.2	6	6.1
	(-)		(15)		(15)		(1)	
Common*	5	62.5	32	55.2	37	56.1	5	83.3
	(-)		(7)		(7)		(1)	
Persons :								
1984-85	66	25.5	374	16.3	440	17.2	35	11.0
	(32)		(116)		(148)		(7)	

Note : (1) *Households/workers that had reported migration during 1984-85 and also in the past are categorized as 'common'.

(2) Figures in parentheses show the number of seasonally out-migrating females.

Similar behaviour has also been recorded among affected families of the Ukai project in south Gujarat. After resettlement, nearly 42 per cent of the families reported seasonal out-migration. Their destination was in the command area of the same project which had uprooted them. The landless households formed nearly two-thirds of the affected households. Mankodi and Gangopadhyay (1983: 89-90) have reported that, before displacement,less than half of the landless labourers were willing to migrate for work; but after displacement, their proportion increased to three-fourths; even those who owned some land joined the migratory team.[4] Thus, the experiences of the Ukai and Panam projects indicate an increase in the incidence of seasonal out-migration after displacement.

Selectivity Process

As in permanent out-migration, there is a selectivity process in seasonal migration too. Age, sex, caste, and economic status (size of holding) are some of the factors which distinguish migrants from non-migrants. As one would expect, it is primarily the principal bread earners who out-migrate when unable to find work during the off-season at home. It implies that males are dominant in the seasonal migration stream. In both affected and non-affected households, the proportion of males reporting out-migration has been very high. This phenomenon existed even in the past when they were migrating from their old villages (see Table 2).

Contrary to this observation, Breman (1985) on the basis of field work in south Gujarat, comments that the seasonal migration of women is grossly underestimated. His data revealed that about 58 per cent of all migrant labourers were women and they constituted majority of the harvest team. His findings do not really contradict our evidence because the proportion of landless households in his study region (Surat district) is quite high and in some areas they constitute the majority. In our data also, the sex ratio of current out-migrant workers was relatively balanced among landless households as compared to affected and non-affected landowners (see Table 2). It reflects the lower availability of work for landless workers than for other households, which induces the entire households of the landless to move.

A few reasons for the relative seasonal immobility of females from landowning households can also be identified. First, females crossing the age of 14 up to the status of single, generally restrict themselves from going out of the village (because of insecurity reasons). Secondly, depending upon the requirements of a household, an adult male member is the first to out-migrate; where his earnings are insufficient for survival, a female (usually the wife of the out-migrating male) migrates for work. In our sample, 95 per cent of females migrating for work were spouses of out-migrating males. Last, female mobility is quite often restricted if the move is of long duration and entirely towards an urban centre. (This factor will be discussed later when we examine the relationship of mobility with distance, and who is left behind in the household.) Above all, there is an inverse relationship between land status and female participation in casual employment. As the size of landholding increases the proportion of women undertaking casual employment declines; hence, women's seasonal-out mobility is also limited.

Another factor which clearly indicates the selectivity in seasonal mobility is age composition (see Table 3). Majority of migrants belong to the younger age group. From the affected households, nearly 80 per cent of male and 90 per cent of female workers going out seasonally during the reference year, were in the age group of 15-34 years. A similar dominance of the young has been noticed in the non-affected households as well. On the other hand, the proportion of non-migrant workers in the age group of 15-34 years in both sexes was markedly low in both affected and non-affected households. A similar pattern has been found in the past also, except for the females in the age group of 25-34 years. Further, mainly male (and not female) workers in the higher age groups (35-44 and 45+ years) participated in seasonal mobility during the year 1984-85. This reflects that age is another factor which restricts the seasonal mobility of females, particularly of those crossing 35 years of age. In the past, there was no female out-migration in the higher age groups. Therefore, after displacement, age specific selectivity among both males and females has increased, and more so in the higher age groups.

Children accompany their parents to the work place only if their mothers also out-migrate. According to our survey data, adult females who accompany out-migrant males participate in gainful activity at the place of work and do not go with them just to look after the children and other chores. During 1984-85, 33 males and 43 females aged less than 15 years from affected landowning households, had joined seasonal out-migration. Except for one male child, all of them had accompanied the adult members of their respective households.

Children particularly those in the age group 10-14, do contribute their labour to various agricultural operations, particularly during crop harvesting. But due to a variety of reasons their work remains under-reported and consequently their work participation is grossly underestimated. Nearly half of the out-migrant children in this age group participated in wage employment at their destinations during the reference period. Those who were not engaged in gainful employment, sometimes contributed to the total family labour when the work was assigned at piece rate. For instance, in South Gujarat, the activities of cotton picking, groundnut harvesting, stripping of sugarcane leaves and their collection, and making of paddy bundles for threshing, involve child labour (Breman 1985). Bhatt observes:

> Children under 10 who are not working collect the dropping of paddy from their fields. They can earn around Re.1.00 to Rs.2.00 per day for selling this paddy to shopkeepers and vegetable vendors. (They accept this paddy and give vegetables and other items in exchange.).... it supplements their income as they mostly get enough vegetables and spices etc., in exchange of this paddy and are not required to spend for these from their wages (Bhatt 1979:33).

Besides such directly productive work, children can be considered indirectly productive as they look after younger siblings, collect firewood, and perform other odd tasks, thus freeing the adults for heavier work. We were not able to notice their direct and indirect participation in productive activities at destinations, because our survey design did not permit us to observe them at their destinations.

Does seasonal mobility differ among caste groups? Studies conducted in the Panchmahals by the Bureau of Economics and Statistics (1974) and Gandhi and Shah (1978) show a higher representation of tribal population among seasonal migrants. Since the area covered by these studies (eastern part of the district) is heavily populated by tribals, the picture does not become clear. In our study region (Godhra, Shehera, and Lunavada talukas), the share of scheduled and non-scheduled population is fairly close to the district average. Therefore, it would be interesting to analyse the pattern of seasonal migration among different caste groups. From Table 4 it is clear that the proportion of scheduled tribes and backward castes (as classified by the Bakshi Commission, Government of Gujarat 1976) among seasonal out-migrant households was higher than that among the non-migrating households in both affected and non-affected categories.

Table 3 : Percentage Distribution of Seasonal Migrant and Non-Migrant Workers by Age Group and Sex

Age Group/ Sex	Affected			Non-affected		
	SM	NM	% Reported SM	SM	NM	% Reported SM
Males			1984-85			
10 - 14	2.0	1.3	45.5	3.8	2.8	33.3
15 - 24	43.1	27.3	46.6	50.0	29.6	38.2
25 - 34	38.3	17.9	54.2	30.8	16.9	40.0
35 - 44	10.3	18.6	23.4	15.4	23.9	19.0
45 +	6.3	34.9	9.1	-	26.8	-
All	100.0	100.0	35.6	100.0	100.0	26.8
Number	253	458		26	71	
Females						
10 - 14	2.1	3.7	28.6	-	-	-
15 - 24	50.0	40.3	46.5	66.7	28.6	66.7
25 - 34	41.5	24.6	54.2	33.3	57.1	33.3
35 - 44	4.3	23.1	11.4	-	14.3	-
45 +	2.1	8.2	15.4	-	-	-
All	100.0	100.0	41.2	100.0	100.0	46.2
Number	94	134		6	7	

Table 3 : (Continued)

Age Group/ Sex	Affected			Non-affected		
	SM	NM	% Reported SM	SM	NM	% Reported SM
Past						
Males						
10 - 14	7.8	6.1	9.3	-	7.8	-
15 - 24	53.0	39.4	9.7	60.0	30.0	10.0
25 - 34	19.6	18.3	7.9	20.0	23.3	4.5
35 - 44	17.6	20.8	6.4	20.0	16.7	6.3
45 +	2.0	15.4	1.0	-	22.2	-
All	100.0	100.0	7.4	100.0	100.0	5.3
Number	51	635		5	90	
Females						
10 - 14	13.3	-	100.0	-	-	-
15 - 24	60.0	23.1	75.0	100.0	66.7	33.3
25 - 34	26.7	61.5	33.3	-	33.3	-
35 - 44	-	7.7	-	-	-	-
45 +	-	7.7	-	-	-	-
All	100.0	100.0	53.6	100.0	100.0	25.0
Number	15	13		1	3	

Note : SM - Seasonal Migrant, NM - Non-Migrant.

Generally, it is observed that lower caste households possess small holdings and poor assets (Visaria and Gumber 1994). Their over-representation among the landless and small holding class is reflected in their moving out of their villages in search of work as soon as the monsoon is over.

Off-farm work and hence seasonal migration are a result of the increased population pressure on land resources. Such migration has increased considerably after submergence due to a significant decline in the size of land holdings. The percentage distribution of households by size class of land holding (presented also in Table 4) shows an influence of the size of landholding on seasonal migration. Both landless and marginal landowning (up to 2 acres) households have a greater tendency to out-migrate. As the size of landholding increases, the share of out-migrant households declines (as depicted in above four acres size class of holding). Among landless households, the representation of women and children in seasonal migration was found to be higher, while among the landowners the percentage of those remaining behind was higher. The latter proportion rises with the farm size. The relationship between size of land ownership and seasonal migration is not absolutely linear. To a certain extent, household size is an independent variable in the sense that with the increase in the number of household members, the temporary 'expulsion' of one or more members becomes both possible and necessary (Breman 1985:211).

Similar selectivity was also observed by Van der Veen (1979) in a South Gujarat village. He found that about 18 percent of young males (aged 20 years and above) were out-migrating seasonally for a period of four to six months to work in brick-kilns or salt-pans located in South Gujarat and around Bombay. Most of them were poor and landless labourers from lower castes.

Determinants

After submergence, there is considerable reduction in the size of land holding of affected households. The question arises as to why all the affected households do not report temporary migration from their home. The observed pattern is linked to wage and employment differentials prevailing in their area of residence. The agricultural wage rate is very low in both partially-affected villages and resettlement sites as compared to that in the agriculturally developed area. At the

Table 4 : Selectivity of Current Seasonal Migrant Households by Caste and Landholding

Caste/ Landholding	Affected			Non-affected		
	SM	NM	% Reported SM	SM	NM	% Reported SM
Caste						
Scheduled Castes	2.8	2.9	40.0	-	2.9	-
Scheduled Tribes	26.2	15.2	55.1	20.0	11.4	42.9
Backward Castes (Bakshi Commission)	11.7	9.3	47.2	20.0	11.4	42.9
Other Backward Castes	20.7	22.1	40.0	6.7	37.1	7.1
Others	38.6	50.5	35.2	53.3	37.1	38.1
All	100.0	100.0	41.5	100.0	100.0	30.0
Size of Landholding (Acres)						
0.0	11.7	9.8	45.9	-	-	-
0.1 - 1.0	17.9	11.3	53.1	20.0	14.3	37.5
1.1 - 2.0	29.7	26.0	44.8	33.3	17.1	45.5
2.1 - 3.0	17.2	18.1	40.3	6.7	22.9	11.1
3.1 - 4.0	14.5	16.7	38.2	20.0	11.4	42.9
4.1 - 6.0	4.8	10.8	24.1	-	17.7	-
6.1 +	4.1	7.4	28.6	20.0	17.1	33.3
All	100.0	100.0	41.5	100.0	100.0	30.0
Number of Households	145	204		15	35	

Note : SM - Seasonal Migrant, NM - Non-Migrant.

time of survey, the rate varied between Rs.5 and Rs.6 per day in cash, or 2.5 kg. of maize in kind. The payment in kind was more prevalent in the affected area than in the resettlement sites in the plains. In the agriculturally developed area the wage rate was between Rs.8 and Rs.10 in cash or 5 kg. of paddy/wheat in kind. However, it is not the agricultural wage rate which is generating the differential pattern; the difference arises from the prevalent non-agricultural wage rate and the duration of employment available in the neighbouring areas.

Table 5 reveals that the households settled in the conventional environment (near the reservoir and remaining in the old villages) had reported a higher incidence of seasonal migration than their counterparts in other settlement areas. The out-migration was the lowest from the households settled in the command area, and next highest from the households settled near the urban area (Godhra town). Both these sites have favourable factors, good transport facilities, and are relatively closer to Vadodara and Kheda districts, which attract seasonal migrants. However, due to the availability of employment in the non-agricultural sector in the neighbouring area, the worker has a choice between going out to distant places and to the neighbouring areas. A majority of the households resettled near the urban area were engaged in construction activity in Godhra town and commuted either by bus or truck, or sometimes just walked down. Similarly Timba and Sevalia are quarry centres, 4 to 7 km. away from the command area sites. The workers from these sites preferred to go for quarry work because the quarry owners provide transport. In the morning, a tractor with a trolley picks them up and drops them back in the evening. The wage differential between non-agricultural activities available in nearby areas and in distant urban areas for the same type of work is quite small. As a result, they prefer to stay at home and their mobility is limited. However, a few households from these sites have shown a tendency to migrate for agricultural work in Kheda district, even when employment in the non-agricultural sector is locally available. One interesting finding came out when we asked them about the underlying considerations. They prefer to earn wages in kind, and in Kheda district most of the payment is made in paddy. After displacement, they are neither able to grow paddy on the new land nor can they afford to buy it in the market. To maintain their previous consumption pattern, they go to Kheda district during the paddy harvesting season so that they can get paddy as wages. For the rest of the year, if required, they would go for non-agricultural work in the

Table 5 : Percentage of Current Seasonal Migrant Households by Size Class of Holdings and Location of Settlement

Location of Settlement	Size Class of Holdings (acres)						No. of Migrant House-holds
	0.0	0.1-2.0	2.1-4.0	4.1-6.0	6.1+	All	
Near the reservoir area	66.7	62.5	47.8	-	-	55.6 (83.3)	30
Near the urban area	66.7	41.4	42.3	11.1	14.3	36.5 (73.0)	27
In the command area	22.2	27.3	23.1	28.6	40.0	26.1 (79.7)	18
Adjacent to canal area	50.0	33.3	58.3	40.0	-	42.5 (92.5)	17
Unsubmerged area	46.7	57.7	36.7	28.6	37.5	47.3 (67.9)	53
All affected	45.9	47.6	39.3	24.1	28.6	41.5 (76.5)	145
Non-affected	-	42.1	25.0	-	33.3	30.0 (38.0)	15

Note : Figures in parentheses are the percentage of households (migrants and non-migrants) reporting casual employment.

nearby areas. That is why some of the male workers have shown three types of activities and females two types of casual employment during the reference year.

During 1984-85, more than two-thirds of the affected households had supplemented their income with casual employment. There were two main sources of casual employment: working in nearby areas and in distant places. Where the proportion of households reporting casual employment in nearby areas or at home was higher, the share of households undertaking it through seasonal out- migration was lower (for such trade-off, see figures in parentheses in Table 5).

Apart from wage and employment differentials between sending and receiving areas, are there other economic factors which distinguish seasonal migrant households from others? Table 6 presents a comparative picture of certain characteristics of these two groups. The factors listed in the table seem to strengthen the prospects for casual wage employment and then result in out-migration. The push factors are lower average and/or per capita size of holding, productivity and area sown more than once, with migrant households than with non-migrant households in both affected and non-affected categories. Among both the affected and non-affected households, the average gross value of crop output of non-migrant households is about twice that of the migrant household; the per capita output of non-migrant households is also almost twice that of migrant households in the affected and thrice in the non-affected category.

The gap in crop output is bridged by migrant households through income earned from casual work. The proportion of net income earned through casual work (after the deduction of transportation charges from the gross wages) to total net income was about two-thirds (66.2 per cent) among the seasonal migrant households in the affected category and nearly half (48.8 per cent) among the non-affected category. The share of casual wage income in the total income of migrant households was higher than that for non-migrant households.

Overall, the average net income from all sources including the contribution of casual wage employment at distant places (migrant households) or at home or in nearby areas (non-migrant households), turns out to be nearly the same for all categories of households. In fact, the average net household income is a little higher, but the per capita income is a little lower in the case of seasonal migrant households (which had a higher than the average family size).

Interestingly, the characteristics of the affected non-migrant households such as landholding, land productivity, cropping intensity and income from casual work as well as its share in total income, are close to those of the seasonal migrant (but not to those of non-migrant) households in the non-affected category. One of the main reasons is that employment opportunities in the old (unsubmerged) villages are limited, and the only alternative left to them is seasonal out-migration even for a short period. The affected non-migrant households participate in some of the employment opportunities available in the neighbouring areas.

Although economic factors do play an important role in extensive seasonal migration, in a few cases non-economic factors were noticed as favouring or retarding it. One person who was too young (aged 14 years), to make an independent move and also was the only male member in the household, went out along with neighbours to gain experience of the outside world. In another case, an adult male was persuaded by his neighbours to accompany them to help prepare a tent for a marriage function in Kheda district. When asked whether he would go out again, he stated: 'Life outside home is very hard; it is better to satisfy oneself with one meal than to go out to earn an extra meal'. Evidently, in these cases the economic push factors were not very strong and the aversion to the first move was high, and there was a clear tendency to postpone the decision to move as far as possible.

Direction and Duration

As stated earlier, a large number of seasonal migrants move to contiguous areas, often to an adjoining taluka or district. If the distance is short, many of them make several moves (to and fro) in a year. Tables 7 to 11 present some of the characteristics of moves of migrants during the reference year to highlight the seasonal fluctuations in labour mobility in different occupations. Further, if a migrant goes to the same destination and engages himself/herself in the same type of work, the seasonal mobility acquires a set pattern. However, such is not the case in reality. Over the time span of a year, a migrant makes several moves to different places and works in different occupations.

The distinguishing features of a move tend to be destination and/or occupation, and the duration of stay at home on return. If a migrant had stayed home for a minimum of two weeks before moving out

Table 6 : Characteristics of Current Seasonal Migrant and Non-Migrant Households

Characteristics	Affected		Non-affected	
	SM	NM	SM	NM
Size of holding (acres)				
Per household	2.1	2.8 *	3.1	3.9
Per capita	0.3	0.5 *	0.4	0.9 **
Per male worker	1.0	1.8 *	1.4	2.5 **
Cropping intensity (Per cent of NCA to GCA)	116	127 *	131	148
Per cent of irrigated area to NCA	7.2	10.4	0.0	8.2
Gross value of crop output (Rs.)				
Per household	1731	3040 *	2626	5131 ***
Per capita	238	504 *	344	1209 **
Per acre of GCA	664	760 ***	773	874

Table 6 : (Continued)

Characteristics	Affected		Non-affected	
	SM	NM	SM	NM
Income from casual work (Rs.)				
Per household	3854 *	1387	2821 *	64
Per worker	1134 *	574	1012 *	32
Per cent to total income	66.2	41.1	48.8	1.2
Ratio to agricultural income	2.2	0.8	1.0	N
Income from all sources (Rs.)				
Per household	5825	5258	5785	5282
Per capita	760	838 ***	734	1144
Per worker	1851	2935 *	2196	3532 ***
Family size	8.0 *	6.9	8.2 *	5.5
Value of assets per household (Rs.)	690	929 *	588	681

Note : (1) SM-Seasonal Migrant, NM-Non Migrant

(2) *, **, ***, respectively shows that the difference in mean values between seasonal migrant and non-migrant households is statistically significant at .01, .05 and .10 level of confidence. N - Negligible.

again, the second move was considered distinct and information about it was recorded separately. Short home visits (of less than two weeks) such as visits to enquire about the relatives left behind or to give them the savings or a part of wages earned through migration were overlooked. Only two migrant households remained out continuously for more than six months and followed different activities at different places round the year.

The direction and the duration of a move are both directly and indirectly related with the distance and the number of persons accompanying the migrant (or the number of persons left at home). If only males go out, they need to worry less about looking after the house. But in households where the adult female, usually the spouse, accompanies the male migrant, they need to decide about who should be left at home to take care of the assets and sometimes young children. According to the field survey, an older/elder relative, particularly a female (mother, mother-in-law or grandmother of the migrant male) is usually assigned this role. The presence of an old woman frees the spouse of the out-migrating male to participate in wage employment at the destination. Thus, besides the married women who accompany their migrant husbands, the members left behind also contribute to earnings by facilitating the migration of more members and lengthening the duration of moves.

The number of persons accompanying the main migrant depends on whether the destination is rural or urban. Females are reluctant to go to urban areas. The city life is hard in terms of both food and shelter. In villages they receive wages in kind (either in terms of paddy or maize) and thus get the main part of their daily meal. Moreover, the space for shelter is not a major problem because they can put up huts on the farms where they work. In urban areas, the distance between work place and residence varies. To take young children along with their mother is troublesome in urban areas. That is why rural work is sometimes preferred to urban work, even though the wage rate for manual work is higher in urban areas. These differences between rural and urban areas retard the mobility of females to towns. In some cases when females accompany the males to work in urban areas, the duration of stay is shortened compared to when only males move.

From Table 7 it is clear that a majority of migrants from affected households had moved more than once during 1984-85. The number of moves per migrant worker had been reportedly lower among the affected households in the past. While recall lapse may be a problem, the circulation of migrants has probably increased after submergence due to lengthening of the slack period. In the past, some of the migrants used to start moving out after the Holi festival, or at the time of harvesting of Rabi crop, but now their move starts as soon as the monsoon is over or just after the Diwali festival (at the time of harvesting of Kharif crop). The number of moves per migrant worker is found to be higher among those moving to a rural area than among migrants to urban areas, because the former are linked with three crop harvest periods. Quite likely, the availability of such opportunities and greater awareness about these, have also contributed to the rise in the frequency of movement.

Before submergence, the majority of moves were towards rural areas, but after submergence these declined considerably. During 1984-85, the share of urban oriented moves in total moves was 57 per cent for males and 35 per cent for females in the affected households; the corresponding numbers for the non-affected households were much higher (81 per cent and 44 per cent, respectively). This has happened due to the widespread increase in construction activity in urban areas available round the year; the crop harvest activity in rural areas on the other hand, tends to be limited. Most of the moves are towards the major urban centres, namely, Vadodara and Ahmedabad. All urban oriented moves are intra-state except one to Ratlam city in Madhya Pradesh. Nearly 90 per cent of moves of both males and females to rural areas were to the contiguous district of Kheda, a majority of them to the agriculturally-developed Anand and Matar talukas.[5]

The outflow of migrants begins as soon as the monsoon is over. However, the time of departure is decided according to the volume of work and the stock of food reserve at home, and the festival schedule. The influx towards rural Kheda begins at the end of October as soon as the paddy crop becomes ready for harvest. This is also the month when the harvesting of their own agricultural crop as well as sowing of the limited winter crop are to be carried out. The quantum of such work at home determines the time schedule of out-migration. The Diwali festival (which usually comes towards the end of October, or in the first week of November) also influences the schedule of move. If they have enough grain harvest from their own land, or cash at home, they like to celebrate the festival. Some of those who leave earlier, come back for a couple of days with some cash to celebrate Diwali.[6] During the weeks following Diwali, there is a heavy outflow

Table 7 : Distribution of Moves and Migrant Workers by Place of Work in Rural and Urban Areas : During 1984-85 and in the Past

Place of work		1984-85				Past			
		Affected		Non-affected		Affected		Non-affected	
		Male	Female	Male	Female	Male	Female	Male	Female
Rural Areas :									
Total	Mo	160	97	7	5	53	18	3	2
Total	Mi	114	68	4	3	42	15	2	1
Mo per	Mi	1.4	1.4	1.8	1.7	1.3	1.2	1.5	2.0
Panchmahals Mo	12	7	-	-	7	4	-	-	
	Mi	11	7	-	-	7	4	-	-
Kheda	Mo	142	89	7	5	37	14	3	2
	Mi	97	60	4	3	29	11	2	1
Anand Taluka	Mo	66	46	-	-	8	4	-	-
	Mi	54	37	-	-	7	4	-	-
Other districts	Mo	6	1	-	-	9	-	-	-
	Mi	6	1	-	-	6	-	-	-

Table 7 : (Continued)

Place of work			1984-85				Past			
			Affected		Non-affected		Affected		Non-affected	
			Male	Female	Male	Female	Male	Female	Male	Female
Urban Areas :										
	Total	Mo	214	52	29	4	11	-	5	-
	Total	Mi	171	42	22	3	11	-	3	-
	Mo per	Mi	1.3	1.2	1.3	1.3	1.0	-	1.7	-
Panchmahals	Mo	4	-	-	-	-	-	-	-	
		Mi	4	-	-	-	-	-	-	-
Kheda		Mo	19	11	-	-	-	-	-	-
		Mi	19	11	-	-	-	-	-	-
Vadodara		Mo	139	30	27	4	7	-	5	-
		Mi	103	21	20	3	7	-	3	-
Ahmedabad	Mo	31	8	2	-	3	-	-	-	
		Mi	28	7	2	-	3	-	-	-
Others		Mo	21	3	-	-	1	-	-	-
		Mi	17	3	-	-	1	-	-	-
All Areas										
	Total	Mo	374	149	36	9	64	18	8	2
	Total	Mi	253	94	26	6	51	15	5	1
Mo per	Mi	1.5	1.6	1.4	1.5	1.3	1.2	1.6	2.0	

Note : For all areas we have taken account of total migrant workers who went out seasonally; thus it is not necessarily a sum of migrants according to rural and urban places of work.

Mo - Moves, Mi - Migrants.

Table 8 : Distribution of Moves by Month of Departure and Return

Month of Migration	1984-85				Past			
	Affected		Non-affected		Affected		Non-affected	
	DM	RM	DM	RM	DM	RM	DM	RM
August	8 (2)	-	-	-	-	-	-	-
September	19 (5)	2 (N)	-	-	5 (6)	-	-	-
October	56 (16)	1 (1)	-	-	2 (9)	-	-	-
November	212 (56)	24 (5)	7 (16)	-	21 (34)	-	3 (30)	-
December	46 (65)	34 (12)	10 (38)	-	1 (35)	8 (10)	1 (40)	-
January	24 (70)	49 (21)	13 (67)	1 (2)	4 (40)	9 (21)	1 (50)	-

Table 8 : (Continued)

Month of Migration	1984-85				Past			
	Affected		Non-affected		Affected		Non-affected	
	DM	RM	DM	RM	DM	RM	DM	RM
February	14	75	2	17	2	-	-	4
	(72)	(35)	(71)	(40)	(43)	(21)	(50)	(40)
March	115	60	13	7	43	3	5	1
	(94)	(47)	(100)	(56)	(95)	(24)	(100)	(50)
April	15	46	-	-	4	12	-	
-	(97)	(56)	(100)	(56)	(100)	(39)	(100)	(50)
May	14	91	-	15	-	24	-	5
	(100)	(73)	(100)	(89)	(100)	(68)	(100)	(100)
June	-	141	-	5	-	26	-	-
	(100)	(100)	(100)	(100)	(100)	(100)	(100)	(100)
All	523	523	45	45	82	82	10	10

Note : (1) DM-Departure Month, RM-Return Month.

(2) Figures in parentheses are cumulative percentages. N - Negligible.

of two types of migrants: those starting their first move of the year and those returning to their respective work places after a brief stay at home. Breman (1985) has estimated that the seasonal migrants constitute nearly 20 to 30 per cent of the working population of the central plains of Gujarat State between the months November to January. Thereafter, the number declines and before the Holi festival (somewhere in the first week of March), most of the migrants return home. Our data on the moves to both rural and urban areas confirm the role of festivals in deciding the time schedule of migration (see Table 8).

The movement of these workers to cities is not very well organized. There is no definite prior information about the destination, the magnitude, nature and duration of work. After arriving at one of the important urban centres, the migrants offer their labour in the labour market. They go early in the morning to the labour market and wait for employers. After an agreement on the wage rate, the migrants accompany the employer. When the work is over, they come back to the market. They are reluctant to accept an offer for a short duration of employment, particularly for less than two weeks. Continuous employment for one month or more is preferred; after such stint(s) for one or two months, they return home to rest for a week or so and then go back to the cities.

On the other hand, the mobility to rural Kheda is somewhat organized though not as much as in the case of contracts arranged for sugarcane cutting by the co-operative factories in South Gujarat, tribal gangs of road workers from Panchmahals in Surat district and the Mukadam (gang leader) system during crop harvest in certain areas of the plains. The organized recruitment with a labour contract for sugarcane cutting does not fit in with the short-term employment on family farms in the plains. According to Breman (1985), migrant labour in agriculture is comparatively much less regulated than in road construction, quarrying and activities of sugarcane co-operative factories. Many of them do not know for which employer (farm owner) they would be working, where they would be going, or how long they would remain there.

The risk involved in such migration is high but as the migrant acquires experience over a period of time, his risk is reduced due to contacts with various employers and the possibility of advance (informal) contracts for future employment. According to our survey, the migrants going to rural Kheda have developed a routine of working for the same farmers again and again. Those who have established good contacts and trust with farmers of Kheda usually receive letters in advance from the farmers as soon as the crop is ready for harvest. Similar observations were made by Bhatt (1979) for the farmers of Kheda. He found that nearly three-fourths of the farmers recruited the migrant labourers through various methods such as writing letters, or going to see them personally, or giving a loan in advance. Nearly three-fifths of the employers employed the same labourers who had worked with them before (Bhatt 1979:17-20). Thus unlike the migrants to urban areas, many of the migrants going to rural areas have prior information about the employer and the time of their own departure.

After submergence, the push factors have become so strong that many of the migrants spend a major part of the year at the destination itself. As shown in Table 9 a majority of the migrants had remained out for six months (38.8 per cent) or more (22.8 per cent) during the reference year to earn their livelihood. However, only 20.3 per cent of the total moves were for six months or more. The remaining migrants had made more than one move. A large number of moves were of short duration ranging from one month to three months. Both male and female migrants reported moves of almost the same duration during the reference year and also in the past. Some of the migrants reporting short duration moves had moved thrice in a year at the time of harvesting. They had made their first move in October-November to harvest paddy crop, the second in February-March to harvest wheat, and the third in May-June to harvest groundnut. In the past, a majority of the migrants from affected households had moved for one or two months at a time, whereas the migrants from non-affected households did not report even a single move of more than three months. Thus after submergence, both the number of moves and their average duration have increased.

Sectoral and Occupational Distribution of Seasonal Migrant Workers

After submergence, the construction activity has emerged as the major sector of employment for migrants. Though the share of moves for construction work was less than that of moves for agriculture work, it accounted for over 50 per cent of the total days of employment and of earned wages (see Table 10). Over a period of time, the share of the agricultural and forestry sector in absorbing seasonal migrants from

Table 9 : Distribution of Moves and Migrants by Duration of Migration

Duration (months)	Affected				Non-affected			
	Male	Female	Person	%	Male	Female	person	%
(A) Migrants : 1984-85								
Up to 1	9	3	12	3.5	1	-	1	3.1
2	24	14	38	10.9	7	2	9	28.1
3	30	12	42	12.1	7	1	8	25.0
4-5	60	9	69	19.9	6	3	9	28.1
6	72	35	107	30.8	5	-	5	15.7
6+	58	21	79	22.8	-	-	-	-
All	253	94	347	100.0	26	6	32	100.0
Average	5.2	5.1	5.2	-	3.6	3.5	3.6	
(B) Moves : 1984-85								
Up to 1	60	40	100	19.1	6	1	7	15.6
2	99	34	133	25.4	15	5	20	44.5
3	92	33	125	23.9	9	2	11	24.4
4-5	45	14	59	11.3	5	1	6	13.3
6	33	16	49	9.4	1	-	1	2.2
6+	45	12	57	10.9	-	-	-	-
All	374	149	523	100.0	36	9	45	100.0
Average	3.1	3.0	3.1	-	2.5	2.3	2.5	-

Table 9 : (Continued)

Duration (months)	Affected				Non-affected			
	Male	Female	Person	%	Male	Female	person	%
(C) Moves : Past								
Up to 1	13	3	16	19.5	1	-	1	10.0
2	29	7	36	43.9	4	1	5	50.0
3	10	4	14	17.1	3	1	4	40.0
4-5	6	1	7	8.5	-	-	-	-
6	2	-	2	2.5	-	-	-	-
6+	4	3	7	8.5	-	-	-	-
All	64	18	82	100.0	8	2	10	100.0
Average	2.7	2.3	2.6	-	2.3	2.5	2.3	-

Table 10 : Percentage Distribution of Moves, Days of Employment, and Income of Migrant Workers by Sector of Activity

Sector of Activity		1984-85		Past	
		Affected	Non-affected	Affected	Non-affected
1. Agriculture	Mo	48.4	26.7	73.2	50.0
	D	41.0	31.4	73.9	52.2
	W	34.8	23.6	64.8	43.8
2. Forestry	Mo	0.6	-	12.2	-
	D	0.6	-	8.8	-
	W	0.6	-	7.9	-
Agricultural Sector (1 to 2)					
	Mo	49.0	26.7	85.4	50.0
	D	41.6	31.4	82.7	52.2
	W	35.4	23.6	72.7	43.8
3. Manufacturing	Mo	2.5	-	1.2	-
	D	2.9	-	2.6	-
	W	3.5	-	4.5	-

Table 10 : (Continued)

Sector of Activity		1984-85		Past	
		Affected	Non-affected	Affected	Non-affected
4. Construction	Mo	46.1	68.9	12.2	50.0
	D	53.0	64.8	10.8	47.8
	W	57.0	73.2	14.4	56.2
5. Transport	Mo	0.8	-	1.2	-
	D	1.2	-	3.9	-
	W	2.3	-	8.4	-
6. Others	Mo	1.7	4.4	-	-
	D	1.3	3.8	-	-
	W	1.8	3.2	-	-
Non-agricultural Sector (3 to 6)					
	Mo	51.0	73.3	14.6	50.0
	D	58.4	68.6	17.3	47.8
	W	64.6	76.4	27.3	56.2

Note : Mo - Moves, D - Number of Days of Employment, W - Total Wage Receipt.

both affected and non-affected households has declined. Seasonal migration has become more urban-oriented, and movers are absorbed in non-agricultural sectors such as construction, manufacturing, etc., Nearly two-thirds of the wage income of seasonal movers from affected households is generated from the non-agricultural sector in urban centres. The rural and urban classification of work places corresponded to agricultural and non-agricultural activities.

Our seasonal migrants mostly belonged to a low economic strata and the majority of them took up manual unskilled labour in construction or agriculture (see Table 11). Less than five per cent of male migrants and no female migrants from the affected and non-affected households were engaged as skilled workers such as drivers, turners, masons, etc., at their destinations, during the reference year or in the past.

The average wage rate for non-agricultural occupations was higher than for agricultural occupations for all migrants during 1984-85 as well as in the past. Women generally received a lower wage rate than their male counterparts in all sorts of manual labour, and the gap was higher in construction (about two rupees) than in agricultural labour.

Income and Saving Through Seasonal Migration

The income of the migrants undertaking agricultural work in rural areas consisted of payments in both cash and kind. In urban areas, payments were entirely in cash. As noted earlier, the migrants to rural Kheda undertaking agricultural work were paid mostly in terms of crop harvest (usually 5 kg. of paddy or wheat per day). In urban areas most of them earned Rs.10 per day in cash for construction work. Because of the difference in the cost of living, migrants to rural areas saved more from their wage income than those going to urban areas. Migrants to rural areas usually got residential accommodation and foodgrains, and sometimes also medicines, vegetables and other miscellaneous perquisites from their employers; such benefits, however, were practically non-existent in urban areas. A migrant worker in rural Kheda was reportedly able to save around 80 kg. of paddy (worth Rs.120) over a month during the October-November harvest season and about the same quantity of wheat (worth Rs.140) during March-April; the wages saved constituted 50 to 60 per cent of the total. In urban areas he saved Rs.3 to 4 per day (30 to 40 per cent) out of the daily wage of Rs.10. Overall, nearly 45 to 50 per cent of wages earned were saved by migrants (see Table 12). The income from seasonal migration constituted about 57 per cent of the total annual income of the affected and 44 per cent of the income of non-affected households reporting migration.

The savings were utilised mostly to meet consumption needs during the lean period of employment, particularly during the monsoon. But the income so earned through migration was not at all adequate to make any substantial improvement in their levels of living. The amount was just not enough to be invested in any productive activity and therefore could not help them to raise their resource base so as to halt the annual routine of seasonal migration.

Summary and Conclusion

The submergence of villages resulting from the construction of the Panam Dam and the associated dislocation have resulted in a decline in the resource base of the affected households. Almost every household has experienced a decline in the size of landholding; the average size has declined from six acres to three acres after submergence and 86 per cent of the households (compared to 47 per cent in the past) now have less than four acres of land. There is also a decrease in ownership of livestock, agricultural implements and machinery after submergence. Further, the newly allotted land is not as productive as the submerged land. The cropping intensity of the new land was reported to be much lower than that of the submerged land.

The three factors, namely, the decrease in the size of operational holdings, productivity and cropping intensity, have forced the affected households to look for non-land based economic activities. More than three-fourths of the affected households in fact have supplemented land based income through casual employment; and in nearly fifty per cent of the affected landed households, casual work has emerged as the main source of livelihood. As casual work was not available throughout the year, at and near the resettlement sites, 42 per cent of the affected households out-migrated seasonally. The dislocation has raised the seasonal mobility among the affected households considerably. They mainly go to Kheda district for the crop harvest and to Vadodara and Ahmedabad cities for construction activities. An analysis of the determinants of the seasonal out-migration shows that a household of a larger family size, smaller size of holding, lower levels

Table 11 : Duration of Employment and Average Daily Wages of Migrant Workers by Occupation at the Place of Work

Occupation		1984-85				Past			
		Affected		Non-affected		Affected		Non-affected	
		M	F	M	F	M	F	M	F
Agricultural									
Labourer :	Mo	156	97	7	5	46	14	3	2
	Mi	110	68	4	3	35	11	2	1
	Av. D	119	115	143	140	102	136	105	150
	Av. W	8.9	8.6	9.6	8.9	4.2	3.8	5.0	3.0
Construction									
Labourer :	Mo	181	52	26	4	10	-	5	-
	Mi	142	42	19	3	10	-	3	-
	Av. D	143	132	99	70	74	-	110	-
	Av. W	11.3	9.4	12.7	10.9	6.2	-	7.0	-
Other									
Labourer :	Mo	24	-	2	-	7	4	-	-
	Mi	17	-	2	-	7	4	-	-
	Av. D	125	-	60	-	77	60	-	-
	Av. W	11.9	-	10.5	-	6.0	3.0	-	-

Table 11 : (Continued)

Occupation		1984-85				Past			
		Affected		Non-affected		Affected		Non-affected	
		M	F	M	F	M	F	M	F
Skilled Labourer :	Mo	13	-	1	-	1	-	-	-
	Mi	12	-	1	-	1	-	-	-
	Av. D	164	-	150	-	270	-	-	-
	Av. W	17.8	-	30.0	-	10.0	-	-	-
All	Mo	374	149	36	9	64	18	8	2
	Mi	253	94	26	6	51	15	5	1
	Av. D	148	122	105	105	100	116	108	150
	Av. W	10.9	9.0	12.9	9.5	5.0	3.7	6.2	3.0

Note : Mo - Moves, Mi - Migrants, Av. D - Average Number of Days of Employment, Av. W - Average Daily Wages (in Rs).

Table 12 : Income and Saving Through Seasonal Migration : 1984-85

Seasonal Income and Saving		Affected	Non-affected
Income :	Per household	3307	2573
	Per capita	406	314
	Per worker	1382	1206
	Percentage of total income from casual work	85.8	91.2
	Percentage of total income	56.8	44.5
Saving :	Per household	1496	1263
	Per capita	184	154
	Per worker	625	592.
	Percentage of seasonal income	45.2	49.1

Note : Income and Saving are shown in Rs.

of irrigation, cropping intensity and productivity, and non-availability of employment in the neighbouring area, is more likely to out-migrate seasonally than others.

Although the seasonal wage income constituted more than half of the total annual income of the majority of affected households, most of the households (60 per cent) seemed to be living below the poverty line. None of the affected households was covered under any poverty-alleviation programme. The forest land allotted by the Government has yet to be transferred to the land revenue department, which in turn would confer the land rights to the allottees until then, they are deprived of the credit from banks or assistance under the various IRDP schemes.

A lot remains to be done to improve the living and working conditions of seasonal migrants. First, these migrant labourers must be organized and it has to be seen that the Interstate Migrant Workmen (Regulation of Employment and Conditions of Service) Act of 1979 should be implemented properly.[7] The scope of ISMW Act should be enlarged to cover both inter-state migrant workers who come of their own rather than through a contractor, and intra-state migrant workers. The other alternative is to take effective measures to improve the socio-economic conditions of migrants at their places of origin. More resources should be diverted to rural backward areas through rural industrialization and industrial dispersal policies and rural development programmes. An effective implementation of the Jawahar Rozgar Yojana (in which at least one adult member gets full time employment) and the 'right to work' as a new employment strategy, would substantially help them to break the vicious circle of migrating season after season for livelihood.

Notes

1. We can cite here a few studies about crop-specific labour in-mobility in different regions at the time of crop harvest. These studies are: in Punjab - paddy and wheat (Chandan 1979; Singh and Iyer 1981 and 1984); West Godavari region in Andhra Pradesh - tobacco (Rao 1978); Shimoga district in Mysore - paddy and sugarcane (Katti 1966); Surat district in Gujarat - sugarcane (Breman 1985); and Kheda district in Gujarat - paddy and wheat (Bhatt 1979; Gandhi and Shah 1978; Jayaraman 1979).

2. As Katti (1966) has observed in Shimoga district (Mysore State), the first batch of migrant labourers arrived in June-July at the time of transplanting of paddy and went back the next month after the completion of work. In the Hirakud Project Command area, they used to make six visits a year at the time of transplanting, weeding, and harvesting during both kharif and rabi seasons (Rao and Sahu 1987).

3. Seven sites were created very near the reservoir in the partially affected villages, while the remaining 12 sites were created outside the affected area. Of the latter, six sites were near the district headquarters (an urban centre) and were linked with a highway; three were adjacent to the canal area; and the remaining three sites were created in the command area of the project and were linked with the national highway and broad gauge railway line.

4. They further commented that it was distressing that these families were going for employment to those farmers who had received the benefits of irrigation at their social and economic cost.

5. According to the Patel Committee Report (Government of Gujarat, 1984), Anand taluka tops among all talukas of Gujarat in terms of the development index.

6. Some of the respondents, when asked why they went out before the Diwali festival, replied with some frustration: 'Diwali for whom? When we do not have enough to eat, how can we celebrate Diwali?'

7. The Act was passed by the central government in 1979 to provide better working conditions to inter-state migrants. The Act applies to any and every establishment and contractor who employs five or more workers from other state(s). The Act made a provision for displacement allowance equal to 50 per cent of the monthly wages or Rs. 75 whichever is higher; a migrant labourer should also get journey allowance, suitable residential accommoda-

tion, medical facilities and payment of wages equal to those of wages paid to other local workers for the same work. Such wages under any circumstances should not be lower than the minimum wage. However, because of the non-cooperation of many states by not framing rules for the implementation, this Act has remained only on paper (for details see Joshi 1987).

References

Bhatt, A. *Study of Working and Living Environments of Seasonal Migrants*. Ahmedabad: The Gujarat Institute of Area Planning, 1979.

Breman, J. *Of Peasants, Migrants and Paupers: Rural Labour Circulation and Capitalist Production in West India.* Delhi: Oxford University Press, 1985.

Amarjit, Chandan. 'Punjab: Plight of Migrant Labour'. *Economic and Political Weekly*, 14, 17, 1979.

Das, A.N. Nilakant, V. and Dubey, P.S. (eds.). *The Worker and the Working Class: A Labour Studies Anthology.* New Delhi: Public Enterprises Centre for Continuing Education, 1984.

Desai, M.B. *The Rural Economy of Gujarat.* Cambridge: Oxford University Press, 1948.

Gandhi, R.D. and Shah, C.H. *Rural Seasonal Migration.* Ahmedabad: The Gujarat Institute of Area Planning, 1978.

Government of Gujarat. Bureau of Economics and Statistics. Final Report on the Survey of Seasonal Migration of Labour in Panchmahals District - 1971-72. *Quarterly Bulletin of Economics and Statistics* 14(1974): 1-25.

Government of Gujarat. *Report of the Socially and Educationally Backward Class Commission I and II.* Gandhinagar: Govt. Central Press, 1976.

Government of Gujarat. *Report of the Committee for the Development of Backward Areas I and II.* Gandhinagar: General Administration Department, 1976.

Gumber, Anil and Visaria, Pravin. *Inter-Village Differences in Social Overheads and Their Correlates in Matar Talvka.* New Delhi: Indian Council of Social Science Research, 1995.

Jayaraman, T.K. Seasonal Migration of Tribal Labour: An Irrigation Project in Gujarat. *Economic and Political Weekly* 24(1979): 1727-1732.

Joshi, V. (ed.). *Migrant Labour and Related Issues.* New Delhi: Oxford & IBH Publishing Co., 1987.

Katti, A.P. *Seasonal In-Migration in Rural Shimoga*. Dharwar: Demographic Research Centre, J.S.S. Institute of Economic Research, 1966.

Mankodi, K. and Gangopadhyay, T. *Rehabilitation, the Economic and Ecological Costs*. Surat: Centre for Social Studies, 1983.

Mehta, D.B. *Seasonal Migration of Labour: A Case of Dangs District* (a summary report). Ahmedabad: School of Planning, Centre for Environmental Planning and Technology, (n.d).

Patel. B.B. 'Seasonal Rural Migration Pattern and Some Alternatives for Effective Protection of Legal Rights of Migrant Labour.' In *Joshi, V. (ed.)*. 1987.

Pillai, S.D. and Baks, C. (eds.). *Winners and Losers*. Bombay: Popular Prakashan, 1979.

Rao, M.S.A. 'Tobacco Development and Labour Migration: Planning for Labour Welfare and Development'. *Economic and Political Weekly* 13, 29(1978): 1183-1186 .

Rao, N.B. and Sahu, M. K. 'Impact of Irrigation on Migration and Work Participation: A Case Study of An Irrigation Project in India.' *Demography India* 16, 1(1987): 90-108.

Shah, C.H. and Patel, B.V. 'Rural Migration: Its Nature and Implications - an Experience of Gujarat (India)'. *Indian Journal of Regional Science* 11(1979): 1-9.

Shah, C.H., Shah, V. and Iyengar, S. *Agricultural Growth and Equity: A Micro-Level Experience*. New Delhi: Concept Publishing Company, 1991.

Shah, Vimal and Shah, C.H. *Resurvey of Matar Taluka*. Bombay: Vora & Co., 1974.

Singh, M. and Iyer, K.G. 'Sweated Migrant Labour for Green Revolution'. *Voluntary Action*, Annual Number 24, 1(1981): 46-51.

Singh, M. and Iyer, K.G. *Migrant Labourer in Rural Punjab*. In Das, A.N. *et al. (eds.)* 1984.

Taniguchi, S., Yanagisawa, H., Shinoda, T. and Oshikawa, F. (eds.). *Economic Changes and Social Transformation in Modern and Contemporary South Asia*. Tokyo: Hitotsubashi University, 1994.

Van der Veen, Klass. *Urbanization, Irrigation and Primordial Attachments*. In Pillai, S.D. and Baks, C. *(eds.)*, 1979.

Visaria, Pravin and Gumber, Anil. *Level and Pattern of Work Participation by Scheduled Castes, Tribes and Others in Western India During the 1980s*. In Taniguchi, S. *et al. (eds.)*, 1994.

8

Urbanization, Development and Communalisation of Society in Gujarat

Sujata Patel

Introduction

The transition from agrarian to industrial societies has the world over inaugurated a period of rapid change and path-breaking developments. If on one hand there has been a slow and steady process towards material prosperity for larger and larger sections of the population, specially after the mid-twentieth century, these changes have been accompanied by misery for a good proportion of the population. Many have had to face extreme poverty and destitution, cope with continuous displacements and migrations, confront epidemics like plague, cholera and small pox, lose families, kin and communities, in addition to contending with changing political, cultural and social upheavals. The structure and pattern of their received identities have not only been interrogated through competing epistemic premises but have almost been destroyed.

The narratives that structure this history is one of protests and support, of adjustment and of confrontation, of resignation and of violence. This has been a common thread linking the stories of communities and cultures widely different, whether in Europe, North America, Australia and Japan or the countries of the South. And yet these narratives show a marked difference in the structure of experience between the North and the South. The difference between these two experiences are rooted not only in the distinctive received patterns of organization, institution and domination-subordination relationship of each region, but also in the historical moment that these became integrated in the process of the global transition and transformation process. The North went through this process earlier and has had some measure of success in controlling the misery of its population, specially after World War II. India and the rest of the South is going through this transition in the late twentieth century and finding it more and more difficult to provide material benefits for the large sections of its poor.

Evidence from the European experience indicates that growing urbanization accompanied by industrialization, together with the processes outlined above, inaugurated a period of violent confrontations and conflict in urban areas. Towns and cities became the site for the emergence of various kinds of protest. Riots and other forms of crowd behaviour reflected unease at the pace of changes and a protest against the near destruction of earlier forms of relationships.

Two significant features distinguished the nature of collective violence in Europe during the initial period of transition and transformation, in the eighteenth and in nineteenth centuries. The first draws our attention to the nature of riots. To a large extent these riots were food riots and represented a collective response of the poor against the state. In the second instance, as some historians have shown, crowd behaviour and collective intervention in the later nineteenth and twentieth centuries concretized to become social movements and specially took the form of the trade union movements. Historians have termed this collective behaviour as initial forms of class organizations representing class interests. (Tilly 1987).

If we compare the European experience with the Indian one, we see many differences. These differences can be evaluated in context to the two phases of the transition process in India, colonial and post-colonial. In both these phases, urban sites became the arena of articulating protest. There is however a difference between the nature and form of protest in these two phases, as the nature of state-society dynamics was different. The state ruled over society through coercion in the colonial period. Thus the protest vocalized in urban areas articulated nationalist aspirations and later became organized to form what we term today as the nationalist movement.[1]

The first two decades in the post-colonial period were decades of relative peace and tranquillity. However after the seventies, once again urban areas exploded with protest against the state. In the late sixties and seventies the cities of India were taken over by protesters demanding more political power, questioning increase in prices and demanding equal distribution of resources. Since the eighties while these problems have remained in the forefront, the nature and form of collective violence have changed. The eighties and nineties have been periods of communal riots. Almost all the big towns and cities of the country have increasingly become communalized and have been caught in communal conflict. This is also true of Gujarat. This paper examines the riots of the eighties in order to understand its roots in contemporary society. It specifically tries to evaluate the form of rioting : communal, and attempts to assess its implications on the transitions and transformation process in Gujarat.

Since 1969, Gujarat state has been caught in the communal conundrum. In 1969 itself, there were 650 deaths due to communal tensions. In the last ten years deaths through communal violence have been increasing. Three urban centres have become prone to communal violence. These are Ahmedabad, Baroda and Godhra, all three in Central Gujarat. Between 1960 and 1993 Ahmedabad had 43 incidents of communal rioting causing deaths of nearly 1100. Baroda had 29 incidents. In 1992 after the demolition of the Babri Masjid, 12 towns and cities erupted in rioting causing 300 deaths. (Varshney and Wilkinson 1995 : 80-82). It is recognized that Gujarat is one of the states most endemic to communal riots. Why? What is the connection between these riots and the transition and transformation process? What does it tells us of the future of the transition and transformation process?

By now we have an extensive literature on riots and specifically communal riots[2]. This literature points to the crisis of the polity and its legitimacy, that has overtaken the Indian State after the sixties. If this is the reason we have to understand why the crisis took place and what its specific features were in Gujarat. But why was there an attempt to resolve this crisis through the communal card? To put it in other words, how were the communal riots reflecting the ideological crisis of the system? Also, why were only some cities embroiled in this communal process? What are the problems of specific urban and local character that has become entangled in these riots?

This paper is an evaluation of the transition and transformation process as seen through the political economy of the riots at three separate levels. For, each level has a specificity that is important to understand in a discussion of the transition dynamics. These three levels are the local, that is, related only to the city; the regional that of the state of Gujarat; and the country. I am arguing that while the structural process of transition affected all three, and thus they are interrelated, the particular manifestations are different. These manifestations have a cumulative effect which then defines the way in which state-society relationship gets expressed subsequently.

I am concentrating my analysis on the urban economic convulsions of the eighties and nineties in order to understand how these have combined with the political crisis of state-society relationship in the country and the Gujarat state. I will be arguing that this crisis led to the articulation of a communalized identity in the city and the state. Part 1 of this paper will examine the crisis of structure accompanied by the breakdown of an ideology defining domination-subordination relationships, faced by the nation-state from the seventies onwards. Part 2 will concentrate on a case, that of Ahmedabad, to understand the urban political-economic processes, the nature of the civil society and its interconnection with communal forces. Part 3 is the conclusion.

1

The period from the late sixties and early seventies to the emergency was a critical period for the economy. The growth of the national income decelerated, the rate of investment dropped, the value of the rupee started falling, there were two years of drought followed by recession with little or no foreign aid. This period was also accompanied by significant changes in the political process. Most analysts have concentrated their attention on the political system, specifically the breakdown of the Congress organization and its impact on the received democratic structures that were institutionalized in the country. I am arguing that this political crisis was part of the economic crisis. In this period which leads to the Emergency, we see the first challenges to the state, and the questioning of existing structure of relationships institutionalized after independence with state showing its inability to reorganize the faction ridden ruling classes to come to a collective ideological and hegemonic agenda[3].

As has been pointed out by various scholars, when the British left, a particular structure of relationship was institutionalized through a hegemonic ideology; this ideology setting the terms of the relationship between the ruling classes, that of them with the state, between the labouring poor and them. However the productive forces that were unleashed from the sixties came to clash with this received structure. Specially, the jump taken through Green Revolution led to a collision of interests on the one hand, between the various factions of the ruling classes and between them and the labouring poor. The state found it extremely difficult to mediate between the ruling classes and the labouring poor and the latter. Class conflicts ensued.

Simultaneously there were changes in the interests and demands of the the industrial capitalist class. In the most colonial period, this class had initiated import substitution and thereby displaced and then attempted to control the imperialist manufacture of traditional consumer goods. However, soon afterwards their aspirations changed. From the fifties they started sponsoring manufacture of capital intensive goods. The state which was earlier adjoined to invest in infrastructure was now asked to make available finance, and broker with foreign finance. The sixties was the period when we saw protests against growing state intervention in industry. It is now that voices for privatisation get articulated. The conflict that emerges in the sixties between the industrial capitalist class and the state is related to ideology with the capitalist class interrogating the social welfare policies of the state which protected the workers.

The green revolution had produced the rich peasantry and in some cases had made the landlords richer. Becoming dissatisfied at their lack of political significance, they started mobilizing various sections of the peasantry as well trader and agriculture based entrepreneurs to enter the arena of politics through peasant and later farmer organizations. Their political confidence was not rooted merely in the change in terms of trade between industry and agriculture, now biased towards agriculture, but was also a reflection of their strength as players on the growing market of consumer goods. Their aspirations were different than the industrial capitalist class. They wanted state subsidies for growth in agriculture, and organization of industry, to cater to the demands of their class as consumers.

This class has continued to grow and their expansion in size and strength over a period of time has been such, that today it brokers to a large extent, the political alignments in contemporary politics. In Gujarat, this process of new class formation is reflected in the growth of the rich peasantry in Saurashtra, who drew their economic strength from the production of commercial crops specially peanuts, and who since the late sixties are playing a major role in the state's politics.

The seventies inaugurated a period of crisis in the state. The stringent questioning of the state by both the industrial capitalist class and the emerging class of rich peasantry led to the rapid decay of its legitimacy. The labouring classes on the other hand started organizing themselves against rising prices and these protests marked the first few years of the seventies. The breakdown of ideology connecting the classes with the state also led to protests from various middle-class groups. In Bihar and Gujarat, there was a growth in the student movement. With more and more clamour set up by various sections of the middle class for a say in the system and the dissatisfaction of the section of the ruling classes, the regime of Indira Gandhi felt threatened. There was a demand for intensifying the domination of the state structure and increase in its power. The split in the Congress and the emergency was the result.

Despite the disaffection of the industrial propertied classes in the early seventies, they still backed Indira Gandhi's Congress. On the other hand the masses deserted the Congress during and after the emergency. The Congress had to evolve a way to get lower class support without displacing upper class interests. Emergency had been one answer but that did not prove successful. After the emergency, more militant struggles started. It is at that time that the Indira Gandhi regime started using the religious card. For, by then the Jan Sangh later known as Bharatiya Janata Party (BJP) had already started becoming popular by mobilizing the populace on religious grounds. The Congress wanting to eliminate a political threat from a rightist party and build a new hegemonic ideology, started evolving a strategy to use religion to mobilize the masses from the BJP.

In Gujarat the situation was a bit different. In the fifties and sixties, the Congress leaders were mainly drawn from the upper castes. They were Brahmins, Patidars from Central Gujarat, the upper sections of the Rajputs and Banias. Their hegemony was initially questioned by the slow mobilization of the Kshatriya block in the fifties. The second challenge to the upper caste Congress came from the peasantry of Saurashtra, as mentioned earlier. The third challenge came from the lower sections of the society, specially after the constitution of the Dalit Panther organization which was mobilizing the *dalits*. With the split of the Congress in 1969, the upper castes moved towards Congress (O). In these circumstances the Congress in Gujarat had to perfect a strategy of mobilization that mobilized the lower sections of society without incorporating the upper castes. The gress attempted to form a block of the largest section of population in the State : Kshatriyas, Harijans, Adivasis and the Muslims. (known popularly as KHAM). Also, recognizing that the Kshatriyas were the largest single caste alike group in the state and that it needed to appease them, it accepted their long term demand to extend reservation to its community.[4]

The construction of this block of mainly those who were poor, backward and deprived, not in class terms, but through caste grouping created its own problems for the regime. Those who were in power and who had supported the Congress earlier and on whose behalf the Government governed were now not part of the ruling groups of the regime. The power of the upper sections of society was based on the control of not only capital and land but also educational institutions and cultural organizations. In fact educational institutions had become the means through which the ruling group was extending its power base and consolidating its class and caste interests. The possible opening up of this critical institution to the backward classes through reservation, spelled disaster for the long-term interests of this group. Their political reaction was to move towards the Janata Party initially and later towards the BJP.

The Indira Gandhi regime thus faced a leadership crisis and its solution was equally swift. It realized that it needed to compete with the BJP in North India and the Janata Party in Gujarat on its own terms. Henceforth the Congress party started using communal politics in a conscious manner to offset the influence of the BJP and draw the upper castes to its influence. This strategy started off by being played out in a hesitant manner from the early seventies and was consolidated by the mid and late seventies, specially after the emergency.

The Indira Gandhi regime tried to fulfil two political tasks together. One was to hegemonize the backward who constituted sixty to seventy per cent of the population (whose votes it needed to remain in power). The second was to retain the membership of the upper castes by articulating a self conscious communal position. It hoped thereby to counter the growing influence of BJP. For some years, the Congress straddled both these positions and thereby attempted to consolidate a large political constituency. But the inherent contradictions between these two strategies made it impossible to represent both together[5].

The events of 1985 in Gujarat indicate the nature of problems that occur when reservation and communalism together become part of state strategies. The Congress won the 1985 elections overwhelmingly. Nearly 85% of the assembly seats were won by members of the lower classes after it had declared that it was extending reservation quota for the backward. The upper castes' wrath knew no bounds. They took over the streets. From the Janata Party which was by then defunct, they shifted their alliance to the BJP. With the simultaneous alienation of the upper caste bureaucracy as also of the upper caste leaders who controlled institutions in the civil society, a legitimacy crisis occurred for the recently elected Government. In this critical situation, a local communal conflict was allowed to surface. The Congress party in this situation could not protect the Muslims and had to compete for upper caste support. The violence thus got escalated and continued for a year until a political compromise was reached. Not only did the Chief Minister lose his job, but the Congress had to accede to the demand that all key ministers should be controlled by the upper castes. This political compromise resolved the immediate crisis but these events left their impact on the politics of the state and of the party.

Henceforth communalized politics dictated the resolution of the city's social and political problems. This violence by creating distances and distrust between the two communities legitimized the isolation of the Muslim community and the consolidation of the Hindu block. It institutionalized communal discourse and thereby made it the politics of the state. The city's history is now being officially re-written in communal categories. When the BJP won the Municipal elections soon after the riots, it changed the name of the city to Karnawati. There were no protests recorded at this change in name. The liberal centre of the state had collapsed and shifted to the right.

2

Why was Ahmedabad city most affected by the communal riots? What were the features specific to the city in its economy and social and cultural organization that act to allow communal politics to redefine the state-society relationship in the city? It is my argument that the growing communalized politics appropriated the discontent emerging as a result of the structural changes occurring in the city, both in the terms of its production system and the urban society. These changes led to the breakdown of the existing structure of governance in the city with new and competing centres of power emerging. In this context the shift of ideological ground towards communal politics by the mainstream parities led to the communalisation of the city, reinforcing divisions based on religion. Almost all tensions whether local or regional, whether between kin groups or *jati* attracted communal flavour. This further gave a fillip to communal politics and the making of communal identities.

What were the specific features in the city, its conflicts, that encouraged and gave space to communal elements? How were they related to political economy and social cultural reorganization of groups in the city?

Most of the violence has taken place in the city and still continues to take place in the walled city. The violence manifests itself as confrontations between two communities fighting for territorial space. Any analysis on communal riots will have to ask questions regarding the process that led to space getting converted to territory, that is how space power and community identity have been constructed historically in the city and how they have and are getting reproduced in the contemporary context through urban development policies and through the growth of productive forces.

Secondly, this violence has mobilized anti-social groups in the city. We have to ask the question as to how this group has grown and found a legitimacy in the city. What kind of economic changes have led to their growth? How are they organized, what is their influence in the city and how are they related to the state structure specifically and the political process generally?

Thirdly, these changes have occurred in context with the changes in the structure of industry. Ahmedabad was known as the Manchester of India. It was producing cloth for the domestic market. Nearly 80% of the workers in the city were employed by the textile industry. This paper asks what have been the changes in the industry, what new industries have developed, how has the structure of work force changed and how has that affected the standard of living and nature of survival in the city[6].

The walled city of Ahmedabad was established by King Ahmed Shah in A.D. 1411 with the aim to establish it as a production centre. To this end he encouraged the settlements of various artisans mainly but not merely related to the textile industry. As skill, occupation and group identity are defined through membership of caste (this includes the Muslim castes also) in pre-capitalist Indian society, the settlements that were established in various sections of the city in the different 'pols' were caste based settlements.[7] The history of space-defined caste identity lies in the specific features of the walled city growth in the medieval period. However, a continuation of such dynamics lies in the way contemporary productive processes have shaped this given notion and incorporated it in defining both boundary maintenance and relationships.

Since the mid-nineteenth century when the city took up a dynamic economic role, the specific spatial contours of the city have been expanding. The textile mills were set up on the east of the walled city with workers' housing being constructed in the east, close to the factories. The growth of the middle classes led to further changes. There was a mobility among the upper castes, specially the banias, both Hindus and Jains and other upper castes who used education as a means to enter the modern structures that colonialism was creating. With their mobility, one section of these castes moved out of the walled city. This process was not caste, class or religion-neutral. The Muslims did not prosper and their space remained restricted to the walled city.

The decades of the thirties and forties of the twentieth century saw the setting up of new bungalow-housing societies for the mobile upper caste groups on the west side of the river Sabarmati. This trend increased after Independence when the western spaces of the city were populated with upper classes and upper caste community based housing societies. The 'pol' culture outlined earlier continued in new forms in these housing colonies[8]. In the walled city upper castes migrants from lower classes took over the empty 'pols' left by the migrating upper castes mobile groups. The tensions in the walled city arose from conflict between the old Muslim settlements and the new entrants in the Hindu 'pols'.

The competition and control of space was never a problem in the city till the late sixties and the seventies. The expansion of the fifties and sixties westwards was regularized through the various town-planning schemes. However, the problems started after the sixties. There was an expansion of the destitute population in the city fleeing agrarian areas as a result of changes occurring there, outlined earlier. Simultaneously, the textile industry, the main industry of the city which had sustained the major proportion of the population had been able to ward off till then, and overcome the cyclical crisis that any industry normally faces. However, after the seventies its fortunes changed. The industry could not only expand but started laying off workers. The tensions that the city saw in the period between 1985-86 relates to this development.

The late sixties saw a major change in the structure of the city's economy[9]. The successful corporate groups of the city had since the forties, diversified into other areas, initially dyes and textile machinery, but moved into capital intensive manufacturing. This new economic investment was spatially located outside the city. Therefore it did not benefit the city's labouring poor. Also, the majority of the textile mills were facing an economic and financial crisis. Having not increased its capital structure it could not modernize and thus went into economic decline. This trend became evident from late fifties, but increased after the Korean war, and when the Ahmedabad textile mills started facing enormous competition. The result was displacement of workers from the industry and their inclusion in the burgeoning 'informal sector' of the city.

Most economists agree that existing statistics do not give a fair idea of the changing contours of the non-organized sector in India. And yet economists have had to use existing statistics to understand this phenomenon for it has come to play a very significant economic role. For Ahmedabad, Meera Mehta's work comparing the census records with the data of the Factories Commission gives us an idea of the importance of this sector in the city's economy.

Examining the changes in the male work force she argues that there is a general decline in their participation in the secondary sector and the increase in their participation in the tertiary sector. The growth of the tertiary sector has been mainly in the activities of trade, commerce and transport. Specifically the census data show a striking decline in the proportion of workers in the manufacturing activities. She concludes that in terms of the earning opportunities of workers in Ahmedabad, there has probably been a decline over the last two decades. On the other hand the share of domestic activities in the service sector has increased. In sheer numbers there is a phenomenal increase in the professional services, including lawyers, teachers and Government employees as a proportion of clerical and worker staff.

On the basis of her analysis, Mehta draws an interesting profile of the changes in the city. She suggests that on one hand, jobs in education have increased. So have domestic services requiring little or no education and services like trade and transport where skill is not needed but initial investment is necessary. On the other hand, there is a general decline in the manufacturing sector specially in the textile industry. The Annual Survey of Industries data for 1960-69 is quoted to show that while capital and output rose, work force declined by

13.9%. On the other hand, there has been an increase of manufacturing in the small scale units which may not employ many labourers, specially in engineering and chemical industries. Most of the latter have little or no unionization and therefore in most cases minimum wages are not being implemented, nor are other social welfare services given.

Qualitative evidence of this secular trend is available in an analysis that investigates the casualisation of the work force in the textile industry. At one time Ahmedabad had 60 mills with 150,000 workers. Over the years the workers started being displaced and by the early 1970s, 10% of the workers had become casualised. Presently recruitment is only on a casual or contract basis. In addition 17 out of 60 mills in the city closed down in 1985. Nearly 40,000 workers had to find alternate employment. This displacement affected nearly 1.20 lakh of the 27 lakh population of the city. A survey conducted by the Gandhi Labour Institute of about 5000 displaced employees who were given aid and alternative employment by the Government showed that even where efforts were made to rehabilitate workers, there was a decline in their daily wages.

These developments led to some very significant changes in living conditions of the workers. There was an increase in the proportion of workers in the non-organized sector of the economy. This sector is mostly unregulated, does not provide for secure and long-term working life, gives little or no benefits through social security, including housing which was earlier provided by the textile industry. It promotes a class which remains unstable in terms of working life and is thereby displaced from the economic organization of the city. Their lack of continuous integration in the specific labour process and in the discipline of this process makes them vulnerable. The economy does not seem to give them a specific status in the society and they remain economically un-integrated role in the social structure. In this context if they become organized in non-class movements they come to play a very destructive role[10].

In Ahmedabad this economic process coincided with the decline in the influence of trade unionism. Simultaneously, the workers started being organized by the various sections of the rightist organizations, the Vishwa Hindu Parishad, the Bajrang Dal and the Hanuman Sena. Also economy organizes the smuggling of alcohol both Indian-made foreign liquor and country liquor, drugs and silver smuggling.[11] From the mid-eighties it has been also involved in the smuggling of guns.

It is difficult to assess the role that this illegal economy plays in the city's daily life, but certainly the political linkages it builds gives it and those who benefit from it a significant role in the city's politics. The official government report (Miyabhoy Commission Report) exploring these activities attests to the role that this group plays in society. It also records that the wealth it has made for itself through illegal means has been invested to build a legitimate space for itself in the society. Thus this group has sponsored educational, religious and cultural organizations. This group contributed extensively in the festivals held in the city creating enormous goodwill for themselves. The Commission points out to the linkages that this group has built with the police hierarchy while it attests to the fact that a section of the police force gets a commission for allowing the group to continue these economic activities.

The trade of bootlegging got a fillip in the seventies. From then on, the bigger among the bootleggers diverted to silver smuggling and drug smuggling. While it is difficult to judge the impact of this economy, certainly it intervened in the circulation of money in the city's economy and has bred a lumpen culture in the context of declining real wages. Also the nexus that it established directly with the police and politicians makes this group a dangerous group having its own mechanism of influence[12].

3

In the sixties the Municipality was ruled by the Communist party whose union had a significant base in the textile industry. The institutionalized mechanism of redress and negotiated settlements that defined the distribution of power and resources between various classes in the society slowly eroded. From the seventies onwards this structure was no longer in place.

The economic changes that the seventies inaugurated has a severe negative impact on the workers' lives. These changes not only destroyed their hopes but increasingly they realized that their voice was not finding either expression nor articulation. The old elite was displaced by a new one who had no interest in the labouring poor. The city's power had shifted into the hands of the fly-by-night operators who made money through illegal activities or in the land market. Simultaneously there was growing mobilization on religious issues and a competition between the Congress and the BJP. to gain acceptance from the upper castes. The political system has lost its power to reign and control any group. In this context of breakdown of legitimacy, local tensions between communities were not only allowed to emerge, but no effort was made to stop them from growing. The inevitable happened. Riots followed.

Between March and July of 1985, there were 178 deaths and 669 were injured. Most of the dead were from the Muslim community. There was complete breakdown of law and order and there were as many as 30 recorded cases of private firing in the same period. There were 50 bomb explosions between May and July 1985. Police records suggest that arson and looting affected 561 houses and shops in the city. Fire brigade records give an estimate of about 2000 private properties being damaged. In terms of money value, the damage was to the extent of 855 lakhs.

These riots left the minorities vulnerable, isolated and forced to accept ghettoization. Much more disturbing has been the shift of development discourse towards the right. The increasing divisions in the city between the poor and the rich was no longer considered worthy of discussion. Nor was it important to frame the policies on urban development in terms of the benefits for the poor[13]. Urban poverty, its problems and ways for its eradication was not part of the agenda. Market philosophy seems to have overtaken commitment to development.

This paper has attempted to show how the collapse of a received hegemonic ideology that integrated the needs of the labouring poor has created a vacuum which the communal ideology attempted to bridge. The latter's attempts to build hegemonic ideology on the discourse of religion cannot provide programmes and policies that reintegrate the concerns that the poor have and through the problem of survival that they face today. A mobilization through religion can only deflect issues.

It is clear that what is needed at this moment is another ideology that can regroup the various sections of society in a transformative process. At this moment this does not seem to be on the horizon. Till this happens we will see merely changes, a transition from one key to another without any transformation of the structure.

Notes

1. This is not to imply that were not other kinds of collective organization and violence that did not get submerged into nationalism. There were For instance, historical evidence suggests an increase of religious tensions and communal riots from the 1930s onwards culminating in the partition riots. However, it is important to note that these were soon eclipsed and dominated by another form, that of nationalist organization. The dominant form was to mould the state-society conflict in terms of nationhood and against colonial and imperial control. In the later phase, that is the post-colonial phase, the story is somewhat different.

2. Communalisation and communal tensions are part of an all-India trend. While its immediate roots can be located in the economic crisis of the eighties combined with the political-ideological process as well as the specific events of the late eighties and early nineties, its long-term historical roots lie in the tangled web that interface religious and national identity in this country. The events of the contemporary decades, the Shah Bano controversy, the Shilanayaas movement, the Mandir-Masjid issue and the effects of the communalization of the state apparatus, the growth of communal parties and specially the spread of the Bharatiya Janata Party, the avowedly Hindu right party and the various organizations supporting growth of communal tensions included under the umbrella coalition of VHP, have all contributed to the making of communal identities which in turn have fed the growth of communal tensions.

3. The arguments used in this section have been drawn from, KB 1985, Sathyamurthy 1985, Baru 1995, and Srivastava 1995.

4. Till 1978, Gujarat had 21% reservation. After accepting reservation for Kshatriyas, reservation increased by 10%.

5. A more detailed exposition of such politics is done in the author's paper, on the Discourse of Communalism 1996.

6. The data put together in this section is from an unpublished manuscript entitled 'The Making of Riots. Ahmedabad 1985-86'.

7. The social and economic life of the caste was regulated within each *pol* through the *panch*. The latter would judicate all disputes both economic and social. The *pol* developed as a spatial formation which incorporated economic, social, cultural and religious functions within its territory by alter medieval period. A study of the *pols* in the mid-twentieth century shows that the *pols* continued to remain the fulcrum of community life in the nineteenth and twentieth centuries. They started taking over new roles. Political mobilization was done through the *pols*. If the leader of the community accepted a

candidate the whole *pol* voted for that candidate. All cultural activities were organized through the *pol* and competition was organized between *pols.*

8. The economic changes created a new sub-strata, a class among the caste which established a spatial settlement in a different space but continued to maintain social cultural and religious ties with the *pol* community.

9. The first major communal riot took place in 1969.

10. This has happened particularly in Bombay where the Shiv Sena has organized the workers.

11. In Ahmedabad this economy had developed a significance presence. In an interview conducted in mid-1985, the additional police Commissioner suggested that this trade generated a turnover of Rs. 15 lakh a day for a big businessman and an average turnover of Rs. 45 lakhs a month for all. (1985 price level).

12. Almost all localities have at least one liquor den. Some localities have 4 to 5. This is where old and young gather to form opinions and establish inter-relationships. Rooms for gambling are set aside. these *'addas'* have replaced street corner discussion groups.

A illicit liquor 'baron' usually retain a number of helpers to conduct his business, some of whom act as 'protectors'. A network of solicitors, retailers and insiders get formalized. Two groups are intrinsic to this trade: panwala and auto rickshaw wallas. While the first acts as a street-corner retailer the other acts as a courier. Youth, specially those that are unemployed gravitate to this activity as wages are extremely high. It gives excitement and is simultaneously a symbol of protest against the society and the frustrations that it breeds.

The anti-socials are also part-time owners of tea stalls. The liquor barons divide the territory amongst themselves and it is a tightly-controlled structure at the top. These top barons induct into territories, individuals who operate from smaller territories. These territories are divided between the top barons and protected by them. The youth hanging around at panwalas and employed in various ways in the trade become protectors of this locality, recreating the link between space, territory and community.

13. The implication of these changes in the discourse is the following: The state's economy was growing at a faster rate than the country's, with an annual average compound rate of SDP at 3.32 in 1960s and 4.69 in 1970s as against all India average of 3.19 and 4.37 respectively. However, in the 1980s, it has declined to 4.37 against the India average of 5.16. The same trend continues in the early years of the nineties. Indira Hirway suggests that this decline has many reasons including drought, crisis in the textile industry as also the riots that have broken out in many urban areas. (Hirway, 1995:2603)

References

K. B. 'Indira Gandhi: An Attempt at Political Appraisal'. *Economic and Political Weekly* (23 March, 1985).

Baru, S. 'Continuity and Change in Indian Industrial Policy', in T.C. Sathyamurthy (ed.). *Industry and Agriculture, 2, Social Change and Political Discourse in India. Structures of Power, Movements of Resistance.* New Delhi: Oxford University Press, 1995.

Hirway, I. 'Selective Development and Widening Disparities in Gujarat'. *Economic and Political Weekly* 30, 41, and 42, (October 14-21, 1995.)

Patel, S. The Making of Communal Riots. (manuscript) Ahmedabad: 1985.

Patel, S. on 'The Discourse of Communalism, Region, Religions, Caste, Gender and Culture in Contemporary India'. 3, *Social Change in India, Structures of Power, Moments of Resistance.* Delhi: Oxford University Press, 1996.

Srivastava, R. 'India's Uneven Development and its Implications for Political Process. An Analysis of Some Recent Trends' in T.V. Sathyamurthi. 1995, op. cit.

Varshney, A. and Wilkinson, S. 'Hindu Muslim Riots in India. What We Know and What We do not Know'. *Towards a Secular India* 4 (October-December 1995): 34-83

Sathyamurthy, T.V. 'Piloting the Nation into the Twentieth Century. Changing Political Context of State Power and Class Contradictions in India'. *Economic and Political Weekly* (July 20, 1985).

Tilly, C. *Repertoires of Action.* Cambridge: Cambridge University Press, 1987.

9

Factory Workers and Their Mobility in Ahmedabad City

Junko Kiso

One of the important ways for the poor in developing countries such as India to overcome their poverty and be upwardly mobile on the socio-economic scale, is to get a job in the organized sector where the workers are generally considered to be relatively well organized, legally protected, and enjoying better labour conditions. However, only a small section of the labour population has been able to enter this sector. In 1991, the total number of workers in India was around 280 million, of which only less than ten per cent were working in the organized sector and only about three per cent were in the organized factory sector. Conversely, this means that fairly large segments of the workers have been, in spite of their desire to enter the organized sector, deprived of an opportunity to do so.

The objectives of the present paper are as follows. The first objective is to explore the characteristics of the workers who were lucky enough to enter the organized factory sector. It is generally accepted that the bulk of factory workers, during the early years of industrialization, consisted of severely depressed peoples _ marginal farmers, landless agricultural labourers, ruined artisans, widows, etc., many of whom came from lower caste groups or were 'untouchables'. Whereas, at present, what are the personal characteristics of the people working in the factories? Who is allocated to which job in the factories?

The second objective is to analyse the recruitment/job access process through which, entrants are differentiated from non-entrants. It is well known that, from the earlier stages of industrialization until Independence in India, middlemen, owing to the shortage of labour in factories and workers' aversion to factory jobs, played a significant role in the recruitment process. This led to the uneven distribution of information about job vacancies, consequently tending to restrict factory employment opportunities to particular people. However, even now, being 'closed' or imperfectly competitive is presumed to be a feature of the factory labour market characterized by excess supply of labour, although the information channels and recruitment procedures are not the same as the earlier ones.

The third objective is to examine the real conditions of external mobility, namely, job changes between factories and/or between industries. Analysis will assess how and to what extent the job changes have actually secured upward socio-economic mobility for the mobile workers.

In connection with these objectives, it may be helpful to briefly introduce results of some earlier studies briefly before moving on to the main subject.

Lambert's (1963) sample survey of workers of five factories in Poona was conducted in 1957. Based on this survey, he analysed the extent of internal mobility, the previous occupational histories of the workers, and the means by which they secured their current jobs. Regarding the first question, a fairly low rate of internal mobility was pointed out. Further he argued that the use of formal channels for securing a job still run a poor second to influence (*Vashila*) which is regarded as an informal channel. Papola and Subrahmanian(1975), based on a sample survey of factories and factory workers which was conducted in Ahmedabad from 1971 to 1972, analysed the labour market and, therefore, made wage structure and labour mobility as the central theme of their study. They concluded that the processes of recruitment in the Ahmedabad labour market showed a characteristic akin to the 'close-shop' system. In addition, a poorly developed promotion system and relatively low extent of external mobility were also pointed out. Purohit's (1989) sample survey of factory workers was conducted in three major industrial centres of economically backward Bharuch district, Gujarat, in 1983. He analysed the mobility of workers across occupations, units, industries, and regions and job information channelling and recruitment practices. The analysis revealed the absence of a well-developed internal labour market, heavy reliance on informal information sources and recruitment practices, and the working of competitive market forces more dominantly in small size units and for low level skill jobs. Harriss, Kannan and Rodgers (1990) have also reported many interesting findings. Based on a survey which was carried out in Coimbatore in 1987, covering not only factory workers but also other types of workers, they analysed the labour market based on models of labour market stratification and segmentation. They concluded that the dominant mechanism in the Coimbatore labour market was that of 'particularism' and its role was stronger in the first job. Labour market stratification and segmentation operated right from the initial entry into the labour market, rather than by a process of 'filtering' after entry. The finding is that mobility is very low both in the short run and over the work history as a whole. Their study is characterized by its methodology, in that they used a labour status approach based on the employment characteristics of workers in the analysis in order to understand the structuring of the urban labour market. The paper by Deshpande and Deshpande (1990) reports the findings of a survey of workers of the manufacturing sector which ARTEP/ILO conducted in Bombay during the first quarter of 1989. This is also a study of labour mobility within and between firms and between industries. They attempted to compare and contrast the extent of mobility by sex.

Thus, various studies have been concerned with the analysis of the Indian labour market, particularly of the factory labour market, from the viewpoint of mobility. However, what does not seem to be presented sufficiently in most of them is an analytical study as who the workers are. Therefore, in the present paper, I shall analyse as to who the entrants are and who are more mobile, giving attention to personal factors such as caste, and ascertain whether labour mobility leads to socio-economic upward mobility for the workers. In other words, what I wish to grasp is whether the factory labour market is functioning as a base for the transformation of society or not.

Methods of the Survey

I conducted field research for five weeks in August and September 1991 in Ahmedabad. In 1981, although Ahmedabad city covered only 1.1 per cent of the area, it accounted for 53 per cent of the total population of Ahmedabad district. The population grew to 2.38 million in 1986 when the area of the city increased more than twice, by the merger of the eastern industrial areas. In 1991, Ahmedabad, whose population had reached 3.30 million, was the largest city in Gujarat and the seventh largest city in India.

Table 1 gives the industrial composition of main workers in Ahmedabad city in 1991. The important industries are manufacturing, processing, servicing and repairing (38 per cent), trade and commerce (25 per cent), and other services (21 per cent). Ahmedabad is clearly an industrial and trading city. The number of working registered factories in the city increased rapidly in the 1960s and 1970s. However, the number of factories decreased after reaching 2,320 units in 1983 and the number of workers also decreased after reaching a peak of 1.86 lakhs in 1982 (AMC, 1990). This decreasing tendency was partly brought about by the excessive concentration of factories inside the city and consequent policies to restrain industrial investment in the city. But the number of factories continued to increase in surrounding areas. This means that the marginalization and relocation of factories has proceeded in these areas. To quote some figures, the number of factory workers decreased by 19 per cent inside the city and increased by 74 per cent outside from 1977 through 1986 (Kashyap 1988 : Table 5). As a result, while more than half of registered factories were still located inside Ahmedabad city, the remainder were located outside in 1985 (Directorate of Economics and Statistics 1987 : 273).

The decrease in the number of the factory workers in the city could also be attributed to a significant extent to the closure of many cotton textile mills since 1982. Ahmedabad city is an old cotton textile centre[1] but it is said that the closure expelled more than 50000 textile workers from the cotton mills by the end of 1984 (Patel 1988 : V; Kashyap 1988:18).

As Table 2 shows, the cotton textile industry still occupies a significant place in the city's industrial economy. It accounts for 21 per cent of the registered factories and 74 per cent of their workers in 1986. Machinery, machine tools and parts, basic metal and alloys industries, metal products and parts, chemicals and chemical products, etc., form the other relatively important industries in the city.

From these main industries, I selected three types of industries for my survey: textiles, engineering and chemicals. Each industry included one each of different sizes of registered factories: large factories (employing 100 or more workers directly) and small factories (employing less than 100 directly). I visited a total of thirteen private factories, which were introduced to me mainly by the office of the Chief

Table 1 : Main Workers Classified by Industry in Ahmedabad City, 1991

Industry	Number of workers	
Agriculture		
Cultivators	3,589	(0.4)
Agricultural labourers	2,755	(0.3)
Livestock, forestry, fishing and hunting	5,740	(0.7)
Mining and quarrying	2,085	(0.2)
Manufacturing, processing, servicing and repairing		
Household industry	6,811	(0.8)
Other than household industry	318,352	(37.2)
Construction	38,966	(4.6)
Trade and commerce	215,950	(25.3)
Transport, storage and communications	77,636	(9.1)
Other services	182,817	(21.4)
Total	**854,701**	**(100.0)**

Note : Figures in parentheses show the component ratios.

Source : Govt.of India, Census of India 1991, *Series-7 Gujarat, Primary Census Abstract,* Gujarat, 1991.

Table 2 : Number of Working Factories and Workers Employed Daily by Industry in Ahmedabad City, 1986

Industry group	No. of factories		No. of workers	
Cotton textiles	452	(20.8)	102,873	(73.6)
Textile production (including apparel other than footwear)	80	(3.7)	1,839	(1.3)
Wood and wood products	167	(7.7)	1,742	(1.2)
Paper and paper products and printing.	145	(6.7)	3,561	(2.5)
Chemicals and chemical products (except petroleum and coal products)	171	(7.9)	2,663	(1.9)
Basic metal and alloys industries	208	(9.6)	4,140	(3.0)
Metal products and parts	181	(8.3)	2.262	(1.6)
Machinery, machine tools and parts (except electrical machinery)	417	(19.2)	7,453	(5.3)
Others	348	(16.0)	13,182	(9.4)
Total	**2,169**	**(100.0)**	**139,715**	**(100.0)**

Notes : Figures in parentheses show the component ratios.
Source : Ahmedabad Municipal Corporation, *Statistical Outline of Ahmedabad City* 1988-89, Ahmedabad, 1990, p.236.

Inspector of Factories, Ahmedabad. From these factories, I selected six which met virtually all of my conditions as well as whose owners/managers willingly consented to my request for their cooperation.

Prior to sampling the workers, all occupations of each factory were stratified into four broad categories: managerial and clerical staff (hereafter MCS), technical staff (hereafter TS), production workers (hereafter PW), and contract workers (hereafter CW). The former three are directly employed by the factories while the latter is supplied to them through contractors. For convenience, I will refer to these as 'worker categories'. Based on the composition by worker category at each factory, I decided on the number of sample workers to be selected from each main, if not every, occupation. Then I picked the workers randomly from the respective main occupational groups, using the factory muster rolls.[2] In the end, 233 workers were chosen for my sample. All the sample workers are male.[3] Each factory's basic characteristics and category-wise composition of the sample workers are presented in Table 3. Each worker was interviewed at his residence in order to guarantee anonymity, to encourage candid responses, and not to disturb their work at the factories.[4] Map 1 shows the location of their residences and factories.

The analysis will be as follows. First I examine personal characteristics of the workers. Next, I discuss how heavily workers still depend on informal networks in order to be employed in the factories. Internal mobility is analysed and finally external mobility of the workers discussed.

Personal Characteristics

Age Structure

The survey reveals that 17 per cent of MCS and 18 per cent of PW are less than thirty years of age, whereas the figure for TS is 30 per cent. Although the majority of them are below fifty, 11 per cent of MCS and TS and 14 per cent of PW are fifty and above. On the other hand, the age distribution of CW shows a unique pattern and has a bias toward the lower age groups. Almost all of them are less than forty and 80 per cent are less than thirty years of age. The average ages of MCS, TS, PW and CW are 38.5, 35, 37.3 and 25.4 years respectively.

Table 3 : Sample Factories and Sample Workers

Factory	A	B	C	D	E	F
Year of initial production	1928	1959	1966	1986	1950	1974
Fixed assets (Rs. in lakh)	675.3	304.1	289	6.6	3.3	70.7
Type of industry	Textile	Engg.	Chem.	Textile	Engg.	Chem.
No. of employees	1260	364	196	87	58	109
Directly employed						
Managerial and clerical staff	56	43	7	4	10	5
Technical staff	51	64	4	1	6	13
Production worker	999	187	122	50	40	74
Casual worker	94	-	-	3	2	-
Indirectly employed						
Contract worker	60	70	63	29	-	17
No. of samples	66	50	40	26	26	25
Managerial and clerical staff	3	5	2	2	4	2
Technical staff	6	10	2	1	4	4
Production worker	52	29	26	17	18	16
Contract worker	5	6	10	6	-	3

Source : Factory Survey (Kiso), 1991

Ahmedabad City and its peripheral area (Location of sample worker's residences and sample factories)

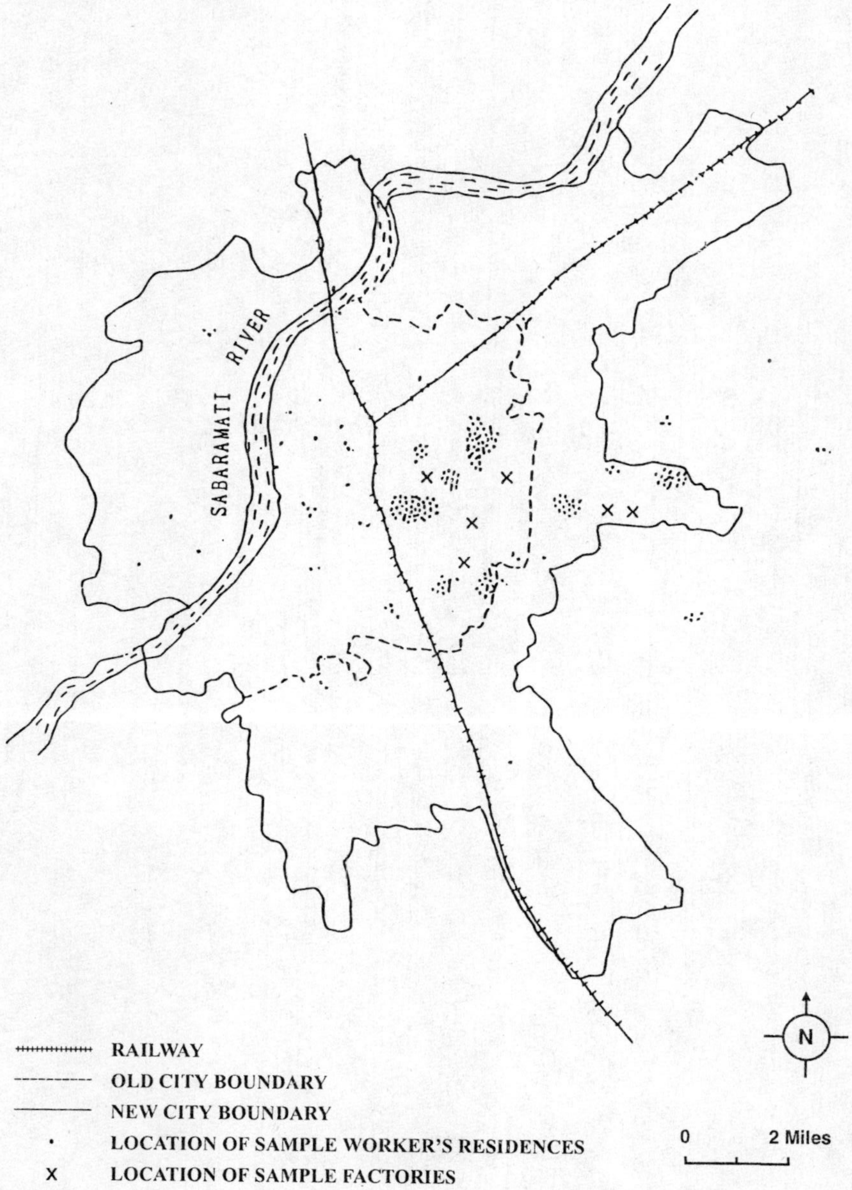

Type and Size of Household

Fifty-seven per cent of the sample workers belong to nuclear families, 27 per cent belong to joint families, while only 4 per cent are single families. The rest belong to 'others' (which are mainly composed of broken joint families and supplemented nuclear families). The percentage of nuclear families is highest in MCS (72 per cent), while the percentage of joint families is relatively high in TS (33 per cent).[5] Regarding household size, the percentage of families with 5 members or less is over 70 per cent in both MCS and TS, and about 53 per cent in both PW and CW.

Place of Origin

As Table 4 shows, almost half of the sample workers come from within the Ahmedabad district and the rest from outside the district. Out of those from outside the district, about half come from Gujarat, 17 per cent from UP, 11 per cent from Maharashtra, and 5 per cent each from Rajasthan and Tamil Nadu. A comparative analysis by the factory shows that factory C draws the highest proportion of its labour from outside the district (88 per cent) and factory F the lowest (24 per cent). Considering that 40 per cent of the workers in factory C come from one district, Panchmahals in Gujarat, one supposes that the territorial network has been at work, especially in the recruitment process of this factory.

Religion and Caste Composition

Of the 233 workers, 93.6 per cent are Hindus, 2.6 per cent are Christians, 2.1 per cent are Jains, 1.3 per cent are Muslims, and 0.4 per cent are Buddhists. Compared to the religious composition of males in Ahmedabad City in 1971 which, although considerably old data, shows that about 79 per cent are Hindus, we can see that the sample workers have a strong bias toward Hindus.

Table 5 presents the caste distribution by worker category.[6] Castes are classified into six groups: (1) upper castes excluding Rajputs, (2) Rajputs, (3) Scheduled Castes, (4) Backward Classes, (5) Scheduled Tribes, and (6) other castes.[7] This classification includes those cases who, although not Hindus, gave their castes.[8] One thing to note here is that among MCS and TS, upper castes are strongly rep-

Table 4 : Percentage Distribution of Workers by Place of Origin

Place of origin	Total	Factory					
		A	B	C	D	E	F
Ahmedabad District	49.4	51.5	60.6	12.5	50.0	53.8	76.4
Outside Ahmedabad District	50.6	48.5	40.0	87.5	50.0	46.2	24.0
Gujarat	27.5	16.7	26.0	67.5	23.1	11.5	16.0
Uttar Pradesh	8.6	16.7	2.0	5.0	11.5	11.5	-
Maharashtra	5.6	7.6	4.0	2.5	-	15.4	4.0
Rajasthan	2.6	4.5	2.0	5.0	-	-	-
Tamil Nadu	2.6	-	4.0	-	15.4	-	-
Delhi	0.9	..	2.0	-	-	-	4.0
Kerala	0.4	1.5	-	-	-	-	-
Andhra Pradesh	0.4	1.5	-	-	..	-	-
Himachal Pradesh	0.4	-	-	.	-	3.8	-
Other Country (Nepal)	1.7	-	-	7.5	-	3.8	-

Source : Same as in Table 3.

resented and lower castes such as Scheduled Castes, Backward Classes, and Scheduled Tribes are few or non-existent. Opposed to this, the lower castes are disproportionally represented in CW; 50 per cent of CW are Scheduled Castes, 33 per cent Backward Classes, while none are from the upper castes. On the other hand, the caste composition of PW falls between these two extremes; every caste group except Scheduled Tribes is more or less evenly dispersed among them.

Another point to note is that persons from particular castes tend to be employed by particular factories. Such examples are Vankars (20 per cent of the sample workers) and Rajputs (18 per cent) in factory A; Rajputs (16 per cent) in factory B; Thakores (30 per cent), Chamars (13 per cent) and Vankars (13 per cent) in factory C; Thakores (31 per cent) in factory D; Patidars (15 per cent) and Marathas (15 per cent) in factory E; Thakores (24 per cent), Vankars (24 per cent) and Chamars (16 per cent) in factory F, etc.[9] Furthermore, a comparable industry-wise analysis shows that only the chemical industry has significant concentrations of particular castes. The share of Chamars, Vankars, and Thakores (of which, the former two are classified as Scheduled Castes and the last is classified as backward classes) are markedly high irrespective of factory size, and these three combined, account for nearly 60 per cent of the sample workers of this industry.[10] On the other hand, in textile and engineering industries, similar concentrations of particular castes do not exist.

Education

The level of education is also distinctly different for each worker category. All of MCS and most of TS have completed at least the secondary level of education. Two-thirds of MCS and more than half of TS have gone to college. On the contrary, 70 per cent of CW have received primary or no education at all, and their highest educational level is secondary, which indicates that the educational requirement is low especially for CW. In the case of PW, 10 per cent of workers have no formal education while nearly half of them have received at least secondary education and 10 per cent have passed the SSC examination.

The survey also reveals a definite relationship between educational level and caste. Exactly half of the workers belonging to the upper castes have passed the SSC examination, while nearly a sixth of the workers belonging to backward classes and only 10 per cent of the

Table 5 : Caste Composition of Workers by Worker Category

Worker Category	All	Upper Caste	Rajput	SC	BC	ST	Other Castes	UC/NA
MCS	18 (100.0)	14 (77.8)	1 (5.6)	-	-	-	3 (16.7)	-
TS	27 (100.0)	18 (66.7)	-	1 (3.7)	1 (3.7)	-	2 (7.4)	5 (18.5)
PW	158 (100.0)	22 (13.9)	23 (14.6)	34 (21.5)	35 (22.2)	3 (1.9)	33 (20.9)	8 (5.1)
CW	30 (100.0)	-	-	15 (50.0)	10 (33.3)	-	4 (13.3)	1 (3.3)
Total	**233** **(100.0)**	**54** **(23.2)**	**24** **(10.3)**	**50** **(21.5)**	**46** **(19.7)**	**3** **(1.3)**	**42** **(18.0)**	**14** **(6.0)**

Note : Figures in parentheses are row percentages. SC - Scheduled Castes, ST - Scheduled Tribes, BC - Backward Classes and UC/NA - "unclassified" and "no answer".

workers of Scheduled Castes have done so. Also, more than 41 per cent of the upper caste workers have received college education, while none of them are uneducated. On the contrary, 24 per cent of backward class workers and 10 per cent of Scheduled Caste workers have received no education at all. Other castes show a pattern similar to the backward classes.

Thus we see that educational levels tend to differ depending on the caste, and educational requirements differ depending on worker categories. We may, therefore, reasonably conclude that these circumstances have strongly affected the relationship between caste and worker category: the concentration of the upper castes among MCS and TS and the lower castes among CW.

Nevertheless, it may be worth mentioning in passing, that their compositions by worker category are not the same, even among each caste group with the same educational level. For example, for those whose educational level is relatively low, secondary level, some of the upper caste workers are MCS or TS but none of them are CW, while more than half of the Scheduled Caste workers are CW but none are MCS or TS. Furthermore, in the case of workers with a college-level education, I found almost all of the upper caste workers to be MCS or TS but the Scheduled Caste workers to be PW only. These findings indicate that caste might have had any influence on the category of work the worker is engaged in, although our information is severely limited.

Job Access in the Factory Labour Market

Some of the personal characteristics described above seem to reflect the peculiarity of the recruitment process.

Table 6 summarizes the recruitment methods by occupation in each factory based on the data collected through interviews. For the moment, I will regard chanels 2-5 as formal methods and Channels 6-11 as informal methods.Channel 1, which is internal recruitment, is excluded from the observation here.) As the table indicates, (1) formal methods are mostly used for MCS and TS; (2) the methods are different among the factories even for the same occupation; (3)in factory B, only formal methods are used for MCS, TS, and PW except for unskilled workers; and (4) in other factories, both methods are used. Let us then attempt to extend the range of observation, based on the worker's answers.

Table 6 : Recruitment Methods by Occupation in Each Factory

	A	B	C	D	E	F
			MCS & TS			
Manager				1,2	2,6	2
Secretary			2		1,2,6	
Accountant		2	10		1,2,6	
Clerk	2,3	2	10	2,9	2,6	
Office assistant					2,6	
Junior assistant				1,2,9		
Store keeper					2,6	
Time keeper					2,6	
Typist		2			2,6	
Labo. in charge						1or2or3
Labo. chemist						2or3
Chief chemist			2			
Production in charge					1,3,6	
Plant in charge						1
Erector					1,6	
Supervisor	2	1,2	2	2,9	1,6	2or3
Statistical quality control				2,9		
Engineer		2,3			1,6	
Draughtsman		2			1,6	
Operator		2				
Technician		2				
Inspector		2				
			PW			
Jobber	8,9			1,2,2,9		1
Weaver	8,9			1,2,9		
Winding mechanics				2,9		
Carpenter	9		10	2,9	1,6	
Cleaner				2,9		
Fitter	2	2,3	10		1,4,3,4	1or2or7
Turner	9				1,4,3,4	
Piecer	8,9					
Warper	8,9					
Sizer	8,9					
Folder	8,9			2,9		

Table 6 : (Continued)

	A	B	C	D	E	F
			PW			
Stamper	8,9					
Doffer	8,9					
Back sizer	8,9					
Mending supervisor				2,9		
Mender				2,9		
Winder				2,9		
Beam drawer				2,9		
Welder	2,3		10		1,4,3,4	1or2or7
Miller					1,4,3,4	
Wireman	2	1	2			
Shaper					1,4,3,4	
Machine operator		2	3		1,4,3,4	
Dye maker		2,3				
Packer		1				
Mason			10			
Boiler attendant						1or2or3
Fireman						1or7
Coal man						7
Worker						2or7
Helper		11			9,5	7
Semi-skilled		2	2,9			
Unskilled		11	2,9			
Peon			10		9	
Security in charge					5	1or2
Watchman		11	10	2	9	7

Notes : Numbers refer to recruitment methods as follows : 1:Internal recruitment; 2:Advertisement; 3:Employment exchange; 4:I.T.I.; 5:Security company; 6:Introduction by relatives or friends of factory owners; 7:Factory notice board; 8:"Employee's son"; 9:Introduction by employees; 10:Recommendation; 11:Contractor.

Source : Same as in Table 3.

Source of Job Information

The first two information channels, namely, advertisement and employment exchange in Table 7, can be regarded as formal, and the remaining six channels except 'others' as informal. Only 13 per cent of the workers have used formal channels. However, such percentages differ to a large extent according to worker categories. The percentage of workers using formal channels is relatively high in MCS (44) and TS (37), which suggests that information channels have been more formalized in this section of factory workers. On the other hand, the percentages in the case of PW and CW are low: 8 in the former and zero in the latter. Contrarily, the percentage of workers who obtained information informally came to 56 in MCS, 63 in TS, 92 in PW, and 100 in CW. (This was a multiple choice question but since all of the workers who used formal channels mentioned only one channel, one can assume that the rest were informed informally.) Of the informal channels, 'employee of the present factory' occurs with the highest frequency, accounting for 65 per cent of respondents in PW, 33 per cent in MCS, and 48 per cent in TS. It may be worth pointing out, in passing, that of the 139 respondents informed by employees of their present factories, 30 per cent also mentioned their friends or neighbours and 43 per cent also mentioned their relatives. It is obvious that in many cases there are some personal relationships between the employees who provided information and the respondents.

Selection Methods

Among selection methods in Table 7, interview is the most formalized method. Of 231 respondents, 23 per cent mentioned this as the method by which they were hired. According to worker categories, the use of this formal method is the highest in TS (59 per cent), followed by MCS (39 per cent), PW (19 per cent), and CW (3 per cent). On the other hand, recommendation which is regarded as an informal method, accounted for as much as 60 per cent in PW. If we take this method (that is, recommendation) and the semi-formal method (that is, interview + recommendation) together, we find that the majority of 231 respondents (60 per cent) have been placed in their factories through recommendation, although the same percentages for MCS and TS were relatively low (45 and 41 respectively).

Recommenders

Table 7 also shows who recommended them. The majority (74 per cent) were recommended by workers of the present factories, followed by previous employees of the factories (6 per cent), contractors (3 per cent), trade unions (2 per cent), and supervisors (2 per cent). If we observe the relationship between respondent and recommender, we find that blood relations account for 38 per cent, which is the highest, followed by same native place (26 per cent) and same caste (15 per cent). The rest were mostly friends.

Castes and Job Access

Let us attempt a comparable analysis of job access by caste group, using the data on PW only in order to remove the bias of category-wise differences.

As Table 8 indicates, some differences were found especially between upper castes and all other caste groups. The use of formal information channels is generally low irrespective of caste group but is slightly higher in the case of upper castes; 18 per cent (4 of 22) of upper castes used formal channels while 6 per cent (2 of 33) of other castes, 6 per cent (2 of 33) of Scheduled Castes, and 3 per cent (1 of 35) of backward classes used this channel. With regard to selection practices, the percentage of persons selected through recommendation is generally high irrespective of caste group. Nearly two-thirds of PW were selected through this practice. In the case of upper castes, however, the percentage of persons selected through interview is also relatively high (41). As for the recommenders, most of them were ordinary factory employees for every caste group, except in the case of upper castes where managerial staff or factory owners (included in 'others') also often appeared as recommenders. Another difference is based on the relationships with the recommenders; 57 per cent of upper castes had mere friendly relations with their recommenders, while most of the other caste groups had blood relations or came from the same native places.

To sum up the inter-caste differences to job access: (1) the extent of formalization of information channels is generally low but relatively high in the case of upper castes; (2) in the selection practices, persons of upper castes tend to be selected more often through recommendation by managerial staff or owners which is obviously more influential

Table 7 : Sources of Job Information and Selection Methods

(Number of employees)

Source of Job Information (multiple answer question)	All	MCS	TS	PW	CW
Advertisement	29(12.5)	8(44.4)	10(37.0)	11(7.0)	
Employment exchange	1(0.4)			1(0.6)	
Factory notice board	2(0.9)			2(1.3)	
Factory owner/ employer	8(3.4)	2(11.1)	1(3.7)	5(3.2)	
Employee of the factory	139 (59.9)	6 (33.3)	13 (48.1)	102 (65.0)	18 (60.0)
Contractor	17(7.3)			8(5.1)	9(30.0)
Friend/ Neighbour	57 (24.6)	5 (27.8)	7 (25.9)	38 (24.2)	7 (23.3)
Relative	83 (35.8)		5 (18.5)	65 (41.4)	13 (43.3)
Others	5(2.2)		1(3.7)	4(2.5)	
Total	**232 (100.0)**	**18 (100.0)**	**27 (100.0)**	**157 (100.0)**	**30 (100.0)**
Selection Methods					
Interview	54 (23.4)	7 (38.9)	16 (59.3)	30 (19.1)	1 (3.4)
Interview + Recommendation	16(6.9)	5(27.8)	4(14.8)	7(4.5)	
Recommendation only	123 (53.2)	3(16.7)	7(25.9)	94(59.9)	19(65.5)
Nothing in particular	35(15.2)	3(16.7)		25(15.9)	7(24.1)
Others	3(1.3)			1(0.6)	2(6.9)
Total	**231 (100.0)**	**18 (100.0)**	**27 (100.0)**	**157 (100.0)**	**29 (100.0)**

Table 7 : (Continued)

Source of Job Information (multiple answer question)	All	MCS	TS	PW	CW
Recommender					
Trade union	3(2.2)			3(3.0)	
Supervisor	3(2.2)		1(9.1)	2(2.0)	
Clerical staff	1(0.7)	1(12.5)			
Worker of a present factory	103 (74.1)	3 (37.5)	8 (72.7)	74 (73.3)	18 (94.7)
Previous employee of a factory	8(5.8)			7(6.9)	1(5.3)
Contractor	4(2.9)			4(4.0)	
Others	17(12.2)	4(50.0)	2(18.2)	11(10.9)	
Total	**139 (100.0)**	**8 (100.0)**	**11 (100.0)**	**101 (100.0)**	**19 (100.0)**
Relationship with the recommender (multiple answer question)					
Blood	52 (37.7)	1 (12.5)	3 (27.3)	44 (44.0)	4 (21.1)
Same caste	20 (14.5)		1 (9.1)	11 (11.0)	3 (42.1)
Same native place	36(26.1)	2(25.0)	2(18.2)	24(24.0)	8(42.1)
Others	37 (26.8)	5 (62.5)	5 (45.5)	25 (25.0)	2 (10.5)
Total	**138 (100.0)**	**8 (100.0)**	**11 (100.0)**	**100 (100.0)**	**19 (100.0)**

Note : Figures in parentheses are percentages to the total number of respondents.

Source : Same as in Table 3.

Table 8 : Sources of Job Information and Selection Methods of PW in Each Caste Group
(Percentage to the Total Respondents in Each Caste Group)

	Upper Caste	Rajput	SC	BC	ST	Other Caste
Source of Job Information (149)						
Advertisement	18.2	4.3	3.0	2.9	33.3	6.1
Employment exchange			3.0			
Factory notice board			3.0			
Factory owner/ employer	4.5		3.0	2.9	33.3	3.0
Employee of the factory	45.5	82.6	66.7	65.7	33.3	63.6
Contractor	4.5	8.7	6.1			9.1
Friend/ neighbour	40.9	26.1	18.2	37.1		12.1
Relative		22.7	39.1	45.5	48.6	54.5
Others	4.5		3.0			6.1
Selection Methods (149)						
Interview	22.7	21.7	15.2	11.4	33.3	12.1
Interview + Recommendation	18.2	8.7		2.9		
Recommendation only	50.0	60.9	60.6	71.4		69.7
Nothing in particular	9.1	8.7	21.2	14.3	66.7	18.2
Others			3.0			
Recommender (100)						
Trade Union	6.7	6.3		3.8		
Supervisor	6.7		5.0			
Clerical staff						

Table 8 : (Continued)

	Upper Caste	Rajput	SC	BC	ST	Other Caste
Worker of a present factory	40.0	68.8	80.0	84.6		82.6
Previous employee of a factory	13.3	6.3	5.0	7.7		
Contractor		12.5	5.0			4.3
Others	33.3	6.3	5.0	3.8		13.0
Relationship with the Recommender (99)						
Blood	21.4	50.0	45.0	34.6		65.2
Same caste	14.3	18.8	20.0	7.7		
Same native place	14.3	12.5	30.0	38.5		13.0
Others	57.1	25.0	10.0	23.1		21.7

Notes : (1) Figures in parentheses are the absolute number of respondents

(2) "Source of Job Information" and "Relationship with the Recommender" are multiple answer questions.

Source : Same as in Table 3.

than that by ordinary employees; while (3) 'blood relation' or 'same native place' proves more important for persons of other caste groups to gain entrance.

Thus, the analysis suggests that the factory labour market is an imperfect competitive market where informal methods to job access are still predominant. It is true that formalization has progressed in a fraction of MCS and TS,[11] but personal connection is definitely important for PW in particular, as they do not generally require a decent education or other qualifications. Therefore, it seems that the bias toward Hindus in the sample workers, the concentration of particular caste groups and the concentration of workers from the same native places in particular factories are the predictable results of these informal entry processes. In addition, it may be presumed that the present composition of the workers by religion, caste, or native place in each factory is affected more or less by the initial recruitment of each factory. To put it another way, given the importance of informal methods of gaining access to factory jobs, not only do the individual's acquired characteristics such as education but also his ascriptive characteristics embedded in society, appear to determine who has access. It seems to depend on whether a group (e.g., caste) he belongs to has a useful connection with any factory and whether the connection is influential enough and highly competitive in the factory labour market.

Internal Labour Mobility: Promotion

As Table 9 shows, 47 per cent of 233 sample workers (109) have ever received a promotion in their jobs; 37 per cent (87) have been promoted once and 9 per cent (22) have been promoted twice. The total number of promotions comes to 131. Looking at the promotees by worker category, PW record the highest (54 per cent), while MCS record the lowest (28 per cent) scores.

As was expected, there was some confusion among respondents about what a promotion is. The respondents were left to decide for themselves and the result is seen in Table 10. Of 131 promotions, 63 per cent involved a change in employment security, 31 per cent involved a change in skill-grade, 56 per cent involved a change in occupational rank, and 67 per cent involved a wage increase. If we regard only the rise in skill-grade or the rise in occupational rank as promotions, the workers who experienced such job changes are 31 and

56 per cent respectively, which suggests that even the 131 promotions may be regarded as an overestimation. In addition, the fact that 33 per cent of 131 promotions did not include a wage increase is also important. The reason is that promotion is expected to be crucial to wage increase, since the regular wage increase, if any, has an institutional or customary ceiling in each skill-grade or each occupation. Nevertheless, this fact reveals that promotion, in reality, does not always bring about a wage increase. From these observations, we may say that internal mobility (that is, promotion) has not so far had enough effect on upward economic mobility, not only in number but also in substance.

Let us try to discuss why promotions are so few, and what factors distinguish promotees from non-promotees. At first, a low rate of internal mobility in the factories is probably attributed to the following factors concerning the technological structure of factories: (1) a well-defined hierarchy of skill-grades does not exist; (2) there is a small number of occupational categories; and (3) occupations are not specialized. In addition, (4) employers lacking intention to train and nurture workers within their factories, and (5) factories having started operation rather recently, are also factors to be taken into consideration. Factor (1) is applicable here to small factories such as D, E and F, and larger factory C, where many workers were not able to provide their skill-grades on our questionnaire. On the other hand, the large factory B has a clear and well-stratified skill-grade ladder, and most workers thereby know their own skill-grades. This is also true, to a considerable extent, for large factory A. Factor (2) is also more applicable to small factories. Factor (3) describes chemical factories like C, and F, where, according to the lists of workers' designations, many workers are grouped into 'worker' or 'labourer' who undertake a variety of simple tasks concurrently. Factor (4) was confirmed to some extent through interviews with employers or personnel staff. Consistently among the sample factories, there are few occupations whose vacancies have been filled exclusively by existing workers through promotion. Although internal recruitment has been treated as one possible way to fill vacancies of certain occupations in small factories, it has not even been a choice in large factories (see Table 6). Finally, concerning factor (5), the extremely low percentage of promotees (4) in the newest factory D seems to be explained mainly by its short length of operation.

Let us now turn to the factors which distinguish promotees from

Table 9 : Number of Promotions

	Number of Promotions			Total
	0	1	2	
Total	**124**	**87**	**22**	**233**
	(53.2)	**(37.3)**	**(9.4)**	**(100.0)**
Worker Category				
MCS	13	5	-	18
	(72.2)	(27.8)	-	(100.0)
TS	16	7	4	27
	(59.3)	(25.9)	(14.8)	(100.0)
PW	73	67	18	158
	(46.2)	(42.4)	(11.4)	(100.0)
CW	22	8	-	30
	(73.3)	(26.7)	-	(100.0)
Factory Size				
Large factories	64	71	21	156
	(41.0)	(45.5)	(13.5)	(100.0)
Small factories	60	16	1	77
	(77.9)	(20.8)	(1.3)	(100.0)

Note : Figures in parentheses are percentage distribution.
Source : Same as in Table 3.

Table 10 : Changes owing to Promotions in Each Factory

Factory	Total No. of Promotions	Number of Changes in Employment Security	Skill Grade	Occupational Rank	Wage (raise)
A	51(100.0)	33(55.9)	9(17.6)	28(54.9)	32(62.7)
B	33(100.0)	16(48.5)	17(51.5)	18(54.5)	20(60.6)
C	29(100.0)	22(75.9)	8(27.6)	16(55.2)	20(69.0)
D	1(100.0)				1(100.0)
E	6(100.0)	2(33.3)	3(50.0)	5(83.3)	5(83.3)
F	11(100.0)	9(81.8)	4(36.4)	6(54.5)	10(90.9)
Total	**131(100.0)**	**82(62.6)**	**41(31.3)**	**73(55.7)**	**88(67.2)**

Note : Figures in parentheses show percentages to the total numbers of promotions in each factory.
Source : Same as in Table 3.

non-promotees. The promotion possibility of workers seems to be affected more or less by features of the individual factories as well as personal characteristics of the workers. Considering the factory features mentioned above, it is predicted that the percentage of promotees would be higher in large factories than in small factories and the result 59 per cent in the former and 22 per cent in the latter appears to support this prediction. Furthermore, the relationships with personal characteristics should be discussed based on the following factors: length of employment, type of occupation, training, level of education, and caste.[12]

The possibility of promotion increases with the length of employment: out of the workers who were employed 10 years or less, 73 per cent have received no promotion, 23 per cent received one promotion, and 4 per cent received two promotions. On the other hand, out of the workers who were employed 11 years or more, 34 per cent received no promotion while 52 per cent received one and 14 per cent two promotions.

As for the type of occupation, promotions are more likely to occur when a worker is engaged in an occupation which is graded for its skill and/or which has higher ranked positions which can be filled internally.

Regarding training, there seems to be no interrelation between promotion and training. Although the reliability of analysis is restricted by the number of trained workers being too small (only 33 workers), half of the trained workers and half of the untrained workers had not got a promotion.

As for the relationship of promotion to level of education, I attempted to analyse PW only. Except for the conspicuous fact that most illiterate workers (10 out of 15) have never been promoted, I could not find any important relationship because the educational level of most PW is low, secondary level or lower.

Regarding the relationship of promotion to caste, again only PW was analysed. The percentage of promotees is higher among Scheduled Castes (62) rather than in upper castes (41) and other castes (52). Promotions measured in relation to years of employment, also do not show any clear relationship to caste. Caste discrimination, therefore, does not appear to affect promotion, although the data facts are not enough to reach definite conclusions.

To sum up, (1)the number of promotions is generally small in the sample factories and the promotion does not always promise upward economic mobility in the form of a wage increase. In these senses, the chance of upward economic mobility in the factories is still severely limited; (2) promotions are basically attributed to the characteristics of skill-grades and occupational structure in the factories, in other words, the underdevelopment of the promotion system; however (3) certain features of each factory or personal characteristics of each worker significantly affect the rate of promotion. Thus we may say that the promotion system has started developing in at least some of the factories.

External Labour Mobility: Job Change

Approximately two-thirds of the sample workers expressed a desire to move to other units if possible and almost all of them expected it would help raise their earnings. One reason for the desire to move to other units seems to be the low internal mobility rate I have discussed above. I shall now examine the frequency and patterns of their past job changes.

Table 11 shows that 60 per cent of the sample workers have changed their jobs at least once, while 40 per cent have never done so. Of the mobile workers, 70 per cent have changed only once and the average rate of job change is only 0.9 per worker for all workers and barely 1.5 even for mobile workers. Therefore, we cannot say that such movements have taken place very frequently although this might be an underestimation owing to under-reporting by some respondents.[13] Let us then see in Table 12 who the mobile workers are. As presumed, in higher age groups, the shares of mobile workers and the average rate of job change are higher. A similar relationship is observed between years of work and job change. Caste-wise, the share of mobile workers and the average rate of job change are the highest among upper castes and followed by other castes, and relatively low among Scheduled Castes, backward classes, and Rajputs. As Table 13 shows, the analysis of job changes in relation to years of work would also support this trend: the rate of workers who have changed jobs at least once in 10 years is the highest in upper castes (41 per cent) and lowest in Scheduled Castes (11per cent). Successively looking at the movements by worker category, the percentage of this type of mobile worker is the highest in MCS (72), followed by PW (62), TS (56) and CW (47): Including immobile workers, the average rate of job change is the highest in MCS with 1.5 per worker followed by TS with 1.1, PW with

Table 11 : Job Changes in Each Worker Category

(Percentage)

Worker Category	Number of Job Changes							Average rate of job changes per worker
	0	1	2	3	4	5	Total	
MCS	27.8	33.3	11.1	16.7	11.1		100.0	1.5
TS	44.4	29.6	7.4	14.8		3.7	100.0	1.1
PW	38.0	42.4	12.7	6.3	0.6		100.0	0.9
CW	53.3	43.3	3.3				100.0	0.5
Total	**39.9**	**40.3**	**10.7**	**7.3**	**1.3**	**0.4**	**100.0**	**0.9**

Note : Figures are row percentages.
Source : Same as in Table 3.

Table 12 : Experience of Job Changes

	No. of All Sample Workers	% of Mobile Workers to All Workers	Average Number of Job Changes	
			Mobile Workers	All Workers
All Age	233	60.1	1.51	0.90
Below 20	4	25.0	1.00	0.25
20-29	60	48.3	1.17	0.57
30-39	90	58.9	1.53	0.90
40-49	52	75.0	1.41	1.06
50-59	22	63.6	1.71	1.09
60 +	5	80.0	2.00	1.60
Years of Work				
Less than 5	21	23.8	1.20	0.29
6-10	35	34.3	1.17	0.40
11-15	49	51.0	1.64	0.84
16-20	37	78.4	1.66	1.30
21-25	26	69.2	1.39	0.96
26 +	29	55.2	2.00	1.10
Caste Group				
Upper Caste	54	77.8	1.86	1.44
Rajput	24	45.8	1.45	0.67
SC	50	50.0	1.20	0.60
BC	46	52.2	1.38	0.72
ST	3	100.0	1.33	1.33
Other Caste	42	66.7	1.54	1.02
UN/NA	14	55.0	1.14	0.57
Worker Category				
MCS	18	72.2	2.08	1.50
TS	27	55.6	1.93	1.07
PW	158	62.0	1.44	0.89
CW	30	46.7	1.07	0.50
Factory Size				
Large factories	156	53.2	1.40	0.74
Small factories	77	74.0	1.60	1.18

Note : UC/NA means "unclassified" and "no answer".
Source : Same as in Table 3.

Table 13 : Frequency of Job Changes

No. of Workers		Frequency (%)						Total
			One job change in					
		Zero	more than 20 yrs	15-19 yrs	10-14 yrs	5-9 yrs	less than 5 yrs	
Total No.	**203**	**93**	**26**	**18**	**22**	**34**	**10**	
Caste Group								
Upper Caste	49	24.5	8.2	12.2	14.3	28.6	12.2	100
Rajput	21	61.9	9.5	4.8	9.5	14.3		100
SC	44	56.8	9.1	13.6	9.1	9.1	2.3	100
BC	40	55.0	7.5	7.5	7.5	20.0	2.5	100
ST	1		100.0					100
Other Caste	37	37.8	27.0	5.4	13.5	13.5	2.7	100
UN/NA	11	63.6	18.2		9.1		9.1	100
Worker Category								
MCS	17	29.4	11.8	5.9	17.6	23.5	11.8	100
TS	24	50.0	12.5		8.3	12.5	16.9	100
PW	133	45.1	15.0	10.5	10.5	17.3	1.5	100
CW	29	55.2	3.4	10.3	10.3	13.8	6.9	100
Factory Size								
Large factories	141	51.8	12.8	8.5	10.6	12.1	4.3	100
Small factories	62	32.3	12.9	9.7	11.3	27.4	6.5	100

Note : Thirty workers were excluded because their years of work were not known.

Source : Same as in Table 3.

0.9, and CW with 0.5 (Table 12). Furthermore, the analysis in relation to years of work also indicates that MCS have changed jobs most frequently. The rate of workers who changed jobs at least once in 10 years of work is the highest in MCS (35 per cent) and more than half of MCS have changed their jobs at least once in 15 years of work (Table 13). Thus, it seems that the above mentioned positive relationship between caste groups and job changes is mainly explained by the fact that many of upper castes are MCS and TS who are more mobile while most of Scheduled Castes and backward classes are CW, who are least mobile, or PW.

It may be presumed that occupational specialty has made MCS and TS more mobile. This view would be supported by an occupation-wise study of Table 14. For example, more mobile occupations include carpenter (2.3 job changes per worker), accountant (2.3), draughtsman (1.6) and engineer (1.4), which are relatively qualified and specialized occupations, while less mobile occupations include winder (0.2), doffer (0.3) and 'worker' (0.5), which require much less skill.

Lastly, observing the mobility by factory size, the percentage of mobile workers in small factories is 74, which is higher than that in the large factories (53 per cent). This difference is reflected in the average rate of job change, being 1.2 per worker in the former and 0.7 per worker in the latter. This suggests that workers in large factories tend to stay in the same factory longer, which is also supported by the fact that the share of workers employed more than 10 years reaches two-thirds in large factories in comparison with one-third in small factories.

Let us now look into the reasons for job changes. Of 227 responses (in multiple answer questions), the main reasons, for job change are: 'low wage/earning' (34 per cent), 'found a better job or post' (27 per cent), and 'closure of the factory' (7 per cent).[14] If we classify all the reasons into three broad groups such as voluntary, quasi-voluntary, and involuntary, each group accounts for 29 per cent, 43 per cent and 12 per cent respectively. We can see, therefore, that many mobile workers have changed their jobs more or less voluntarily, expecting a rise in social or economic status.

In order to find whether job changes have actually affected their upward mobility, it will be useful to examine the content of job changes. This analysis will be concerned with changes of sector, industry, employment security, and wage, in that order. As for sectors, I grouped all units (including self-employed) into agriculture and industries other than agriculture. The units of the latter are further divided into two sectors: formal sector (where employees number 20 or more) and informal sector (where employees number less than 20).[15]

Table 15 shows that of 212 previous jobs, agriculture accounts for 15 per cent of all workers, formal sector 50 per cent, which is the highest, and informal sector 34 per cent. Looked at in more detail, the percentage of agriculture is quite low in both MCS and TS while much higher in CW (40) and PW (17). The informal sector accounts for 37 per cent for MCS, 21 per cent for TS, 37 per cent for PW, and 20 per cent for CW. On the other hand, the percentage of the formal sector is 56 per cent for MCS and 79 per cent for TS, which are higher compared to PW (44 per cent) and CW (40 per cent). In addition, if we look into the sector changes more concretely, we find that 48 per cent of the 212 job changes included no sector change, while 7 per cent included a change from formal to informal (which is regarded as downward mobility) and 27 per cent included a change from informal to formal (which is regarded as upward mobility). As far as the sector changes are concerned, therefore, we can infer that job changes have more often occurred with upward mobility than downward mobility and that MCS and TS have showed a stronger tendency to move within the formal sector as compared to PW and CW. Let us see then the industrial content of previous units from the same table. It can be seen that manufacturing accounted for 68 per cent of the total previous units and it accounted for more than 50 per cent in all worker categories. Also, the percentage of manufacturing is conspicuously high in TS, while the percentage of agriculture is relatively high in CW. In addition, although it is not presented in this table, movement from other factories of the same industry have occurred most frequently with the workers of the textile industry. Table 15 also shows that, while 40 per cent of employment was regular, temporary employment and casual employment account for 33 per cent and 11 per cent, respectively. This suggests that there has been an upward tendency in this sense as well because 82 per cent of the sample workers are employed regularly at present. Finally, by comparing the last wage of the previous job with the first wage of the next job, we can see that 50 per cent of the job changes brought with them a wage increase, while 25 per cent resulted in a wage decrease and 9 per cent showed no change. Thus, it can be concluded that most of the mobile workers have attained some economic rise through a job change.

Table 14 : Number and Frequency of Job Changes of Workers in Each Occupation

Occupation	No. of Sample Workers	Average No. of Job Changes	Frequency of Job Changes: Zero or once in more than 20 yrs. (%)	Frequency of Job Changes: Once in less than 10 yrs. (%)
Accountant	3	2.3	0	100.0
Checker	3	0.6		
Cleaner	3	1.0		
Clerk	9	1.2	50.0	12.5
Doffer	6	0.3	80.0	0
Draughtsman	3	1.6	66.7	33.3
Engineer	5	1.4	20.0	80.0
Fitter	16	1.1	46.2	23.1
Helper	19	0.6	70.6	11.8
Jobber	8	1.0	62.5	12.5
Machine Operator	20	1.1	38.9	27.8
Mistry (Carpenter)	3	2.3		
Peon	4	0.7	50.0	25.0
Piecer	3	0.6	100.0	0
Plant Operator	3	0.6		
Secretary	3	0.6		
Supervisor	13	0.7	75.0	16.7
Sweeper	5	0.6	80.0	0
Watchman	7	0.7	60.0	20.0
Weaver	15	0.7	70.0	10.0
Winder	8	0.2	75.0	12.5
Wireman	4	1.5	25.0	50.0
Worker	34	0.5	65.5	17.2

Note : Includes the occupations with three and more sample workers. Regarding "Frequency of job changes", the percentages are not shown if three and more workers could not give information on it.
"Frequency of job changes" refers only to the workers who have changed jobs more frequently and those who have changed less frequently. Hence the figures in each row do not aggregate 100%.
Source : Same as in Table 3.

Table 15 : Sector, Industry and Employment Security of Previous Jobs

	All	MCS	TS	PW	CW
Sector					
Agriculture	31 (14.6)	1 (3.7)		24 (17.0)	6 (40.0)
Formal sector	106 (50.0)	15 (55.5)	23 (79.3)	62 (44.0)	6 (40.0)
Informal sector	71 (33.5)	10 (37.0)	6 (20.7)	52 (36.9)	3 (20.0)
Not known	4 (1.9)	1 (3.7)		3 (2.1)	
Industry					
Agriculture	31 (14.6)	1 (3.7)		24 (17.0)	6 (40.0)
Manufacturing (including repairing)	144 (67.9)	16 (59.3)	26 (89.7)	94 (66.7)	8 (53.3)
Construction	4 (1.9)	7 (25.9)		4 (2.8)	
Trade & restaurants & hotels	23 (10.8)	2 (6.9)	13 (9.2)	1 (6.7)	
Transport, storage & communications					
Other Services	9 (4.2)	3 (11.1)	1 (3.4)	5 (3.5)	
Not known	1 (0.5)			1 (0.7)	
Employment Security					
Regular worker	84 (39.6)	19 (70.4)	14 (48.3)	49 (34.8)	2 (13.3)
Contract worker	5 (2.4)			4 (2.8)	1 (6.7)
Temporary worker	69 (32.5)	4 (14.8)	13 (44.8)	48 (34.0)	4 (26.7)
Casual worker	23 (10.8)	2 (7.4)		17 (12.1)	4 (26.7)
Apprenticeship	3 (1.4)	1 (3.7)	2 (6.9)		
Not known	28 (13.2)	1 (3.7)		23 (16.3)	4 (26.7)
Total number of previous jobs	**212 (100.0)**	**27 (100.0)**	**29 (100.0)**	**141 (100.0)**	**15 (100.0)**

Note : Figures in parentheses show percentages to the total number of job changes.

Source : Same as in Table 3.

Summary

A summary of some important findings of this paper are given below.

(1) We found workers from various caste groups working in the factories in Ahmedabad. But the caste composition was different among the worker categories. While a relatively higher percentage of MCS and TS came from higher caste groups, most of CW came from low caste groups or Scheduled Castes. Those in the PW category were distributed more evenly among various caste groups. As presumed, educational levels of the workers differed depending on the worker category; educational levels of MCS and TS were found to be relatively high.

(2) The methods of job access in the factory labour market have been relatively formalized for jobs like MCS and TS which require relatively high skill-grade or higher educational level. As a result, many workers with higher caste rank, whose educational levels tend to be comparatively high, are found in these two categories. In other words, it may be safely said that Scheduled Caste workers, whose educational levels generally tend to be lower, tend to be excluded from these upper ranked jobs through such formalized recruitment processes, rather than through discrimination against them. Needless to say, further investigation on how and to what extent caste affects the educational level is necessary.

(3) The recruitment methods have been hardly formalized for PW, for whom neither high educational level nor special qualification is required. Instead, the informal network based on religion, caste or blood relations, etc., has been most important for workers to gain access to factory jobs as PW. It does not mean, however, that caste appears to operate as an ascriptive factor or through its influence on access to education. It rather operates as nothing more than a framework of social division. The most important thing is whether the caste group the worker belongs to has any connection with the factory labour market and whether the connection is influential enough even in the labour surplus situation. In this sense, paradoxically enough, for persons of upper caste groups who generally tend to lack connections with production workers because of their relatively late emergence as PW in the factory labour market use of formal channels and acquiring more effective connections are presumed to have been the only ways to enter the factories as PW.

(4) The promotion system is generally underdeveloped which indicates that although workers may get a chance to enter the factories, their economic rise in terms of promotion within each factory is very restricted.

(5) Many workers wish to move on to other units with the main object of a wage increase. But workers in large factories are less mobile as far as past job changes show. This seems to be partly attributed to the comparatively greater degree of introduction of the promotion system in those factories, in addition to various other advantages.

(6) Job changes have brought to most mobile workers better economic conditions by means of changes in employment security, sector, and wages. But one thing to note here, is that while it is true that some informal (sector) workers have moved up to the formal sector, this is not possible for all informal (sector) workers. The reason is that for those who lack any personal connections, the opportunities of upward movement would be extremely restricted because of the prevalence of the informal methods of recruitment.

Notes

1. In India, there were 1,035 cotton textile mills in April 1988. Of them, 117 mills (11 per cent) are concentrated in Gujarat, which is one of the important centres for the cotton textile industry. Among the 117 mills, 90 are composite mills and 27 are spinning mills. More than half of them (67 mills) are located in Ahmedabad city. (AMC: 1990 : 239) See, B.B. Patel, *Workers of Closed Textile Mills*, New Delhi, Oxford & IBH Publishing Co. Pvt. Ltd., 1988, p.v, and Kashyap, op.cit., p.18.

2. For factory A, a complete factory muster roll which includes names, addresses, and occupations of all the workers was not available because of its large number of employees. Therefore, I requested a factory manager to prepare a list of workers which reflects the composition by main section and by main occupation in the factory and which includes twice as many workers as the scheduled sample. Half the workers were randomly chosen from this list in order to reduce some arbitrariness in selection.

3. Female workers are also working as production workers in some sample factories such as textile factories as well as working as clerical staff in one engineering factory. But in this research, only male workers were selected as the sample in order to avoid the effects of sex on the analysis.

4. Worker interviews were conducted by the author and six local investigating staff. One of them provided support to the author, who does not understand Gujarati, as an investigator-cum-interpreter.

5. The respondents are not necessarily heads of their households. Taking this into consideration, four types of households are defined as follows.

Single: himself only

Nuclear family:

1. himself, spouse
2. himself, unmarried children
3. himself, spouse, unmarried children
4. himself, parent(s)
5. himself, parent(s), unmarried brother(s)/sister(s)

* 'Himself' is not married in the cases of Nos. 4 and 5.

Joint family:

1. himself, (spouse), married children, their spouse(s)
2. himself, (spouse), married brother(s)/sister(s), their spouse(s)
3. himself, spouse, parents
4. himself, parents, married brother(s)/sister(s), their spouse(s)

* In the case of a worker who does not have a spouse in 1 and 2, his household is regarded as a joint family only when he has two and more

married children in 1 and two and more married brothers/sisters in 2. In the case of 4, it does not matter whether 'himself' is married or not.

** Combinations of two or more cases are also valid.

*** These are valid irrespective of presence of other kin or the others.

Others: all except cases mentioned above.

6. Although some sample workers might not have declared their correct castes, either intentionally or unintentionally, castes were analyzed basically based on their responses. But for Rajputs, see note 11.

7. The castes which each group includes are as follows. (Figures in parentheses show the number of persons.) Upper Castes (54) [Patidar (21), Brahmin (11), Jain (5), Panchal (5), Vaishnav Hindu (4), Kayastha (1), Lohana (1), Mudaliar (1), Tiwari (1)]; Rajputs (24) [Rajput (21), Darbar (2), Gulsia (1)]; Scheduled Castes (50) [Vankar (30), Chamar (16), Bhangi (1), Bhuiya (1), Pasi (1), Rohit (1)]; Backward Classes (46) [Thakore (30), Valand/Barber (6), Bawa (4), Padmasali (3), Koli (1), Rabari (1), Raval (1)]; Scheduled Tribes (3) [Nayaka (3)]; Other Castes (42) [Maratha (14), Pattni (4), Luhar (3), Suthar (3), Bhavsar (2), Chaudhary (2), Jeswal (2), Kadia (2), Sheikh (2), Vaishya (2), Goswami (1), Naik (1), Patthan (1), Rana (1), Sadhu (1), Soni (1)]. Although it is said that Rajputs in Gujarat are originated from the royal families of large and powerful kingdoms in Gujarat and neighbouring Rajasthan, I excluded Rajputs from upper Castes in my classification. The reason is that Rajputs have positively amalgamated with the lower caste and tribal people through marriage and political solidification, while there has been a trend of Rajputization in certain lower caste and tribal people on the other hand. As a result, the category 'Rajput' is characterized by its flexibility. It seems to be extremely difficult either to consider Rajputs as a traditional ruling caste or to distinguish persons who feign Rajput from indigenous Rajputs. For example, it is said that the Rajputs' relationship with the Kolis is very strong and some Kolis have been claiming to be Rajputs. See A.M. Shah and I.P. Desai, *Division and Hierarchy: An Overview of Caste in Gujarat*, Delhi, Hindustan Publishing Corporation, 1988. In addition to these six groups, furthermore, a category UC/NA was prepared. Reference was also made to their sub-castes when it was difficult to classify just by caste names given by respondents. But some castes still remain unclassified into proper groups. These, together with 'no answer', are put into UC/NA. It should be added that the above classification might not be perfect, although it was done with the greatest possible care.

8. The main reasons are as follow: (1)other religions are not necessarily opposed to the observance of caste; (2)Backward Classes include some non-

Hindu groups; (3)converts from Hindus to other religions often reply their caste names.

9. Let me here add a little explanation about these main castes. Vankars and Chamars are classified into Scheduled Castes and the former's 'inherent' occupation is weaving and the latter's is leather works. Thakores are included into Backward Classes and whose main occupation is agriculture or agricultural labour. Patidar is a dominant land owning caste in Gujarat state. Maratha is a relatively economically influential cultivating caste whose origin is Maharashtra state.

10. The concentration of Scheduled Castes and the lower castes in the chemical industry is probably due to the characteristics of the industry: more dangerous and hard work; lower skill requirements; predominance of employment through personal connections. The last point is a question to be discussed later.

11. It is true that some of the respondents (especially some of MCS and TS) actually used the formal methods as main methods to job access but this finding does not deny the possibility of the personal connections to have influenced the process.

12. It appears that sex usually has some effect on promotion. But it is out of consideration in this paper because all the sample workers are exclusively male.

13. In questions concerning job history, we requested the respondents to mention the length of employment of all jobs (When started and when terminated) in order to prevent omitting any job. Nevertheless, some respondents may possibly have failed to mention all jobs. The possibility of their omitting jobs is likely to be higher for those which were short-term or intermittent or in which the respondents are engaged as family workers.

14. The closure of factories was mostly the closure of the large textile mills mentioned earlier.

15. The number of employees, 20, is an tentative criterion. Units other than agriculture, when the number of employees could not be identified, were clubbed with the informal sector if their employment status was 'self-employed' or 'family worker'.

References

1. Ahmedabad Municipal Corporation (AMC). *Statistical Outline of Ahmedabad City 1988-89*. Ahmedabad: AMC 1990.

2. Deshpande, S. and L.K. Deshpande. *Labour Mobility in Bombay's Manufacturing Sector*. New Delhi: ILO/ARTEP, 1990.

3. Directorate of Economics and Statistics. *Statistical Abstract of Gujarat State*, 1985 and 1986. Gandhinagar: Directorate of Economics and Statistics, 1987.

4. Kashyap, S.P. 'Industrial Perspective for Ahmedabad Metropolitan Region.' Paper presented at the TRF Seminar on Ahmedabad 2001: Imperatives Now Towards a New Metropolitan Management Strategy, 1988.

5. Harriss, J., Kannan. K.P. and Rodgers, G. *Urban Labour Market Structure and Job Access in India: A Study of Coimbatore*. Geneva: ILO, 1990.

6. Lambert, R.D. *Workers, Factories, and Social Change in India*. New Jersey: Princeton University Press, 1963.

7. Papola, T.S. and Subrahmanian, K.K. *Wage Structure and Labour Mobility in a Local Labour Market*. Ahmedabad: Sardar Patel Institute of Economic and Social Research, 1975.

8. Purohit, S. *Industrializing Economy and Labour Market in India (A Study of Bharuch District)*. New Delhi: Mittal Publications, 1989.

10

Elite Attitudes Towards the Poor : Patidar Entrepreneurs in Rural Central Gujarat

Mario Rutten

Economic and social integration, and the antithesis of the exclusion of the lower classes in rural India is, as in every society, to a large extent controlled by members of the economic elite. Large farmers, traders, and rural industrialists often occupy the main social and political positions in local society through which economic benefits, knowledge, and prestige are distributed to, or withheld from the poorer sections of the population. Moreover, the former are among the main providers of employment in the countryside and it is upon them that a large part of the rural labour force depends for its survival. The economic, social, and political dominance of the rural business elite makes it an important actor in the process of social integration, or exclusion, of distinct categories in society, especially those at the lower end. In order to understand the present position of the weaker sections of society in rural India and to find ways to improve their condition, it is therefore important to have some knowledge of the views and perceptions fostered by the entrepreneurial class towards the poor in society.

In this paper I focus on the economic elite in rural central Gujarat, particularly on the class of large farmers and small-scale industrialists in the countryside of the Charotar tract, an intensively irrigated and agriculturally-developed area which forms a part of Kheda district.[1] Most of these farmers and industrialists belong to the

Patidar community, an upwardly mobile, middle-ranking peasant caste which makes up about fifteen to twenty per cent of the district population. Although the Patidar community can be found in several regions of Gujarat, its main concentration is in the Charotar tract. Since the early part of this century, this community has been able to acquire economic, social, and political dominance at the local, regional, and state level. Within the economic elite of central Gujarat today, in the fields of agriculture, trade, and industry, members of the Patidar community form the large majority of the business population.[2]

The paper starts with a description of recent changes in social distance between the economic elite and the other sections of rural society. These findings show that, as a result of changes in labour relations, educational background, and residential location, members of the entrepreneurial families in central Gujarat are quickly losing direct contact with the remaining village population: relations between the large farmer or industrialist and his workers are increasingly being mediated through a stratum of labour contractors; more and more members of the younger generation are sent away to secondary and even primary schools outside the village; and more and more families are deciding to shift their residence to a separate location away from the village residential area. Underlying this widening social distance between the rural business elite and the village population are changes in the views and perceptions of the rural rich towards the weaker sections of society. In section two, I discuss these views and perceptions which have become more callous in their nature: considering itself to be the backbone of rural society, the economic elite views its life in the lap of luxury as a personal achievement and the presence of the poor as a nuisance and obstacle to further progress. In its view, the poor are not victims but the millstone around India's neck, who should not receive any government support but instead should be disciplined and kept firmly under control. In the final section of the paper, I trace the historical background to these recent changes in social distance and views among the rural entrepreneurial class in central Gujarat, and briefly compare their perceptions on the poor with the findings on rural elites in other regions of Gujarat and India.

Social Distance

An important characteristic of the labour management practised by rural entrepreneurs in central Gujarat is the use of an intermediate stratum of labour contractors or subcontractors. Many of the large farmers and small-scale industrialists today no longer employ their labourers directly and on an individual basis, but hire them through intermediaries or as small teams. In most of these cases, the farmer or industrialist enters into an agreement with a contractor or team of workers to perform specific operations in his fields or factory, such as ploughing, planting, weeding, or harvesting plots of land, loading or unloading trucks with raw materials or finished products, producing a fixed number of articles, or finishing off products. For this, they pay a fixed amount agreed on in advance. Control over production remains in the hands of the large farmer or industrialist who decides on the type and timing of the whole range of operations and usually provides all of the capital required, including financial advances to the intermediary who often does not have the reserves to pay the wages and other allowances of the hired labourers. As a result, many of the labourers are not employed directly by these rural entrepreneurs, but operate as outworkers who are employed as teams or by an intermediate stratum of labour contractors who have been commissioned to carry out part of the production process in which they are responsible for recruitment and actual supervision of the workforce.

This picture of employment arrangements - which relies heavily on the piece-work and outwork systems - illustrates the way in which large farmers and rural industrialists in central Gujarat have transferred the adverse effects of fluctuations in production to the labour force. By thus organizing the recruitment of labour and the work on their farms and in their factories, they have solved the problem of fluctuations in supply and demand of labour, while still exercising control over the production process. As far as possible, they recruit labour on terms which allow them to hire and fire as it suits them, while they accept no responsibility whatsoever for the fate of their workers. These piece-work and outwork systems enable them to shift the onus of supplying work and for the terms of employment to an intermediate group of labour contractors, or, as far as piece-work is concerned, to a team of workers. Although not a new phenomenon, the creation of an intermediate stratum has become an important aspect of the management of large farms and small-scale factories in central Gujarat, in which direct contact and responsibility for the welfare of the labourers working in the fields or factories is increasingly abdicated to an intermediate layer in society.

By contracting out the labour-intensive parts of the production process, the rural entrepreneurs in central Gujarat avoid having to recruit labour and to provide daily supervision on their farms or in their factories. The piece-work or contract system means that they need to carry out inspections only retrospectively, either at the end of the day, or, in some cases, at the end of the week. Many of these families are involved in several economic activities at the same time and often have interests in various sectors of the economy simultaneously: farmers who trade in agricultural products or own a small-scale factory; industrialists who are engaged in commercial ventures and invest part of their industrial and commercial profits in the purchase of agricultural land. While performing their economic activities, these farmers and industrialists have turned themselves more and more into managers who spend a substantial amount of time attending to the external side of their affairs. A significant part of their day's work consists of making contacts and maintaining relations within government organizations, banks, and co-operatives in order to keep up-to-date with marketing trends, and to secure access to capital and material inputs. By paying short visits to their fields or factories and having regular conversations with their middlemen, these entrepreneurs are able to acquire the information they need to take decisions and to give instructions on the work to be done. Not having sufficient relatives to supervise the execution of the work, as a result of the size of the enterprise and the composition of the family, their frequent absence from the village leaves them relatively little time to supervise production processes themselves, and the situation is exacerbated if they are engaged in several business activities in different sectors of the economy simultaneously. Partly for these reasons, large farmers and rural industrialists in central Gujarat resort with mounting frequency, to making use of an intermediate stratum of labour contractors or subcontractors who relieve them from the burden of recruitment and direct supervision. This is installing a system of labour management which diminishes direct contact between the economic elite and the rural labour force, while it enables the entrepreneurial class to continue to perform the major managerial functions on their farms and in their factories.

The distance between members of the economic elite and the remaining village population is widening not only in the field of labour relations, but has also extended into the field of education. Most of the larger-sized, Patidar-dominated villages in the Charotar tract are economically well-developed and have their own primary and secondary schools.[3] Many of these secondary schools are private institutions which were often founded in the 1960s, partly through donations from the economic elite, especially members of the Patidar community. From an early stage, these families recognized education as a valuable addition to the family 'property' and could afford to send their children to the newly-established village schools. Over a period of time, an increasing number of these children have pursued higher education in the nearby towns of Anand and Nadiad. Consequently, most members of the Patidar entrepreneurial families in central Gujarat today are well-educated; especially among the younger generation, both male and female, a diploma course or university degree is no longer exceptional, but has in fact become a quite common level of education.

Until recently, almost all entrepreneurial families in the countryside relied on the availability of primary and secondary education in their own village. During the last ten to twenty years, however, an increasing number of them have supplemented local education with extra, private teaching facilities, such as individual tuition, or sent their children to private primary and secondary schools outside the village. For the sake of their school-going children, over the past few decades more and more entrepreneurial families have bought a house in Anand or Nadiad, to which, part of the family has moved. Some families have started to send their children to English-language schools, while several of them have even begun to send their children for that purpose to boarding-schools outside Kheda district or even outside Gujarat (such as Mount Abu and Panchgani). The purpose of this preference for primary and secondary education outside the village is to provide their children not only with an educational but also with a socio-cultural background which will help them to acquire the necessary knowledge and contacts among the urban middle class to run the family's economic interests in the future. Therefore, many of the younger generation among the rural entrepreneurs, operate within a regional network of economic and social relationships on a day-to-day basis, while they hardly ever have, or have had in their youth, frequent and direct interaction with members of the poorer sections within their home village, including those belonging to their own community.

This widening social cleft between the economic elite and the majority of the village population is further deepened by the recent tendency among the entrepreneurial families to shift their residence to new and distinct geographical locations away from the village. Until recently, the houses of the economic elite in the countryside of the Charotar tract were situated in the centre of the village, which has always been the residential area of the higher castes, in particular of the Patidar community. Hampered by a scarcity of building space in these residential areas, many entrepreneurial families have constructed new houses on specially designated plots just outside the village, while others have moved to one of the district towns. At present, there are separate housing localities on the edge of almost all the larger villages of the Charator tract, most of them being organized within the framework of a co-operative or private housing society. The initiative for establishing these societies came mostly from members of the economic elite in the village. The societies themselves were often established in the 1960s and 1970s, although most of the houses were usually constructed in the 1980s and 1990s. Membership of most of these societies is restricted to families belonging to the higher castes, especially to members of the Patidar community.[4] It is on these plots of land that the entrepreneurial families have been able to give expression to their newly-acquired wealth by building spacious bungalows two to three storeys high, with all kinds of luxurious facilities and furnished with expensive consumer durables.

The shift of residence away from the village centre to separate localities with a socially and economically homogeneous population has meant a further decline of direct contact between the economic elite and the majority of the village population. On top of their frequent absence from the village during the daytime and their abstention from supervision of the work process, their isolated residences leave the large farmers and rural industrialists very limited opportunities to mix or even keep in regular touch with other sections of rural society. Only occasionally and for a very brief visit only, do the male members of the entrepreneurial families still come to the village square in the evening: they usually stay in their car or on their scooter or motorcycle, send out their order for pan, chat for a while with relatives or friends, and then leave again. Slowly but surely, they withdraw from social life in the village and restrict their interaction with the village population to brief contacts with intermediaries, usually within the confines of their offices or on the verandah of their newly-constructed bungalows located outside the village residential area.

Taken as a whole, the recent changes in residential location, labour management, and education among large farmers and rural industrialists in central Gujarat have brought about a widening social distance between the economic elite and the remaining village population, especially the poorer sections among them, as is illustrated by the following case study.

The family of Ambalal Patel (aged 63) owns twelve acres of agricultural land in one of the larger-sized villages of the Charotar tract. Although Ambalal has already handed over the management of the farm to his two sons several years ago, he still spends most of his days near the family's farmhouse on the outskirts of the village. Whenever I met him there he was always somewhere in the fields, checking work in progress at close quarters and discussing the condition of the crop with the labourers. In the 1960s, Ambalal and his brother jointly owned about nine acres of land. At that time, they were usually in the fields throughout the working day, supervising the day-to-day execution of the agricultural work and often doing part of the manual work, such as irrigating the fields, tending the motor pump, and driving the tractor themselves. At the busiest times, during planting and harvesting both brothers could often be seen working alongside their agricultural labourers.

Today, Ambalal's two sons Ashok (37) and Suresh (29) manage the agricultural operations of the family from the verandah of their house or from behind their desk in the office of their factory. Almost all the labourers working in their fields are not employed directly by them, but are hired by one of their four labour contractors to whom they have given their land on contract; each of them is responsible for the labour on two to four acres of land for which they receive a small share in the gross produce. Given this organization of the agricultural work in the field, supervising the execution of the work is not part of Ashok's and Suresh's daily work. Only once in every three to four days, one of the brothers may visit the farmhouse on his scooter or in his car. During those brief visits, they usually analyse the condition of the crop from a distance and hardly ever talk with the labourers directly. When necessary, they address them only through their contractors. It is far more usual for the contractors to come to see the brothers in their office from where they also manage the floor tile factory that the family established a few years back. In this business also, they make use of a piece-work and contract-labour system which allows them to limit their supervision of production to inspections at intervals of several days. By thus instructing their contractors as to the timing and type of operations to be carried out, Ashok and Suresh are able to perform the major managerial functions and to exercise control over the process of production from a distance, both on their farm and in their factory.

A large part of the working day of both Ashok and Suresh is spent outside the village. Part of their time away from home is devoted to buying agricultural inputs or raw materials for their factory, but most of it is concerned directly or indirectly with selling their agricultural products or marketing their finished floor tiles. For this purpose they spend several days a week visiting agrarian traders, building contractors, and government officials in the major cities of Gujarat and sometimes in other states as well. Such activities mean that Ashok and Suresh are hardly ever in the village during the daytime. If they do not come home late, they usually spend their evenings in their office or sometimes at home in front of the television. Up to ten years ago, the family still lived in their ancestral house in the centre of the village. At the insistence of Ashok and Suresh, who wanted to convert part of the family's newly-acquired wealth into a luxurious and more respectable life-style, they then moved to a new three-storey bungalow on the edge of the village. Since then, Ashok and Suresh have tended to turn their backs on the village itself. "I sometimes feel like a visitor in my own village", Ashok told me once after he had returned home from a business trip lasting a few days. "I mostly drop in at the centre of the village for very brief visits only, usually in connection with a family occasion. It is only every so often that I go to the village square in the evening to get some pan or cigarettes and mix with old friends. I therefore can't keep up with the latest bit of news about what's happening in the village, and to be honest, I don't really care."

This tendency to turn away from village society shown by Ashok and Suresh will probably be even stronger among the next generation in their family. Ashok and Suresh went to the village primary and then secondary school until they had obtained their S.S.C. examination, after which they went to high school and college in Anand. A few months ago, the brothers decided that their children will go to primary and secondary schools in Anand from next year onwards. To facilitate this resolve, the family has bought a bungalow in Anand where Suresh will live with his wife and their own children, taking care of Ashok's children as well. When I asked Suresh about their reasons for sending their children to schools in Anand, he answered: "Private schools in Anand have a good reputation and their standard of education is very high. Besides, our children will be able to meet many children from good families at such schools. This might be good for our company and it will help our sons later when they will take over or set up a new kind of business for themselves. As Anand is only twenty minutes by car, this change will not affect the management of our family business. Quite apart from this, I personally like the idea of a move to Anand as most of my friends live there. In fact, I often feel that I have more friends in Anand than here in the village."

Callous Views

The data in the first section show that the widening social distance between the economic elite and the rural poor in central Gujarat can be attributed partly to changing management practices, to the overcrowding of the village residential areas, and to the perceived need for higher education to protect the elite's economic interests in the near future. Alongside these business considerations and other economic-related reasons, this recent increase in social secession of the rural elite is closely related to changes in their social behaviour, and in their views and perceptions towards the poorer sections in society. This is especially true of their preference for management practices which rely heavily on the use of an intermediate stratum of labour contractors. Underlying this preference are indeed economic reasons, but there is also an increasing reluctance among the large farmers and rural industrialists to take part in manual labour and to rub shoulders with those who do. The concentration on managerial tasks by the male members of the entrepreneurial families is part of their transition to a new life-style in which the performance of physical labour is regarded as demeaning, the direct supervision of the work of lower social classes as unpleasant, and the performance of managerial tasks as enhancing one's status. Disengagement from performing manual labour on the farm or in the factory indicates wealth and enhances the status of the family. Being the manager-owner of a farm, trading company, or industrial enterprise, without having to perform manual labour, or even better, without having to come into too - close a contact with those who do, is considered to be a position worth striving for.

This tendency among the rural entrepreneurs in central Gujarat to withdraw, for social reasons, from direct contact with the village population not only applies to their involvement in labour management on their farm or in their factory, but also to their participation in socio-political institutions at the local level. Until recently, local organizations such as the village panchayats (councils) and the local educational boards were controlled by members of the economic elite, especially by those who belonged to the Patidar community. Occupying positions of political dominance, these entrepreneurial families were among those responsible for establishing public facilities in the larger-sized villages of the Charotar tract in the 1950s and 1960s. Many of them were actively involved in getting public funds and private donations to lay on electricity, to put in water pipes, and to construct school buildings. In most cases, they themselves were the main beneficiaries of these facilities: the connections to the water and electricity mains were confined to the residential areas in the centre of the village predominantly inhabited by the Patidar caste, and the schools were attended mostly by children of this same community.

In contrast to this early involvement and participation in the village panchayats and other local organizations, present-day members of Patidar entrepreneurial families are not interested in local politics or social welfare. They have no ambition to stand for the village panchayat and are not interested in the issues discussed during its meetings. Those entrepreneurs who are members of local educational boards seldom attend the meetings. This low level of participation does not mean that the entrepreneurs are satisfied with the present-day level of public facilities in their own village. On the contrary, most families believe that over the past ten to twenty years, the level of public facilities in their village has declined substantially, quoting as examples the overdue maintenance needed on the village roads, on the water supply system, and on the school-buildings. Although they acknowledge these problems, they emphasize that they are not willing to donate money to the village panchayat or local educational board, something which they are regularly asked to do. They are no longer interested in local politics and do not consider the deterioration of public facilities in the village to be their concern.

This withdrawal from local politics and lack of concern for education and public facilities on the part of the Patidar entrepreneurial families is related to changes in the power balance at the village level and the rise in economic position of the families concerned. The gradual shift in power in favour of the lower castes in Kheda district and Gujarat in the 1960s and 1970s affected the balance of power in the village panchayats in the Charotar tract, where the Kshatriyas were eventually able to capture the majority of the seats.[5] Following the decline in power of the Patidars, most Patidar entrepreneurs began to distance themselves from local politics, which to them had become a low-status profession, dominated by members of the lower castes. It was also at this time they became less dependent on the very public facilities which they themselves had helped to build up. Following their economic success in the 1960s and 1970s, these entrepreneurial families were able to acquire modern in-house facilities such as watertanks, bathrooms, and wash-basins, and were in a position to send their children to private educational institutions outside the village. Nowadays, therefore, they are less affected by the malfunctioning of public facilities at the village level. More than anything else their interest lies in the pursuit of profit, in agriculture, trade and industry, and in this goal, they feel, positions of local power do not count for much.

In line with their interests in agriculture, trade, and industry, the rural entrepreneurs in central Gujarat are increasingly voicing their grievances and supporting agitations against government policies at the regional, state, and national level. Although most of the large farmers and rural industrialists manage to evade taxes and circumvent government regulations, and although some have even benefited directly from government subsidies, they have a very negative attitude towards the agricultural and industrial policies of the state and national governments. On many occasions, they publicly emphasize that their interests are not served by government policy, worse they are in fact being frustrated. Considering themselves the backbone of the rural economy, providing employment and income to the village population, they have no compunction about claiming a larger share from the government budget in terms of subsidies while, rather perversely, they feel strongly that they should be left alone to run their economic enterprises without any government interference in the form of labour laws, price regulations, taxes, and so on.

In the field of industry, the resentment of the industrial families towards government policy is shown in complaints asserting that they are 'harassed' by tax officers and labour inspectors, and are not eligible for subsidies which, they say, are given only to factories in backward talukas and to families with poor, low-caste backgrounds. In the field of agriculture, these feelings are expressed in complaints about the imposition of land ceilings, the high level of minimum wages, low prices for agricultural products, and high irrigation rates and power tariffs. In their line of reasoning, any attempt by the government to intervene in these matters, especially in the relationship between employer and labourer, is seen as a direct attack on their freedom of economic movement as entrepreneurs, and on their privileged position as members of the dominant class. They view themselves as the 'sons of the soil' who bring prosperity to the countryside and should therefore receive full support from those in power. They utter a growing litany of complaints about the growing laziness, independence, and impudence of those they hire for work in their fields or factories. As members of the entrepreneurial class, they are of the opinion that the state apparatus should be used to teach the labouring classes discipline rather than support those who are not able to help themselves and are not willing to pay respect to their superiors on whom they depend for survival. In their view, the poor and lower classes in rural society are not to be considered victims but major obstacles to future economic development, whose members should not receive any Government assistance - however marginal - but should be disciplined and kept firmly under control.

It is not only in connection with their economic interests that entrepreneurial families openly voice their grievances against Government policy, this is also betrayed in their social interests. Entrepreneurial families of the Patidar community, especially, have been very outspoken in their criticisms of the social policy pursued by the state and national governments to facilitate access for lower castes to higher professional education and to employment in the public sector through a quota arrangement system of positive discrimination. When this quota of reserved places in education and Government was increased in 1985, they strongly supported the anti-reservation demonstrations which took place in Gujarat in the two years following.[6] Although none of the entrepreneurs participated in any of these demonstrations themselves, they encouraged members of their own community who expressed their willingness to participate, to do so and sometimes offered them the use of their scooter or car with driver. They displayed the same attitude when the reservation policy gave cause for similar protests in various parts of the country in the early 1990s. According to the members of the Patidar entrepreneurial families in central Gujarat, it should not be caste or economic backwardness that form the criteria for selection and admission to higher education and government positions, but intelligence and level of examination marks. They claim that the recent participation of children from the lower castes in 'their' primary and secondary schools has resulted in a decline in the level of education in the village. For this, they blame the Gujarat Government which has tried, by using positive discrimination, to increase the educational opportunities of those who belong to the lower castes.

These complaints about the Government's social policy from the Patidar entrepreneurial families do not imply that they consider their interests best served by emphasizing caste solidarity. Although they usually interact with members of their own community in the village, there is a tendency among the Patidar entrepreneurs to express their discontent openly when their poorer caste-fellows try to lay claim to financial and social caste-solidarity. By shifting their residence away from the village centre and by gradually withdrawing themselves from social and political positions in village society, they are distancing themselves not only from the lower classes in rural society, but also from their poorer caste-fellows, trying not to antagonize them unnecessarily. They are in fast wasting their breath as this tendency is clearly noticed and viewed negatively by the poorer sections within the Patidar community.

Partly fuelled by callous views about the weaker sections in society, over the years the economic elite in the countryside of the Charotar tract has distanced itself to an ever greater extent from the majority of the village population. The younger generation is raised in homes outside the village residential area, educated in private schools in urban localities, and is hardly ever in direct contact with members of the labouring classes working in their family's fields or factories. It would therefore be fair to say that both in terms of business contacts and social life, members of the entrepreneurial families in rural central Gujarat operate on a supra-village or regional level. As part of this, they have adopted a regional middle-class, social frame of reference in which the underlying assumption is that the positions of local status and power do not count for much, at least not for those who are making financial fortunes. They view themselves as part of an elite whose economic and social future does not depend on their local contacts but whose interests coincide with members of the regional or even national middle class, both rural and urban. To be part of such an extended social network also requires an emphasis on caste, kin, and rural ties, but of a different order than earlier. Instead of strengthening sub-caste divisions and relationships with other communities in the village, the Patidar entrepreneurial families in the Charotar tract emphasize an upper caste-class solidarity, based on loyalties between those families who are economically well-off and belong to the upper social stratum in society. As a result, they consider themselves members of a larger community consisting of mainly rich, upper caste families whose freedom of movement is not limited to village, sub-caste, and kin ties, but who operate at a regional or even national level. Following their recent success in agriculture, trade, and industry, they view themselves as the backbone upon which the rural order depends for progress and stability, and whose economic and social interests should be served and not frustrated by the Gujarat and Indian governments whose policies often strike, they feel, at the heart of their very interests and thereby against the interests of the society at large.

The lower classes and the government's educational and social policy were among the topics which the members of the entrepreneurial families in the villages of central Gujarat frequently brought up themselves in the conversations I have had with them over the years. Many of them lament the growing laziness and independent attitudes of the labourers working in their farms or factories. "Nowadays, the labourers are lazy, they just don't bother showing up for work if they don't feel like working. They say they are ill, but they are just being lazy and stay home because they have been drinking the night before and have to sleep it off." During the last years it has even become worse because of the Government, one of them once told me. When I asked him to explain, he answered: "In the past there was a harmonious relationship between the farmer and his labourers. We provided them financial support when necessary and they were loyal to us and always willing to do some extra work. But ever since the Government has started to implement the minimum wage policy, the labourers have become impudent and no longer show their employers any respect. They demand minimum wages, but do not want to work eight hours for these; they come to work late in the morning and leave early in the afternoon. The Government would do better to spend more time on teaching the labourers to fulfill their duties towards their employers than to antagonize the relationship between the farmer and the labourers."

Government intervention in the field of education has also strengthened the entrepreneurial families in their conviction that the Government policy is diametrically opposed to their interests. They claim the standard of education in the villages has deteriorated tremendously since the lower castes began to attend the village schools. "And what's worse", one of them once angrily pointed out to me, "The Government in India as a whole has become totally dominated by the lower castes. The policy of the Congress Party has always been to give

Government jobs and provide admission to engineering and medical courses to people from backward castes, even though most of them are not qualified for these positions. The only reason is that they want to get these peoples' votes. Because of this, in the future our health will depend on unqualified doctors. Even now, we have to say 'Solanki Saheb' when we visit a Government office (Solanki being a common surname among the Kshatriyas in Gujarat). Can you imagine it! 'Solanki Saheb', these people can't even write their own name properly! I tell you, *sarkar emni baju chhe!* (the Government is on their side)."

On various occasions, members of the entrepreneurial families stated that in their opinion a new climate of corruption and a lowering of standards began to make themselves felt in politics when the Kshatriyas first set foot on the political scene in Kheda district in the 1960s. Once sitting in a factory office with two industrialists, one of them told me: "In the beginning, the changes were only minor, but in next to no time the Kshatriyas became more active and began to run 'our' village. I remember my uncle telling me: 'What's the use of spending all my time in politics when the lower castes are in power. Whatever your father, grandfather, and I built up, these uneducated people are unable to manage. They have no interest other then their own self-interest; whenever they can, they use money of the panchayat for their own benefit'. To this, his business partner added: 'This is the reason that I am not interested in politics. Nowadays, it is dominated by the lower castes. The sarpanch of our village is a Bariya (low-ranking Kshatriya). He is an *anghutha chhap* (thumb print), he can't even write his own name. Kshatriyas are all uneducated and have no idea of how to run an organization. They only get elected because there are so many of them. Succumbing to mismanagement, nothing works properly in our village today: for example, the supply of water is irregular because the panchayat has run up a debt with the electricity board. Luckily, we are not affected by it. We have our own water tank which ensures that we have running water throughout the day. Personally I think we businessmen should not get involved in politics. There is nothing to be gained by it. We are better off using our time and energy developing our businesses instead of wasting them in building up what these lower castes will break down in no time at all, either through mismanagement or plain corruption."

In more general terms, the members of the economic elite in the villages of the Charotar tract are of the opinion that it is not poverty which is the problem but the poor themselves. "India could have been among the leaders of the world if there weren't so many poor people", one young entrepreneur told me once. "Hamstrung by their presence, India has become the beggar of the world. It all started with (Mahatma) Gandhi. Have you seen pictures of him, the way he used to dress? Like a beggar! It was he who started with the idea that we should help the poor, and see for yourself, where it has led us. Instead of giving support to those who give employment to the poor, through its reservation policy and interventions in agriculture and industry, the Government has oppressed those very people who could easily have turned India into a developed country. India would have been a much better country if the English had only stayed on here. Look at Hong Kong for example: a rich country which is highly respected throughout the world. What our Government has done is to take money away from the hardworking farmers and businessmen, and to give it the lower classes. But that doesn't mean that you eradicate poverty, it only means you spread poverty over more people and end up having more poor people. Today, India is a beggar on the international scene. Our leaders have to hold out their hands to the World Bank and beg for money. My friends who live in the USA often tell me that foreigners look down upon us because we come from a poor country. If only we had less poor people in India, India would no longer be notorious throughout the world only for its poverty and people like us would receive the respect we deserve."

A New Frame of Reference?

The widening social distance between the economic elite and the majority of the village population in central Gujarat, and the callous views cultivated among these rich entrepreneurial families towards the lower classes in rural society, discussed in the two earlier sections, are based on values, standards, and practices which often go back several generations. This is especially true of the characteristics of withdrawal from manual work, the increase in social secession and supra-local orientation, and the emphasis on expressions of an anti-government attitude. The tendency to move away from performing manual labour has a long tradition among the better-off members of the Patidar community. As part of a process of upward mobility, a small elite of landlords, traders, and money-lenders had already begun to disengage themselves from performing agricultural work in their fields in the second half of the nineteenth century. As part of this same process, this oligarchy among the Patidars tried to set themselves apart and gain prestige through the enforcement of social customs, such as demanding excessively large dowries for marriage, putting a ban on widow remarriage and on exchange marriage, and increasingly secluding and confining the women of the family to their homes. It was partly through these early forms of social secession that this small elite distanced themselves from the remaining village population in an effort to preserve and strengthen their privileged descent and superior status (Bates 1981: 789; Clark 1983: 19-22; Hardiman 1981: 41).

This early social secession was concomitant with a supra-local orientation among the members of this business elite. The profitable trade in tobacco especially - the most important commercial crop in this region - spelled early prosperity for the elite families and brought their members into contact with other parts of India at a relatively early stage. Even before Independence, these families were establishing branch-offices in cities like Calcutta, Nagpur, and Pune to sell their tobacco (Desai 1948). One of the male members of the family would move in his turn, taking his wife and children with him, to the new place, to set up a separate household within the joint family. Consequently, members of the older trading families have long-standing business contacts and well-established social networks in other parts of India, which go far beyond family ties and caste relationships. It was partly as a result of this exposure to the outside world that these families began to place a higher value on education at an early stage. Among a small part of the business elite in the Charotar tract, for several decades it has therefore been common practice to send their children to educational institutions and hostels outside the village.

The expression of strong dissatisfaction with Government policy by the entrepreneurial families in the Charotar tract today also has a relatively long tradition. Within the Patidar community particularly, it is part of an overall anti-Government attitude and reaction to power at the supra-local level. Members of this community formed part of the vanguard of the nationalist movement against British rule (Hardiman 1981), and provided the main leadership for movements and groups against central Congress Party elites which dominated Gujarat politics in the 1950s and 1960s (Wood 1973: 330). During these years, they developed an instinctive dislike for the Congress-dominated Government's professed philosophy of welfarism through taxes, and could not appreciate the logic that some social groups could not climb the economic ladder on their own and, therefore, needed support (Somjee 1978: 113).

Although the widening of social distance between the economic elite and the majority of the village population in central Gujarat is based on older patterns of behaviour, it is also symptomatic of a transition to a new life-style which has only recently become more widespread among the upper stratum of village society. Less than thirty years ago, for instance, most of the male members of the Patidar entrepreneurial families were still performing agricultural labour in their own fields, which earned them a reputation as 'good cultivators' who led a life of simplicity and frugality (Pocock 1972: 62). Forming part of a socially rising caste, an increasingly larger section within the Patidar community benefited from the introduction of new agrarian technology and modern inputs, a process which began in the early 1960s, and this group was subsequently able to infiltrate the ranks of the economic elite gradually through a process of upward economic and social mobility. The raising of one's social status by the expedient of withdrawal from manual labour and social secession is therefore not a new phenomenon among the economic elite in the Charotar tract, but is one which has only recently become more widespread among a larger-sized group of newly-rich entrepreneurial families operating in agriculture, trade, and rural industry.

The urban type of life-style and the supra-local orientation are also relatively new phenomena among the larger part of the economic elite. It was in the 1960s and 1970s especially, that migration by members of the Patidar community to the cities in Kheda district increased substantially (Trivedi 1992: 33-4), a phenomenon which was closely related to a new tendency among a wider section within the Patidar community to send their children to schools outside the village as part of the recent upward economic and social mobility of these families. The same can be said about the strong anti-Government attitude among the economic elite, of which its more callous expression is also the outcome of recent changes. Viewing the Government as an enemy which was increasingly imposing restrictions on their freedom of economic movement, members of the economic elite began to lend their support to the farmers' demonstrations and the agitations against reserved places in Gujarat in the 1970s and 1980s (Bose 1987; Shah 1987), and subsequently many have recently shifted allegiance to the Bharatiya Janata Party. Although based on earlier patterns of behaviour, a reactionary view of life has become more explicit and more widespread among the rural business community of central Gujarat. An important characteristic of this view of life is an espousal of callous views, in which the presence of the poor is seen as a nuisance and an obstacle to further progress, and the Government's attempts to intervene to make a partial correction to the distorted economic and social balance in rural society are viewed as a dangerous threat to stability.

This tendency in central Gujarat towards widening social distance between the economic elite and the majority of the village population, and towards increasing espousal of callous views among the rich entrepreneurial families towards the weaker sections of society, accords with studies on other parts of India. In his research on south Gujarat, Jan Breman, for example, extensively discusses the behaviour and views of the economic elite towards the lower classes in rural society. His conclusions about the characteristics of the members of rich Patidars and Anavil Brahmins in south Gujarat are in line with the features of the Patidar entrepreneurs of central Gujarat, as described in this paper:

> What strikes me each time I return to the area is the unqualified social-Darwinist outlook of the prosperous farmers. This is illustrated by the harshness of their behaviour as individuals towards the landless and the shocking judgements they delight in making in public. Naturally, as members of the dominant caste they permit no doubts regarding their personal superiority, and added to this, they react with condemnation and bitterness to what they perceive as the untrustworthiness of their subordinates, and their reluctance to work. ... In social interchanges with others (the) attitude (of the elite) is characterized by bluntness and arrogance... (and) they show a brutal indifference or even callousness towards those classed as being socially lower (Breman 1985: 430, 108; see also Breman 1993).

An indication that such a 'social-Darwinist outlook' is not specific to the behaviour and attitudes of rural elites but is also present among the urban middle classes in India is shown by the study of James Manor, on the causes and effects of the poisoning disaster by illicit liquor in Bangalore in July 1981. According to Manor : "nothing ...has yet persuaded most middle class people in this and other Indian cities that they are causally involved in the suffering of indigent strangers such as slum dwellers, and that the remote consequences of their actions may prove damaging the poor. ... In Bangalore, it has not become generally accepted...that under urban, industrial conditions, poverty was not so much a reflection of individual moral worth, but that it might hit anyone who found himself without steady employment. Most middle class people in Indian cities, like most prosperous people in rural India, tend to the view – derived in part from caste prejudice – that poor, low status groups are largely to blame for their unhappy state" (Manor 1993: 167-68).

Sad though such attitudes are, it may well be that the tendency towards the abrogation of one's social responsibilities is not confined to Gujarat, or even to India alone. When comparing the views of the middle class residents in Bangalore with those in western countries, Manor emphasizes that "Middle class Americans...have tended increasingly in recent times to retreat from their former belief in the interdependence of all groups within urban society. They have retreated still further from the idea that the sufferings of the urban poor are, in part, the result of elite actions and, hence, the responsibility of elites. Many have gone to the extent of blaming the poor."[7] Wider surveys would probably indicate this to be a global tendency among (newly rich) middle classes everywhere.

Notes

1. The findings presented in this paper are based on field work conducted in 1983-84 and 1986-87, supplemented by impressions during short return visits in 1992, 1995, and 1996. For an account of the results of the 1983-84 research, see Rutten (1986); for an account of he 1986-87 research (and a short revisit in 1992), see Rutten (1995).

2. See for an account of various aspects of the social, political, and economic characteristics of the Patidar community in the Charotar tract of central Gujarat, Hardiman (1981), Pocock (1972), and Rutten (1995).

3. According to the Census of 1981, almost 50 per cent of the total rural population of the Charotar tract lived in villages larger then 5,000 inhabitants, while almost 20 per cent lived in villages larger than 10,000 inhabitants. This figure is considerably above the average for Gujarat State as a whole. Many of these villages are dominated by the Patidar community which usually accounts for 15 to 20 per cent of the village population, while often owning more than half of the total agricultural land. This economic dominance of the patidar community in the agriculturally developed villages in the Charotar tract was already the case during the first decades of this century, when about 130 of the 200 Charotar villages of Kheda District were dominated by Patidars (Hardiman 1981:33).

4. This dominance of the societies by Patidars is illustrated by their names. Many of these private housing societies have included the name of 'Sardar Patel' after India's first Minister of Home Affairs, Vallabhbhai Jhaverbhai Patel, who was a Patidar from Kheda district. Others are named after religious sects which are popular among the members of the Patidar community, as for example the Swaminarayan Sect which has a centre in the Charotar village of Vadtal.

5. For an account of the political rise of the Kshatriya community in central Gujarat, and their power struggle with the Patidars, see Shah (1975; 1983).

6. After the 1975 assembly poll, which was the high water mark of Patidar power, the Congress party in Gujarat evolved the KHAM strategy to expand its political base by winning votes among the Kshatriyas, Harijans, Adivasis, and Muslims. The reserved quota for direct recruitment of Scheduled Castes went up from 12.5 per cent in the 1950s to 15 per cent in the 1970s and for Scheduled Tribes from 5 per cent to 7.5 per cent, in proportion to the rise of their population. On top of that, separate quotas of 10 per cent were introduced for other backward castes in 1978 on the basis of the outcome of a specially appointed commission by the Gujarat Government. This empha-

sis on positive discrimination within the overall KHAM strategy led to a victory for the Congress party in the 1980 elections, which resulted in the dominance of the Kshatriyas at the highest political level in Gujarat and the appointment of Natvarsinh Solanki as the first Kshatriya chief minister. In January 1985 this Government decided to increase the quota for 'other backward castes' from 10 per cent to 28 per cent, thereby bringing the total quota of reservation in education and government jobs from 31 to 49 per cent. This decision - which was based partly on the Rane Commission report following the first anti-reservation protest in 1981 - triggered off new riots which started in Ahmedabad in 1985 and quickly spread to other cities and rural areas of Gujarat (Shah 1987; Sheth and Menon 1986).

7. Manor (1993 : 172). In his discussion of the elite perceptions on the poor in Western countries, Manor builds his argument around the concepts and ideas developed by Abram De Swaan in his study of the evolution of social policy in Western Europe and the United States (De Swaan 1988).

References

Bates, C.N. 'The Nature of Social Change in Rural Gujarat: The Kheda District, 1818-1918'. *Modern Asian Studies* 15, 4 (1981): 771-821.

Bose, Pradip Kumar. 'Kulaks on the Rise'. *Economic and Political Weekly* 22, 25 (1987): 974-76.

Breman, Jan. *Of Peasants, Migrants and Paupers: Rural Labour Circulation and Capitalist Production in West India*. Delhi: Oxford University Press, 1985.

___. *Beyond Patronage and Exploitation: Changing Agrarian Relations in South Gujarat*. Delhi: Oxford University Press, 1993.

Clark, Alice 'Limitations on Female Life Chances in Rural Central Gujarat'. *The Indian Economic and Social History Review* 20, 1 (1983): 1-25.

Desai, M.B. *The Rural Economy of Gujarat*. Bombay: 1948.

De Swaan, Abraham. *In Care of the State: Health Care, Education and Welfare in Europe and the USA in the Modern Era*. Oxford: Polity Press, 1988.

Hardiman, David. *Peasant Nationalists of Gujarat: Kheda District 1917-1934*. Delhi: Oxford University Press, 1981.

Manor, James. *Power, Poverty and Poison: Disaster and Response in an Indian City*. Delhi: Sage Publications, 1993.

Pocock, David. *Kanbi and Patidar: A Study of the Patidar Community in Gujarat*. Oxford: Clarendon Press, 1972.

___. *Mind, Body and Wealth: A Study of Belief and Practice in an Indian Village*. Oxford: Basil Blackwell, 1973.

Rutten, Mario. 'Social Profile of Agricultural Entrepreneurs: Economic Behaviour and Life-Style of Middle-Large Farmers in Central Gujarat'. *Economic and Political Weekly* 21, 13: A-15 - A-23 (1986).

___. *Farms and Factories: Social Profile of Large Farmers and Rural Industrialists in West India*. Delhi: Oxford University Press, 1995.

Shah, Ghanshyam. *Caste Association and Political Process in Gujarat; A Study of Gujarat Kshatriya Sabha*. Bombay: Popular Prakashan, 1975.

___. 'Socio-Economic Stratification and Politics in Rural Gujarat', in Lakdawala D.T. (ed.). *Gujarat Economy: Problems and Prospects*, Ahmedabad: Sardar Patel Institute of Economic and Social Research, (1983): 169-92.

___. 'Middle Class Politics: Case of Anti-Reservation Agitations in Gujarat'. *Economic and Political Weekly* 22, 19,20,21, (Annual May Number, 1987).

Sheth, Pravin. *Patterns of Political Behaviour in Gujarat*. Ahmedabad: Sahitya Mudranalaya, 1976.

___. 'Caste, Class and Political Development: An Overview', in Lakdawala D.T. (ed.). *Gujarat Economy: Problems and Prospects*. Ahmedabad: Sardar Patel Institute of Economic and Social Research, (1983): 19-210.

Sheth, Pravin and Menon, Ramesh. *Caste and Communal Time-Bomb*. Ahmedabad: Golwala Publications, 1986.

Somjee, A.H. 'Social Mobility among the Patidars of Kaira'. *Contributions to Asian Studies* 12, (1978): 105-13.

Trivedi, Jayprakash M. *The Social Structure of Patidar Caste in India*. Delhi: Kanishka Publishing House, 1992.

Wood, John R. *The Political Integration of British and Princely Gujarat; The Historical-Political Dimension of Indian State Policies*, Ph.d. thesis. New York: Columbia University, 1973.

11

Differentiated Diversification of Occupations in a Multi-Caste Village

Tsuguo Nakasato

Unemployment in India today is not only limited to the rural areas but encompasses the entire country. Affected by urbanization, the market economy has penetrated deep into the villages which can no longer function without cash income. During the last thirty years, population has increased tremendously and employment opportunities have become increasingly limited. The majority of villagers fail to get employment round the year in rural areas.

The Green Revolution which began from the end of the 1960s and is based on irrigated farming with a multicropping pattern, has certainly increased demand for labour to a large extent. However, the increase in population has exceeded the demand for labour in rural India. Moreover, in some areas, there is a tendency towards single cash cropping pattern because of profit-making factors. In these areas, the demand for agricultural labour is stagnant and may actually be decreasing (Nakasato 1992:31-67).

Recent studies indicate a certain degree of progress in the diversification of employment among the backward classes including the Scheduled Castes (SCs) and the Scheduled Tribes (STs) (Fujiwara 1992, Fukunaga 1993, Yanagisawa 1985, Rakesh Basant and Harish Joshi 1994). This phenomena, however, is still partial and limited to certain regions. It should be noted that the number of agricultural labourers, the majority of whom belong to the backward classes, has been increasing during the past thirty years (Patel 1981:273-311). The growth in population of the backward classes, forming the bulk of the poor in rural India, may have intensified the problem of rural unemployment.

In this paper, the conditions of employment in a village in central Gujarat are traced. This study was carried out with reference to four factors: (1) growth in population of the backward classes, (2) development of market-oriented farming, (3) development of urbanization which has brought about a steady progress in the informal sector, and (4) spread of education in rural society. Besides these factors, the paper also discusses the extent to which the strong influence and the control over the backward classes by dominant castes in village society has impeded the progress in the diversification of employment among the backward classes.

Attempts have also been made to clarify the occupational changes that have occurred during the thirty years since 1961. Ambav was selected as the sample village, because one of the monographs of the 1961 census provided detailed data on occupations in this village (Trivedi 1968:16). A household survey of the village was undertaken in order to compare the situation with that of the 1961 monograph. However, data could be collected from about 91 per cent of the village households because of certain practical difficulties.[1]

Ambav : Some Features

Ambav is a prosperous, multicaste village in Thasra taluka of Kheda district in central Gujarat. The village is situated on the right side of the alluvial plain of the Mahi river. According to the census of 1991, it has an area of 315 hectares and a population of 1512. The railway station, which is on the Anand-Godhra railway line, and the state highway are very close to the main settlement site. Taluka headquarters Thasra is only four kilometres away from the village and is approachable by rail and road in all seasons. The village is situated about 40 kilometres away from Anand, the largest centre of the milk industry in India (Kaira District Co-operative Milk Producers Union 1988).

The village consists of three settlements as can be seen in Map 1 (a) the superior main old settlement, where mainly Patidars, the landowning caste, dwell; (b) the bazaar, running parallel to the state highway on the north, newly set up as a result of growing urbanization; and (c) the new settlement of the Bharwards (shepherds) who have recently migrated into the village from Kathiawar.[2]

Population and Caste

Ambav is a medium-sized village of the district (Chhaya 1982:xxxiv). As can be seen in Table 1, population in 1961 was a mere 589. According to the 1981 census, population rose 2.35 times to 1387. However, the population growth since the 1980s has showed down (0.9 per cent). It has declined because of a fall in the birth rate. Moreover, some Patidars and others have migrated in search of new profitable jobs to cities like Mumbai and Ahmedabad. Urban jobs are regarded as highly lucrative by the villagers. A few persons have emigrated even to the United States and the Gulf. Female population rose from 40.2 per cent of total population in 1961 to about 46.8 per cent in 1981. Population density has increased from 419 persons to 441 persons per sq. km. during 1961-81.

Ambav is a multi ethnic village. Hindus, Muslims, Christians and Sikhs have long been living together. Muslims in the village are divided into four 'castes': Shaikhs, Pathans, Maliks and Vohras. Vohras are said to be mostly descendants of Hindu converts (Trivedi 1968:6). Christians in the village are Roman Catholics, converted from Vankars, a Scheduled Caste, in 1952. Some of them have recently immigrated to get better jobs (Trivedi 1968:7).

Table 1 : Households and Population of Ambav

Year	HHs	Person	Male	Female	AIR
1951	-	547	304	243	-
1961	98	589	352	237	0.8
1971	-	961	-	-	6.3
1981	247	1387	738	649	4.4
1991	-	1512	-	-	0.9

Notes : HHs - Number of Households
Source : Official Census Data

Settlement Pattern of Village Ambav

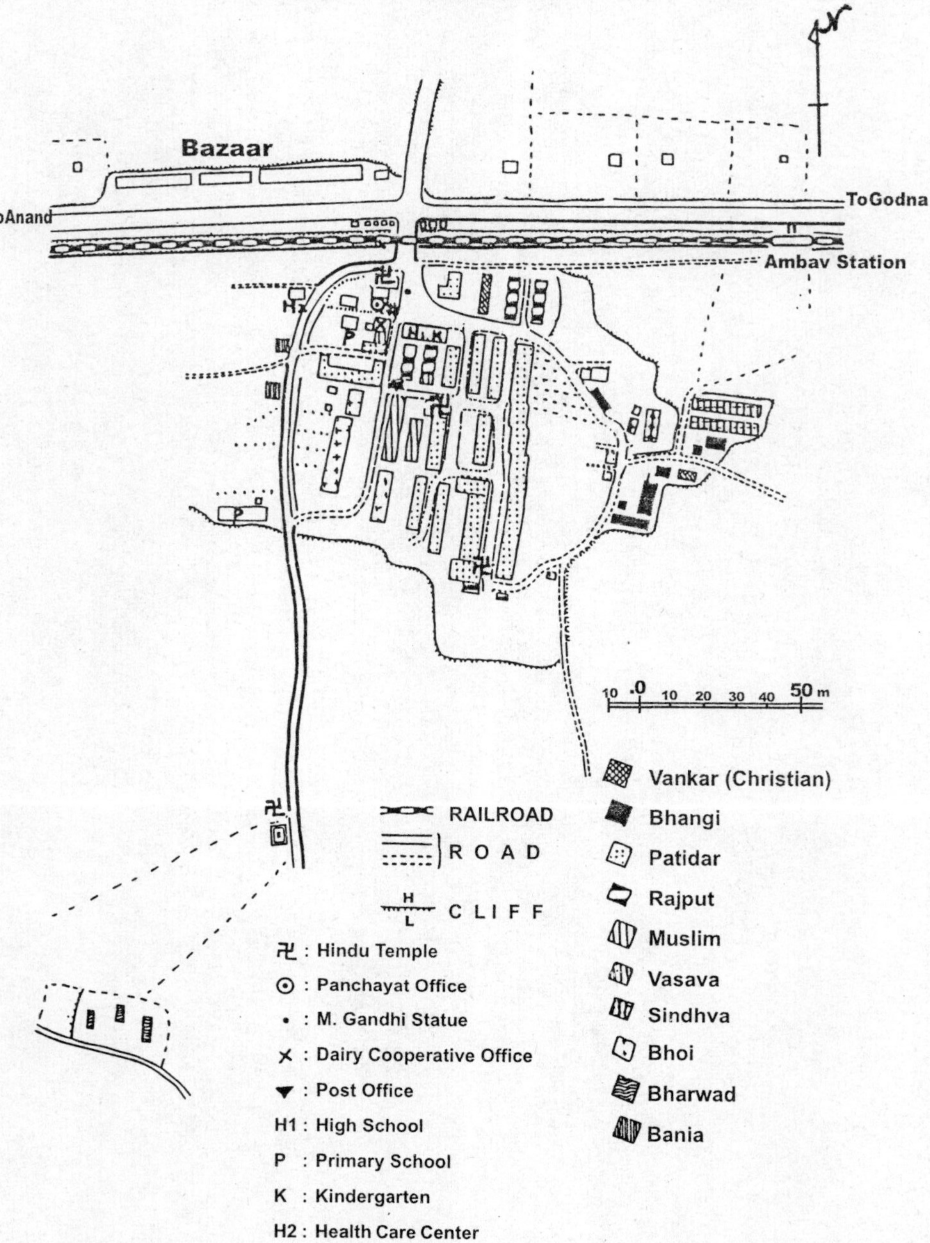

Comparing the data of the 1961 census with our survey in 1991, we can distinguish the following characteristics as shown in Table 2: While the population of Hindu and Muslim communities has shown an increase, the Christian community has recorded a decline. A Sikh family has settled down at the new bazaar settlement. The ratio of SC and ST households to the total number of Hindu households has increased from 12.0 per cent to 28.6 per cent, while the population ratio has increased from 10.0 per cent to 26.1 per cent. While Muslim households and population have shown an increase, Christian households and population have actually decreased.[3] Twelve *jatis* of Hindus have been added recently. Excluding Bharwads and Bahariyas[4] the number of new migrants of each *jati* is very small.

Newly Developed Features

Since 1961, the population growth of Ambav has been mainly because of natural and social increases of backward class population including SC and ST. At present, there are 15 *jatis* of backward classes.[5] Of these, nine *jatis* have immigrated since 1961. The population share of backward classes increased from 29.0 per cent in 1961 to 44.2 per cent in 1991. For example, in the Bhangi community, population has increased from one household in 1961 to 11 households in 1991. The Bhangi population increased, as a result of natural growth, from four persons and one household in 1961, to 40 persons and six households in 1991. Five new Bhangi households came in from neighbouring villages as agricultural labourers.

The new *jatis* which have migrated into the village since 1961 include more than 10 households of Bharwads, a community of shepherds, came from Kathiawar, five households of Bahariyas from Panchmahals, and other STs from neighbouring mountainous regions as stone quarry labourers.

Development of Market Oriented Farming

Agricultural development in Ambav can be divided into : rainfed farming and irrigated farming. Surface irrigation came to the village in the 1970s.

Ambav is located in Kheda district, an advanced region in agriculture and dairy farming. The construction of the Mahi canal has greatly facilitated the development of agriculture in the district. Work

Table 2 : Population of Ambav by Religion and Jati

Religion	1961				1991			
Jatis	HHs	Person	Male	Female	HHs	Person	Male	Female
1 Hindu	75	470	284	186	196	1107	600	507
Patidar	30	208	132	76	52	283	152	131
Rajput	27	149	86	63	41	264	148	116
Bhoi	5	44	25	19	15	114	55	59
Valand	2	15	11	4	2	10	5	5
Bania	1	6	2	4	2	8	4	4
Suthar	1	1	1	0	1	4	2	2
Bharwad					14	77	45	32
Brahman					3	10	8	2
Prajapati					2	12	7	5
Bhalia					2	13	9	4
Luhar					1	11	5	6
Rathodia					1	4	3	1
Katara					1	3	2	1
Bhabhai					1	2	1	1
Nair					1	1	1	0
Other					1	2	1	1
SC								
Sindhva	3	22	13	9	12	64	32	32
Bhangi	1	4	2	2	11	67	34	33
Rohit					1	1	1	0
ST								
Vasava	5	21	12	9	24	120	63	57
Bahariya					5	20	12	8
Damor					1	6	5	1
Nayaka					2	11	5	6
2 Christian	14	65	37	28	10	38	19	19
3 Muslim	9	54	31	23	18	122	75	47
4 Sikh					1	6	4	2
Total	**98**	**589**	**352**	**237**	**225**	**1273**	**698**	**575**

Source : Village survey monograph 1961
Field survey 1991 (Nakasato)

on the Mahi Right Bank Canal Project began in 1949 and construction of the head works was completed in 1958-59 (Rajyagor 1977:241). Cutting across the village, the project was expected to meet the irrigation needs of the village. However, since the majority of the arable land was situated at a greater height than the canal, many areas could not get water. Well irrigation was almost absent because of high construction costs as the sub-soil water was deep (Trivedi 1968:21). Apart from the village well, two wells were dug by two Patidar farmers who thus derived the benefit of irrigation. According to the village survey monograph of 1961, only about 20 acres or 2.4 per cent of the arable land was under irrigation.

The cultivated area of cotton was the largest at 180 acres (27.5 per cent of net sown area) followed by that of tobacco. It is, thus, possible to deduce that the crop pattern of the village was cash-crop oriented.

Regarding landownership, the Patidar community owned 71.2 per cent of the total arable land of 572.36 acres. The Rajput community owned 14.2 per cent, Muslims and Bhois 3.0 per cent each, and Christians 2.7 per cent. Each Patidar household owned an average of 14.03 acres which was three to four times larger than that of other communities.

The shift from rainfed farming to irrigated farming seems to have taken place in the first half of the 1970s, because the canal system covering a command area of 178,705 hectares with a main canal of 46 miles length, and 6 branches of 140 miles length was completed by September 1973. In addition, at least three new wells for irrigation were dug in the 70s, as shown in Table 3. At the time of our survey, about 70 per cent of the total arable land was under well and canal irrigation. The crop pattern underwent a change from cultivation of four crops to cultivation of two main crops (tobacco and rice) thanks to the availability of irrigation facilities and cheap labour. These two crops represented 78.5 per cent of the net sown area in 1989 (Table 4).

Looking at the distribution of landholdings, about 45 per cent of the total of 226 households surveyed are landholders (Table 5). Out of these 102 land holders, 44 are Patidars who own 70.4 per cent of the total arable land. Although tobacco and rice cultivation is increasing in the village, it remains to be seen whether this trend will continue in the future.

An analysis of our field data shows that the costs of chemical fertilizers and labour wages account for more than 50 per cent of the

Table 3 : Wells for Irrigation in Ambav

	Name of Owner	Jati	Year	Depth in Feet Pre. M	Depth in Feet Post. M
1	J. B. Patel	Patidar	1940	N. A.	N. A.
2	Panchayat		1940	70	75
3	B. C. Patel	Patidar	1942	65	70
4	M. H. Patel	Patidar	1972	65	70
5	R. C. Patel	Patidar	1972	65	70
6	C. B. Patel	Patidar	1973	65	70
7	H. H. Patel	Patidar	1989	80	90

Note : M : Monsoon
Source : Field Survey of 1992 (Nakasato)

Table 4 : Net Sown Area of Main Crops

	Crops	1961 (Acre) (%)	1989 (Acre) (%)
	Paddy	101(15.4)	211.3(35.8)
Grain	Jowar	23(3.5)	0.0(0.0)
	Bajri	46(7.0)	79.3(13.4)
	Bavto	20(3.1)	0.0(0.0)
Pulses	Tuver	16(2.4)	10.8(1.8)
&	Wal	15(2.3)	0.0(0.0)
Tobacco	Tobacco	121(18.5)	251.9(42.7)
	Groundnut	90(13.7)	0.0(0.0)
Non-	Cotton	180(27.5)	6.5(1.1)
food	Suudhiyu	26(4.0)	0.0(0.0)
	Kodra	0(0.0)	8.0(1.1)
	Char	0(0.0)	8.6(1.4)
	Castor	0(0.0)	10.1(1.7)
	Others	17(2.6)	3.6(0.6)
Total		**655(100.0)**	**590.1(100.0)**

Source : 1961 (Village survey monograph 1961)
1989 (Talati data 1990-91)

Table 5 : Landholding Patterns by Jati in Ambav

Religion	No of	Landholdings			bigha	House		
Jatis	HHs	IL	UIL	Total	(%)	Own	Rent	Other
1 Hindu	196	487.4	254.5	741.9	91.7	172	17	7
Patidar	52	420.5	148.7	569.2	70.4	46	5	1
Rajput	41	32.4	66.3	98.7	12.2	37	2	2
Bhoi	15	13.0	22.5	35.5	4.4	14	0	1
Valand	2	3.0	0.0	3.0	0.4	2	0	0
Bania	2	3.0	0.0	3.0	0.4	2	0	0
Suthar	1	0.0	0.0	0.0	0.0	1	0	0
Bharward	14	0.0	0.0	0.0	0.0	14	0	0
Brahman	3	0.0	0.0	0.0	0.0	1	1	1
Prajapati	2	0.0	0.0	0.0	0.0	1	1	0
Bhalia	2	0.0	0.0	0.0	0.0	1	1	0
Luhar	1	0.0	0.0	0.0	0.0	1	0	0
Rathodia	1	0.0	0.0	0.0	0.0	1	0	0
Katara	1	0.0	6.0	6.0	0.7	0	1	C
Bhabhai	1	4.0	0.0	4.0	0.5	0	1	0
Nair	1	4.0	0.0	4.0	0.5	1	0	0
Other	1	0.0	0.0	0.0	0.0	0	1	0
S.C.								
Sindhva	12	0.0	8.0	8.0	1.0	12	0	0
Bhangi	11	0.5	0.0	0.5	0.1	8	1	2
Rohit	1	0.0	0.0	0.0	0.0	1	0	0
S.T.								
Vasava	24	0.0	0.0	0.0	0.0	24	0	0
Bahariya	5	1.0	0.0	1.0	0.1	5	0	0
Damor	1	0.0	2.0	2.0	0.2	0	1	0
Nayaka	2	6.0	1.0	7.0	0.9	0	2	0
2 Christian	10	7.0	3.1	10.1	1.2	10	0	0
3 Muslim	18	30.3	26.5	56.8	7.0	14	4	0
4 Sikh	1	0.0	0.0	0.0	0.0	0	1	0
Total	**225**	**524.7**	**284.1**	**808.8**	**100.0**	**196**	**22**	**7**

Note : IL : Irrigated Land
UIL : Unirrigated Land

Source : Field Survey 1991 (Nakasato)

total cost. Landholders of communities other than Patidars have only an insignificant role in the development of market oriented agriculture in the village.[6]

Development of Urbanization and Formation of the Bazaar Settlement

The bazaar settlement in Ambav came up under the influence of urbanization of the village. The old settlement of Ambav is gradually declining with the formation of the bazaar situated along the state highway.

At the time of our survey, the bazaar consisted of forty-four establishments (Table 6). Its formation can be roughly divided into three stages according to the number and varieties of establishments.

Table 6 : Type of Shops and Their Numbers in Ambav Bazzar

	Type of Shop (Business)	Number of Establishments
1	Pan and Bidi	7
2	Auto Services	7
3	Quarry Works	6
4	Hotel	6
5	Saw Mill	4
6	Transport Services	4
7	Tyre Services	2
8	Hair Saloon	2
9	Cycle Repairings	1
10	Oil & Electrics	1
11	Others	4
	Total	**44**

Source : Field Survey of 1992 (Nakasato)

(a) The first stage (up to the 70s) : During this period, two stone quarries, one stone transport company, and one hair cutting saloon were set up. According to Table 7, among the twenty-eight establishments surveyed, four were set up at this time. These were run by persons from outside the village. The first establishment was a transport business run by a Muslim who benefited from the locational advantages of the site. Stone and sand used to be loaded into trucks from the pier of the Mahi river. Two stone quarries were then established along the state highway by a Brahmin and a Patidar. The quarry run by the Patidar was built on personal land and was the biggest in the bazaar with twenty-five employees at the time of our survey. The village panchayat leased out the land for other establishments. The labourers were brought in from outside the village.

(b) The second stage (from 1980-89) : The remarkable feature of this stage was that seven out of 12 establishments were set up by the villagers of Ambav themselves. They are run by Rajputs, Patidars (two each), Muslim, Bhangi and Valand (1 each). These were a saw mill, a fuel shop, pan and bidi shop, a hair cutting saloon, a cycle repair shop, an electrical repair shop, and a watch repair shop. Outsiders set up a hotel, a pan and bidi shop, a transport company, a salt factory, and a truck repair shop.

(c) The third stage (after 1990) : Four pan and bidi shops, three tyre repair shops, one furniture shop, one electrical repair shop, and one quarry were set up. Out of these establishments, the furniture shop and tyre repair shops are owned by the villagers. It is interesting to note that a businessman from Ahmedabad has set up quarry work in the bazaar. The outsiders commute to the village for business purposes. Another feature of this stage is that several small scale businesses have sprung up in the village. These are the stages of the formation of the bazaar settlement and the resultant urbanization in the village. The function of these establishments in the bazaar has rarely any relation to the daily lives of the villagers of the old settlement.

However, even within the old settlement, development of commercial activities has become important, especially for the landless labourers. This is because their employers stopped giving them meals and instead doubled their daily wages to Rs. 10 since 1982. Responding to their needs, three grocery shops, four vegetable shops and one pan and bidi shop were established within the old settlement. The

Table 7 : A List of Establishments (Business and Shops) in Ambav

Location of Settlement	Stage	Sl. No.	Type of Business	Age of Owner	Religion	Jati	Owner from	Year of foundation	Items	No. of Empl-yees	Annual Income Rs.
		1	Transport	55	M	Muslim	Dholka	1965	Stone, Sand, Metal	5	N. A
	First	2	S. Quarry	78	H	Patidar	Ghodra	1966	Stones	25	N. A
	Stage	3	S. Quarry	43	H	Brahman	Thasra	1972	Stones	3	20000
		4	Saloon	55	H	Barber	Thasra	1975	Hair cutting	0	9000
		5	T. Reparing	N. A	M	Muslim	Indore	1980	Truck	2	25000
		6	W. Reparing	18	M	Muslim	Ambav	1982	Watches	0	4800
		7	Saw Mill	45	H	Patidar	Ambav	1982	Wood	3	N. A
		8	Hotel	45	M	Muslim	Bhalej	1984	Rice, Mutton, Chapati	2	40000
	Second	9	Fuel	57	H	Bhangi	Ambav	1985	Woods	0	15000
	Stage	10	Saloon	34	H	Barber	Ambav	1986	Hair Cutting	1	12000
		11	C. Reparing	35	H	Patidar	Ambav	1987	Cycles	0	7200
New		12	Pan & Bidi	30	H	Rajput	Anandp	1987	Pa. Bidi, Stationary	0	18000
Bazzar		13	E. Reparing	N. A	H	Rajput	Ambav	1987	Dynamo	0	15000
Settlement		14	Transport	45	M	Muslim	Malvan	1988	Stone, Sand	4	35000
		15	Salt Powder	45	H	Patidar	Mehsana	1988	N. A	0	N. A
		16	Pan & Bidi	25	H	Rajput	Ambav	1988	Pan and Bidi	0	2400

Table 7 : (Continued)

Location of Settlement	Stage	Sl. No.	Type of Business	Age of Owner	Religion	Jati	Owner from	Year of foundation	Items	No. of Empl-yees	Annual Income Rs.
		17	T. Reparing	30	N. A	N. A	Ambav	1990	Tyre Repair	. 1	15000
		18	Furniture	50	H	Haryanvi	Ambav	1990	N. A	1	N. A
		19	S. Quarry	55	J	Jain	Ahmedal	1990	Stone	6	N. A
		20	Pan & Bidi	30	M	Muslim	Angari	1990	Pa, Bidi, Stationary	0	20000
	Third	21	T. Reparing	20	H	Patidar	Jarsad	1990	All type of Wheel	0	4000
	Stage	22	Pan & Bidi	26	H	Rajput	Ananpu	1990	Pan, Bidi, Masala	0	12000
		23	Pan & Bidi	32	M	Muslim	Angadi	1991	Pan, Bidi, Stationary	0	14500
		24	Repair	26	M	Muslim	Godhra	1992	Wiring Dianand	0	24000
		25	Auto Service	30	M	Muslim	Bhalej	1992	N. A	0	12000
		26	Pan & Bidi	20	H	Rajput	Unlet	1992	Pan, Bidi, Masala	0	18000
		27	T. Reparing	50	H	Nayar	Thasra	N. K	Tyre Reparing	0	40000
		28	Snacks	N. A	H	Rajput	Sukhi	N. K	N. A	1	45000
		1	Grocery	22	H	Patidar	Ambav	1955	Rice, Wheat, Soap	2	12000
Within		2	Grocery	52	H	Patidar	Ambav	1982	Wheat, Rice, Soap	0	15000
The Main		3	Pan & Bidi	28	H	Darbar	Sarnal	1982	Pan, Bidi, Cigarate	0	9000
Old		4	Vegetable	37	H	Rajput	Ambav	1983	Vegetable, Mashala	1	2000
Settlement		5	Vegetable	28	H	Rajput	Ambav	1987	Vegetable, Curds	0	6000
		6	Grocery	65	H	Patidar	Ambav	1990	Rice, Wheat, Bidi	0	17000
		7	Vegetable	N. A	M	Muslim	Ambav	1991	Vegetable, Buscuits, B.	0	6800
		8	Vegetable	37	H	Rajput	Ambav	1992	Vegetable, Mashala	0	3000

Source : Field Survey of 1991, 1992. (Nakasato)

grocery shops are operated by Patidars who also lend money to agricultural labourers. Most of the villagers of the old settlement frequently visit these shops rather than those of the bazaar to meet their daily requirements.

Differentiated Diversification of Occupation among Communities

Table 8 shows changes in the occupational pattern that have taken place in the past 30 years in Ambav. Data of our survey of 1991 are compared with those of the village survey monograph of 1961 in which occupations were roughly divided into four categories: agriculture, agricultural labour, livestock and miscellaneous works.(Trivedi 1968:16).

In 1961 among the total of 98 households in the village, fifty-six households (57.1 per cent) were engaged in agriculture. Among these households, 28 were Patidars, followed by 15 Rajput households. The two communities accounted for 76.8 per cent of the total farm households in the village. They dominated agricultural activities in Ambav.

Seven households of Christians, seven households of Rajputs, one household of Bhangi and one household of Patidar were engaged as agricultural labourers. Only one household, a Bhoi, was engaged in livestock rearing as the main occupation. Miscellaneous work such as railway service, school teacher, government service, basket making, carpentry, etc., was carried out by 6 Muslims, 5 Vasava Bhils, 5 Rajputs, 3 Bhoi households, (Trivedi 1968 :26-27).

At the time of the 1961 survey, a simple occupational structure prevailed in the village. In brief, Patidars and Rajputs were the principal landholders while the backward classes were mainly engaged in agricultural labour and miscellaneous works. The occupational pattern has undergone several changes in the past thirty years. The most striking feature is that there has been a dramatic increase in the agricultural labour households. Among 225 households, as many as 80 (35.6 per cent) are currently engaged in agricultural labour.

In concrete terms, the number of landowning households fell to 54 mainly because of a decrease in the number of Rajput landowners who shifted their occupation to agricultural labour. Moreover, Vasava Bhils (24 households), and the SCs also shifted to agricultural labour. Of the 82 households engaged in miscellaneous works, 16 households belong to Patidars, again a very conspicuous phenomenon. Rajput and

Table 8 : Occupational Patterns by Jati

Religion		1961						1991					
	Jatis	HHs	P	A	AL	L	M	HHs	P	A	AL	L	M
1 Hindu	Patidar	30	208	28	1	0	1	52	281	36	0	0	16
	Rajput	27	149	15	7	0	5	41	264	7	19	0	15
	Bhoi	5	44	1	0	1	3	15	114	2	4	0	9
	Valand	2	15	1	0	0	1	2	10	1	0	0	1
	Bania	1	6	1	0	0	0	2	8	1	0	0	1
	Suthar	1	1	0	0	0	1	1	4	0	0	0	1
	Bharwad							14	7	0	0	9	5
	Brahman							3	10	0	0	0	3
	Prajapati							2	12	0	0	0	2
	Bhalia							2	13	0	1	0	1
	Luhar							1	11	0	0	0	1
	Rathodia							1	4	0	1	0	0
	Katara							1	3	0	0	0	1
	Bhabhai							1	2	0	0	0	1
	Nair							1	1	0	0	0	1
	Other							1	2	0	0	0	1
S. C	Sindhva	3	22	2	0	0	1	12	64	0	10	0	2
	Bhangi	1	4	0	1	0	0	11	67	0	11	0	0
	Rohit							1	1	0	1	0	0
S. T	Vasava	5	21	0	0	0	5	24	119	0	22	0	2
	Bahariya							5	20	0	0	0	5
	Damor							1	6	0	0	0	1
	Nayaka							2	11	0	0	0	2
2 Christian		14	65	5	7	0	2	10	38	2	8	0	0
3 Muslim		9	54	3	0	0	6	18	122	5	3	0	10
4 Sikh								1	6	0	0	0	1
Total		98	589	56	16	1	25	225	1273	54	80	9	82

Note : P - Persons, A - Agriculture, AL - Agricultural Labourer, L - Livestock, M - Miscellaneous

Source : Village survey monograph 1961, Field survey 1991 (Nakasato)

Muslim households engaged in miscellaneous activities have also gone up. Moreover, the number of people engaged in these activities has increased as the bazaar was set up in recent years and several people from neighbouring villages have come to work here.

In our survey, we have classified occupations into six types on the basis of nature of employment (self-employed or employee) and the nature of job (permanent or temporary).

Out of the total population of 1273 people in the 225 households, 525 (41.2 per cent) worked as main workers. Occupations of the 525 main workers by Jati are shown in Table 9. Of these, 421 are males, representing 80.2 per cent of total main workers. Female workers numbering 104 represent 19.8 per cent. It is worth mentioning that more than 50 per cent of the Female workers belong to SCs and STs. Of the total of 525 workers, self-employed workers are 161 (30.7 per cent). Of the 161 self-employed workers, 52.2 per cent belong to the agricultural sector mainly operated by Patidars, 29.8 per cent to businesses operated by *jatis* other than SCs, STs and Christians, and 14.9 per cent (all come from the Bharward community) to livestock rearing. Traditional caste occupations of barber, carpenter and potter are performed by five persons.

On the other hand, employee workers account for 69.3 per cent of the total workers, and can be divided into temporary workers and permanent workers. Temporary workers account for as much as 63.6 per cent of the total workers. As can be seen in Table 10, the majority are engaged as agricultural labourers and account for 77.5 per cent of the total temporary workers. This is the most numerous class among the labour force of Ambav. Of the remaining temporary workers 9.0 per cent are engaged as quarry labourers and 6.9 per cent are employed in transport activities.

All the workers of the STs, SCs and Christians except one person, work as temporary labourers, accounting for 48.5 per cent of temporary workers and 43.7 per cent of them belong to Rajput, Bhoi, and Muslim communities.

Increasing Demand for Labour

The answer to the conspicuous increase in agricultural labourers is found in the new agricultural pattern emerging after the introduction of irrigation facilities in the village. Compared to the single cropping pattern under rainfed farming, irrigated farming increases the demand for labour by 2-3 times. In the case of Ambav, not only the total number of agricultural labourers but also yearly contracted labourers have increased rapidly since 1961. In 1961 agricultural labourers were mainly of two types : Bhagia, who were employed on a yearly contract basis and Dadio, who were employed as daily wage earners (Joshi 1986:6-8). Three households worked as Bhagia out of a total of 32 families working as agricultural labourers (Trivedi 1968:26). Those employed full-time as agricultural labour numbered about 50 (Trivedi 1968:16) out of a total labour force of 204 in 1961, i.e., about 20 per cent. However, their ratio shot up to 49.3 per cent in 1991. At present, almost all these labourers are employed under the Dadio system.

Table 11 shows the production cost of tobacco cultivation by operations. Preparatory tilling is done by tractors and bullocks before transplantation and interculture. The other stages of operations, namely, manuring, harvesting and drying and collection, transplanting, irrigation, topping and using pesticides, and preparation for the market, require human labour. Labour costs (56.5 per cent) are much higher in the total costs as compared to seeds and sapling costs (15 per cent) and fertilizer costs (13.4 per cent) according to the data of 1961 (Trivedi 1968:23). In contrast, out of the total production cost per hectare of Rs. 9680 in 1986, labour costs (including the operational cost of tractors and livestock) had actually fallen to 40.4 per cent. In other words, labour costs show a decline owing to increase in fertilizer cost in terms of its dosage.

Wages of agricultural labour were comparatively high compared to the state minimum wage until the mid 1980s, as shown in Table 12. Since then, wages have been controlled by Patidars who aim to save on labour costs and are aided by excess supply of labour within the village.

The area under tobacco in 1989 increased more than twice from 121 acres in 1961 to 252 acres. Moreover, there is a trend for timely use of labour to complete production process for the market. Therefore, the demand for labour will no doubt increase.

The area under rice cultivation increased from 101 acres in 1961 to 211.3 acres in 1989. In 1961, only 20 acres were under irrigation. Rice is a labour-intensive crop. While labour costs were 36 per cent of the total cost under rice cultivation, that was only 18 per cent for tobacco cultivation. In other words, rice cultivation has doubled its capacity to absorb labour than tobacco cultivation.

As far as profits are concerned, tobacco cultivation is more

Table 9 : Main Workers by Type of Employment and Jati in Ambav

Religion & Jatis	No.of HHs 1991	Population			Self-Employed										Employed				Total Main Workers		
					A		B		C		D		E		F		G				
		P	M	F	M	F	M	F	M	F	M	F	M	F	M	F	M	F	P	M	F
1 Hindu	196	1107	600	507	76	2	23	1	5	0	17	1	24	1	197	86	25	1	459	367	92
Patidar	52	283	152	131	57	2					13	1	7	1	5		10	1	97	92	5
Rajput	41	264	148	116	13						2		6		63	21	6		111	90	21
Bhoi	15	114	55	59	3								1		21	5	4		34	29	5
Valand	2	10	5	5	2				3										5	5	0
Bania	2	8	4	4	1								2						3	3	0
Suthar	1	4	2	2											2				2	2	0
Bharvad	14	77	45	32			23	1					4				2		30	29	1
Brahman	3	10	8	2							2		3		1		1		7	7	0
Prajapati	2	12	7	5					1						3				4	4	0
Bhalia	2	13	9	4											4		1		5	5	0
Luhar	1	11	5	6					1				1						2	2	0
Rathod	1	4	3	1											1	1			2	1	1
Katara	1	3	2	1											1	1			2	1	1
Bhabhai	1	2	1	1											1	1			2	1	1
Nair	1	1	1												1				1	1	0
Other	1	2	1	1											1	1			2	1	1

Table 9 : (Continued)

Religion & Jatis	No.of HHs 1991	Population			Self-Employed										Employed				Total Main Workers		
					A		B		C		D		E		F		G				
		P	M	F	M	F	M	F	M	F	M	F	M	F	M	F	M	F	P	M	F
SC Sindhva	12	64	32	32											18	11	1		30	19	11
Bhangi	11	67	34	33											18	18			36	18	18
Rohit	1	1	1	0											1				1	1	0
ST Vasava	24	120	63	57											42	19			61	42	19
Bahariya	5	20	12	8											10	5			15	10	5
Damor	1	6	5	1											1	1			2	1	1
Nayaka	2	11	5	6											3	2			5	3	2
2 Christian	10	38	19	19	1										11	4			16	12	4
3 Muslim	18	122	75	47	4	1								3	29	7	4		48	40	8
4 Sikh	1	6	4	2										2					2	2	0
G. Total	225	1273	698	575	81	3	23	1	5	0	17	1	29	1	237	97	29	1	525	421	104

Note : A : Agriculture, B : Livestock, C : Caste occupation, D : Factory, E : Small business, F : Temporary labourwork,
G : Permanent labour work.

Source : Field Survey of 1991, 1992 (Nakasato).

Table 10 : Distribution of Temporary Labourers by Jati and Type of Employment (1991)

Type of Employment	(Sex)	Raj-put	Va-sava	Bha-ngi	Sin-dhva	Mus-lim	Chri-stian	Bhoi	Others	Total
Agricultural	M	51	37	18	18	20	15	11	6	176
Labour	F	21	18	18	10	6	5	4	1	83
Quarry	M	3	3	0	0	0	0	0	15	21
Labour	F	0	0	0	0	0	0	0	9	9
Transporting	M	6	2	0	0	3	2	0	4	17
Saw Mill	M	2	0	0	0	0	0	0	3	5
Labour	F	0	0	0	0	0	0	0	1	1
Factory Labour	M	0	0	0	0	1	3	0	1	5
Hotel	M	0	0	0	0	2	0	0	1	3
Labour	F	0	0	0	0	0	0	0	1	1
House Servant	F	0	1	0	1	0	0	0	0	2
Bidi Rolling	F	0	0	0	0	1	0	0	0	1
Other Labour	M	1	0	0	0	3	1	0	5	10
Total		**84**	**61**	**36**	**29**	**36**	**26**	**15**	**47**	**334**

Note : M:Male, F:Female
Source : Field Survey of 1991, 1992 (Nakasato)

Table 11 : Minimum Wage for Daily Worker and Annual Farm Servant

	Wage Rate (State)		Wage Rate (Ambav)	
Year,Date	Daily	Yearly	Daily	Yearly
1972.08.15	3.00 (Rs)	1200 (Rs)		
1976.01.05	5.30	2000	5.00 + 2 meals	
1982.10.02	9.00	3200	10.00 + alfa	1000.00 + (2meals)
1986.02.04	11.0	4000		2000.00 + (2meals)
1990.08.01	15.00	5400		
1992.10			15.00	

Source : State Government and Field Survey of 1991, 1992.

Table 12 : Production Cost of Tobacco Cultivation per Hectare

	Type of Operations	Total Cost(Rs.)	Bidi Tobacco (A)	(B)	(C)
1	Tillage	669.6	11.5	29.4	59.1
2	Manuring	2947.8	6.0	1.6	7.2
3	Transplanting	607.8	65.5		
4	Irrigation	1209.6	11.1		
5	Weeding	257.0	100.0		
6	Interculture	227.7	35.4	64.6	
7	Topping	462.0	100.0		
8	Pesticide	0.8	84.5		
9	Drying & Collection	681.4	83.3	12.7	4.3
10	Preparation for Marketing	24.2	100.0		
11	Miscellaneous	6.0	N. A.		
12	Others	2766.5	N. A.		
	Total	**9860.4**			

Note : (A): Manual Labour (B): Bullock (C): Tractor

Source : Economics of Tobaco Production in Middle Gujarat (1985-86) profitable than rice cultivation. However, its income and price are not as stable as that of rice. Also, tobacco cultivation weakens the soil and, as a result, the Patidar farmers cultivate rice and tobacco alternatively. In this way, with the development of irrigation farming in Ambav, labour-intensive agriculture has developed with an eye on the market. For landowners, rising costs of fertilizers and electricity for irrigation in recent years have formed a large chunk of production costs, and as a result profits are decreasing and agricultural operations are no longer considered to be profitable. Some tobacco planters have underlined the following reasons : (a) increasing labour cost, (b) increasing price of chemical fertilizer, (c) fluctuation in market price, and (d) increasing miscellaneous costs. There is a clear tendency to diversify to others businesses like motor repair and sawmill among the prosperous Patidars. Investment in other enterprises and migration to other regions has already started in the Patidar community.

Under these changing conditions, there is no way but to control the wages of agricultural labour. On the other hand, a protest against their low wages was staged at the time of our survey in September 1992. About 21 members of the Sindhva community went on strike against the daily wages of Rs. 10.[7] Officials from Taluka headquarters mediated and in a meeting it was decided that: a) Rs. 15 would be given as minimum daily wage as set by the Government, b) tea and *bidis* would not be served by the employers, and c) labourers would be employed for 8 hours per day. At present, the Patidar land owners are facing a turning point in the cultivation of tobacco and rice in view of the rising costs and declining profit.

Impact of the bazaar and increasing demand for informal labour

The formation of the bazaar and increasing demand for informal labour reflects the urbanization of the village society. It has not only increased the demand for labour but has also brought about a change in the quality of labour in a village which has traditionally been dependent on agriculture.

In the bazaar, there are 44 shops of 11 types. In the old settlement, there are 8 shops of three kinds. On the whole, there are 52 shops and factories of 13 kinds in the village.

As can be seen in Table 8, out of 28 shop owners who live in the new settlement, only 9 live in the village. Seven out of the 8 establishments in the old settlement are owned by the residents of the village. The 16 shop owners living in Ambav, employ only 9 labourers while the 20 shop owners from outside Ambav employ 57 labourers. Thus it can be understood that shop owners of Ambav tend to manage small businesses which do not have the capacity to absorb a large number of labourers.

There are 22 Patidars, 8 Rajputs, 5 Brahmins, 4 each of Bharwads and Muslims, 3 Valands, and 2 Banias in various business. However, there are no STs, SCs, and Christians engaged in business activities.

The dominant community of Patidars has responded to urbanization in an effective way. A section of Rajputs and Muslims is engaged in small capital businesses.

Spread of Education and Employment Opportunities

One of the reasons why diversification of employment cannot be seen in the case of SCs, STs, and the backward classes, is apparently illiteracy, and a low level of education. Ambav has a private high school which is a rare thing. In 1992, 92 students were enrolled in this school, of whom 38 were girls. The first middle school was set up in 1915 (Trivedi 1968:43).

Regarding the main occupation and education level of the work force of 525 people in the village, the following can be pointed out: (a) there is a clear distinction between the literate and illiterate groups, (b) the persons who went to high school are self-employed in agriculture and business and those employed are working as labourers in permanent jobs, while (c)the persons who studied till middle school are employed in trade and the transport business in the bazaar. The illiterate are employed as casual agricultural labourers and in the quarries and saw mills.

In other words, people with higher education are employed in stable and secure jobs. However, there is doubt about education providing profitable and secure jobs in the future. Out of 100 persons with high school education, 58 belong to the Patidar community, clearly an overwhelming number. Out of 120 persons with middle school education, Patidars and Rajputs accounted for 27 persons and the majority of the 120 primary school graduates are Rajputs and Bhois. Illiterate

Table 13 : Divesification of Employment among Patidar HHs

HH No	Age 1	No 2	Land holding Irr	Land holding Unir	Total Bigha	No. of Workers	Type of Occupation A	B	C	D	E	F	G	Place of Birth Ambav	O.V.S.D	O.D
1	31	5	31	7	38	1	1							Ambav		
2	85	6	36	0	36	2	2							Ambav		
3	55	3	24	11	35	1					1				Thasura	
4	33	5	20	10	30	1	1							Ambav		
5	35	9	28	0	28	2	2							Ambav		
6	72	18	28	0	28	5	2			1	1		1	Ambav		
7	85	9	8	20	28	3	1				1	1		Ambav		
8	49	7	25	0	25	3	3							Ambav		
9	55	8	10	15	25	2							2	Ambav		
10	59	7	10	10	20	2	2							Ambav		
11	38	9	8	8	16	2	1						1	Ambav		
12	70	5	10	5	15	2	2							Ambav		
13	76	2	14	0	14	1	1							Ambav		
15	65	5	1.25	10.25	11.5	2	1						1	Ambav		
16	40	3	11	0	11	1	1							Ambav		
17	28	4	10	1	11	2	1						1	Ambav		
18	25	3	10	0	10	1	1							Ambav		
19	29	3	10	0	10	3	3							Ambav		
20	60	5	6	4	10	4	2					2		Ambav		
21	65	4	6	4	10	1	1							Ambav		
22	60	5	5	5	10	3	2					1		Ambav		
23	62	6	9	0	9	3	3							Ambav		
24	47	4	8	1	9	1	1							Ambav		
25	46	5	7	2	9	1							1	Ambav		
26	70	8	0	9	9	4	4							Ambav		

27	52	3	3.5	5	8.5	1							1	Ambav		
28	62	6	6.5	1.5	8	2	1				1			Ambav		
29	54	10	5	3	8	2	2							Ambav		
30	56	4	1.25	6	7.25	1	1							Ambav		
31	45	5	5	2	7	1	1							Ambav		
32	38	4	4	3	7	1	1							Ambav		
33	42	5	4	3	7	1	1							Ambav		
34	57	6	4	3	7	1	1							Ambav		
35	45	4	6	0	6	1	1							Ambav		
36	50	1	6	0	6	1	1							Ambav		
37	62	3	6	0	6	1	1							Ambav		
38	72	6	6	0	6	2	2							Ambav		
39	58	8	5	0	5	4	4							Ambav		
40	52	6	4	0	4	1	1							Ambav		
41	50	4	2	2	4	1	1							Ambav		
42	57	4	3.5	0	3.5	2	1							Ambav		
43	31	4	3	0	3	1	1						1	Ambav		
44	35	4	3	0	3	1	1							Ambav		
45	45	3	2	0	2	1							1		Thasura	
46	29	4	0	0	0	1							1		Thasura	
47	35	4	0	0	0	1				1						Kuch
48	38	2	0	0	0	2				2						Kuch
49	42	12	0	0	0	3				3						Kuch
50	52	10	0	0	0	3				3						Kuch
51	55	6	0	0	0	5				4	1					Kuch
52	60	3	0	0	0	2					2				Thasura	
Total		**283**	**424**	**153.7**	**577.7**	**97**	**59**	**0**	**0**	**14**	**8**	**5**	**11**			
Average	51.2	5.4	8.1	2.9	10.9											

Note : A (Agriculture), B (Livestock), C (Caste occupation), D (Factory), E (Small business), F (Temporary labour werks), G (Permanent labour), O.V.S.D (Other village in the same District), O.D (Other District), (1) Age of the head of HH, (2) Number of HH members.

Source : Field survey of 1991, 1992. (Nakasato)

workers mainly belong to the Rajput, Vasava, Bahariya, and Bhangi communities.

It can be inferred from this, that employment conditions are related more to *jati* affiliations than literacy. For example, there are people from SCs and STs who have received high school education but are engaged as agricultural labour. Moreover, even to avail jobs under the reservation policy, they have to pay bribes.

It is arguable that instead of equating labour problems with only education, they could be better understood in the context of the multi-caste structure.

Lack of Diversification of Employment among Backward Classes

We can see that diversification of employment is progressing in the case of the Patidar community (Table 13). New Patidar households who have no land in the village are engaged in stone quarries and other businesses. It is also important to note that the Patidar households with larger landholdings tend to show a higher degree of diversification of employment.

Further, diversification to some extent is found in Rajput, Banias and Muslim communities. These communities owned small tracts of land during the 1961 survey, which some of them had to sell to cover debts. Currently, some of them are engaged in small business activities and are active in the panchayat.

However, diversification can hardly be seen in the case of the backward classes which are landless. Active and passive reasons impede diversification of employment in the backward classes.

Among the active reasons, dominance of the Patidar community in the traditional agricultural society can be cited. As a result, economic changes in the village are effected by the Patidars overwhelmingly. As mentioned earlier, they are engaged in the cultivation of labour intensive crops and, as a result, they attract cheap labour not only from within the village but outside as well.

Patidars on the other hand, have also established economic and social ties with the outside villages as some members of the community have migrated to cities for jobs and business to supplement their incomes. Those residing in the village and engaged in agriculture, tend to diversify to other businesses and control the wages of the labourers they employ. The labourers are also given incentives such as loans and food which are not available in other jobs. Thus, in such a society, backward classes do not have the means to diversify their economic activities.

Passive reasons impeding diversification of employment among the backward classes include the attitude toward life. They consider their life satisfactory as long as their basic needs (food, clothing, and shelter) are met and as long as they can educate their children. That they do not own land has been from time immemorial, a way of life for them.

Except the Sindhva community, the rest do not dare to oppose the low wages openly offered by Patidar employers. Moreover, they lack the will to diversify to other jobs in the stone quarries and saw-mills, for they consider them to be dangerous. Today, year-long employment is difficult to get and they are mostly idle during summer.

Conclusion

The village society of Ambav is distinctly divided into two : the dominant community and the dominated communities. Whereas diversification of employment has progressed in the dominant community of Patidars, it is limited in some dominated communities like the Rajputs and Muslims. In the other dominated communities, i.e., the SCs, STs and the backward classes, diversification is conspicuously absent. They are still engaged as labourers in agriculture and in the informal sector.

The sharp increase in population has been caused mainly by the increase in the SCs, STs and the backward classes. It should be emphasized that they have almost completely failed to diversify their economic activities. Moreover, the employment pattern of the persons living in the old settlements based on agricultural activities has rarely changed. The new settlers, meanwhile, live and work in the bazaar.

There is little relation between the bazaar settlement and SCs, STs, and the backward classes in the old settlement. The former has not absorbed labour from within the village. It is clear that the majority of labourers in the bazaar has come from other villages.

While education ensures improved employment opportunities among the dominant community, it seems to bear hardly any advantage among the SCs, STs and the backward classes.

The dominant Patidar community, with a stable base in agriculture in the village has ventured to cities and some to even foreign countries, and, thus, has established economic ties outside the village. Even today, they continue to dominate the village community. The dominated communities have not been able to coup up successfully in their efforts to raise their wages. Patidars, on the other hand, unitedly prevent a wage hike, using their own caste panchayat extending to the neighbouring villages. Most of the dominated communities are obliged to obey the paternalistic control of the dominant Patidars.

Acknowledgements

I am deeply indebted to Prof. Taniguchi who gave me invaluable support throughout. I am also grateful to Prof. T. Shinoda and Prof. S Nakayama and other members of this project for their cooperation.

I am grateful to Prof. B. B. Patel of the Gandhi Labour Institute, Prof. Desai of Gujarat University and Prof. T. Shah, the then Director of IRMA, for their comments and suggestions. I thank my Research Assistants from Gujarat University for their contributions and hard work and Ms Y. Kumano for data input. I am grateful to Ms S. Sharma for her help with the English translation. Last but not least, I am grateful to Dr. N. K. Vyas and his family for their wonderful hospitality year after year.

Notes

1. We were not able to get a map showing the location of households which was necessary for our survey from the Panchayat. We were not able to complete the survey of the Bazaar to our satisfaction. This was chiefly due to the lack of cooperation on the part of the people engaged in business activities in the village. Since the households of the bazaar have greater mobility, and some of them were single occupants, the data were very crucial. Unfortunately, even the Sarpanch did not have information regarding these households. Adding to these reasons, we also had time limitations on our part.

2. Even before 1987, a few bamboo huts belonging to the Bharwads had existed in the same place and were only used during seasonal migration for grazing their cattle and sheep. As a result, they could not be surveyed in the 1961 census.

3. Though they are agricultural labourer households, all the men except two in their thirties, were educated and compared to other communities their literacy rate is higher. This is deeply related to the decline in their population, especially in the period between the latter half of the 70s and the first half of the 80s.

4. The word Bahariyas means outsiders. The Bahariyas of Ambav belong to the Scheduled Tribes who have all come as stone quarry labourers from the village of Suliyat in Panchmahal district. Three households immigrated five or six years ago and the other two households came 3 months ago. They live in small huts.

5. Backward classes consist of Bharwards, Valands, Bhois, Bhalias, Prajapatis, Rathodias, Rajputs (Takore) and Gujarati-Christians in the village, besides the Scheduled Castes of Sindhvas, Bhangis and Rohits and Scheduled Tribes of Vasavas, Bhahariyas, Nayakas and Damors.

6. The rainfed arable land mainly belongs to the Rajput, Bhoi and Muslim communities. Most of them grow bajri, jowar and pulses for their home consumption.

7. Following is a letter dated 27.8.92 written to the Labour Minister by a member of the Vasava community during the strike against low wages: "In our village, condition of adivasi, Vasava is very bad. We work for whole day and yet get only Rs 10. It is not possible to manage expense with this rate. Outside villagers come and do work here. We don't get enough labour work in such inflationary situation, we can't afford to such wages. So we appeal to the Government that we should get the Government recognized minimum wages."

References

Basant, Rakesh and Joshi Harish. 'Employment Diversification in an Agricultural Developed Region : Some Evidence from Rural Kheda, Gujarat'. In Pravin Visaria and Rakesh Basant (eds.). *Non-Agricultural Employment in India - Trades and Prospects*. New Delhi: Sage Publication, 1994.

Breman, Jan. *Patronage and Exploitation*. New Delhi: Manohar Publications, 1979.

Breman, Jan. *Of Peasants, Migrants and Paupers*. Delhi: Oxford University Press, 1985.

Campbell, J.M. *Hindu Castes and Tribes of Gujarat*, 2 vols. Vintage Books, 1988.

Chen, M.A. *Coping with Seasonality and Drought*. New Delhi: Sage Publications, 1990.

Chhaya, R.S. *Census of India,* 1981 (Series-5, Gujarat). *Village & Townwise Primary Census Abstract-Kheda District*, 34, 1982.

Fujiwara, K. (ed.) *Agriculture and Rural Changes in Drought Prone Area in India*, Annual Report of Research Center for Regional Geography, Hiroshima University, (in Japanese) 1992.

Fukunaga, M. *Society, Caste and Factional Politics : Conflict and Continuity in Rural India*. Delhi: Manohar Publications, 1993.

Guha, Sunil. *Rural Manpower and Capital Formation in India*. New Delhi: Academic Books, 1969.

Hardiman, David. *Peasant Nationalists of Gujarat-Kheda District 1917-1934*. Delhi: Oxford University Press, 1981.

Joshi, V.H. *Economic Development and Change in a South Gujarat Village*. Baroda: Maharaja Sayajirao University of Baroda, 1966.

Joshi, Vidyut. *Bonded Labour in Gujarat*. Ahmedabad: Gandhi Labour Institute, 1986.

Lakdawala, D.T. (ed.). *Gujarat Economy: Problems and Prospects*, Ahmedabad: Sardar Patel Institute of Economic and Social Research, 1981.

Mukhtyar, G.C. *Life and Labour in a South Gujarat Village*, Calcutta: Longmans, Green and Co Ltd, 1930.

Nakasato, T. 'Development of Agriculture and Rural-Urban Interaction in Former Zamindari Village-Dikhatpura', in Fujiwara, K. (ed.). *Agriculture and Rural Changes in Drought Prone Area in India*, Annual Report of Research Center for Regional Geography, Hiroshima University (in Japanese), 1992.

Rajyagor, S.B. (ed.). *Gujarat State Gazetteers, Kheda District*, Ahmedabad: Government of Gujarat, 1977.

Singh, Bhanwar. *Agrarian Structure, Technology Change and Poverty*. New Delhi: Agricole Publishing Company, 1985.

Satyanarayana, G. *Changing Agrarian Structure and Labour Relations*. Jaipur: Rawat Publications, 1992.

The Kaira District Co-operative Milk Producer's Union Limited. *The AMUL Story - A Saga of Co-operative Effort, Anand*, 1988.

Trivedi, R.K. *Census of India 1961, Village Survey Monograph AMBAV*, 1968.

Yanagisawa, H. *Socio-economic Changes in a Village in the Paddy Cultivating Area in South India*, Institute for the Study of Languages and Cultures of Asia and Africa, 1985.

12

Changing Pattern of Rural Artisans in Gujarat : Need for a Fresh Policy?

Amita Shah

Introduction

Background

Rural artisans have been an integral part of the socio-economic fabric of Indian villages. Characterized by home-based enterprises using local material and traditional technologies, rural artisans were regarded as rendering services to the village community and were paid in part by a share of the crop (Gadgil, 1974). Servitude was the predominant feature of the artisan class and most of them were classified under the lower strata (i.e. 'shudras') of the social hierarchy (Ghurye, 1969). In Gujarat, artisans are known as 'vasavayas' which means those associated with the process of settlement or bringing land under the plough (Gohil, undated). Artisans, as different from craftsmen, belong to specific caste groups, namely, weaver, tanner, cobbler, potter, carpenter, blacksmith. To a large extent, these caste groups have been classified as socially and economically backward communities in the state.[1]

Historically, artisans (i.e. the 'service' castes) were linked in a clear hierarchial relationship with the agriculturists who, by virtue of having control over land, were able to keep others dependent on them

(Streefkerk, 1982). While the form of these relationships varied significantly over space and time, the exploitative elements were present in most situations (Breman, 1974). The changes however, were more significant during the colonial rule, setting the downward trend and the process of de-industrialisation (Chattopadhyaya, 1975). Nevertheless at the time of independence, the economy was still vested with a fairly large and widespread segment of rural artisans (Roy Chaudhari, 1968). The crucial elements characterizing this segment were as follows:

- their presence was essential to sustain a self-sufficient rural economy
- their growth was mainly dependent on the development of agriculture and allied activities. Frequent drought conditions therefore exerted a disintegrating influence on the artisan-sector (Gadgil, 1974).
- servitude and patronage on the one hand and a decentralized production system on the other, constrained mobilization of capital and entrepreneurial skill (Singh, 1990). Moreover, low social status of some of the artisans (like those belonging to the scheduled castes) might have further aggravated these constraints.
- traditional arrangements of mutual rights and obligations were undergoing constant changes in the light of the overall changes taking place in the economy
- the process of transformation resulted in a gradual shift towards urban centres (Gadgil *op.cit*) and an advance integration with the market economy (Bhattacharya, 1984).

Most of these characteristics have been closely associated with the early phase of capitalist production. However, these activities get transformed into higher forms of production as industrialization proceeds. Eventually, the artisan-based activities especially those scattered over the countryside, would disappear (Singh, 1990). Such transformation also takes place in the less industrialized countries (Stately and Morse, 1965). In its simple form, the changes emerge through the transition of artisan industry, replacement of household industry and development of modern small scale industries along with large scale production. In the process, the artisan-based production tends to get integrated with the mainstream industrial production by establishing product as well as spatial linkages (Shah, 1990). Thus, a shift from home-based to workshop/factory enterprises and from rural to semi-urban/urban locations is a natural phenomenon and perhaps, a desirable goal in the process of capitalist development. Moreover, it can pave the way for an upward mobility as well as social integration among the artisan households. Overall, therefore, the changing pattern of artisan-based production can be seen as a positive phenomenon.

Sectoral Transformation : The Indian Experience

The changing forms of capitalist production are also interfaced with a sectoral shift in workforce composition. This brings into its fold two important features: (i) the manufacturing sector may absorb at least a major part of the population released from agriculture; and (ii) the increase in labour absorption may go along with a shift from household to non-household activities Kuznets (1966). To a large extent, such transformation has already started in the Indian economy though with certain variations. For instance, between 1981 and 1991 the share of agriculture in the total workforce has marginally declined. Against this, the share of the tertiary sector has increased, whereas, the manufacturing sector has shown a decline during this period (Visaria, 1994). But, within the manufacturing sector the household industries have experienced a decline not only in relative but also in absolute term (Bhalla, 1996). Also, the decline is sharper in urban as compared to the rural areas. It may however, be noted that the workers shifting from the household sector are mainly absorbed in the non-household segment of the unorganized sector; employment in the organized (factory) sector has not increased substantially (Ramaswamy, 1994). This has happened in spite of its increasing share in the total value added.[2]

The pattern of sectoral shift is somewhat different in Gujarat. Unlike the situation at the all-India level, manufacturing employment has shown a marginal increase between 1981-1991. This has been attained mainly because of the significant increase in rural non-household sector, a large part of which seems to have taken place in the unorganized sector.[3] This indeed, suggests a more dynamic situation obtaining in Gujarat's manufacturing sector (Basant, 1994) within which artisan-based activities are an important constituent.

On the whole, the pattern of sectoral transformation in Gujarat suggests a more advanced stage of capitalist development as compared to the all-India situation. Nevertheless, the low growth of employment in the manufacturing sector, notwithstanding the rapid increase in value added, may cause serious concern. An important policy imperative therefore is to further boost the growth of rural industries (Bhalla, 1996) since it is the only segment within the manufacturing sector where employment has grown positively and substantially. This of course, is a difficult task and calls for a significant shift from the policies followed in the past (Tyabji, 1989). The task may become further difficult in the wake of the recent move towards liberalization. Given this backdrop, it might be useful to understand the changing pattern of industrial production and its implications for the different segments, especially in the rural non-household and non-factory manufacturing sector. The following analysis examines some of the important features of Gujarat's industrial sector with a special focus on the rural artisan-based activities.

Objectives and Coverage

The main objectives of this study are:

1. To discern changes in the structure of the rural industries sector and the role of artisan-based activities therein.

2. To examine the status of artisan households across districts with different levels of industrial development.

3. To review the policy approach and suggest changes for ensuring a sustainable growth of employment in the rural manufacturing sector.

Data and Coverage

The study is mainly based on secondary data pertaining to the different segments of rural industries sector, namely the directory manufacturing enterprises (DME); the non-directory manufacturing enterprises (NDME); and the own-account enterprises (OAE).[4] To ascertain the changes over time, data have been collected for two points of time, i.e. 1989-90 (the latest year for which these data are available) and 1978-79.

Identification of artisan-based activities has been made at two-digit level of industrial classification for which state-level data are published. This includes nine industry groups that have a close correspondence with the activities of the traditional rural artisans such as weavers, carpenters, cobblers/flayers, blacksmiths and potters. Since caste-wise classification of rural enterprises is not available at the state level, it is assumed that a large proportion of the persons engaged in these activities might belong to the traditional artisan castes.

The analysis pertaining to the artisan households is based on a primary survey conducted during the late eighties.[5] The survey covered all the major categories of artisans (except for weavers) listed above. Of the total nineteen districts in the state, the analysis is confined to four districts, namely, Ahmedabad, Baroda, Kheda and Banaskantha. In terms of typology of development these districts represent the largest industrial centre with a traditional (i.e. textile) base, modern industrial centre, developed agricultural sector and economic backwardness respectively. In the four districts, the survey covered nearly 50,000 artisan households from 4637 villages.

The analysis is divided into five sections including this introduction. The next, section 2 focuses on the changing structure of the rural industrial sector and the artisan-based activities in Gujarat. This is followed by an examination of the important features of artisan households in the four districts, followed by a case study of Khadi and Village Industries in the state. Section 4 discusses some of the important policy issues emerging from the analysis. And the last section, 5, presents a summary of the major findings.

Structure of Manufacturing Sector and Artisan-Based Production: Changes Over Time

The Transition

Since the eighties, Gujarat's manufacturing sector has undergone a significant transformation attaining higher stages of capitalist production. This is reflected through a fairly smooth transition of its industrial base from the traditional (i.e. textile) to the modern (i.e. chemical) products, accompanied by capital intensive technology and a relatively higher rate of urbanization.[6] This process has brought into its fold, changes in the forms of production organization within the manufacturing sector. For instance, by 1993-94 nearly three-fourths of the value added (state domestic product) in the manufacturing sector originated from the organized (factory) enterprises. This proportion is higher than that observed at the all-India level (i.e. 61 per cent). Along with this shift capital intensity has also increased significantly; between 1980-81 and 1990-91, capital/labour ratio in the organized sector has increased significantly (Hirway, forthcoming). The growth of the organized sector however, is concentrated in the Ahmedabad-

Vapi belt (known as the 'Golden Corridor'). This would have created strong agglomeration economies in the sub-region which accounts for about 72 per cent of the total employment generated in the organized sector. Compared to this, the growth of the household sector - the major segment within the unorganized sector- appears to be more broad based. For instance, the 'golden corridor' constitutes less than 60 per cent of the total employment generated in household sector as compared 72 per cent in the organized sector.

Changes in the Unorganised Sector

The growing organized sector seems to have exerted a significant influence on the structure of the unorganized sector. This is reflected through the changing size as well as rural-urban distribution of manufacturing activities within the unorganized sector (see Table 1). It is observed that the OAE-segment (which closely corresponds but is not equivalent to the household sector) has undergone significant decline not only in terms of its share in employment but also in terms of the number of enterprises, fixed assets and value added.

The shift from the OAE-segment is largely in favour of the next segment in the size hierarchy, i.e. NDME. The DME-segment however, has lost its share in terms of employment, fixed capital and value added. It is likely that a large number of DME, especially in the urban areas have outgrown the employment-size and shifted to the category of the organized sector. This may suggest a bi-polar structure whereby at the lower end the OAE-segment is getting transformed into NDMEs and at the upper end, the DME-segment is possibly merging with the organized sector. Of course, there are no direct evidences indicating such an upward movement among individual units in DME. Generally, the tendency is to avoid such shifts from DME to the registered factory sector because of the liabilities associated with the factory laws. Hence, another possibility is a refrogression of DME-units towards NDME. This kind of backward movements, especially of the less efficient DME-units, is somewhat less likely because NDME had emerged as a more dynamic sector with higher growth in labour as well as capital productivity compared to the DME-sector. Instead, what appears more logical is an upward movement of the more officient DME-unit to the next size class in the factory sector. There are evidences that the small-scale units in the factory sector have increased its share both in employment and gross value added; and

Table 1 : Share of Different Segments Within Unorganized Manufacturing Sector in Gujarat: 1978-79 and 1989-90

Enterprise Categories	% Share in							
	No. of Units		Employment		Fixed Asset		Gross Value Added	
	78-79	89-90	78-79	89-90	78-79	89-90	78-79	89-90
Home-based (OAE)	76.5	66.3	36.1	35.5	38.7	24.1	25.0	16.3
NDME	12.4	22.0	16.6	25.5	22.6	44.1	13.7	42.4
DME	11.1	11.7	47.3	39.0	38.7	31.8	61.3	41.3
Total Un-organized Sector	100.0	100.0	100.0	100.0	100.0	100.0	100.0	100.0
Organized*	3.6	2.0	51.8	30.0	89.6	78.6	80.7	64.7
Un Orga-nised	96.4	98.0	48.2	70.0	10.4	21.4	19.3	35.3
Total Manu-facturing Sector	100.0	100.0	100.0	100.0	100.0	100.0	100.0	100.0

Source :

a. OAEs and NDMEs-NSSO, 45th and 33rd Rounds.

b. DMEs-CSO, Reports on Unorganized Manufacture: Directory Establishments, 1978-79 and 1989-90.

c. Factory Sector, CSO, Annual Survey of Industries, Summary Results for Factory Sector 1978-79 and 1989-90.

The NSSO-CSO estimates do not match with the Census estimates of main workers. This is because of the non-comparability of sectoral categories (i.e. household-non-household vs. OAE-NDME-DME), coverage (Census vs. Sample), definition of worker (main vs. all) etc. Therefore, the NSSO-CSO estimates have been used to capture the relative magnitude across different segments rather than indicating absolute values.

* Excluding gas, electricity, water supply and storage.

have also show much higher growth in labour productivity vis-a-vise that in the DME (Shah, 1997 Table 1). Moreover, in the late eighties, DME's share in total employment in the unorganized sector seems to have increased whereas, its share in gross value added has declined. This tends to indicate that those who remained as DME-units in the termonal year (i. e. in 1989-90) were those which could not move further up. Unlike this moving backward to NDME could have been relatively easier, the fact that this option has not been exercised by these units, can be interpreted as relative absence of backward movement from the DME-sector.

On the other hand, an earlier analysis (Nagaraj, 1985) of the factory sector did suggest higher growth and better profitability among the smaller size class. To the extant that it implies a dynamic situation in the small-scale factory sector it stands to reason that, it might have pulled some of the more efficient DME- units in an upward direction. In any case, higher growth of factories in the smaller size does indicate that many of the new entrants, on the border line, might have chosen to enter the more dynamic smaller size class in the factory sector, rather than join the rank of the stagnating declining DME sector. The transition from NDME to DME segment seems to be weak. Is this because of the entry barriers faced by the NDMEs while crossing the threshold size and join the DMEs? If so, the phenomenon may have significant implications for the growth of the traditional artisan-based activities.

Rural-Urban Distribution

The dynamism observed in the NDME-segment is reflected further in terms of its relatively higher share in urban as compared to rural areas. In 1989-90, the share of urban-NDME, is more than twice that of rural-NDMEs in terms of all the four variables. Moreover, in terms of employment, its share has declined in rural areas whereas it has increased in urban areas. This suggests a relatively higher urban base of NDMEs vis-a-vis the other two segments. For instance rural enterprises constitute only 21 and 7 per cent of the total employment and gross value added within NDMEs respectively [Table 2 (a)]. These proportions are lower than both OAEs as well as DMEs. Relatively larger share of rural enterprises among the DMEs might further support the earlier contention that a large proportion of these enterprises, particularly in the urban areas, have shifted to the category of orga-

Table 2 (a) : Share of Rural Enterprises in Unorganized Sector in Gujarat: 1978-79 and 1989-90

Enterprise	Category	% Share in			
		No. of Units	Employment	Fixed Capital	Gross Value Added
OAE	1978-79	58.7	37.7	48.7	43.6
	1989-90	59.7	55.8	62.5	44.2
NDME	1978-79	34.1	29.2	30.4	21.4
	1989-90	28.4	20.8	16.0	7.1
DME	1978-79	N.A	N.A	N.A	N.A
	1989-90	26.9	22.2	14.6	14.6
All	1978-79	N.A	N.A	N.A	N.A
	1989-90	48.9	37.2	27.5	16.3

Source : Same as in Table 1.

nized (factory) units. The data also suggested that, over a period of time the share of rural enterprises has declined in the case of NDMEs whereas it increased in the case of OAEs. (For DME, this comparison is not possible owing to non-availability of data separately for rural and urban areas). Taken together these data suggest that not only the shift in unorganized manufacturing sector has taken place from OAEs to NDMEs, it has also moved from rural to urban areas.

Artisan-Based Activities

Traditionally, artisan-based activities take place within the household sector. Hence, these activities could be expected to be concentrated the most in the OAE-segment. Over time however, they may be shifted to higher forms of production and also to urban areas. Table 2(b) provides estimates regarding the share of artisan-based activities across different segments of the unorganized sector. It is observed that OAEs constitute about 80 per cent of the enterprises, 53 per cent of employment and 31 per cent of gross valued added generated in artisan-based activities. Evidentally, these proportions are higher than the OAEs' share at the aggregate industries level both in rural and urban areas. Also, it is observed that the OAEs' share is higher in rural, as compared to that in urban areas. Of the three segments, NDMEs have lowest share in all the three variables. In the case of NDMEs, these industries have a lower share than that at the aggregate level taking all industry groups together.

Within each segment, the concentration of artisan-based activities is also highest in the case of OAEs followed by DMEs and then by NDMEs (Table 3). Among OAEs these activities constitute more than 40 per cent of enterprises as well as employment and about 38 per cent of gross value added. For NDMEs these proportions are only 20 and 14 per cent respectively. Of the various activities, most important among the OAEs are wood and wood products (carpentry), non-metallic mineral products (pottery), and repair services. The pattern is somewhat different among NDMEs and DMEs where metal and light engineering products are more important than in the OAEs. Over a period of time, however, the importance of artisan-based activities has declined both in OAEs + NDMEs combined and also in DMEs (see Table 4). Surprisingly, the decline is sharper in the OAE+NDME combined than in the DME segment. Most probably, this phenomenon might be a reflection of changes within the NDMEs rather than in

Table 2 (b) : Share of OAEs, NDMEs and DMEs in the Artisan-Based Activities in Rural and Urban Gujarat : 1989-90

Enterprise Category	% Share in								
	No. of Establishment			Employment			Gross Value Added		
	R	U	C	R	U	C	R	U	C
OAE	92.7 (80.8)	56.2 (52.3)	80.4	78.1 (53.1)	27.1 (24.9)	53.0	69.3 (44.5)	15.4 (10.9)	30.7
NDME	4.2	26.8	11.8	6.7	27.9	17.1	10.6	39.0	30.6
DME	3.1	17.0	7.8	15.2	45.0	29.9	20.1	45.6	38.7
All	100.0	100.0	100.0	100.0	100.0	100.0	100.0	100.0	100.0

Note : Figures in parentheses indicate percentage share in all-industries taken together.
Source : Same as in Table 1.

Table 3 : Share of Major Industry Groups Among Artisan Based Activities: 1989-90

Indy Groups NIC Product Code Group	OAEs			NDMEs			DMEs		
	No. of Units	Emp.	GVA	No. of Units	Emp.	GVA	No. of Units	Emp.	GVA
23 Cotton Textile	6.4	6.1	2.6	2.2	2.8	1.1	1.5	1.5	1.6
27 Wood	23.3	22.7	21.0	3.4	3.4	1.7	3.4	2.7	0.6
29 Leather	3.5	2.8	2.9	0.2	0.1	0.1	0.4	0.2	0.1
32 Non-Metallic Mineral	6.8	9.8	4.8	2.2	2.7	0.7	7.9	8.5	4.1
33 Basic Metal	0.0	0.0	0.0	0.8	0.9	0.8	2.6	2.6	3.3
34 Metal Products & Parts	2.4	1.5	2.1	5.3	4.3	2.1	2.7	1.9	1.6
35 Machinery & Parts	0.8	0.9	1.4	2.9	2.8	2.6	5.7	4.7	6.7
37 Transport Equip. Parts	0.2	0.3	0.1	0.5	0.6	3.9	0.9	0.7	0.6
39 Repair of Machinery	2.9	3.0	3.2	3.1	3.0	1.2	0.4	0.5	0.4
Sub Total	46.3	47.1	38.1	20.6	20.6	14.2	25.5	23.3	19.0
All Industries	100.0	100.0	100.0	100.0	100.0	100.0	100.0	100.0	100.0

Note : Emp. = Employment; GVA = Gross Value Added.

Source : Same as in Table 1.

Table 4 : Change in the Share of Major Industry Groups in the Artisan-Based Activities, 1978-79 and 1989-90

Industry Groups	% of Share					
	No. of Units		Employment		GVA	
	78-79	89-90	78-79	89-90	78-79	89-90
OAEs + NDMEs						
23 Cotton Textile	5.4	5.3	4.6	4.7	3.9	1.6
27 Wood	12.0	18.4	3.1	14.5	9.2	7.1
29 Leather	4.4	2.6	3.1	1.7	3.5	0.9
32 Non-Metallic Mineral	5.7	5.6	4.2	6.8	3.5	1.9
33 Basic Metal	0.3	0.2	6.2	A	0.7	0.6
34 Metal Products & Parts	2.1	3.1	4.2	2.7	2.8	2.1
35 Machinery & Parts	0.8	1.3	5.1	1.7	2.6	2.4
37 Transport Equip. Parts	0.1	0.3	5.4	A	0.1	2.9
39 Repair of Machinery	17.9	2.9	2.7	2.9	15.9	1.8
Sub Total	48.7	39.7	38.6	35.0	42.2	21.3
All Industries	100.0	100.0	100.0	100.0	100.0	100.0
DMEs						
23 Cotton Textile	4.2	1.5	3.9	1.5	4.0	1.6
27 Wood	8.3	3.4	7.8	2.7	13.2	0.6
29 Leather	0.1	0.4	0.1	0.2	0.1	0.1
32 Non-Metallic Mineral	3.2	7.9	3.6	8.5	2.7	4.1
33 Basic Metal	1.8	2.6	1.6	2.6	2.3	3.3
34 Metal Products & Parts	2.8	2.7	2.2	1.9	3.3	1.6
35 Machinery & Parts	3.9	5.7	3.2	4.7	5.6	6.7
37 Transport Equip. Parts	0.3	0.9	0.3	0.7	0.4	0.6
39 Repair of Machinery	1.3	0.4	0.9	0.5	1.0	0.4
Sub Total	25.9	25.5	23.6	23.3	32.6	19.0
All Industries	100.0	100.0	100.0	100.0	100.0	100.0

Source : Same as in Table 1.

OAEs. Evidences from an earlier study also suggested that between 1961 and 1981, all the constituents of the non-household sector (to which NDME sector is a part) had grown; the growth however was higher among modern industries as compared to traditional ones (Basant and Kumar, 1990).

Economic Ratios

The changing structure of the unorganized manufacturing sector also gets reflected in terms of the selected economic indicators as observed in Table 5 through 7. The following aspects are important.

1. At the aggregate level, economic ratios are positively associated with the scale of production, i.e. they increase from QAEs to NDMEs to DMEs (Table 5). However, in 1989-90, labour productivity among NDMEs was found to be higher than the DMEs. Similarly, in 1989-90 most of these indicators were higher among urban enterprises as compared to their counter parts in the rural areas.

2. The pattern is almost unchanged in the case of artisan-based industries. However, compared to the aggregate industries, the artisan-groups by and large have lower labour productivity (Table 6).

.3. Although, employment size is almost similar across different artisan-based activities, gross value added per enterprise shows significant variations. Among OAEs, these variations have significant implications since they reflect variations in earnings of the artisan households engaged in different activities. Table 7 indicates that the gross value added is higher than Rs. 20,000 in six out of the nine industry groups except for textiles (Rs. 5,109), basic metal products (Rs. 7,330) and transport equipment parts (Rs. 7,808). These earnings are significantly lower than the income level which is being used to define the poverty line (i.e. Rs. 11,000) for rural households.[7]

The above analysis thus, highlights some important features of the changing composition of the unorganized manufacturing sector and the changes being experienced by the artisan- based activities within it. However, before discussing the policy implications, it might be useful to understand the functioning of the artisan activities at the household level. The next sections attempts this.

Table 5 : Selected Ratios for Different Segments of the Unorganized Manufacturing Sector in Gujarat

Sector/ Area	Economic Ratios						
	FA/ Emp.	GVA/ Emp.	Emo/ Emp.	Emo/ GVA	FA/ Unit	Emp/ Unit	GVA/ Unit
OAE							
Rural							
78-79	3.83	3.02	N.A	N.A	2.58	0.67	2.03
89-90	7.67	5.20	N.A	N.A	11.78	1.53	7.98
Urban							
78-79	2.44	2.36	N.A	N.A	3.86	1.58	3.73
89-90	5.82	8.28	N.A	N.A	10.47	1.80	14.90
Combi							
78-79	2.97	2.61	N.A	N.A	3.11	1.05	2.74
89-90	6.85	6.56	N.A	N.A	11.25	1.64	10.77
NDME							
Rural							
78-79	3.92	2.29	0.09	0.04	9.97	2.54	5.81
89-90	13.39	8.04	2.63	0.33	34.77	2.60	20.89
Urban							
78-79	3.72	3.47	0.27	0.08	11.82	3.18	11.03
89-90	18.49	27.73	6.96	0.25	69.49	3.76	104.44
Combi							
78-79	3.78	3.13	0.22	0.07	11.19	2.96	9.26
89-90	17.39	23.64	6.06	0.26	61.70	3.55	83.82
DME							
Rural							
78-79	N.A	N.A	N.A	N.A	N.A	N.A	N.A
89-90	4.39	7.02	4.50	0.64	52.35	11.92	83.76
Urban							
78-79	N.A	N.A	N.A	N.A	N.A	N.A	N.A
89-90	95.99	18.55	69.24	0.38	95.99	9.71	180.17
Combi							
78-79	2.27	4.89	2.53	0.52	21.56	9.50	46.47
89-90	8.21	15.02	6.33	0.42	84.24	10.27	154.20

Notes : Variables used for economic ratios. Value in '000 Rs; Employment in Nos. F.A - Fixed Asset, Emp. - Employment, GVA - Gross Value Added, Emo - Emoluments, Unit - Enterprise

Source : Same as in Table 1.

Table 6 : Labour Productivity Among Major Industry Groups in the Artisan-Based Activities in Gujarat : 1989-90

(Rs.'000)

Industry Groups NIC-Code	GVA/Emp.								
	OAE			NDME			DME		
	R	U	C	R	U	C	R	U	C
23	2.9	2.8	2.9	10.6	9.9	9.9	20.4	16.6	16.9
27	5.7	8.1	6.2	8.9	12.2	11.9	12.0	2.9	3.5
29	5.1	10.0	6.9	11.0	11.8	11.8	-	9.1	9.1
32	3.2	4.4	3.3	6.4	6.7	6.5	5.2	11.1	7.3
33	..	3.9	3.9	10.1	22.1	22.0	39.3	18.6	18.8
34	13.2	7.5	9.4	12.1	11.5	11.6	11.5	13.2	12.9
35	6.2	11.9	11.2	3.6	24.3	23.1	26.7	20.8	21.0
37	-	3.1	3.1	20.3	168.4	163.2	17.5	12.1	12.2
39	4.3	11.1	7.3	6.5	10.7	9.9	16.0	9.9	10.7
All Indus..	5.2	8.3	6.6	8.0	27.7	23.6	7.0	18.5	15.0

Note : R - Rural; U - Urban, C - Combined

Source : Same as in Table 1.

Table 7 : Employment and Value Added per Enterprise in Major Industry Groups in the Artisan-Based Activities in Gujarat 1989-90

Industry Groups	Employment/Unit (No.)			GVA/Unit ('000 Rs)		
NIC-Code	OAE	NDME	DME	OAE	NDME	DME
23	1.5	4.5	9.9	5.1	85.5	464.9
27	1.6	3.5	8.2	22.1	68.8	111.9
29	1.3	3.3	6.0	21.4	93.2	54.3
32	2.3	4.4	11.1	17.9	52.9	224.9
33	1.9	4.0	10.4	7.3	131.3	1104.0
34	1.0	2.9	7.2	21.1	60.6	194.6
35	1.8	3.5	8.5	31.6	97.5	476.5
37	2.5	4.6	8.0	7.8	855.6	208.9
39	1.6	3.4	13.4	24.2	58.1	276.4
All Industries	1.5	3.5	10.3	10.8	83.8	154.2

Source : Same as in Table 1.

Status of Rural Artisans: Micro Level Evidence

Artisan Households: Findings of a Survey

Evidences in the previous section suggested that despite the significant transformation taking place in the unorganized sector, a large proportion of the artisan-based activities is still concentrated in OAEs (i.e. the predominantly homebased enterprises) especially in the rural areas. The following analysis highlights some of the important features of artisan households in the four districts of Gujarat. The average number of artisans (surveyed) per village is 11; the highest in Banaskantha (i.e. 15) which is a backward district and the lowest in Baroda (i.e. 7) which is predominated by modern industries. Among the different activities, carpentry has the largest spread across villages, followed by pottery and leather work (Table 8). Over two-thirds of the surveyed villages have at least one artisan from these three categories; the coverage of blacksmithy and light engineering is limited to 56 and 41 percent respectively. The last two categories however, may have a significant overlap, hence, may not be considered as separate categories. Overall it is observed that only eight percent of the surveyed villages do not have an artisan unit in any one of the above five categories. This proportion is somewhat higher than the official estimate of 75 percent at the state level (Parthasarathy, 1993). A part of this could be attributed to the inclusion of the light engineering group which normally, is not considered as artisanal activity.

The other important features emerging from the survey data could be highlighted as follows:

1. About 80 percent of the units are operating within the household premises though, the proportion is somewhat lower (i.e. 67 percent) in Ahmedabad (Table 9).

2. To a large extent, artisans are catering to rural markets. Over 70 percent of the artisans, except for leather workers, sell their products within their own villages.

3. Despite the predominance of local markets, a large proportion (i.e. 52 percent) of artisans in all the five categories have changed the quality of their products.

4. The dynamism on the production front however, is not adequately matched by improvement in production technology. Artisans, by and large, have continued to work with old tools/equipment. The

Table 8 : Extent of Artisan-Based Activities Among Four Districts in Gujarat

Artisan Activities	% of Villages Having Artisan Household				
	Ahmedabad	Baroda	Kheda	Banas-kantha	All
Pottery	76 (494)	46 (750)	64 (619)	86 (1175)	66 (3038)
Carpentry	49 (215)	82 (1342)	77 (748)	70 (959)	71 (3264)
Blacksmithy	62 (405)	45 (733)	46 (441)	74 (1015)	56 (2594)
Leather Work	61 (399)	50 (827)	67 (649)	82 (1126)	64 (3001)
Light Engineering	37 (242)	43 (707)	46 (440)	39 (530)	41 (1919)
At Least One of the Above	89 (579)	89 (1466)	98 (891)	98 (1337)	92 (4265)
All Villages	100 (650)	100 (1639)	100 (968)	100 (1368)	100 (4625)

Note : Figures in parentheses indicate no. of villages having the specific category of artisan households.

Source : Rural Technology Institute, Primary Survey Results.

Table 9 : Distribution of Artisan Households Working in House-Premises and Incorporating Changes in Finished Products

Artisan Activities	Ahmedabad	Baroda	Kheda	Banas-kantha	All
		PERCENT			
(a) Working in House-Premises					
Pottery	66.2	82.8	76.9	78.0	77.0
Carpentry	73.3	89.3	80.9	87.6	85.8
Blacksmithy	57.7	80.6	70.2	87.2	81.0
Leather Work	66.2	65.1	68.4	85.0	75.5
Light Engineering	65.5	83.1	60.5	87.5	75.5
All	67.0	81.0	72.5	84.7	79.2
(b) Changed the Finished Products					
Pottery	51.5	46.3	65.4	53.2	54.5
Carpentry	67.2	53.7	63.8	43.8	53.1
Blacksmithy	63.1	45.9	75.0	51.3	53.4
Leather Work	47.9	30.2	56.9	47.7	46.7
Light Engineering	58.2	50.0	60.9	61.1	56.9
All	54.9	53.2	62.4	49.0	51.8

Source : Same as in Table 8.

important reasons for not acquiring new tools/equipment are non-affordability (due to high prices) and lack of information. It is likely that these constraints may have hampered product and/or market development.

5. As large as 55 per cent of the labour force in artisan households are either partially or fully unemployed (Table 10). This proportion is more or less the same across districts. Fully unemployed persons constitute nearly 24 percent of the total labour force among these households. The proportion of fully unemployed is highest in the backward district, i.e. Banaskantha and lowest in Baroda characterized by modern industries.

The high incidence of unemployment causes serious policy concerns. To what extent have the existing policies contributed to employment generation in the traditional artisan based rural industries? This has been examined in the light of the performance of Khadi and village Industries (K&VI) programme in Gujarat.

Khadi and Village Industries Programme: A Case Study

K&VI programme is a national-level comprehensive strategy for supporting traditional rural industries including the artisan-based activities. It provides a package of policy support to the voluntary organizations which in turn manage the whole range of activities namely finance, production, distribution, technology and training.

The policy package mainly includes protective measures like preferential purchase, subsidies on retail sale, tax rebates etc. In Gujarat the programme covers twenty-one product groups including the hand-spinning and weaving of cotton textile, i.e. Khadi. The two most distinct features of this programme are: (a) employment generation through minimum use of mechanisation; and (b) decentralized production structure through the maximum use of local skills/material/resources.

Apart from the K&VI programme, the state Government has also setup special boards for the development of handloom and handicrafts. Besides this, there are organizations like the Directorate of Cottage Industries, Rural Technology Institute and Gujarat Rural Marketing Corporation to take care of the different aspects of rural industries including the artisan-based activities. But these organizations deal with only a specific aspect e.g. technology, without much

Table 10 : Extent of Fully and Partially Unemployed Persons* in Artisan Households

Artisanal Activities		Ahmedabad	Baroda	Kheda	Banas-kantha	All
Pottery	U**	13.0	9.0	25.2	75.8	43.9
	UD***	87.0	91.0	74.8	24.2	56.1
Carpentry	U	21.5	13.0	22.9	78.9	32.4
	UD	78.5	87.0	77.1	21.3	67.6
Blacksmithy	U	18.3	23.0	30.5	76.9	42.6
	UD	81.7	77.0	69.5	23.1	57.4
Leather Work	U	25.8	19.0	22.3	78.8	57.5
	UD	74.2	81.0	77.7	21.2	42.5
Light Engineering	U	23.4	20.0	42.3	68.0	31.3
	UD	76.6	80.0	57.7	32.0	68.7
All	U	19.6	14.0	24.5	78.1	42.7
	UD	80.4	86.0	75.5	21.9	57.3
% of U + UD in Total Labourforce Within the Artisan HHs		57.7	54.9	51.5	57.5	55.5
% of U in Total Labour force Within the Artisan Households		11.3	7.7	12.6	44.9	23.7

Note : * Within the age-group 15-60 years.

** U = Fully Unemployment; *** UD = Partially Unemployed

Source : Same as in Table 8.

co-ordination among them. Also, these programmes, unlike K&VI, cater to the scattered artisans/rural enterprises rather than supporting the voluntary organizations which in turn takeup entrepreneurial responsibilities and associated risks. In this context, K&VI programme has the special distinction of providing a comprehensive policy support to the traditional industries for generating employment in the rural areas.

Some of the important aspects of the activities supported under the K&VI programme can be highlighted as follows:

1. By the mid-nineties, K&VI sector had generated about one lakh jobs mainly in the rural area. This works out to be about six percent of the total employment generated in the unorganized manufacturing sector in Gujarat.

2. Of the total employment generated, Khadi and village industries share about 60 and 40 per cent respectively. Among the various village industries, contribution of artisan-based activities is nearly 50 per cent (Table 11). Over a period of time, the total employment has increased both in Khadi and village industries with a marginal increase in the share of artisan-based activities.

3. In 1994-95, the average earnings per worker varied between Rs. 1,700 in leather work to Rs. 11,000 in carpentry-blacksmithy. The average earnings however, worked out to be just the same as that of an agricultural worker, earning an average wage of Rs. 25 per day for 182 days in a year.

4. Nevertheless, what is of critical importance about the employment in K&VIs is that it can be made available at the doorstep and to the persons having limited mobility e.g. old persons, women, handicapped etc. In 1994-95, nearly 70 percent of the employment generated in Khadi has gone to women of which 45 percent belong to backward communities. In village industries, these proportions are 29 and 76 per cents. Overall the share of backward communities is 66 and 79 per cent in the total employment generated in Khadi and village industries respectively.

5. To a large extent the products of K&VI sector are sold in towns and cities. It is however, difficult to ascertain the extent to which they cater to the rural consumers who might purchase these products from the marketing outlets located in towns/cities. But given the nature of the products, it is likely that a substantially large proportion of the production might be catering to the relatively better off consumers in the urban areas.

Table 11 : Employment and Wage Earnings in K&VI Activities in Gujarat

(Rs. '000)

	Employment No.	% Share	Wages	Wage Rate
1982-83 to 1985-86				
A. Khadi	42892		651.32	1.52
B. Artisan Based Activities				
Carpentry-Blacksmithy	1923	6.8	92.50	4.81
Leather Work	3306	11.7	48.25	1.46
Earthen Work	7757	27.4	132.92	1.71
Sub Total	12986	45.9	273.66	2.11
C. Other Village Ind.	15323	54.1	273.43	1.78
D. All Village Ind.	28308	100.0	547.09	1.93
1992-93 to 1995-96				
A. Khadi	53823		1716.19	3.19
B. Artisan Based Activities				
Carpentry-Blacksmithy	3151	8.3	343.85	10.91
Leather Work	17293	11.4	286.70	1.66
Earthen Work	11172	29.3	376.22	3.37
Sub Total	18647	49.0	1006.77	5.40
C. Other Village Ind.	19436	51.0	915.68	4.71
D. All Village Ind.	38082	100.0	1922.46	5.0

Source : Gujarat State Khadi and Gramodyog Board, Annual Reports, Various Issues, Ahmedabad.

Together the above evidences suggest that the K&VI sector is able to generate only limited employment both in terms of extent (i.e. the number) as well as intensity (i.e. the magnitude of earnings). Yet, its contribution might be important in so far as it covers a special segment of the weaker sections including women.

The Policy Dilemma

The above analysis with respect to the traditional rural industries suggests that the existing policies, by and large, have failed to generate additional employment. On the other hand, the mainstream industrial development seems to have triggered off a process of transformation, shifting a large number of homebased activities to the higher forms of production and to the urban areas. Among those who still operate in the rural areas, a large proportion is likely to be linked with the modern organized industries having an urban base (Shah, 1986; Basant *et.al.*, 1991). While these changes could be seen as a positive phenomenon, the issue of attaining faster growth in employment within the manufacturing sector still remains a matter of concern. What went wrong especially when the original objective for promoting rural industrialization was to create additional employment opportunities (Gadgil, 1974; Tyabji, 1989)? The answer probably, is a mismatch between the policies which governed the process of rapid industrialization and those that influenced the traditional rural industries within that. This section tries to discuss this policy dilemma.

The initial vision, under the spell of Gandhian ideology, was to develop a dynamic and yet (mainly) 'rural-linked' industrial sector that is spread widely across villages and grows along with the development of the agricultural sector.[8] It was envisaged that agricultural development would not only precede but also set the stage for developing rural industries mainly through demand as well as input linkages (Robinson, 1977). It was further envisaged that the rural industries would respond to these growth impulses by adhering to labour intensive (or 'appropriate') techniques of production such that they can meet the growing demand by simultaneously creating employment to absorb a large proportion of the rural labour force which may fail to get full time employment in agriculture. Thus, the emphasis was more on generating supplementary employment and within rural areas so as to accommodate the seasonality in agricultural operations. The policies of protection and decentralized production structure therefore were consistent with this framework of agriculture-led development with (almost) full employment within village economies. The fact that agriculture was not allowed to play its leading role in the process of economic development may therefore provide a major explanation for the failure in terms of generating large-scale supplementary employment in the rural industries sector. This is what reflected in a mismatch between the overall strategy of industry-led growth and the specific measures that aimed at promoting 'rural-linked'[9] industrialisation. This would imply that unless the basic conditions are changed, the present set of policies of protection and decentralization, may not yield significant results; at best, they may contribute marginally in terms of providing employment to the weaker sections.

Alternatively, the Government may expedite the process of transformation which is already under way. One of the approaches adopted in the past has been to promote industrial dispersal and provide linkages to the traditional industries operating in the rural areas. Accordingly, various policy measures (e.g. industrial estates, growth centres and fiscal incentives) were evolved to attract modern industries in the rural/backward regions. The impact however, has remained selective and/or limited (Mohan, 1993). Generally, lack of infrastructure has been viewed as the major stumbling block. Moreover, creating such infrastructure on a large scale appears to be difficult especially if the pay-offs are (likely to be) limited and confined only to fewer locations (Bhalla, 1993). For, industries unlike agriculture, are strongly influenced by agglomeration economies, hence do not grow anywhere and everywhere as observed in the case of spatial concentration of the organized industries in Gujarat. This is true not only of the modern organized industries but also of the traditional/small scale industries. The recent evidences from a large number of countries indicate that small scale industries tend to be concentrated over the product specific spatial clusters. This pattern is also observed in the case of Indian small scale industries including the traditional artisan-based or craft-based activities (Government of India, 1997). Here, enterprises of different sizes and organizational forms grow through a complex pattern of inter-firm networking and collectivism (see, Schmitz, 1995).

Given this characteristic therefore, creating a widespread industrial infrastructure in the rural areas may not be as rewarding as that in the case of creating a broad-based support network for agriculture. Nevertheless, having moved significantly on to the path of modern industrialization, a more feasible strategy might be to promote clustering of enterprises or artisans rather than promoting them individually across a large number of scattered locations. This would imply that the emphasis should shift from rural-linked to urban-linked, from villages to spatial clusters and from individuals to networking among them. It is plausible that, collectively these enterprises might be able to overcome some of the entry-barriers, such as credit and information constraints, that might be hampering the growth as observed in the case of transition from NDMEs to DMEs. Of course, this kind of strategy may not necessarily generate a large number of additional supplementary employment in the rural areas. But, it may certainly provide better employment in terms of time as well as income criteria.

Summary and Conclusions

The foregoing analysis examined the process of transformation of rural unorganized manufacturing sector in which artisan-based activities are important components. In the backdrop of the industrial sector growing on the pattern of capitalist form of production, the analysis highlighted certain dynamic changes that have characterized the process of transformation. For instance, it indicated the shift from the household to the non-household sector in which the relatively smaller enterprises (i.e. employing less than six workers) are playing a significant role especially in terms of employment generation. Over a period of time, these enterprises have also shifted to urban areas and thereby improved their productivity as well as earnings. The next segment in the size-hierarchy (i.e. employing between six to nine workers) does not seem to be expanding so rapidly. This may be because a significant part of the growing enterprises in this segment might have crossed the threshold size and joined the rank of the organized sector. Thus, the changing size-structure suggests a bi-polar situation where the NDMEs and the organized modern enterprises are growing at the expense of own-account enterprises and the DMEs respectively.

Despite this upward shift, a substantially large proportion of artisan-based activities still take place in the own-account enterprises and in rural areas. Conversely, the OAE-segment is predominantly characterized by the traditional artisan-based activities. These enterprises, by and large, make moderately good earnings except for those involved in cotton textile, basic metal products and transport equipment parts. Their earnings can be improved if they move to a higher scale of production and to urban areas where they can reap the benefits of spatial clustering and collective efficiency.

The pertinent question emerging from this analysis is: will the non-household sector, especially in the non-factory enterprises continue to absorb the work force that gets released from the very small enterprises? If the macro trends are any guide, then the answer is not very encouraging. The immediate concern therefore is to improve the scope of these activities so as to ensure a sustained growth of employment irrespective of size and spatial characteristics. The analysis of artisan households and K&VI programme highlighted certain important features in this context. For instance, it was observed that the average earnings of the own-account enterprises is moderately good. But, this does not ensure employment to all the members within working-age groups in an artisan household. Similarly, employment generated by K&VI sector is neither extensive nor intensive though, it has a substantial scope for providing supplementary employment among the weaker sections and women. Overall, the K&VI programme is likely to yield limited results because of the in-built disadvantage in terms of technology and product-quality. It can succeed only if the right kind of objective conditions are created whereby agriculture takes the lead and village economies are placed at the centre of the developmental strategy.

In the absence of this, a more feasible approach could be to expedite the process of integration of the traditional artisan-based activities with the mainstream industrial production. The process is already on; the need is to modify and strengthen it further. One of the possible ways of attaining this, is to promote clustering of rural artisans/industries and help them overcome some of their constraints like access to information, technology and infrastructural facilities through collective dynamism. Earlier, some efforts were already made by the supporting organizations to promote groups or co-operatives of rural artisans by organizing common facility centres, technology parks, sale-exhibitions etc. A more comprehensive approach and specific emphasis on collective efficiency may perhaps, bring better results. Till then protective measures may have to continue, to provide at least some employment to those who need it the most.

Acknowledgements

The author is grateful to Shri Hasmukh Joshi, Shri Bhalsingh Parmar and Ms. Ila Mehta for their help in data collection and processing. Thanks are also due to Ms. Sheela Devadas and Ms. Vasanthi V.A. for a competent typing support.

Notes

1. Of the major artisan groups, weavers and leather workers often belong to the scheduled castes. The other three categories, namely, carpenters, blacksmiths and potters by and large, are classified as 'other backward' castes (Government of Gujarat, 1994).

2. Between 1980-81 to 1990-91 the share of the organized sectors in value added increased from 54 to 61 per cent (Visaria and Jacob, 1995).

3. The estimates of employment in organized (factory) and unorganized (non-factory) sector are not readily available. For Gujarat, the estimates given by the Annual Survey of Industries suggest that between 1980-81 and 1990-91, the number of employees in the organized sector had declined from 6,99,427 to 675,447. However, according to the estimates of the Chief Inspector of Factories (CIF) the number of workers engaged in the working factories had increased by 20 per cent during the same period. Employment in the unorganized sector can be derived by substracting the CIF-estimates from the number of main workers estimated by the Census of India. The estimates derived by adopting the above procedures suggest that employment in the unorganized sector had increased by 40 per cent, almost double than the rate observed in the case of the organised sector. It may however, be noted that this procedure is likely to underestimate (not over-estimate) the employment in the unorganized sector because (a) it leaves marginal workers (constituting 15% of the total main workers in the census-estimates), a large part of which is likely to be in the unorganized sector; and (b) the CIF-estimates for employment in the organized sector is likely to be on the higher side as compared to the estimates given by the Annual Survey of Industries.

4. The three segments of the unorganized manufacturing sector are defined as follows:

Own Account Enterprise (OAE) not employing any hired labour; Non-Directory Manufacturing Enterprises (NDMEs) - employing 1-5 workers; Directory Manufacturing Enterprises (DMEs) - employing 6-9 workers. Ofcourse, there is no one to one correspondence between the unorganized and the small scale sector. For, the former is defined according to employment size, whereas the later is defined in terms of investment size. It is, however, likely that a large part of the unorganized sector, except for a few units mainly in DME sector, might be covered under the small scale sector. The official definition for small scale sector till the late eighties was investment in fixed assets up to Rs. 35 lakhs, and Rs. 45 lakhs for anullary units. Given this definition, at least a part of the registered factory sector is also covered under on all scale sector. In 1989-90, around 80 per cent of the factaries had invested less than the above limit. These units however, contributed approximately 35 per cent of the total workers and 18 per cent of the net value added in the factory sector. Such data however, are not available at the state level.

5. The survey was carried out by Rural Technology Institute (RTI), the state supported organisation for promoting development and diffusion of technology especially for rural artisans. The survey covered all the artisan-households in the five categories.

6. Gujarat is forging ahead in terms of modern industries involving new investments in highly capital-intensive technologies. The recent evidences suggest that on realization of intended investment levels, the state would achieve the top rank, overall and in terms of per capita industrial output (Kashyap, 1995; also Hirway, forthcoming).

7. At 1990-91 prices, the poverty line for rural households has been defined at Rs. 11,000 per annum (GOI, 1995).

8 Following the linkage approach developed for non-agricultural employment, rural industries could be categorized into four:

a. Rural located - Rural linked

b. Rural located - Urban Linked

c. Urban located - Rural Linked

d. Urban located - Urban Linked

The 'rural-linked' approach refers mainly to (a) and (c) above (Saith, 1992). Also see, Papola (1978).

9 This has been clearly brought out by Charan Singh's critique on the Nehruvian policies (Singh, Charan, 1978). In turn he argued for drawing a demarcating line between cottage and small scale industries, the latter to be curbed or regulated in the interests of the former. What is implicit in this argument is a clear-cut initiative in favour of small commodity producers, and therefore a radical move against the logic of small industries policy (Tyabji, 1989, pp. 196).

References

Basant, Rakesh. 'Economic Diversification in Rural Areas: A Review of Processes with Special Reference to Gujarat'. *Economic and Political Weekly* 29, 39, (1994).

Basant, Rakesh and Parthasarathy, R. 'Correlates of Inter-Regional Variations in Rural Non-Agricultural Employment in Gujarat'. *Indian Journal of Labour Economics* 34, 2, (1991).

Basant, Rakesh and Kumar, B.L. 'Non-Agricultural Employment in Gujarat: A Review of Evidences'. *Working Paper No. 28.* Ahmedabad: The Gujarat Institute of Area Planning, Gota, 1990.

Bhalla, Shiela. 'Workforce Restructuring, Wages and Want: Recent Events, Interpretations and Analysis'. *Indian Journal of Labour Economics* 30, 1, (1996).

Bhalla, Shiela. 'Patterns of Employment Generation in India'. *Indian Journal of Labour Economics* 36, 4, (1993).

Breman, Jan. *Patronage and Exploitation: Changing Agrarian Relations in South Gujarat India.* Berkely, 1974.

Chattopadhyaya, R. 'De-industrialization in Indian Reconsidered'. *Economic and Political Weekly* 10, 1, (1975).

Gadgil, D.R. *The Industrial Evolution of India in Recent Times: 1860-1939.* New Delhi: Oxford University Press, 1974.

Ghurye, G.S. *Caste and Race in India.* Bombay, 1969.

Gohil, Shankar (undated). *Rural Artisans in Gujarat: A Study of Their Status and Role of Support Agency*, (mimeo). Gota, Ahmedabad: Gujarat Institute of Development Research.

Gokhale Institute of Politics and Economics. *Writing and Speeches of Professor D.R. Gadge an Planning and Development*, (1967-1971). Pune, 1973

Government of India. *Report of the Expert Committee on Small Enterprises.* New Delhi: Ministry of Industry, 1977.

Government of India. *Concurrent Evaluation of IRDP.* Ministry of Rural Areas and Employment, Administrative Intelligence Division, New Delhi: 1995.

Government of Gujarat. Government Resolution 'SSHP-4394-191-A'. Gandhinagar: Ministry of Social Welfare, 1994.

Hirway, Indira (forthcoming). *Economic Growth Policies and Patterns of Industrialisation in Gujarat (mimeo)*, Ahmedabad: Gandhi Labour Institute.

Kashyap, S.P. 'Industrial Scene in Gujarat - A Contrast of Two Patterns'. *Anvesak* 25, 1, (1995).

Kumar, A.V., Vani B.P., and Vyasulu, Vinod. 'Structure of Employment as seen from 1981 and 1991 Census: A Preliminary Look'. *Economic and Political Weekly* 30, 38, (1995).

Kuznets, Simon. *Modern Economic Growth: Rate Structure and Spread*. Yale University Press: New Haven, 1966.

Mohan, Rakesh. 'Industrial Location Policies and their Implications for India'. Studies in Industrial Development. New Delhi: Ministry of Industry, Government of India, 1993.

Nagaraj, R. 'Trends in factory size in Indian Industry, 1950 to 1980 : Some Tentative Infereness'. *Economic and Political Weekly* 20, 8, (1985).

Papola, T.S. 'Rural Industrialisation: Issues and Evidence', in T.S. Papola *et.al.,* (eds.). *Studies on Development of Uttar Pradesh, Occasional Paper No. 1*. Lucknow: Giri Institute of Development Studies, 1978.

Ramaswamy, K.V. 'Small Scale Manufacturing Industries: Some Aspects of Size, Growth and Structure'. *Economic and Political Weekly* 29, 9, (1994).

Ray Chandhari, T. 'A Reinterpretation of Nineteenth Century Indian Economic History'. *The Indian Economic and Social History Review*. 15, 1, 1968.

Robinson, Joan. 'Employment and the Choice of Technique', in Krishnaswamy, K. *et.al.* (eds). *Society and Change*, Bombay: Oxford University Press, 1977.

Saith, Ashwani. *'The Rural Non-Farm Economy: Processes and Policies'*. Geneva: International Labour Office, 1992.

Schmitz, Hubert. 'Collective Efficiency: Growth Path for Small-Scale Industry'. *The Journal of Development Studies*. 31, 4, (1995).

Shah, Amita. 'Scalar Linkages in Industries: Implications for Productivity and Employment'. GIDR working Paper No. 90. Gota, (Ahmedabad): Gujarat Institute of Development Research, 1997.

Shah, Amita. 'Linkages Between Small and Large Industries: Some Evidences from Gujarat'. *Artha Vijnana*. 32, 2, (1990).

Shah, Amita. 'Rural Industrialisation in Gujarat', *Indian Journal of Regional Science*. 18, 1, (1986).

Shirikov, G.K. *Industrialisation of India*, Moscow, 1973.

Singh, Charan. *India's Economic Policy: The Gandhian Blueprint*. New Delhi: Vikas Publishers, 1978.

Singh, Manjit, *The Political Economy of Unorganized Industry: A Study of the Labour Process*. New Delhi: Sage Publications, 1990.

Staley Engine and Morse, Richard. *Modern Small Industry for Developing Countries*. New York, 1965.

Streefkerk, Hein. *Industrialization in Rural India: Artisans, Trader and Tribals in South Gujarat*. Bombay, 1985.

Tyabji, Nasir. *The Small Industries Policy in India*, Calcutta: Oxford University Press, 1989.

Visaria, Pravin and Jacob, Paul. *The Informal Sector in India: Estimates of its Size, and Needs and Problems of Data Collection. Working Paper No. 70*, Gota, Ahmedabad: Gujarat Institute of Development Research, 1995.

Visaria, Pravin. The Sectoral Distribution of Workers in India 1961-1991 in Visaria, P. and Basant, R. (*eds.*). *Non-Agricultural Employment in India. Trends and Prospects*. New Delhi: Sage Publication, 1994.

13

Measuring Women's Development in Gujarat : Some Conceptual Issues and Empirical Results

Indira Hirway and Darshini Mahadevia

A significant aspect of Gujarat is, its less than satisfactory performance in social development. And this is closely related to the overall characteristics of the State. It is observed, for example, that Gujarat lags behind in rural literacy, drinking water, measures against crime against women, communal riots, etc. as compared to many other states.

It seems that Gujarat's growth is a typical case of promotion of industrial growth with less attention paid to social development and sustainable development.

In this way, Gujarat cannot proceed on this path of growth for long, as fast degrading environment, stagnant agriculture and the socio-economic groups which have been more or less bypassed by the growth process will put limits to any further growth.

This paper focuses on one such lagging group of the population, namely, women; and assesses their lack of development, in the context of the growth process of the state economy. This paper starts with discussing the concept and measurement issues of gender development; then presents empirical data on gender development in Gujarat and attempts to draw inferences for corrective actions.

Measuring Gender Development

Two most commonly used gender development measures today are GDI (Gender Development Index) and GEM (Gender Empowerment Measure) developed by the UNDP and computed for a large number of countries every year in their Human Development Reports. The genesis of these indices lies in the concept of human development as defined by the UNDP. The Human Development Reports since 1990, have brought into focus, the human aspect of development in recent years. Especially the report of 1995 has discussed gender development and argued that development that is not engendered, is in danger.

The UNDP defines human development as 'a process of expanding people's choices by formation of human capabilities through investing in people' (UNDP 1990). The Human Development Index (HDI) measures human development as a composite index of three basic components, namely, longevity measured in life expectancy at birth, knowledge measured in literacy rate and mean years of schooling and access to resources measured in per capita income adjusted for Purchasing Power Parity (PPP). In the same way, the GDI measures achievements of women with respect to the same capabilities, while taking note of inequality in the achievements of men and women. The UNDP has also presented the GEM which measures the use of the capabilities of women in taking advantage of the opportunities in life.

The UNDP computes the values of HDIs. GDIs and GEMs for a large number of countries every year. However, looking at the values and at the concepts and methods used in this computation, we believe that it is not quite relevant nor valid for the developing countries of the South. Our major objections against these concepts are as follows:

1. To start with, the formulation of HDI, GDI and GEM is too narrow compared to the broad and dynamic concepts of human / gender development. The two indices do not reflect the new human-centred development paradigm as presented in HDRs and they also overlook the much accepted understanding that human capabilities include much more than freedom to live, ability to read and write, and access to goods and services. A multi dimensional view of society and human advances in economic, social, cultural, political and environmental spheres is not reflected in these measures.

2. Also, the variable selection only reflects on the achievements with respect to personal capabilities and their private returns to the individuals. For example, there is an implicit belief that 'returns to education' lead to improvement in productivity, and to expansion of real opportunities to participate in economic activities. This 'economism' which is the basis of forming GDI, is expected to even-

tually increase the GDP. In other words, the index does not talk of social capabilities and macro or structural capabilities of women.

3. Good health, good education and control over resources will, and provided they can, maximize the country's GDP in the given structure of the national and global economy. However, the revival of the world economy through better human and gender development within the given (unequal) North-South structure of the global economy dominated by the North and the MNCs and TNCs of the North, will not bring in gender justice, social justice or equity. The given global system will perpetuate and even enhance the inequalities of all types, including gender inequalities. At the national level also, improved productive capabilities through higher HDI/GDI will not ensure a better deal for women. Thus, human and gender development measured without any reference to the structural aspects of development does not ensure justice, on the contrary it supports and promotes the Northern model of development which promotes Structural Adjustment Programme (SAP) as a precondition for the development of the poor countries of the South. Such an ideological underpinning of the HDI/GDI was, perhaps, not aimed at by the UNDP, but it has crept in quietly. The new models of development demanding equitable, participatory, holistic and sustainable development, as well as gender justice are not reflected in the measures of the HDI and the GDI.

4. Overemphasis on income: The HDI and the GDI, both, give one-third weightage to income irrespective of its composition and distribution. By now, many criticisms have been levied at the use of income as a measure of welfare. In short, income is not a satisfactory measure of welfare as well as capabilities, because: (a) income increases with many unnecessary economic activities, which are negative for human / gender development; at includes military expenditure, income from illegal activities such as crimes, unrest, drugs, as well as expenditure on diseases, (b) income increases with the depletion caused by thoughtless exploitation of national resources and passing on the costs of pollution to the society, and (c) income does not include unpaid family work, voluntary services etc. In short, though income reflects the control of a person over his resources to an extent, it cannot be given one third weightage in computing the index.

5. Poverty, Inequality and Patriarchy: Two of the major concerns of the South are poverty and inequality, which are not reflected in the human / gender development indices. Per capita income does not adequately reflect the incidence of poverty and deprivation prevailing

in these countries. Nor does it depict the widespread exploitative inequalities that exist here. Any development measure that does not pay any attention to these aspects will not properly measure the human/gender development in the countries of the South. In the same way, education as an important aspect of women's development has been accepted in all the four approaches; welfare, efficiency, equality and empowerment, within the gender theory. However, it is realized that women's education alone cannot empower them to change gender relations within a patriarchal society and the given economic order. The strategic gender need is, the relieving or sharing the burden of the social reproduction sector that women solely carry on their shoulders. This will release tremendous potential of women towards achieving gender development. The other important dimension in a woman's life is fear of violence against her during all stages of her life. Neither income, nor education nor better health can remove this fear or make the families and society share her burden of social reproduction. What is required is doing away with the structural limitations of the patriarchal system imposed on women.

The structural limitations imposed by patriarchy on women's development are very well known now. The UN Convention on the Elimination of Discrimination Against Women (CEDAW) adopted in 1979, as well as the Forward Looking Strategies (FLS) adopted at the Nairobi Conference in 1985 accepted that women's empowerment needs significant structural changes to shake patriarchy. Neither the GDI nor the GEM reflect any of these. In short the GDI and GEM measures under the framework of the existing development paradigm, which the feminists have criticized for being topsy-tarvy, and market dominated model imposed by the North on the South cannot really reflect the development and empowerment achieved by the women of the South.

6. Selection of Variables and Indicators : The variables selected for computing the GDI and the GEM are individual level variables reflecting individual level achievements only. They do not reflect any macro or structural variables, which are also crucial in enlarging opportunities and choices for people, including women. Also, the individual level variables selected by the UNDP are too few. Inclusion of only three variables, namely, income, health and knowledge leave out quite a few other variables crucial even for individual level development. For example, freedom and liberty which may not necessarily have a positive and significant association with literacy are important

variables for human and gender development. In the same way, housing, employment, safety and security are also important variables, specially for women.

There are problems with regard to the selection of indicators as well. For example, health (of women) cannot be adequately reflected in LEB (life expectancy at birth) alone, as LEB does not measure all the critical dimensions of women's health during her life cycle. Instead or along with it, IMR-F (Infant Mortality Rate of Females), MMR (Maternal Mortality Rate) and incidence of disease should be used. All these three indicators reflect the current dynamics and have immediate policy implications.

Towards An Alternative – Women Development Measure

The conceptual lacunas in the GDI from the perspective of the developing countries and the feminists discussed above, suggest a need for evolving an alternative concept and measure of gender development. This new measure should (a) represent the concerns of poor women in the South, (b) measure gender development in a comprehensive way, and (c) be useful in drawing policies for gender development. We have termed this new concept as Human/Gender Development Measure (GDM) to distinguish it from the UNDP's GDI. For women, we call this measure WDM (Women Development Measure), as we measure women's development independent of men's development.

We have seen above that human / gender development is reflected in, not only the individual level characteristics, but also in the macro and structural characteristics of a society. That is, the choices available to women for achieving their potential are enlarged not merely by their individual level achievements but also by favourable structural and macro level achievements of the society. We therefore propose two level WDM: WDM-I, which measures individual level development of women and WDM-II, which measures macro level development of women. In the following we discuss the components of the WDM-I and WDM-II, variables considered for each of the components, rationale for the selection of variables among the larger set of variables available, and the empirical exercise of construction of the indices for the fifteen states of India.

WDM - I : We propose that the WDM - I include the following components and the variables :

(1) Income Component Represented by Per Capita Income: Per capita income indicates the capability of individuals to access goods and services. For women, remunerative employment, as against predominant unpaid employment, is a way towards their visibility, social recognition, development and empowerment. Women's incomes in the low income households are critical for keeping the families above the poverty line, which itself has a spin-off effect in terms of women's development. With their income, women can also purchase labour-saving devices, so necessary for alleviating women's drudgery at the household level, which is generally not in the agenda of any family unless women push for it. A woman's income in the family therefore reflects her control over resources to a considerable extent, though not quite totally, as women often do not have control over their own earned income.

(2) Educational Attainment Component: Educational attainment reflects the knowledge status of an individual, which is a goal as well as an enabling condition of human / gender development. Education can and has proved to have expanded choices and opportunities in life. For women in developing countries, education is a means to empowerment. Since much has been written on women's education and its impact on fertility, infant mortality and the survival of female child, we are not elaborating on these points here.

(3) Health Status Component: The third important dimension of women's development is the health status of women. Good health is not only an achievement in life but also an enabling condition for enjoying better opportunities for development. For women, who are also responsible for the reproduction of new life, good health status is a must. We selected several variables to measure women's health; life expectancy at birth, the infant mortality rate of females, maternal mortality rate as well as incidence of disease and the use of polluting fuels. The last is very important in the context of women in the developing economies as the extensive use of polluting fuels that create indoor air pollution does harm women's health, though it is not always reflected in statistics on morbidity, or total disease.

(4) Housing Status Component: The housing status of women reflects their safety and security on the one hand and their better health and productivity on the other hand. For a large section of women in the developing economies, home is also a work place, a

means of enhancing their income. It is therefore an important variable that measures gender development. Two sets of indicators wish for measuring housing status across the states. These are availability of housing measured in terms of the percentage of people living in a serviceable house (i.e. not houseless or living in non-serviceable *katcha* houses) and the availability of the three basic facilities, drinking water, electricity and toilet, within or near the house. The three basic facilities are very important for women as their availability reduces women's drudgery and ensures their better health and hygiene.

(5) Employment Diversification: Employment diversification of women reflects the extent of opportunities available to them in the labour market. The level of occupational diversification of the female labour force is observed to be very limited in the developing economies where most women are employed in farm and farm-related activities. Larger diversification implies diverse skills, higher wages and more importantly, better access to development.

(6) Empowerment of Women: Since empowerment is a very wide concept, there can be many variables to indicate the level of achievement in this area. Empowerment can be viewed at two levels, household level to overcome intra-household inequality and at the societal level to overcome inequalities at that level. Due to non-availability of relevant data to measure empowerment adequately, only two areas have been considered here: atrocities and violence against women as represented by the incidence of rapes, dowry deaths, murders, suicides and unnatural deaths of women, and participation by women in economic and political organizations. UNDP uses the percentage of women-holding seats in Parliament as one of the components of the GEM. But this variable will not be adequate in a developing country where women's participation in the national Parliament is very low. We have therefore used additional indicators for measuring political participation by women: percentage of women contesting as well as being elected to Parliament and the State Assembly and percentage of women voting in different elections.

We have formulated indicators to measure women's development in the above areas. A comprehensive list of the indicators is given in Table 1:

Table 1: List of Variables Considered for Constructing WDM-I

1. Per Capita Income of Women (Per Capita Women's DP)
2. Life Expectancy at Birth (LEB), Female
3. Maternal Mortality Rate (MMR)
4. Infant Mortality Rate, Female
5. Morbidity Rate per 1000, Female
6. Percentage of households using polluting fuels
7. Percentage of households (rural) using wood as domestic fuel
8. Natural Growth Rate
9. Total Fertility Rate (TFR)
10. Literacy Rate, Female
11. Retention Rate after Class VIII, Female
12. Non-enrolment Rate, Female
13. Percentage of population houseless and living in institutions and *katcha* houses.
14. Percentage of households with access to safe drinking water
15. Percentage of households with access to toilet
16. Percentage of households with access to electricity
17. Percentage of households not having access to either of the above three facilities
18. Female Workforce Participation Rate (FWPR), Main + Marginal
19. Female WFPR, Main
20. Percentage non-farm employment, Female
21. Percentage women employed in the organized sector
22. No. of rapes per lakh of female population
23. No. of accidental deaths per lakh of female population
24. No. of suicides committed by women per lakh of female population
25. No. of dowry deaths per lakh of female population
26. No. of unnatural deaths per lakh of female population
27. Percentage of women voting in Parliamentary elections
28. Percentage of women voting in the State Assembly elections
29. Percentage of women contested in the Parliamentary elections
30. Percentage of women elected in the Parliamentary elections
31. Percentage of women contested in the State Assembly elections
32. Percentage of women elected in the State Assembly elections
33. Female to Male Ratio in the population (FMR)

WDM-II : The WDM-II measures the women's development at the macro level. Five components have been considered for measuring it. These are stated below:

(1) Environment and Ecology: The environment and ecology of any region has a direct influence on the life opportunities of people. This parameter can be broadly classified into two categories, namely, status of natural resources such as land, water and vegetation, and status of pollution of air, water and land. The former affects the intensity of natural calamities such as droughts and floods and also the productivity of land and land-based activities, while the latter affects the quality of natural environment available to people. The former can be measured in terms of environmental degradation, i.e. changes in areas under deserts / droughts, wasteland, forests, etc., and changes in quantity and quality of ground and surface water while the latter can be measured in terms of the extent of air, water and land pollution arising out of industrial development and other such activities.

The state of natural environment has a relationship with women's development, specially rural women who depend on these for their and their family's survival. In times of natural resource degradation and in the absence of any radical changes in society, they are forced to spend more time on activities related to family survival and hence have to neglect their health and education. Since much is written about women and environment and impact of environmental degradation on women's life, we are not discussing these arguments.

(2) Community Level Facilities: There are certain community level amenities and facilities which have a direct impact on the quality of life that people enjoy and the extent to the access that people have for developmental opportunities. Broadly, these are (a) availability of street lights, *pucca* approach road, all-weather bus services, electriity/ energy, postal and telecommunication facilities (b) availability of a fair price shop, a flour mill, a chemist shop, etc. (c) availability of potable drinking water, sanitation and public hygiene, etc., and (d) pre-primary and primary schools and primary health facilities. These variables are different from those considered for constructing individual level GDM. For the GDM-I, the basic facilities considered were at the household level attached to an individual house.

(3) Institutional Participation: Institutional participation by women at different levels suggests decentralization of decision-making in society. It ensures empowerment of people at lower levels. This,

once again results in a higher level of freedom and liberty, better enjoyment of human rights and less exploitation of people at the bottom. Only in a decentralized and participatory system can ordinary women come into the public sphere. Participation of women can be through the cooperatives, self-help groups (SHGs), trade unions, political parties and economic groups such as the DWCRA groups. Data with respect to none of these except the first one, that too for both men and women, were available for all the states. Since the DWCRA groups often exist on paper and have not proved to be a genuine means of women's institutional participation, we have not used these data. Thus, for the time being, only one variable, namely, participation of the population in credit cooperatives is considered for depicting overall environment of institutional participation.

(4) Social Environment: Social environment and human rights are an area which is crucial for human development as this area has implications for freedom and liberty as well as for law and order enjoyed by a community. In many instances, better social environment enhances human capabilities. For example, removal of untouchability in its true sense can enhance educational opportunities for SCs in India. Repeated communal riots or wars can force a whole generation to a life with poor safety and security. Education and health are also neglected in times of war or civil strife, besides inflicting direct casualities. The major variables here would be the incidence of communal violence and riots, the incidence of crimes in general, as well as the incidence of atrocities on backward castes, women and minorities. A high crime rate in any society discourages women from fully participating in the non-domestic domain and realizing their capabilities. Besides, human rights have their own intrinsic value to human beings.

(5) Inequalities of Assets and Incomes: Inequalities of distribution of assets and income have important implications for human development as the higher the extent of the inequalities, resulting in a concentration of assets / incomes in a few hands, the lower will be the bargaining strength of people with no / low assets or incomes. This will imply relatively low levels of wages and remuneration for those with poor assets; lower access of the no / low asset population to credit markets as well as to development opportunities in general; and in extreme cases, acute exploitation of vulnerable sections at the lower end of the asset and income distribution. The countries with relatively equal distribution of assets and incomes will provide its population,

relatively, equal access to developmental opportunities on the one hand, and reduce chances of extreme exploitation and acute deprivation of the weaker sections of the society on the other.

The list of the variables used for computing WDM-II is listed below in Table 2.

Table 2 : Variables Considered for WDM - II

1. Percentage of talukas of the state under DPAP and DDP programmes.
2. Percentage of area under waste lands.
3. Percentage of area under forests.
4. Percentage of forest area under degraded forests.
5. Percentage of villages with an all-weather approach road.
6. Percentage of villages with electricity.
7. Percentage of villages with a fair price shop.
8. Percentage of villages with some medical facilities.
9. Area / population served by a post office.
10. Percentage of women as members of cooperatives.
11. Incidence of rapes per lakh women population.
12. Incidence of murders and attempted murders in the state.
13. Gini coefficient of ownership of land holding in the state.
14. Range coefficient of variation of the distribution of per capita bank credit across districts in the state.

Construction of Women Development Indices for Gujarat

Using the above concepts and indicators we compute below the women development indices for Gujarat.

As a first step towards understanding the level of women's development in Gujarat in comparison to the development in other major states in India, we have computed state level indices for the major fifteen states in India.

Our first step was to construct a correlation matrix of all the variables listed in Tables 1 and 2. This was done in order to identify the relevant variables for the construction of the two indices, for the fifteen major states in India. The correlation matrix helped us in identifying the significant variables, multicollinearity among the variables, and in selecting the critical variables for constructing the indices. The selected variables along with their weightage are presented in the Tables 3 and 4 respectively.

WDM-I and WDM-II for the fifteen major states in India were constructed by, more or less, employing the same method used in the construction of the HDI by UNDP. Since our objective was to construct women development measures independently for women alone, (that is without reference to male-female disparity), we did not use any ε (epsilon), a value attributing to the preference given by any society on gender equity. Also, the value 2 of the epsilon given by UNDP in HDR 1995 is arbitrarily assigned. Hence also, we have not used ε. This is an important departure from the method used in the construction of the GDI.

The steps followed for the construction of the indices are described below:

1. To start with, variables scores were calculated for all variables using the following formula

$$I = \frac{\text{actual value - min. value}}{\text{max. value - min. value}}$$

where I is the variable score for the index, min. value is the minimum value observed in the fifteen states and max. value is the maximum value observed in the fifteen states.

2. The negative variable scores were converted into positive scores by subtracting each of these from one. This was done in order to have all the variables as positive variables.

3. Sectoral indices were constructed for each of the components by giving appropriate weightages stated in Tables 3 and 4.

4. WDM-I and WDM-II, which are the composite indices of the component indices, were computed for each of the fifteen states and for all-India, by giving equal weightage to each of the component (sectoral) indices and adding up the scores.

The data for the variables used in constructing WDM-I and WDM-II are given in Tables 3 and 4 and the composite and component indices of WDM-I and WDM-II, along with the ranking of states are presented in Tables 5 to 8. The major observations emerging from the tables are discussed below:

The performance of Gujarat, in relation to other states, varies considerably across different aspects of women's development (Table 5). For example, Gujarat ranks second in per capita SDP (women's share), third in maternal morbidity but ninth in percentage women

Table 3 : Selected Variables and Weightages Given for Constructing GDM - I

Component	Selected Variables	Weightage within Component Index
Income	1. Per Capita share of earned income of women in SDP	100%
Health Status	1. Life Expectancy at Birth or Maternal Mortality Rate	40%
	2. Incidence of morbidity	40%
	3. % households using polluting fuels	20%
Educational Attainment	1. Literacy rate (+7)	33%
	2. Retention rate after class VIII	33%
	3. % girls not-enrolled in age 6-11 years	33%
Housing Status Diversification	1. % households having no access to either individual water, or toilet	100%
Empowerment	1. Incidence of rapes per lakh population of women	25%
	2. Incidence of unnatural deaths (dowry, suicides and murder) of women per lakh population of women	25%
	3. % Women voting in the Parliament elections	25%
	4. % Women voting in the State Assembly elections	25%

Table 4 : Selected Variables and Weightages Given for Constructing GDM - II

Component	Selected Variables	Weightage within Component Index
Environment and	1. % talukas under DDP and DPAP programmes	50%
Ecology	2. % state area under wastelands	50%
Community Level Basic Facilities	1. % Villages with all weather approach road	100%
Institutional Participation	1. Members in credit co-operatives per 1000 population	100%
Social	1. Incidence of rapes per lakh population of women	50%
Environment	2. Incidence of murders and attempted murders per lakh population	50%
Inequalities	1. Concentration ration of land ownership	50%
	2. Range coefficient of variation of per capita bank credit across districts	50%

voting and tenth in the incidence of unnatural death of women. (inverse ranking) These fluctuating ranks across the different components of women's development indicate that Gujarat is neither consistently high nor consistently low in gender development.

Some of the other interesting aspects of women's development in Gujarat as emerging from the table are discussed below:

1. As for as the per capita income of women is concerned, Gujarat is far ahead of the other states, including states like Punjab and Haryana which have a much higher per capita income. This is because the work-force participation rate as well as the relative agricultural wage rate of women (as compared to the same of men) is much higher in Gujarat. In fact, the detailed data on agricultural wages in Gujarat show that in most of the districts there is wage parity between men and women for the same work.

2. As regards the health of women in Gujarat it is interesting to note that though maternal mortality is relatively low in the state, ranking third after Kerala and Maharashtra, the morbidity rate as well as life expectancy at birth (LEB) are not very favourable. This perhaps implies that Gujarat has achieved considerable control over the mortality arising out of child birth, but has yet to do a lot in terms of protecting general health and mortality of women.

3. The general neglect of women in the state arising out of socio cultural factors is greatly reflected in the high incidence of unnatural death of women in Gujarat. This incidence is 26 in the state against 23 in all India. Also, the incidence of rapes per lakh population in the state is relatively high. The state ranks ninth in this regard.

4. In the case of female education, the picture of Gujarat is rather interesting. Though Gujarat ranks fifth among the states in female literacy and fourth in non-enrolment rate of girls, it lags far behind most of the states in terms of the retention rate of girls up to standard eighth. This suggests that the drop-out rate of girls is fairly high in the state. This once again shows that women enjoy lower social status in the state.

5. As regards the other aspects of gender development, such as housing, employment, facilities in the house, etc., the performance of Gujarat is sluggish, i.e. it does not rank in the top five for these indicators.

To sum up, the state which enjoys fourth rank in per capita income and which is on the verge of being number one in industrialization, does not show an equivalent performance in terms of human development, and especially women's development.

Table 5 : Variables for Constructing GDM - 1

	State	Per Capita SDP 1991-92	LEB (1988-91)	MMR (1982-86) per lakh live births	Morbidity Rates per 000	% HHs using polluting fuels	Literacy Rate 1991
		X1	X2	X3	X4	X5	X6
1	Andhra Pradesh	1515	62.33	402	123.86	85.70	32.70
2	Assam	1003	55.23	1028	79.08	92.61	43.00
3	Bihar	633	57.00	813	97.77	97.05	22.90
4	Gujarat	1722	61.49	355	85.70	68.69	48.60
5	Haryana	608	61.97	435	78.21	80.78	40.50
6	Karnataka	1411	63.61	415	108.96	80.84	44.30
7	Kerala	573	73.80	234	184.71	93.34	86.20
8	Madhya Pradesh	1036	54.71	535	117.04	90.21	28.90
9	Maharashtra	2405	64.30	393	72.49	66.00	52.30
10	Orissa	777	55.15	778	222.43	95.02	34.70
11	Punjab	569	65.30	435	126.79	72.98	50.40
12	Rajasthan	1003	58.69	938	132.41	87.92	20.40
13	Tamil Nadu	1087	60.80	319	77.53	82.16	51.30
14	Uttar Pradesh	518	49.64	931	105.10	80.35	25.30
15	West Bengal	431	59.53	551	87.75	91.01	46.60
	India	1295	59.4	555	108.18	84.10	39.30

Table 5 : (Continued)

Retention Rate after class VIII	Non-enrollment rate	% has neither sanitation electricity individual water	Non-farm Emplt. 1991	Rapes per lakh pop. 1991	Unnatural Death of Women 1991	% Women voting in Parliament elects.Av. 1977,80,84	% in Assembly elects. Av.. 1974-75/77 1978/79-80
X7	X8	X9	X10	X11	X12	x13	x14
33.54	21.31	26.12	17.29	2.03	21.27	59.77	67.69
28.20	13.84	34.75	37.06	4.52	10.59	47.34	57.95
17.27	32.79	36.80	9.11	2.13	7.70	47.89	42.84
33.54	8.49	15.00	24.33	1.52	25.77	52.22	48.71
67.95	1.34	10.23	28.32	1.96	13.68	63.84	63.99
30.28	25.33	15.03	24.59	0.76	34.06	56.90	65.21
99.43	0.00	34.19	58.41	1.42	22.86	72.59	75.83
45.85	49.38	31.19	11.52	8.13	34.64	45.22	41.16
43.70	18.69	13.42	17.24	2.38	47.80	55.73	56.00
40.96	26.53	47.58	19.08	2.01	22.37	41.69	36.45
57.22	10.36	2.25	66.92	0.67	8.17	62.83	63.19
27.66	42.67	32.65	12.44	3.83	14.05	48.93	47.23
58.80	7.71	15.25	25.29	1.15	33.14	67.07	60.35
52.37	45.50	23.65	16.00	2.18	11.97	47.60	39.07
56.04	26.71	12.01	45.91	1.44	33.64	66.96	51.66
43.22	29.00	24.54	21.19	2.42	22.99	55.00	53.76

Source : X1 : Based on Dreze and Sen (1995), Table A.3 and Shivkumar (1996), pp, 891. X8 NCAER (1994).
X2, X6 : EPW, Research Foundation (1994), pp. 1300-07.
X3 : Dreze and Sen (1995).
X4 : Sundar (1995), Tables 1 and 2
X5, X7, X9 : CMIE (1996a), pp. 188-90 and 276-84.
X10 : Based on Census, 1991.
X11. X12 : Based on Statistics from Crime Bulletin.
X13, X14 : Based on India, Ministry of Human Resource Development (1988), pp. 174-84.

The macro level variables pertaining to women's development in Gujarat also do not present very favourable results (Table 6). In fact, the performance here is relatively worse than the performance reflected in individual level variables.

To start with, Gujarat is eleventh in terms of environmental variables. About one-fourth of the talukas in Gujarat are under DPAP (Drought Prone Area Programmes) or DDP (Desert Development Programme) implying that these talukas are problem areas in terms of environment. About 47 per cent of the land in Gujarat is waste land which includes land without vegetation cover and land under DPAP and DDP. This highly unfriendly environment poses a serious challenge to women's development as this increases women's drudgery in collecting fuel, fodder and water, and affects their health, education and nutrition adversely. It has been observed that about 50 to 60 per cent of the villages in the state do not get potable drinking water in the summer of even a normal year. If the year is abnormal (as three out of five years are abnormal in the state), this percentage goes up to eighty raising women's drudgery to extreme. The unfriendly environment encourages massive seasonal migration which again harms the education of children.

As regards basic amenities such as approach roads, drinking water, primary schools, health / medical facility, etc., Gujarat shows an average position. The table provides data on the villages connected with all - weather approach road - which shows that Gujarat ranks fourth after Kerala, Punjab and Haryana.

In terms of social environment as well as equity (across regions), however, the performance of Gujarat is not very satisfactory. As shown in the statement, Gujarat ranks very low in both these sectors among the major states in India : twelfth in equity and seventh in violence against women.

Tables 7 and 8 present sectoral as well as composite indices of women's development for the major states in India. It shows that on the whole women's development in Gujarat is more constrained by macro variables than by micro variables. That is, the macro constraints such as poor environment and ecology, less safety against violence of different types, and wide regional disparities do pose serious limits to women's development in the state.

The final composite indices, namely WDM-I and WDM-II hide a lot of the details of the sectors aspects of women's development. However, as crisp measures of the overall position of the state in women's development, they do say a lot. Tables 7 and 8 show that the rank of the state is fourth and seventh respectively in WDM-I and II. What emerges from these ranks is that the level of women's development acquired in Gujarat is not commensurate with the rank of the state in the growth of GDP and per capita income. The ranks also indicate the macro constraints, unless removed through appropriate policy interventions, it will create serious hurdles in the development of women in the state.

Intra-State Variations in Women's Development

As seen earlier, wide regional disparities in growth persist in the Gujarat economy. One observes wide inter-district disparities in the different aspects of women's development also. While the achievements in terms of education and literacy, health and nutrition as well as housing are better in the 'Golden Corridor' (the region from Mehsana to Vapi which is prosperous agriculturally and industrially), these are much below the average in the desert and semi-desert areas of Kachchh, Banaskantha, Sabarkantha, and western Mehsana, as well as in the eastern tribal belt from Panchmahals to Dangs. In the same way the incidence of poverty also is the lowest in the 'Golden Corridor' while the same in the other region is much higher.

The performance of the relatively prosperous regions/districts, however, is not all that good in terms of violence against women. The higher incidence of rapes, molestation and unnatural deaths (including dowry deaths) of women in the relatively prosperous districts of the state are, however, partly due to better reporting in these regions and partly due to the 'curses' of the prosperity. As far as macro variables are concerned, once again women's development is low in the regions which are degraded environmentally, and are also backward with respect to infrastructure and basic facilities. For example, the macro constraints on women in Kachchh, Banaskantha, Sabarkantha, Surendranagar, etc., or in Panchmahals and Dangs are indeed serious enough to create an adverse impact on their development in health, education, nutrition, etc.

To sum up, the wide inter-district variations in women's development seem to arise from the macro variables such as environment and ecology, infrastructure etc. as well as from socio-cultural variables. One should also carefully look into the quantity and quality of expenditure on social sectors in the state to understand the performance of gender development.

Table 6 : Data Used for Constructing GDM - II

	State	% Talukas Under DDP & DPAP	% Area as Wasteland 1988	% Villages connected with all weather roads 1992-93	Membership credit socty. per 1000pop. 1986-87	Murder + Attempt to Murder 1991	Reported Rapes per lakh (Av. of 1990-92	Land Concentration (Gini's Coefficient)	Concentration of Per Capita Bank Credit
		Y1	Y2	Y3	Y4	Y5	Y6	Y7	Y8
1	Andhra Pradesh	20.91	67.31	43.00	196	6.67	2.08	0.737	0.9309
2	Assam	0.00	19.41	64.60	78	5.38	4.00	0.558	0.8721
3	Bihar	9.14	28.54	34.90	88	10.00	1.93	0.687	0.8113
4	Gujarat	23.85	46.95	73.60	145	6.03	1.29	0.693	0.8960
5	Haryana	40.74	47.01	99.10	124	5.67	2.10	0.735	0.6224
6	Karnataka	40.57	42.71	32.90	181	4.35	0.74	0.685	0.6373
7	Kerla	0.00	45.18	100.00	338	3.15	1.33	0.700	0.7957
8	Madhya Pradesh	10.68	30.40	23.40	121	10.29	7.83	0.650	0.9279
9	Maharashtra	17.45	39.92	52.90	203	5.90	2.37	0.707	0.9874
10	Orisa	12.42	48.21	15.10	139	4.60	1.77	0.615	0.7271

Table 6 : (Continued)

State	% Talukas Under DDP & DPAP	% Area as Wasteland 1988	% Villages connected with all weather roads 1992-93	Membership credit socty. per 1000pop. 1986-87	Murder + Attempt to Murder 1991	Reported Rapes per lakh (Av. of 1990-92	Land Concentration (Gini's Coefficient)	Concentration of Per Capita Bank Credit
	Y1	Y2	Y3	Y4	Y5	Y6	Y7	Y8
11 Panjab	0.00	24.48	98.80	120	23.32	0.62	0.735	0.7130
12 Rajasthan	48.73	39.15	21.20	138	6.52	3.75	0.623	0.8897
13 Tamil Nadu	11.20	59.03	63.20	261	5.15	0.88	0.761	0.8152
14 Utter Pradesh	9.70	37.04	42.80	111	14.08	2.39	0.627	0.9151
15 West Bengal	9.97	30.67	41.40	78	3.32	1.66	0.700	0.9766
All India	**14.40**	**36.15**	**40.70**	**144**	**7.85**	**2.49**	**0.714**	**0.8520**

Source : Y1 : CMIE (1996b).
Y2 : Based on Ministry of Environment and Forests, Report on Developing India's Wastelands.
Y3 : Tata Services Limited (1989).
Y4 : Based on CSO (1989).
Y5, Y6 : Based on Bulletin of Crime Statistics.
Y7 : India, Ministry of Agriculture (1992).
Y8 : Based on CMIE (1993).

Table 7 : Sectoral and Composite Indices of GDM - I with Rankings

	State	Income		Education		Health		Housing	
		Index	Rank	Index	Rank	Index	Rank	Index	Rank
1	Andhra Pradesh	0.5493	3	0.3178	11	0.5462	8	0.4734	9
2	Assam	0.2897	8	0.3987	8	0.5036	10	0.2830	13
3	Bihar	0.1025	10	0.1247	14	0.4544	11	0.2378	14
4	Gujarat	0.6540	2	0.4849	5	0.7436	2	0.7187	5
5	Haryana	0.0900	11	0.6317	2	0.6937	3	0.8240	2
6	Karnataka	0.4966	4	0.3362	9	0.6384	6	0.7181	6
7	Kerala	0.0719	12	1.0000	1	0.5245	9	0.2954	12
8	Madhya Pradesh	0.3064	6	0.1590	13	0.4092	14	0.3616	10
9	Maharashtra	1.0000	1	0.4760	6	0.8427	1	0.7536	4
10	Orissa	0.1754	9	0.3228	10	0.1043	15	0.0000	15
11	Punjab	0.0700	13	0.5775	4	0.6695	4	1.0000	1
12	Rajasthan	0.2899	7	0.0874	15	0.4488	12	0.3294	11
13	Tamil Nadu	0.3323	5	0.6063	3	0.6672	5	0.7132	7
14	Uttar Pradesh	0.0440	14	0.1934	12	0.4206	13	0.5279	8
15	West Bengal	0.0000	15	0.4431	7	0.5619	7	0.7847	3
	India	0.4379		0.3386		0.5498			

Table 7 : (Continued)

Employment Diversification		Empowerment		Composite - I		Composite - II	
Index	Rank	Index	Rank	Index	Rank	Index	Rank
0.1415	10	0.7066	4	0.4733	9	0.4558	9
0.4834	4	0.5354	9	0.4002	10	0.4156	10
0.0000	15	0.5418	8	0.2413	14	0.2435	13
0.2634	8	0.5219	10	0.5882	4	0.5644	4
0.3323	5	0.7735	3	0.5733	6	0.5575	5
0.2677	7	0.6383	6	0.5288	7	0.5159	7
0.8528	2	0.8803	1	0.6042	3	0.6042	2
0.0417	14	0.1405	15	0.2638	13	0.2364	14
0.1406	11	0.4306	12	0.6201	2	0.6072	3
0.1724	9	0.3639	13	0.1956	15	0.1898	15
1.0000	1	0.8379	2	0.6991	1	0.6925	1
0.0576	13	0.4817	11	0.2651	12	0.2825	12
0.2798	6	0.6826	5	0.5756	5	0.5469	6
0.1192	12	0.4875	14	0.3069	11	0.2988	11
0.6366	3	0.6136	7	0.5194	8	0.5066	8
0.2090		0.5639		0.4474		0.4346	

Note : Health - I and Composite - I are with MMR and Health - II and Composite - II are with LEB.

Table 8 : Sectoral and Composite Indices of GDM - II with Rankings

State		Environment		Basic Facility	
		Index	Rank	Index	Rank
1	Andhra Pradesh	0.2855	15	0.3286	8
2	Assam	1.0000	1	0.5830	5
3	Bihar	0.8109	3	0.2332	11
4	Gujarat	0.4678	11	0.6890	4
5	Haryana	0.2938	14	0.9894	2
6	Karnataka	03405	12	0.2097	12
7	Kerala	0.7310	6	1.0000	1
8	Madhya Pradesh	0.7757	5	0.0978	13
9	Maharashtra	0.6069	8	0.4452	7
10	Orissa	0.5720	9	0.0000	15
11	Punjab	0.9471	2	0.9859	3
12	Rajasthan	0.2939	13	0.0718	4
13	Tamil Nadu	0.4715	10	0.5665	6
14	Uttar Pradesh	0.7164	7	0.3263	9
15	West Bengal	0.7801	4	0.3098	10
	All India	**0.6774**		**0.3015**	

Table 8 : (Continued)

Institutional Participation		Social Environment		Equality		Composite	
Index	Rank	Index	Rank	Index	Rank	Index	Rank
0.4533	4	0.8110	8	0.1661	13	0.4089	11
0.0000	15	0.7100	11	0.2849	4	0.5156	5
0.0388	13	0.7394	10	0.2508	7	0.4146	6
0.2582	6	0.8824	6	0.2055	12	0.5006	7
0.1780	9	0.8352	7	0.3213	3	0.5236	4
0.3971	5	0.9622	1	0.3388	1	0.4497	9
1.0000	1	0.9511	2	0.2522	6	0.7868	1
0.1641	10	0.3229	15	0.2110	11	0.3143	14
0.4793	3	0.8106	9	0.1528	15	0.4990	8
0.2340	7	0.8847	5	0.3290	2	0.4039	12
0.1616	11	0.5000	14	0.2760	5	0.5741	3
0.2307	8	0.6990	12	0.2437	8	0.3078	15
0.7022	2	0.9325	3	0.2119	10	0.5770	2
0.1281	12	0.6065	13	0.2289	9	0.4012	13
0.0012	14	0.9239	4	0.1617	14	0.4353	10
0.2543		**0.7537**		**2170**		**0.4408**	

Inference for Corrective Interventions

One major conclusion about women's development in Gujarat is that the economic growth in the state has neither ensured human development nor guaranteed women's development. That is, the economic growth in the state has not automatically been translated into human/woman development. It appears that the state Government has to make special efforts to promote human/woman development.

One important factor that seems to have worked against the development of women is the narrow character of the economic growth in the state. If the growth is broad-based, balanced and sustainable environmentally, economically and socially, the chances of the growth becoming translated in human/woman development are much higher. Gujarat has to go a long way to achieve this growth rate.

Women's development also depends on several structural characteristics of the society/economy including the hold of patriarchy. Gender sensitivity on the part of policy makers and administration can counter this hold considerably. Somehow, Gujarat's achievements in this respect are limited, with the result that it is lagging behind in women's development.

To sum up, Gujarat has a long way to go to achieve equitable development with respect to gender development. This calls for corrections in the macro growth path as well as in micro policy/programme formulation and implementation.

References

Central Statistical Organization. *Statistical Abstract*. Ministry of Planning. Government of India, 1989.

Centre for Monitoring of Indian Economy (1993). *'District Profiles'*. Bombay, 1989.

———. 'India's Social Sector'. Bombay, 1996a.

———. 'India's Agricultural Sector. A Compendium of Statistics'. Bombay, 1996b.

Desai, M. 'Income and Alternative Measures of Well-being' in D.G. Westendorff and D. Ghai (eds.). *Monitoring Social Progress in the 1990s*. For UNRISD, Averbury, Aldershot, Hong Kong, Singapore, Sydney, 1995.

Dreze, J. and A. Sen. *India: Economic Development and Social Opportunity*. Delhi: Oxford University Press, 1995. *EPW* Research Foundation : 'Social Indicators of Development for India - II: Inter-State Disparities'. *Economic and Political Weekly (May 21, 1994): 1300-07.*

Hirway, I. and Mahadevia, D. 'Critique of Human Development Index : Towards an Alternative', paper presented at the workshop on HDR 1995. New Delhi, March 1996.

Hirway, I. and Mahadevia, D. 'Critique of Gender Development Index : Towards an Alternative'. *Economic & Political Weekly* (Oct. 26, 1996).

Shiva Kumar, A.K. 'UNDP's Gender-Related Development Index : A Computation for Indian States'. *Economic and Political Weekly* 31, 14, (1996):887-97.

United Nations Development Programme : *Human Development Report, 1990*. Oxford: Oxford University Press, for UNDP, 1990.

——. *Human Development Report, 1991*. Oxford: Oxford University Press, 1991.

———. *Human Development Report, 1992*. Oxford: Oxford University Press, 1992.

———. *Human Development Report, 1993*. New Delhi: Oxford University Press, 1993.

———. *Human Development Report, 1994*. New Delhi: Oxford University Press, 1994.

———. *Human Development Report, 1995*. New Delhi: Oxford University Press, 1995.

———. *Human Development Report, 1996*. New Delhi: Oxford University Press, 1996.

14

Employment Status of Women in Gujarat in a Drought vs Normal Year

Jeemol Unni

Introduction

The state of Gujarat consists of very diverse agro-climatic regions. While South Gujarat has a wet climate and rich alluvial soil, the furthest western region encompasses the Little Rann of Kutch with desert conditions. A large part of Gujarat is a semi-arid zone with little rainfall during the year. Besides, Gujarat also has a tribal belt and a long coastal region with problems of salinity ingress. An added curse on most of the Gujarat region is the frequent occurrence of drought.

The impact of drought on the livelihood of the people is immense. With the failure of the monsoon, agricultural activities are disturbed. The agricultural year 1987-88, saw the culmination of three consecutive years of drought. The Government of Gujarat was forced to declare 1987-88 as a year of scarcity. However, it did a commendable job of providing massive scarcity relief work programmes throughout the drought-affected regions. A large proportion of the population dependent on agriculture was forced to work on these relief sites. Women, in particular, worked on relief work programmes in large numbers.

A primary survey was conducted by GIDR in 1988-89 in 30 villages belonging to five districts of Gujarat, one each in the five agro-climatic regions of the state. Since the reference year 1987-88 for which the data had been collected, turned out to be a year of severe drought, a high proportion of households reported themselves to be primarily dependent on scarcity relief works for their livelihood. About thirty per cent of households surveyed in Mehsana and Bhavnagar districts reported participation in the relief work programmes. In 1994-95 we decided to re-survey some of these villages to study changes in the employment status of the people. The reference year 1993-94 was a normal agricultural year and none of the households reported themselves to be engaged in relief work programmes.

Obviously, the occupational status of the workers, particularly those dependent on agriculture, is greatly affected by the rainfall pattern in the reference year. As we shall see, the work participation of women in particular is affected by this. In this paper we shall study the changes in the employment status of women in the drought, vis-a-vis the normal year, in the sample villages.

Survey and Sampling Design

In order to capture various levels of diversification of occupations in the villages, the five districts surveyed in 1988-89 were chosen on the basis of the share of non-agricultural workers in the rural work force, as reported in the 1981 Population Census. The districts were chosen to represent low, medium and high share of rural non-agricultural male workers. From these five districts, two talukas each with the highest and lowest proportion of non-agricultural workers were selected, based on the size of the village to represent villages with small, medium and large population size.

The sample households were selected at the third stage. For this purpose, a houselisting of all the households in the study villages was conducted. This constituted the sampling frame from which the households were selected for survey. During the houselisting, information was collected on the major source of household income during the previous year (1987-88). Based on this the households were stratified into four categories, namely, cultivators, agricultural labourers, household industry (engaged in manufacturing, including skilled self-employed workers such as masons) and others. All the households engaged in household industry were surveyed. Besides, one-fifth of the cultivator and agricultural labour households and one-third of 'other' households were randomly selected for primary survey.

For the re-survey in 1994-95 Mehsana was chosen as representing several interesting features of the agro-climatic environment and the growth of non-agricultural employment in Gujarat. Firstly, Mehsana falls within the corridor of highly diversified districts identified by Sheila Bhalla (1993). It runs from Delhi, through Haryana, Rajasthan and Gujarat, all the way to the coast at Bombay. The nature of non-agricultural activity engaged in by the rural population and the incomes accruing to such enterprise in this region can be gauged from the primary survey.

Secondly, two villages selected in Kalol Taluka are close to Ahmedabad city and Gandhinagar. The impact of urbanization on the diversification of economic activities in these villages can be assessed.

Thirdly, in the original survey, two talukas were selected from each district having a relatively high and low percentage of non-agricultural workers. This interestingly, picked up two diverse regions of Mehsana district - an irrigated tract (Kalol) and a semi-arid dry tract (Harij). This captures the important agro-climatic diversity of Gujarat state, discussed earlier, which consists of both wet agriculturally developed, and dry undeveloped regions. The study would enable us to analyse the employment patterns of rural households in such diverse environmental conditions.

The houselist of the 1988-89 survey has been retained as the sampling frame for the 1994-95 survey. All the households surveyed in 1988-89 in Mehsana district were re-surveyed in 1994-95. However, there was a net decline in the total number of households surveyed due to outmigration and deaths. The formation of new households through splitting did not fully compensate for this loss. As mentioned earlier, the households in each of the villages were stratified into four categories according to their major source of income reported during houselisting. From each stratum a fixed proportion of households was selected with equal probability as ultimate sampling units. For estimation purposes, the inverse of these fixed proportions was used as weights in the earlier survey. These weights are five for cultivator and agricultural labour households, one for household industry and three for other households.

Since we have re-surveyed all the households in one district, our sampling frame remains the same as in the previous survey. Hence, for estimation and comparison with the previous survey, we also apply the same weights in the current survey data.

Occupational Structure and Economic Diversification

Occupational Structure of the Households

The weighted distributions of all households by their major source of income in the year 1987-88 and 1993-94 are presented in Table 1, separately for the villages in Kalol and Harij Taluka. The most striking difference in the distribution of households by their major source of income is the disappearance of scarcity relief as a source of income in 1993-94, since it was a normal agricultural year. About twenty-seven per cent of households in Mehsana district were dependent on this activity in 1987-88.

A steep decline in the proportion of non-agricultural households is observed between the two years, from nearly 50 to 27 per cent. In 1993-94, 81.2 per cent of the sample households dependent on scarcity relief in 1987-88 were agricultural households, engaged mainly in cultivation and agricultural labour. If we redistribute this proportion of households dependent on scarcity relief to agriculture, then the percentage of agricultural households in Mehsana district in 1987-88 rises to 72.1 per cent, and non-agricultural households declines to 27.8 per cent. These proportions are close to the 1993-94 figures of 73.5 per cent agricultural and 26.5 per cent non-agricultural households. Thus the dramatic change in the main occupation of households in the two survey years is only a phenomenon brought about by drought conditions in 1987-88.

The proportion of households dependent on scarcity relief programmes in 1987-88 was about 61 per cent in the villages of the backward Harij Taluka, compared to only 9 per cent in Kalol Taluka. The decline in proportion of non-agricultural households between the two years, observed earlier, is much more striking in Harij Taluka. However, these households were also re-distributed mainly into agricultural activities in the normal year 1993-94.

Work Participation of Men and Women

The household is a major decision-making unit for the allocation of the time of the individuals. So far we have studied the changes in occupational structure of the household in terms of their major source

Table 1 : Percentage Distribution of Households by Major Source of Households Income by Taluka of Mehsana

Major Source of HHs Income	1987-88 Kalol	Harij	Mehsana	1993-94 Kalol	Harij	Mehsana
All Agricultural Households	65.0	22.0	50.6 (72.1)	70.8	78.4	73.5
Cultivation	39.1	13.6	30.6	21.3	31.4	24.9
Allied Agri.	4.5	1.5	3.5	22.9	13.0	19.4
Agri. labour	21.3	7.[illegible]	16.5	26.6	33.9	29.2
Non-Agriculture Households	35.0	77.8	49.4 (27.8)	29.2	21.6	26.5
Scarcity HHs	9.2	60.7	26.5	-	-	-
Other Non-Agri. Labour	3.9	2.0	3.3	2.6	2.1	2.4
Reg. Emp. in Non-agri.	8.7	2.7	6.7	12.5	7.1	10.7
SE in Manufacturing	4.0	4.4	4.1	2.8	3.2	2.9
SE in Trade, Hotel, etc.	5.1	4.5.	4.9	4.2	3.7	4.0
Others	4.1	3.5.	3.9	7.0	5.6	6.5
All HHs	100.0 (2059)	100.0 (1033)	100.0 (3092)	100.0 (1893)	100.0 (1008)	100.0 (2901)

Note : Figures in parentheses refer to the estimated number of house holds. HHs refers to Households.

Source : GIDR surveys of 1988-89 and 1994-95.

of income. In any particular year, however, an household may be engaged in more than one economic activity. The diversification of economic activities in the household can occur through two processes. The household may diversify its activities by increasing the number of members to work in different economic activities. Or it may diversify by the participation of each member in more than one economic activity.

Tables 2 and 3 present the work participation ratios (WPR), that is, the proportion of workers to the total population, by the major source of household income and operational land status groups. In order to understand the gender dimension to changes in the occupational structure and economic diversification, the analysis at the level of individuals is done separately for men and women.

The overall WPR was not very different by gender in 1987-88 in Mehsana district. However, in 1993-94 while male WPR remained more or less constant, female WPR fell by five percentage points. In an earlier paper, I had hypothesized that women's work participation may be higher in a year of severe scarcity (Unni 1988). In the current study, 1987-88 was a year of severe drought, whereas 1993-94 was a normal agricultural year. The participation of women in the workforce was relatively higher in the year of drought substantiating the earlier hypothesis.

We had observed earlier that a large proportion (61 per cent) of households in Harij Taluka were predominantly dependent on scarcity relief work for their livelihood in 1987-88. It is quite significant that when WPRs are looked at separately for villages in the two talukas, the female WPRs fell from 60.5 in 1987-88 to 48.7 per cent in 1993-94 in Harij Taluka. This further substantiates the hypothesis regarding a high female work-force- participation in a year of drought. The male WPRs remain more or less constant between the two years in both sets of villages. With only 9 per cent of households in Kalol Taluka dependent on scarcity relief works in 1987-88 there is only a slight fall in female WPRs in these villages in 1993-94.

When WPRs are compared across households by their major source of income, the decline in female participation in predominantly non-agricultural households is most striking between the two years. This again is due to the high work participation in scarcity households in 1987-88. WPRs of both men and women have increased considerably in households with other sources of income between the two years.

Table 2 : Worker Population Ratios by Major Source of Household Income

Major Source of HH Income	Kalol Males	Kalol Females	Harij Males	Harij Females	Mehsana Males	Mehsana Females
1987-88						
Cultivation	52.4	53.7	58.4	63.7	53.5	55.5
Allied agri.	64.5	55.8	71.4	80.0	65.4	58.6
Agri. labour	53.6	54.9	56.1	64.3	54.0	56.1
Agri. HHs	53.5	54.1	58.3	64.4	54.3	55.8
Scarcity work	60.4	62.4	57.6	63.1	58.3	62.9
Non-agri. wage labour	56.9	42.7	63.8	61.1	58.4	46.2
Regular employ. in non-agri.	45.5	34.5	53.3	73.8	46.3	39.2
SE in manu-facturing	60.6	34.7	51.9	41.4	57.5	36.9
SE in Trade, Hotel etc.	53.2	35.9	65.5	32.1	56.8	34.7
Others	10.3	30.1	28.6	20.6	19.8	27.0
Non-agri. HHs	53.3	46.7	56.9	59.3	55.3	51.8
All HHs	53.4	51.6	57.3	60.5	54.8	53.9
1993-94						
Cultivation	51.6	54.1	58.4	48.1	54.8	51.3
Allied agri.	54.1	49.8	55.9	52.4	54.5	50.4
Agri. labour	54.8	54.4	58.2	53.2	56.1	54.0
Agri. HHs	53.6	52.7	57.9	50.7	55.2	52.0
Scarcity work	-	-	-	-	-	-
Non-agri. wage labour	55.6	65.3	59.4	46.5	56.9	59.6
Regular employ. in non-agri.	51.9	34.1	56.2	36.8	52.9	34.6
SE in manu-facturing	58.1	45.0	60.6	33.8	58.9	41.1
SE in Trade, Hotel etc.	63.8	45.9	64.6	27.7	64.1	40.1
Others	46.5	37.4	55.2	54.9	49.5	43.0
Non-agri. HHs	53.8	39.7	58.6	39.9	55.1	39.8
All HHs	53.6	49.0	58.0	48.7	55.2	48.9

Note : SE - Self Employed, HH - Household.

Source : Same as in Table 1.

WPRs by operational land status categories are presented in Table 3. The decline in female WPRs between 1987-88 and 1993-94 is more striking among the landed rather than in the landless category. This is perhaps due to the forced work participation of women among the landed households, even the large ones, in a year of drought and their withdrawal in a normal year.

Multiple Activities per Worker

The second process of diversification suggested earlier was through an increase in the number of activities per worker. Tables 4 and 5 present the average number of economic activities per worker by the major source of household income and operational land status categories.

On an average, both men and women were engaged in 1.7 economic activities per worker in 1987-88. The number of economic activities per worker reduced to 1.4 for men and 1.5 for women in 1993-94. The results were more or less similar when the workers were considered separately by the talukas to which they belong.

In the villages of Harij, however, male workers in cultivation, regular and wage workers in non-agriculture and self-employed in manufacturing on average undertook about 2.0 economic activities per worker in the drought year.

Table 3 : Worker Population Ratios by Operational Land Status Categories

Land Status	1987-88		1993-94	
Categories	Males	Females	Males	Females
Landless	53.3	48.0	51.2	43.6
Small Holdings	53.7	53.6	59.4	50.6
Medium Holdings	55.4	60.9	56.0	54.5
Large Holdings	58.1	60.3	54.7	50.6
Landed	55.7	57.6	57.2	51.6
Total	**54.8**	**53.9**	**55.2**	**48.9**

Note : Small Holding = Up to 1 hectare;
Medium Holding = 1-2 hectare;
Large Holding = More than 2 hectares.

Source : Same as in Table 1.

Table 4 : Average Number of Economic Activities Per Worker by Major Source of Household Income

Major Source of HH Income	Kalol		Harij		Mehsana	
	Males	Females	Males	Females	Males	Females
1987-88						
Cultivation	1.6	1.7	2.0	1.9	1.7	1.8
Allied Agri.	1.7	1.4	1.8	1.5	1.7	1.4
Agri. Labour	1.6	1.6	1.4	1.6	1.7	1.6
Agri. HHs	1.6	1.7	1.8	1.8	1.7	1.7
Scarcity Work	2.2	2.1	1.8	1.7	1.9	1.8
Non-Agri. Wage Labour	1.7	1.7	2.0	2.5	1.8	1.9
Regular Emply. in Non-Agri.	1.3	1.3	2.1	2.1	1.4	1.5
SE in Manu-facturing	1.5	1.6	2.0	1.4	1.6	1.5
SE in Trade, Hotel etc.	1.5	1.4	1.6	1.3	1.5	1.4
Others	1.0	1.3	1.3	1.0	1.2	1.2
Non-Agri. HHs	1.7	1.7	1.8	1.7	1.8	1.7
All HHs	1.7	1.7	1.8	1.8	1.7	1.7
1993-94						
Cultivation	1.5	1.6	1.5	1.7	1.5	1.7
Allied Agri.	1.5	1.6	1.4	1.6	1.5	1.6
Agri. labour	1.4	1.5	1.3	1.3	1.4	1.4
Agri. HHs	1.5	1.6	1.4	1.5	1.4	1.6
Scarcity Work	-	-	-	-	-	-
Non-Agri. Wage Labour	1.7	1.5	1.4	1.3	1.6	1.5
Regular Emply. in Non-Agri.	1.3	1.4	1.2	1.6	1.3	1.4
SE in Manu-facturing	1.2	1.1	1.5	1.3	1.3	1.2
SE in Trade, Hotel etc.	1.4	1.5	1.3	1.1	1.4	1.4
Others	1.2	1.4	1.6	2.0	1.4	1.6
Non-Agri. HHs	1.4	1.4	1.4	1.6	1.4	1.4
All HHs	1.4	1.5	1.4	1.5	1.4	1.5

Note : SE - Self Employed; HH- Household.

Source : Same as in Table 1.

This decline in the number of multiple activities by men and women in a normal year can be explained in terms of fluctuating income levels in these years. In a year of drought relatively lower incomes accruing to various agricultural and non-agricultural activities encourages diversification in order to obtain reasonable levels of income. This is more so in the backward villages. In a normal year when the main activity of the worker is able to provide sufficient income for the household, the need to engage in multiple activities reduces.

By the major source of income of the household, women in agricultural households undertook more economic activities in a normal year compared to non-agricultural households in the district as a whole. This was, however, not true for the backward villages in Harij taluka. Here again, the difference in the agro-climatic conditions in the two regions can explain this difference. In the better endowed region, all agricultural activities such as crop cultivation and animal husbandry provide a number of opportunities for work both in self and wage employment. In the backward region women have to find multiple jobs in the non-agricultural sector to meet their daily needs.

The average number of economic activities per male and female worker in households with operational land was higher than among the landless in both years (Table 5). This was true for men and women in both regions. The availability of land appears to help diversification of economic activities.

While the number of economic activities per worker declined for both men and women between 1987-88 and 1993-94, the proportion of workers undertaking a secondary activity also declined (Table 6). This supports our earlier hypothesis that in a normal year, the urgency to undertake multiple activities in order to meet their livelihood needs is reduced. This could be due to better returns in the main activity itself and more days of employment available in a normal year as compared to a drought year.

It is observed, however, that the percentage of women who undertake a subsidiary activity is higher in both a drought and a normal year, as well as in both the developed and backward regions compared to men. This is possible for various reasons. In agricultural households women have to undertake a variety of activities in crop cultivation as well as looking after the cattle. The main activity engaged in by both men and women of the household does not provide enough income, which forces the women to engage in all kinds of activities to meet

Table 5 : Average Number of Economic Activities Per Worker by Operational Land Status Groups

Land Status Groups	Kalol Males	Kalol Females	Harij Males	Harij Females	Mehsana Males	Mehsana Females
1987-88						
Landless	1.4	1.4	1.4	1.4	1.4	1.4
Small	1.9	1.8	2.1	2.0	2.0	1.8
Medium	1.7	1.8	2.2	2.0	1.8	1.9
Large	1.8	1.9	2.1	2.0	2.0	1.9
Landed	1.8	1.8	2.1	2.0	1.9	1.9
All	1.7	1.7	1.8	1.7	1.7	1.7
1993-94						
Landless	1.1	1.2	1.3	1.2	1.1	1.2
Small	1.6	1.7	1.6	1.8	1.6	1.7
Medium	1.5	1.7	1.5	1.8	1.5	1.7
Large	1.5	1.6	1.5	1.6	1.5	1.6
Landed	1.6	1.7	1.5	1.7	1.5	1.7
All	1.4	1.5	1.4	1.5	1.4	1.5

Source : Same as in Table 1.

Table 6 : Percentage of Workers with a Subsidiary Activity

Survey Villages in	1987-88 Males	1987-88 Females	1993-94 Males	1993-94 Females
Kalol Taluka	54.2	60.0	41.3	51.4
Harij Taluka	60.1	61.7	35.7	47.9
Mehsana District	56.4	60.7	39.2	50.1

Source : Same as in Table 1.

their livelihood needs. This would imply that it is the responsibility of the women to make ends meet in the household.

Industrial and Status Distribution of Workers

The industrial distribution of workers by main activity is presented in Table 7. There was a major shift of male and female workers from the non-agricultural sector to the agricultural sector between 1987-88 and 1993-94. Among the non-agricultural sectors it was the construction industry which registered a major decline in the proportion of workers. It is obvious that this shift was due to the workers engaged in scarcity relief works in the drought year moving to the agricultural sector in the normal year. It was in the backward Harij Taluka, particularly among women, that these shifts were most noticeable, since a very large proportion of households here were engaged in scarcity relief works in the drought year. In fact, 62 per cent of the women workers in the villages in Harij taluka reported themselves to be engaged in the construction sector in the drought year.

Table 8 presents the distribution of the workers by main activity status in 1987-88 and 1993-94. There is a major shift in the work force from manual wage employment to self employment particularly in Harij Taluka. This again was perhaps mainly due to less emphasis on cultivation in the year of drought, 1987-88. Wage work on scarcity relief programmes was the major activity in a large proportion of households, particularly in Harij Taluka. However, in a normal year these workers returned to their usual self employed activities, either in agriculture or non-agriculture.

At the beginning of this section we had suggested an economic diversification process either by the increase in number of workers in the household or an increase in the number of activities per worker. However, this trend need not be linear in time. The analysis earlier suggests that diversification due to a distress situation led to an increase in female workers in a year of drought. Similarly, one observed a decline in the number of activities per worker in a normal year compared to a drought year. Overall, diversification of activities through these two processes in a year of drought points to the possibility of distress as a major cause for it. Women seem to bear the burnt of these adjustments in the household.

Table 7 : Industrial Distribution of the Work Force by Main Activity

Major Source of HH Income	Kalol Males	Kalol Females	Harij Males	Harij Females	Mehsana Males	Mehsana Females
1987-88						
Agriculture	66.9	84.9	34.9	34.7	55.2	65.4
Mining & Quarrying	0.2	-	-	-	0.1	-
Manufacturing, Repair						
a. Hhld	3.4	1.5	3.0	1.1	3.3	1.3
b. Non-Hhld	4.2	0.1	0.6	..	2.9	0.1
Electricity, Gas & water	0.5	-	-	-	0.3	-
Construction	12.7	11.9	54.3	62.3	28.0	31.4
Trade, Hotel, etc.	5.6	0.5	3.4	0.9	4.8	0.6
Transport, Storage & Comm.	2.8	-	1.5	-	2.3	-
Financing, Insurance, Business Service etc.	0.2	-	-	-	0.1	-
Community, Social & Personal Services	3.5	1.2	2.3	1.0	3.0	1.2
All Workers	100.0 (2974)	100.0 (2639)	100.0 (1721)	100.0 (1675)	100.0 (4695)	100.0 (4314)
1993-94						
Agriculture	77.8	97.4	86.3	94.7	81.0	96.5
Mining & Quarrying	-	-	-	0.4		0.1
Manufacturing, Repair						
a. Hhld	2.2	1.5	2.9	1.5	2.5	1.5
b. Non-Hhld	6.9	0.0	0.9	0.4	4.7	0.2
Electricity, Gas & Water	0.8	-	0.3	-	0.6	-
Construction	2.8	-	1.2	0.6	2.2	0.2
Trade, Hotel, etc.	2.8	0.4	3.2	0.9	3.0	0.5
Transport, Storage & Comm.	2.8	-	1.3	-	2.2	-
Financing, Insurance, Business Service etc.	0.5	-	-	-	0.3	-
Community, Social & Personal Services	3.3	9.7	3.9	1.4	3.5	0.9
All Workers	100.0 (2844)	100.0 (2457)	100.0 (1729)	100.0 (1255)	100.0 (4573)	100.0 (3712)

Note : Figures in parentheses refer to the estimated number of persons in each group.

Source : Same as in Table 1.

Table 8 : Dis ribution of the Work Force by Main Activity Status

Activity Status	Kalol		Harij		Mehsana	
	Males	Females	Males	Females	Males	Females
1987-88						
Employer	1.0	0.7	0.2	0.4	0.7	0.4
Self-Employed	57.5	65.9	33.0	31.8	48.5	52.7
Casual Wage Labour	31.7	32.6	59.1	66.9	41.7	45.9
Regular Employees	9.8	0.8	7.7	1.0	9.1	1.0
All Employees	41.5	33.4	66.8	67.9	50.8	46.9
All Workers	100.0	100.0	100.0	100.0	100.0	100.0
1993-94						
Employer	-	-	-	-	-	-
Self-Employed	61.4	80.0	60.5	71.4	61.1	77.5
Casual Wage Labour	26.1	19.5	23.5	27.6	25.3	21.8
Regular Employees	12.5	0.6	16.1	1.0	13.6	0.7
All Employees	38.5	20.1	39.6	28.6	38.9	22.5
All Workers	100.0	100.0	100.0	100.0	100.0	100.0

Source : Same as in Table 1.

Days of Employment and Underemployment in a Normal Year

The analysis so far has emphasised the changes in the occupational status and the number of economic activities undertaken by men and women in a drought vis-a-vis a normal year. However, in order to understand the employment status of women it is necessary to know the intensity with which these activities are conducted. That is, it would be useful to know how many days of work are available to the men and women during the agricultural year in the two regions and the extent of underemployment.

Data on employment in various agricultural and non-agricultural activities was collected in great detail in the re-survey of 1995. Data on the number of days and average hours per day was collected for each worker separately for up to three activities. Information on his/her activity status, industry or sector of work, and occupation or type of work, was recorded for each economic activity. These data for a normal year are analysed below.

Days of Employment

Table 9 presents the total days worked in a year, average number of hours per day and the standardized average eight hour days worked in the year for each main activity cum occupational group of male and female workers. The total days worked in a year represents the average of all days engaged in economic activity irrespective of the number of hours. Therefore, even one hour of economic activity during the day, would be treated as one working day. The maximum number of days would thus be 365 days, and this includes days in both the main activity engaged in by the worker, as well as any subsidiary activity he/she might engage in.

The total working hours in a day include hours engaged in both the main and subsidiary economic activity of the worker. The average working hours per day actually implies the intensity of the employment which can be computed for each activity. A standard working day is assumed to be of eight hours. The standardized working day is calculated by multiplying the total days by the average number of hours worked and dividing this by eight.

On an average, women in the surveyed households work for 290 days in the year, while men work for only 255 days. However, on an average women have reported 5.1 hours of work per day whereas men reported 6.5 hours. This lower intensity of work reported by women is partly because they also bear the burden of doing the household work. While activities related to the feeding and care of animals have been included in our estimates of work, other household activities such as fuel collection, fetching water, etc., have been excluded.

The result of these lower working hours is that the number of standard working days available to women (175) is lower than that available to men (205). That is, on an average, women in the surveyed households, obtain work for only less than half the year.

The days and hours of work are computed separately for the main activity/ occupation of the worker. While on an average among men, the non-agricultural workers obtain more total days of income generating work than agricultural workers, this is not so among women. The average working hours and hence the standardized working days among men is also greater among the non-agricultural workers. This is not so among women workers.

Men and women engaged in animal husbandry have some duties to perform every day at least for an hour or two, hence their total days of work is very large. Workers, self-employed in trade, hotels or personal services also similarly engaged themselves almost throughout the year. The worst off in terms of availability of days of work are the agricultural labourers, both men and women.

We hypothesized earlier that the number of days of employment available to workers in the two talukas with differing agricultural environments are likely to be different. Thus, we observe that in the better-irrigated Kalol Taluka with proximity to large cities, the days of employment, both total and standard are higher among men and women, than in the less developed Harij Taluka. Even then, women in the Kalol Taluka obtained work for only about half the year.

When looked at in terms of sectors, men in agriculture obtained on average similar standard days of work in both Talukas, about half the year. Men and women in Kalol Taluka are also similarly engaged in agriculture, 188 and 185 days respectively. Male non-agricultural workers in both Talukas obtained more days of work than agricultural workers, while female non-agricultural workers did not. However, the number of days available to non-agricultural male workers in Kalol Taluka (301) is much larger than in Harij Taluka (257).

Table 9 : Total Days, Average Working Hours and Standard Days Per Worker by Main Activity/Occupation Group

Main Activity Occupation	Male				Female			
	Cases	Total working days	Average working hours	Standard Days	Cases	Total working days	Average working hours	Standard Days
Mehsana District								
Cultivation	1993	256	6.0	184	443	249	5.8	175
Allied Agri.	439	328	5.2	210	2271	356	4.6	200
Agri. Labour	1270	199	7.0	180	847	142	6.2	106
Agriculture	3702	245	6.3	186	3561	292	5.1	175
SE in Manufacturing	129	272	7.2	242	56	198	4.7	113
SE in Trade/Hotel	101	336	8.0	335	20	284	5.8	194
SE in Personal Services	63	353	6.0	267	3	330	3.3	143
Wage and Salaried N.A.	554	295	7.8	292	51	261	6.3	215
SE in Others	24	301	8.1	305	21	321	5.3	203
Non-Agri.	871	300	7.6	288	151	250	5.4	172
Total	4573	255	6.5	205	3712	290	5.1	175

Table 9 : (Continued)

Main Activity Occupation	Male				Female			
	Cases	Total working days	Average working hours	Standard Days	Cases	Total working days	Average working hours	Standard Days
Kalol Taluka								
Cultivation	1282	268	6.2	197	327	257	5.9	180
Allied Agri.	259	324	5.2	203	1565	357	4.8	206
Agri. Labour	698	197	6.7	166	482	163	5.8	118
Agriculture	2239	253	6.2	188	2374	303	5.1	185
SE in Manufacturing	83	289	7.4	263	38	219	4.5	121
SE in Trade/ Hotel	63	337	8.2	347	9	308	4.7	186
SE in Personal Services	33	353	6.7	298	-	-	-	-
Wage and Salaried N.A.	412	302	8.0	302	20	317	6.3	62
SE in others	14	306	8.0	306	16	346	4.4	192
Non-Agri.	605	307	7.8	301	83	277	5.0	174
Total	2844	264	6.6	212	2457	302	5.1	184

Table 9 : (Continued)

Main Activity Occupation	Male				Female			
	Cases	Total working days	Average working hours	Standard Days	Cases	Total working days	Average working hours	Standard Days
Harij Taluka								
Cultivation	711	233	5.7	161	116	229	5.7	159
Allied Agri.	180	333	5.3	221	706	335	4.2	186
Agri. Labour	572	201	7.4	197	365	113	6.7	91
Agriculture	1463	233	6.3	182	1187	269	5.1	154
SE in Manufacturing	46	239	6.8	205	18	155	5.1	97
SE in Trade/Hotel	38	335	7.6	316	11	264	6.5	201
SE in Personal Services	30	352	5.2	233	3	330	3.3	143
Wage and Salaried N.A.	142	273	7.5	260	31	225	6.3	189
SE in others	10	293	8.2	302	5	240	8.0	240
Non-Agri.	266	286	7.2	257	68	218	6.0	168
Total	1729	241	6.5	194	1255	266	5.2	155

Note : SE - Self Employed; NA - Non-Agriculture.
Source : Same as in Table 1.

Underemployment

The average of standard working days does not give any indication about the extent of underemployment among men and women in the two talukas and in the various activities. The distribution of the working days available to workers would present a better picture of underemployment. About 270 days of employment can be considered near full-employment, or approximately 22 days a month. Less than 100 standard days of work can be considered severe underemployment. Since 180 days represent half the year, 100-180 days of work can be considered as underemployment. The distribution of total and standard days is presented in Table 10.

A comparison of the distribution of total and standard days is quite striking, particularly among women. About 70 per cent of the women and 50 per cent of the men are engaged in some economic activity every day. But when looked at in terms of standard days, only 28 per cent of the men and 12 per cent of women are fully employed. About 20 per cent of men and women are severely underemployed getting less than 100 days of work. Another 26 per cent of the men and 36 per cent of women can be said to be underemployed.

Again comparison between the two talukas shows underemployment to be much more severe in the less developed Harij Taluka. In fact in this taluka only 22 per cent of the men and 5 per cent of women are fully employed.

The distribution of standard working days by the main activity of the worker is presented in Table 11. It is clear that a larger proportion of agricultural workers are underemployed compared to non-agricultural workers. More than 60 per cent among the male non-agricultural workers in all occupations, except for self employment in manufacturing and personal services, had full employment. About 40-50 per cent of the latter two also had full employment. In contrast, only 19-20 per cent of male agricultural workers were fully employed. The participation of women workers in non-agricultural activities is quite small both in terms of number of workers and days of employment available to them, even in the better developed Kalol Taluka.

In Kalol Taluka, the employment situation of male non-agricultural workers is even better, in terms of full-employment. Underemployment among male non-agricultural workers in Harij Taluka exists to some extent among those self-employed in manufacturing and per-

Table 10 : Underemployment Among Men and Women

(Percentage)

Days	Male		Female	
	Total Days	Standard Days	Total Days	Standard Days
Mehsana				
<100	8.3	20.4	11.1	21.0
100-180	23.1	26.2	11.9	35.9
180-270	18.5	25.4	6.4	28.0
270-365	50.1	24.2	70.3	10.9
>365	..	3.9	-	1.2
Kalol				
<100	7.1	17.9	8.1	21.3
100-180	20.0	24.5	10.5	34.7
180-270	19.4	25.9	7.0	28.0
270-365	53.5	28.5	74.3	14.0
>365	..	3.2	-	1.4
Harij				
<100	10.3	21.4	17.9	29.2
100-180	28.2	28.9	14.5	38.3
180-270	17.0	24.4	5.3	28.0
270-365	44.5	17.2	62.3	3.7
>365	-	5.1	-	0.8

Source : Same as in Table 1.

sonal services and wage-employed in the latter. One of the factors which helps non-agricultural male workers in Kalol Taluka to obtain better level and intensity of employment is its proximity to the urban areas like Kalol, Ahmedabad and Gandhinagar. For self-employed workers this provides a market for their goods. In the earlier GIDR survey we had observed that some of these workers commuted to urban areas.

Conclusion

It has been hypothesized that poor households adopt certain survival strategies to tide over difficult periods (Corbett, 1988). Even in normal times the diversity of actions and strategies of the poor and vulnerable to ensure their livelihood have been highlighted (Chambers 1989; Beck 1989; Heyer 1989). In an earlier article I had argued that the poor are not passive actors on the stage of life. They also make concerted efforts to improve their status (Unni, 1994).

The most striking change in the occupational distribution of households in a normal vis-a-vis drought year was the disappearance of scarcity relief programmes as a source of income. This change is also observed for the occupational distribution of individual men and women. In fact, in this paper we observed that the poor households, in times of stress adopt two kinds of employment strategies. Firstly, persons generally outside the labour force, such as women and children, enter the visible work force. This can be observed as an increase in the number of workers per household in a year of scarcity. Secondly, the members of the household each undertake more than one economic activity. This can be observed as a higher number of economic activities per worker in a year of poor agricultural output.

As discussed in the introduction, the agro-climatic diversity of the region is captured by the two talukas surveyed. The impact of drought was perhaps felt more in the backward semi-arid Harij taluka. Consequently, nearly 60 per cent of households surveyed were engaged in scarcity relief works in the drought year, as compared to only 9 per cent in the developed taluka. The entry of women in the work force in the drought year, and their withdrawal in the normal year is also more striking in the backward taluka.

In general, a larger proportion of women participated in a subsidiary activity as compared to men, irrespective of drought and relative development of the region. Perhaps it is the responsibility of the

Table 11 : Underemployment (Standard Days) Among Workers by Main Activity/Occupation (Percentage)

Main Activity/	Male			Female		
Occupation	<180	180-	>270	<180	180-	>270
Mehsana						
Crop Cultivation	49.8	31.2	19.0	53.5	28.7	17.8
Allied Agriculture	41.7	36.4	21.9	50.2	35.2	14.6
Agri. Labour	62.9	17.6	19.4	87.6	11.2	1.2
SE in Manufacture	32.5	25.6	41.9	89.3	8.9	1.8
WE in Manufacture	6.8	19.5	73.6	100.0	-	-
SE in Trade	7.0	8.9	84.2	60.0	-	40.0
WE in Trade	-	-	100.0	33.3	-	66.7
SE in Services	20.6	30.2	49.2	100.0	-	-
WE in Services	17.0	12.8	70.2	-	-	100.0
SE in NA	-	33.3	66.6	52.4	47.6	-
WE in NA	24.7	14.2	61.1	70.4	11.1	18.5
All	46.6	25.4	28.1	56.9	28.0	12.1
Kalol						
Crop Cultivation	43.7	31.4	24.8	51.6	25.7	22.6
Allied Agriculture	49.1	28.2	22.8	48.3	32.9	18.9
Agri. Labour	64.1	24.2	11.7	81.6	16.4	2.1
SE in Manufacture	25.3	21.7	53.0	92.1	5.3	2.6
WE in Manufacture	7.6	16.4	76.0	66.7	-	33.3
SE in Trade	1.6	6.3	92.1	-	-	-
WE in Trade	-	-	100.0	25.0	-	75.0
SE in Services	3.0	30.3	66.7	-	-	
WE in Services	-	-	100.0	-	-	100.0
SE in NA	-	21.4	78.6	68.8	31.3	-
WE in NA	19.4	15.6	65.0	66.7	33.3	-
All	42.4	25.9	31.7	56.0	28.0	16.0

Table 11 : (Continued)

Main Activity/ Occupation	Male			Female		
	<180	180-	>270	<180	180-	>270
Harij						
Crop Cultivation	60.9	30.8	8.3	58.6	37.1	4.3
Allied Agriculture	31.2	48.3	20.6	54.5	40.4	5.1
Agricultural Labour	61.6	9.6	28.8	95.6	4.4	-
SE in Manufacture	45.7	32.6	21.7	83.4	16.7	-
WE in Manufacture	-	-	100.0	100.0	-	-
SE in Trade	15.8	13.2	71.1	54.6	-	45.5
WE in Trade	-	-	100.0	37.5	-	62.5
SE in Services	40.0	30.0	30.0	100.0	-	-
WE in Services	40.0	30.0	30.0	-	-	-
SE in NA	-	50.0	50.0	-	100.0	-
WE in NA	34.7	11.6	53.6	72.3	-	27.8
All	50.3	24.4	22.3	67.5	28.0	4.5

Note : SE - Self Employed; WE - Wage Employed, NA - Other Non-Agriculture.

Source : Same as in Table 1.

women to make ends meet, consequently any available additional activity is undertaken.

In a normal year the average number of activities undertaken by women was also slightly higher than that of men. Consequently, the total number of days on which a women worked is greater than that of men. However, the intensity of work available to women was lower, so that the effective (or standard eight hour) average days available to women were less than half the year. A larger proportion of women were also underemployed compared to men.

In terms of broad sectors, men workers in non-agricultural activities obtained more total days of work than in agricultural activities. However, among women workers the agricultural activities provided more total days of work. The average working hours and standardized working days among men were also higher in the non-agricultural sector, while among women these were higher in the agricultural sector.

In terms of the agro-climatic environment, the developed taluka, with better irrigation and proximity to large urban centres, provided better opportunities for work to both men and women. Underemployment was also very severe in the underdeveloped taluka. Again women were the most affected by severe underemployment.

Acknowledgements

The data analysed in this paper were collected as part of a project sponsored under the United Nations Development Programme and the International Development Research Centre of Canada Research Project on Strategies and Financing for Human Development. The financial and other support provided by these organizations and the Government of India is gratefully acknowledged. I also thank late Professor T.N. Krishnan, National Co-ordinator of the Project, for granting permission to use these data.

I am grateful for the able support provided by Harish Joshi in data collection and processing. Upendra Upadhyay, Balu Parmar, Gani Meman and a team of investigators helped in the survey and coding work. Jignasu Yagnik solved many of our computer problems, while Ms. Sheela Devadas has word-processed the paper efficiently. I am thankful to all of them and other colleagues of the Gujarat Institute of Development Research for keeping the spirit of enquiry alive. However, the responsibility of any errors of fact and interpretation rest with me alone.

References

Bhalla, Sheila. 'Patterns of Employment Generation'. *The Indian Journal of Labour Economics* 36-4, (1993): 506-524.

Beck, Tony. 'Survival Strategies and Power Amongst the Poorest in a West Bengal Village'. *IDS Bulletin* 20, 2, (1989): 23-32.

Chambers, Robert. 'Vulnerability, Coping and Policy'. *IDS Bulletin* 20, 2, (1988): 17.

Corbett, A. 'Famine and Household Coping Strategies'. *World Development* 16, 9, (1988): 1099-1112.

Heyer, Judith. 'Landless Agricultural Labourer's Asset Strategies'. *IDS Bulletin* 20, 2, (1989): 33-40.

Unni, Jeemol. 'Agricultural Labourers in Rural Labour Households, 1956-57 to 1977-78: Change in Employment, Wages and Incomes'. *Economic and Political Weekly* 26 (1988): A-59-A-68.

_____. 'Inter-Linkages Between Poverty and the Labour Market in Rural India'. *The Indian Journal of Labour Economics* 37, 4, (1994): 623-638.

15

Shifting Perspectives on Widows' Issues in Gujarat

Varsha Bhagat-Ganguly and Amrita Shodhan

Introduction

Widows : Lonely and Deprived

Hindu widows in India face discrimination as 'inauspicious' creatures. Other religious groups, Muslims, Christians, Parsis, Sikhs and tribals do not hold widows to be impure or unworthy in theory. However, widows in these groups are also often treated with the same kind of denigration as Hindu widows, specially in rural areas. Hindu social and religious theory accords widows an inferior status to women in general and they continue to suffer from social, religious and economic deprivation even in practice.

For the widow the death of the husband means : the loss of love and security, single parenthood, increase in family and social responsibilities and a curb on her own sexual needs. According to Hindu social-cultural norms, widows are forced to wear simple clothes and avoid any kind of ornaments, cosmetics, etc. In the nineteenth century, upper-caste widows had to shave (tonsure) their heads, eat food without salt, wear white/red/blue, simple clothes, sleep on the ground and generally live out their lives in social seclusion. Some of these norms are still in practice.

Widows in India face multiple marginalizations. Their difficult lives pose questions regarding the incidence of widowhood, duration of widowhood, the link between widowhood, poverty and the struggle for survival, aging and widowhood and the issues of female-headed households. Widows are vulnerable because of various types of social restrictions such as limited freedom to remarry, insecure property rights, social restrictions on mobility and lifestyle, restricted employment opportunities, and limited social support; all these over and above negative religious beliefs and practices.

The total number of widows in India is extremely large - more than 25 million at the time of the 1981 census. The proportion of widows to the total female population is 8.2 per cent in India while it is 7 per cent in Gujarat, which means out of every 14 or 15 women, one is a widow in India. In Gujarat, the population of widows in the total female population is as large as the proportion of Scheduled Castes and female agricultural labourers in the total population. In contrast the population of male widowers is 2.3 per cent of the population in India while 2.1 per cent in Gujarat.

The question of this large difference in the number of male widowers and female widows remains largely unanswered. The explanation that the male widower can remarry without any protest from society begs for greater investigation into the prospects for widows. Can the permission to remarry solve the problem of widows? To understand this issue we shall examine the social reform movement of the nineteenth century. This movement made widow remarriage a campaign issue and advocated it as a solution to the problems of widowhood in a very systematic way. Subsequent to this major campaign, widowhood did not remain an important issue for those concerned with social change. This paper analyses the shifts in the way in which widowhood is an issue of social concern.

Social Reform in the Nineteenth Century

The nineteenth century is considered to be a landmark century for events related to the position of women in Indian society. The reform movement is popularly associated with the campaign against *sati,* struggles for widow remarriage and the importance given to women's education. Each issue is linked to its sponsor's name, like abolition of *sati* and Raja Rammohan Roy, promoting widow remarriage and Ishwarchandra Vidyasagar, raising the age of consent and B. M. Malabari and others.

Social reform was grounded on humanitarian principles and the natural rights doctrine developed in the European liberal tradition. The debate and effort for social reform to change the status quo in society was also justified through Hindu *shastras* (scriptural texts). As a result of the campaign against *sati* and for widow remarriage, two laws were enacted by the British Government in India. The act of abolition of *sati* was enacted in 1829, while the act legalizing the marriage of Hindu widows was promulgated in 1856, the age of consent to marriage was raised in 1891. The debate and efforts to encourage remarriage were initially started in eastern India and later on spread to the other parts of India.

Following the banning of *sati* in 1829, the Bengali social reformers believed it to be their 'responsibility' to settle the question of upper caste widows whose only option now was to lead miserable marginalized lives. Almost all the lower castes allowed widows to remarry, however for Brahmins in Bengal and Brahmins and Baniyas in Gujarat, Hindu scriptures strongly condemned widow remarriage. In text upon text the widow is seen as a threat to the social and moral order.

Widow Remarriage in Gujarat

Gujarat became a separate state in 1960, earlier it was a part of Bombay province in western India. Although it was a part of Bombay, it has a distinct history of social reform in the last century. The distinctions are mainly based in language, and territorial criteria. These events of the nineteenth century, which took place in present-day Gujarat are considered to be a part of Gujarat social reform movement; the oral and written sources available in the Gujarati language are now identified as part of the social reform movement in Gujarat and the people who were Gujarati speaking or belonged to Gujarat are also part of the reform movement in Gujarat.

After the 1856 act legalizing the marriages of Hindu widows, the widow remarriage campaign became an important movement. The reformers supported the widows who wanted to re-marry and the men who were ready to marry widows. Despite protests from the local people or their caste fellows, there were instances of widow remarriage in different parts of Gujarat. At many places, 'mandals' or 'associations' were established to promote and support widow remarriage. In 1865, *The Vidhava Punarvivah Uttejak Sabha* was established in

Bombay and in 1868, *Punarlagna Association* was established in Ahmedabad to promote widow remarriage (Dhruv 1936).

The first reported high-caste widow remarriage was in 1862 but it was unsuccessful, as the man who married the widow, deserted her very soon. He reportedly deserted her because he did not receive the kind of monetary support he thought he would when he married a widow. No more details are available about this marriage. In 1871, a Bhatia (upper caste) widow named Dhankorbai, married Madhavdas Rughnathdas in Bombay. Her marriage is considered to be the first successful upper caste widow remarriage. This marriage took place under the auspices of the *Vidhava Punarvivah Uttejak Sabha* (Trivedi 1974). Between 1878 and 1934, a total of 214 widow remarriages were registered under the auspices of the *Punarlagna Association* of Ahmedabad (Dhruv 1936). However the widow remarriage debate started much earlier than the first marriages in the sixties and seventies. We shall examine various aspects of these debates below.

Various Aspects of Widow Remarriage Movement

The debate started in 1840s and many people joined in with different arguments. The earliest such discussion was held in Surat. It was held under the auspices of the Manav Dharma Sabha, the first 'secular' group (Mahipatram 1879). Durgaram Manchharam, a teacher in the vernacular Government school in Surat organized and led the *Manav Dharma Sabha*. Widows and their condition formed one of the topics of interest - others were questions like improvement of human qualities, the removal of evils like belief in magic and superstition. In May 1843 Durgaram read an essay to the meeting on the subject of widow remarriage. It was followed by a discussion (Mahipatram 1879 : 111-117).

The issues raised in this discussion were reflected over and over again in later discussions of the question of widow remarriage in the nineteenth century. Those who supported reform argued that remarriage was a solution for the woes of widowhood. In the 1850s and 60s reformers wrote poems to describe the agonies of widows, while some wrote essays and made presentations with description of injustices and inhuman social practices widows had to follow. These were published in journals and newspapers or read to interested groups (Narmadshankar 1888; Dalpatram 1905).

Most looked at remarriage as the only solution and absorbed by it, they spent all the rest of the time trying to convince others about the possibilities of high caste remarriage. They argued that widow remarriage was not against the sacred Hindu scriptures but was in fact approved by them. They supported their arguments with quotations from Hindu scripture - *smritis* and *shastras*, in favour of widow remarriage (Narayan 1882, 1886; Vaishya 1897). These were vociferously opposed in rival journals and letters to the editors by those who opposed remarriage. Those who opposed remarriage used scripture and tradition to uphold the practice of enforced widowhood and others employed modern medical notions (Trivedi n. d.; Dave 1892; Shah 1936). In this period men advertised in magazines and newspapers for a match, stating their preference for a widow.

Advocating Remarriage of Child Widows

A striking feature of the debate was the overwhelming concern of the reformers for child widows. They were far more interested in the question of virile widows than in the problems of older widows. The question of widow remarriage was crucially linked to the problem of child marriages. They argued that women who were young and married before puberty suffered widowhood not for any fault of their own and before they had 'experienced' life. Remarriage was an option only for young women whose marriages were not consummated as they were widowed before puberty.

When the Age of Consent Act, seeking to fix the legal age of marriage was discussed in the 1880s and 1890s, it was also crucially linked with the question of enforced widowhood. Thus all those who wrote on the subject, like Malabari, talked about widowhood and child marriage in the same breath. The Government concerned about this vociferous campaign also collected opinions on the subject titled 'Papers relating to Infant Marriage and Enforced Widowhood in India' (Government of India 1886)

In contrast to male reformers who discussed the problem mainly from the point of view of child widows, Rukhmabai, a young woman caught up in the age of consent and marriage controversy, and the step-daughter of Sakharam Arjun, a prominent reformer, wrote about widows very sensitively. In a letter to *The Times of India* about enforced widowhood, she distinguished between different widows by age, listing the differences in their problems, suggesting different ways to deal with them (Varde 1982).

Question of Uncontrolled Sexuality and Widow Remarriage as Solution

Another striking feature of the widow remarriage debate was the amount of time spent on describing the sexual vulnerability of widows and the problems resulting from it.

Besides those who saw the genuine sexual vulnerability of widows, many taking up this subject wrote as if the widow was to blame. They described widows as sexually insatiable and the source of sexual corruption. In a slightly later text, a child widow is held to be responsible for the sexual corruption of a young bride. Malabari, talking about the corruption of a certain portion of Gujarati society described how Moghi Thakrani, a young bride was corrupted by her widowed aunt. This widow acted as a pimp for the Vallabhacharya religious priests and preceptors and brought the bride to the temple for the priest (Malabari 1889). A similar tone of writing on the subject of a widow who was convicted of infanticide near Surat provoked Tarabai Shinde into writing a spirited defense of women in 1882 (Shinde 1994).

The Idiom of Shastra Used by the Reformers

When Ishwarchandra Vidyasagar and others started advocating widow remarriage, they cited *smritis* and *shastras* favouring widow remarriage. In the 1850s and 1860s in Gujarat, reformist young men advocated widow remarriage in poetry, essays, and presentations of discussion groups. In advocating the cause of widows, translations of the Bengali texts were used in essays. They also quoted appropriate Sanskrit *shastras* to convince people that widow remarriage was permissible and therefore should be promoted in contemporary society. The reformers early on tried to engage prominent religious heads like the Vallabhacharya Maharajas in 'shastrartha'. In 1861 Narmadshankar Lalshankar set out to examine the *shastras* publicly on the subject of widow remarriage with Jadunathji Maharaj (Narmadashankar 1983). Narayan Hemchandra, wrote *Vidhava no Vakil* and *Punarvivah Shastra Sammat Chhe*. Thus while the reformers were inspired by their liberal western principles, they were also employing the Sanskrit idiom in their debates.

Protesting Against Widow Remarriage with Medical Notions

On the other hand those protesting against the permission to remarry for high caste widows based their arguments on tradition and *shastra*. In fact they tried to denigrate the reformers as lacking in true respect for the *shastras*. Thus Jadunath Maharaj in the above mentioned encounter with Narmada accused the latter of not believing that the *Shastras* were *Ishvarkruta,* i.e. the word of God.

However, the so-called champions of tradition also employed modern medical notions to argue against remarriage. Some Ayurvedic medical practitioners [*vaidyas*] opposed widow remarriage with the argument that it would be instrumental in creating miscegenation. They borrowed from western sexologists to say that the first intercourse crucially transforms the entire reproductive system of the female and hence reproduction with a different man would result in hybrid children. One Vaidya Jatashankar quotes a European sexologist and argues that '... the act of fecundation is limited in its effects but that it is an act which affects the whole system, the sexual system especially; and in the sexual system the ovary to be impregnated hereafter is so modified by the first act, that later impregnations do not efface that first impression (Trivedi n. d.).'

Forfeiture of Husband's Property after Remarriage

The question of widow remarriage was also crucially linked to the question of their rights in family property. It has been suggested that *sati* was a preferred practice in Bengal to prevent widows from inheriting their husband's property. Under the *Dayabhaga* system (a Sanskrit treatise for inheritance of property), widows in Bengal inherited half the husband's property, and in the case of no issue she inherited all of it. In Bombay province, widows received only a proportional share in the family property along with her sons and husband's brothers in accordance with the *Vyavahara Mayukh* (a commentary on the *Mitakshara* - a old Sanskrit treatise).

When upper caste reformers advocated remarriage for these widows, they made sure that the woman forfeited her property rights to the husband's family on remarriage. The law that the British passed in 1856, enabling upper caste widows to remarry included this provision. Her economic support after marriage came from the new husband. There were no public policy provisions for widows, however traditional community philanthropy, recognized widows as destitutes and made a special provision for them under caste and communal norms.

Unexpected Consequences of Reform Movement : Marginalizing Lower Castes

The need for public recognition of widow remarriage was urgent only among the upper castes, specially Brahmins and Baniyas. Among many other castes, remarriage of widowed and divorced women was permitted according to the rules of each caste; most of the castes had their `Bandharan' (Constitution) formulated by the *Nyat Panchayat* (Caste Council). The subsequent marriage of widowed or divorced women was called *Naatru* or *Ghargharanu* and not treated as equivalent to the first marriage. The rituals and social exchanges at the time of remarriage of widows were different from those of the first marriage. The rules were prescribed also for the custody of children and inheritance of property in the respective caste constitution.

Most castes allowed the woman to retain her rights to the first husband's property even after remarriage (Steele 1827). These lower caste practices were ignored by the reformers concerned about upper caste widows' lot. When the British framed the act enabling widow remarriage in 1856, they also ignored lower caste practices and disallowed widows to retain their first husband's property (Carrol 1989).

Instead of considering the rules of each caste distinctly, and adopting the relevant portions from the existing practices of lower castes supporting women, they generalized the norms for the remarriage of widows. Consequently, the remarried woman, who earlier used in keeping with to receive share in property in keeping with caste rules, lost her right to inherit her first husband's property. This further marginalized lower caste widows. Such consequences, revealed the privileged and self-absorbed character of the upper caste reformers.

Association of Women with Reform

Very few widows participated in the public debate on remarriage but their responses were very sharp and apt. A twenty-one year-old, Brahmin widow from Bharuch district, wrote an appeal in 1854 published in the daily, Bombay Telegraph. She said that she was recently widowed and ready to marry again though Brahmins and Baniyas were against her. She said that the worst part of being widowed was having to shave her head at the hands of a male barber. She appealed therefore to the Government to stop the practice of enforced shaving of the widow's hair. She also suggested that any barber proved to have shaved a widow's hair against her wishes should be punished (Rast Goftar 1854 : 268).

Another widow published a poem in 1856 in the *Rast Goftar*, a reformist newspaper. The poem was addressed to the religious head to permit high-caste Hindu widows marriages (Rast Goftar 1856 : 23). At the same time she wrote about the problems of fifty year old men marrying nine year old girls, thus, laying the blame for widowhood not only on child marriages in general and women's sexuality, but on the practice of unequal marriages.

Besides the active advocacy of remarriage for widows, education and teaching was seen as an important avenue for providing a better life to widows. Women took this up as an option very actively. Jivkorbai, a widow who had remarried and fled her hometown for Bombay became a teacher in a Municipal school for girls and the school was known by her name (Gujarat Vidyasabha 1934).

Pandita Ramabai, also a young widow, started a society for the education of women in 1882 in Poona. In 1889 she founded the school for widows in Poona (Dongre and Patterson 1963). Shivgauri and Bajigauri women who were widowed in childhood, provided the funds and started an orphanage and shelter for widows - the Vanita Vishram in Surat in 1907. Others, men also started education centres focusing on widows. One of the most prominent of these was D. K. Karve's centre in Poona.

These women and some men concentrated on the question of creating support structures for women. It is also remarkable that these women who were active were all widows themselves. Other widowed women while they did not support only widows created institutions for women. Of these, the most noteworthy is the first girl's school in Gujarat which was started by a rich widow - Harkunvar Shethani in Ahmedabad in 1842.

Shifts and Trends in the Campaign for Women's Reform

The remarriage campaign in the nineteenth century was primarily about and for child widows and upper-caste widows. The reformers were not aware or were not ready to take up the issue of the misery of widows of lower castes where widow re-marriage was already permitted and practised. In fact the manner in which the widow remarriage act was framed was harmful to women of many lower castes who were traditionally allowed to remarry. With the passing of the act which applied to all Hindu widows, these lower caste women lost their traditional right to inherit from their first husband's property.

Remarriage of child widows was meant to prevent sexual corruption of the widows and through them, of society. Today the age of marriage is generally much higher than before and child mortality is much lower, therefore the problem of child widows is not as acute. Given this restriction however, remarriage of young upper caste widows is more easy today than before in big cities, highly educated families. To that extent the reformers have been successful in their campaign. However remarriage of older women, specially women with children is still looked down upon. One recently conducted survey of widows of rural Gujarat however reveals that the upper caste widows in rural areas do not think of remarriage because it is considered to be against religious norms (Bhagat-Ganguly 1994). Permission to remarry therefore continues to mark the difference between upper castes and lower castes.

In addition, the positive aspect of lower caste practices where they permitted women to retain their rights in their first husband's property was also denied by the reformers. Thus if we know the nineteenth century to have had a beneficial effect on widows of the upper castes, on those of the lower castes to the extent that they came under the purview of organized law, the nineteenth century was not beneficial.

Women in the nineteenth and twentieth centuries while not opposing remarriage, attempted to create stronger support structures for widows to enable them to live out their single lives better. They supported and initiated attempts to provide widows with a profession and shelter away from the exploitative home and family environment. They seem to feel that remarriage is not an easy option for widows.

While looking critically at the campaign for remarriage, one of the contributory factors found, was that the social reform agenda was separated from the political agenda in the Congress Session in 1892. Perhaps, this was because of the politicization around the age of consent controversy (Kosambi 1991). Contemporary opponents of social change based their opposition on anti-colonial political agenda. For example, Tilak argued that social change should not be mediated by the foreign Government. Thus for later advocates of reform like Gatulalji, who came from a liberal reformist family, change became a personal matter rather than one of public action.

A social reformer, Gatulal Dhruv, writing about widow remarriage movement in 1930, looking at the last 60 years (1870 to 1930), clearly says that remarriage should be left to the individual's choice. This is a shift from the previous reformist stance and activities. It also reflects the decline in general public concern with social reform issues.

With Gandhi the social agenda came back on the political scene. He used the Hindu idiom to discuss social reality. In his world view, renunciation and celibacy were highly valuable practices. While not opposing widow remarriage, in accordance with his glorification of celibacy he praised widows who were able to maintain it (Makanji 1967). Thus remarriage was always a last choice for those women who were unable to live up to the ideal. He categorized women by age and relaxed the norms of celibacy for those young girls who were widowed without the realization of conjugal life. With this attitude the disgust and the sense of shame and burden with which widows were regarded was replaced by a sense of piety and sanctity, while remarriage as a matter of choice for ameliorating widow's lives continued to loose its importance.

In the early nineteenth century the acceptance of widow remarriage was a question of caste practice posed by Borradaile when he examined the castes of Gujarat to establish customary laws. He saw this practice as distinguishing the Brahmins and Baniyas from the other 'lok' - people in general (Shodhan 1992).

With the establishment of Sanskritic and Brahminic ideals for all of Indian society in the nineteenth century through various means - legislation, reform and public discussions - numerous castes that did not follow prescriptions and proscriptions of Sanskrit shastras began to adopt them as models for 'good civilized' Hindu behaviour. Pathare Prabhus of Bombay, Kanbis of central Gujarat and others banned widow remarriage in an attempt to 'reform' social practice (Srinivas 1974). These early twentieth century changes show the ineffectiveness of nineteenth century reformers in the context of the lower castes.

In the later half of the twentieth century, Srinivas and other sociologists described this reform as 'upwardly mobile sanskritization'. Their evaluation of this trend of caste reform uses remarriage as a sign of demarcation between 'forward or upper' castes and 'backward or lower' castes. The Commission set up in Gujarat in 1974 under the chairmanship of A. R. Baxi for the identification of 'Other Backward Classes' considers the tradition of widow remarriage as an indicator of backwardness.[1] This use of remarriage as an indicator of social backwardness recognizes the stigmatized status of remarriage. However it also further reinforces the stigma against remarriage.

Present Situation of Widows

Widows of Gujarat in the Last Decade of the Twentieth Century

The widows, one of the largest socially neglected groups have failed to get political recognition. If one asks about the major changes during the last 100 years, one can generally say that widow remarriage (even though socially stigmatized) is still considered as a solution to the problem and the issue of sexuality is at the centre of the debate on widows. The problems of custody of children and the right to inherit the husband's property are as acute as in the last century. Largely speaking apathy towards widows has not been reduced nor have any supportive structure or infrastructure been developed to solve their problems. Their economic hardships are aggravated. The absence of public intervention or public policy has worsened the situation. The castes, which allowed widow remarriage in the last century, still allow it but the hold and influence of caste leaders has increased. The increase in their influence has not led to substantive changes in the lives of women, though they do make for small reforms, for example in the rituals to be followed at the time of birth, marriage or death.

Keeping in view the importance of this social problem a study[2], was conducted in Gujarat to champion the cause of widows. The study has revealed that an overwhelming majority of widows in rural areas are against remarriage; almost ali struggling for survival as they are poor, indebted and with no assets to fall back on, illiterate, unskilled; many of them are not supported by the family and Government. The study stressed the need for social security as widows face multiple marginalizations.

Widow Remarriage in Present Times

In present times, upper caste widows specially from rural areas don't remarry at all. The castes (as per their caste constitutions) which allow widow remarriage, are in two forms - either *diyarvatu* (levirate alliance - to marry younger brother-in-law) or *Naatru* or *Ghargharanu*. Some castes have changed their constitutions and stopped the practice of *diyarvatu*. The idea behind *diyarvatu* is to keep the widow within the same family. If she remains in the family, her share in property and her children will be retained. Also the widow being seen as a potential violator of the sexual and moral order will be taken care of as she remains in the family. The issue of reproduction and sexuality of a widow is then no more a threat to the family, as it is now under their control. Her labour or income or any contribution will lie with her husband or his family.

Remarriage is not as fruitful for the widow as it is to her in-laws. If she remarries within the family, she is an unwanted insider. The members of the family, specially the women, feel that the widow has gained more which she actually doesn't deserve. If she remains a widow, she can be asked to leave the family or she is treated as not a family responsibility any more. For a natal family, a widow or a remarried widow remains an outsider as she has left her natal home. Moreover, the stigmatized status of remarriage doesn't let her be a respected person.

Widows' Perception of the Problem and Solution

The trend observed is that most of the widows are not willing to remarry, but most of them are ready to support the widows who are willing to remarry. Almost all said that only a widow who is virgin or childless or young or destitute should remarry. It is generally said that 'samji jay te Naatru na kare' meaning 'those who are wise don't remarry'. This actually reflects the dilemma of widows about remarriage; lack of surety of having a successful remarriage. Women prefer independence and would like to avoid discriminatory, ill-treatment or dependence which are likely to follow remarriage.

Many castes, specially the scheduled castes, scheduled tribes and some lower castes have provisions (mentioned in their caste constitution) for inheritance of property. Traditionally, the distribution of the property has been done by the community leaders. The decision of the leaders is treated as final, it can be challenged or changed only in case of a serious dispute. Generally, women may not participate in such meetings and even if they do, they hardly have a say. This creates a disadvantageous situation for them.

Very few cases were observed during the survey where a widow has fought for her rights to get her due share in the family property. Not a single case was found where she has succeeded. If a widow gets a share after the death of her husband, it would be either partial or she will be harassed and pressurized to give up the share. It is also seen that even though a widow gets a small piece of land as a share in the property, she is not considered the owner and is only allowed to manage her property, specially cultivable land.

Vulnerable Groups

The younger the widow, the longer the widowhood and more severe the problems, is a simple equation to understand the problems of widows. The younger widow is more vulnerable to sexual harassment and faces more economic hardships. A widow with a child or children means the chances to remarry are rare and a choice she may not opt for.

Older widows face acute economic problems as their physical capacities to work and earn are reduced. If child(ren) do not take care of her, it further intensifies her social and psychological problems. There are charity institutions which provide shelter, economic assistance to widows, but these are not adequate in terms of the gravity of the situation and the requirement of widows to survive with dignity. For example, the *waqf* board for Muslims widows. Some Hindu temples spare a small amount for widows but many of the widows are reluctant to accept as it is not a dignified act to survive on such meagre help.

Shelter homes for widows and destitutes (mainly for elderly people and known as 'Old Age Peoples Home') are mainly located at urban places in Gujarat; with the idea that rural areas provide traditional' support to widows and hence rural widows do not face such problems! These centres have limited resources and capacity, to solve problems, as they have limitations in understanding their social, psychological needs. Also the traditional, religious belief about widows as inauspicious, always has forced widows to be out of sight of people. The same reason has played a role in people subconsciously negating the idea of actively supporting widows.

Problem of Social Security

In the nineteenth century, a widow's economic necessities were to be provided for by her family. Thus the stress was on re-marriage. From the 1870s there was a trend towards absorbing widowed literate women as teachers in girls' schools. This can be seen in Karve's centre in Poona. Later, some women saw economic independence and career as solving the problems of widowhood, as mentioned earlier.

In spite of this early beginning for widows' economic independence few modern organizations working towards the improvement of women's lives focus on this issue. Post-independence, the Government has taken some of the burden for social welfare, however even this is inadequate. The Government of Gujarat has a social security scheme for widows which is nothing but a piecemeal solution of a serious problem.

Widows have no priority in Government schemes nor on employment programmes. Very few institutes are established in Gujarat for destitute, old widows and these are in a pathetic situation, mainly because of lack of funds and failure to comprehend the multifaceted problems of widows (Bhagat - Ganguly 1994).

The Government of Gujarat has only one scheme to support destitute widows, deserted and divorced women; minimum for one year and maximum for three years provided a woman undertake the training for income generation. The total amount spent was Rs. 12,228,140 during the year 1994-95 for 7,323 single women under the category mentioned earlier.[3] This brings only 0.5 per cent single women as beneficiaries of the scheme for one year as their social security!

The scheme has been launched since 1979 and has undergone a few marginal changes regarding the amount offered to single women and its official procedures. But largely speaking, the insensitivity of Government has played a sad role in looking at the problem in totality, also in providing the type of support widows look for.

Conclusion

After Independence, the Indian Government took some measures to improve the social and economic status of women. In the last decade of the century, India adopted a new economic policy for further socio-economic development. Despite five decades of modernization,

urbanization and industrialization, our traditional outlook has not changed. The question of widows remains largely ignored in the absence of the social reform movement. Women's contribution for the betterment of widows' lives has remained a narrow stream which has not grown further.

Not all widows face these types of problems and ill treatment, except perhaps for a branding as ritually 'inauspicious'. Many older widows who live with their sons and their families enjoy their respect and love. A few older widows are supported by their daughters. The major changes observed in upper castes widows residing in big cities, are changes in dressing, food habits and their free mobility. However, the family and social responsibilities are as great as ever before.

The largest group of widows face the above mentioned problems and need support in the form of 'social security'. The need for social security is emphasized in the context that the deprivation of resourceless or poor people is generally passed on to the next generation. Indebtedness, none or little education, lack of family or community support, etc., makes it hard to create resources for a better life.

Notes

1. The commision set up in Gujarat for the identification of `Other Backward Classes' in 1974 and published its report in 1978. It is widely known as `Baxi commission' by the name of its chairperson.

2. The study was conducted in 1993 by Varsha of SETU : Centre for Social Knowledge & Action, Ahmedabad with the help of 4 voluntary organizations - Shramajivi Samaj, Bhiloda; Saurashtra Shramik Parishad, Junagadh; Ahmedabad Study Action Group - Antyodaya Yojana, Dholka and Vedchhi Pradesh Sewa Samiti, Valod.

3. A Summary prepared by Social Defence, Department of Social Welfare, Government of Gujarat, 1996, to answer the question raised in the State Legistative Assembly.

References

Dhruv, Gatulal. 'Pachhala Saath Varshma Vidhva-Vivahni Pragati'. Parekh Hiralal (ed.). *Lady Vidyaben Manimahotsav Abhinandan Granth,* Ahmedabad: Gujarat Vernacular Society, 1936.

Shah, Chunilal. 'Kautumbik Jivanma Vidhavanu Sthan'. Parekh Hiralal (ed.). *Lady Vidyaben Manimahotsav Abhinandan Granth,* Ahmedabad: Gujarat Vernacular Society, 1936.

Trivedi, Navalram. *Samaj-Sudharanu Rekhadarshan*, Ahmedabad: Gujarat Vidyasabha, 1974.

Nilkanth, Mahipatram. *Durgaram Charitra,* 1. Ahmedabad: Ahmedabad United Printing and General Co., 1879.

Bulger, Drimitrius. (trans), Nanavati Hiralal. *Lord William Bentinck,* Mumbai: 1895.

Parekh, Hiralal. *Gujarat Vernacular Societyno Itihas.* 2, Ahmedabad: 1933.

Dave, Harikrishna. *Vidhavavapannishedh Lakhanarne Javab.* Ahmedabad: 1892.

Narmadashankar, Lalshankar. *Narm Kavita.* Gujarati Press Series, Mumbai: 1888.

Dalpatram. *Dalpatkrut Kavya.* Ahmedabad, 1905.

Narayan, Hemchandra. *Vidhvano Vakil*, Ahmedabad: 1882.

____. *Punarvivah Shastra Sammat Chhe.* Mumbai: Nirnay Sagar Press, 1886.

Trivedi, Vaidya Jatashankar. *Vidhava-Vivah Vishe Vichar*, Ahmedabad: Gujarat Arya Aushadhshala (n.d.).

Kekhushro, Hormasji. *Punar-Vivah Prabandh,* 1855.

Chaudhari, Maitrayee. 'Nineteenth Century, Social Reform Movement and the Women's Question'. *Women's Link.* New Delhi, 1994.

Dongre Rajas Krishnarao and Patterson J.F. *Pandita Ramabai.* Madras: The Christian Literature Society, 1963.

Rosalind O'Hanlon. *A Comparison Between Women and Men,* Oxford University Press: 1994.

Sengupta, Padmini. *Pandita Ramabai Saraswati: Her Life and Work.* Asia Publishing House, 1970.

Desai, Tanubhai Devidas. 'Gujaratio ane Hindu Kaydama Teoni Vishishtatao'. *Journal of Gujarat Research Society* 4, (1939): 197-199.

Shodhan, Amrita. 'Rakhmabai : A Woman's Voice in the Age of Consent Controversy'. *Stri Jivanvishayaka Sthityantar: Mumbai Parisar (1876-1950),* Bombay: SNDT University, 1992.

Government of India, 'Papers Relating to Infant Marriage and Enforced Widowhood in India'. Selections From the Records Series No 3. Calcutta: Government of India, 1886.

Kosambi, Meera. 'Girl Brides and Socio-Legal Change: Age of Consent Bill (1891) Controversy'. *Economic and Political Weekly* 26, 31 and 32. (1991): 1857-1863.

Bhagat-Ganguly, Varsha. *Vihoni:Gramin Gujaratni Vidhvao*. Ahmedabad: Setu, 1994.

Makanji, Lallubhai. *Gandhiji–Strioane Strijivanani Samasyao*, Ahmedabad: Navjivan Prakashan Mandir, 1967.

Mahipatram, Rupram. *Durgaramnun Charitra*. Ahmedabad: Ahmedabad United Printing and General Co., 1879.

Vaishya, Balabhai. *Shu Punarlagna Sashastra Chhe?*, Ahmedabad: 1897.

Carroll, Lucy. 'Law, Custom, and Statutory Social Reform: the Hindu Widows' Remarriage Act of 1856'. J. Krishnamurty (ed). *Women in Colonial India: Essays on Survival, Work and the State*. Delhi: Oxford University Press, 1989.

Vaide, Mohini. *Dr. Rukhmabai: Ek Arta* [In Marathi]. Mumbai. Popular Prakashan, 1982.

Malabari, Behramji Merwanji. *Gujarat and the Gujaratis: Pictures of Men and Manners taken from the Life*, 3rd ed Bombay: Fort Printing Press, 1889.

Shinde, Tarabai. 'Stree Purusha Tulana in 1882'. Rosaline O'Hanlon, *Stree Purusha Tulana*, Oxford University Press, 1994.

Narmadshankar, Lalshankar. *Mari Hakikat Ane Anya Atmakathaniya Lakhano*. Dhirubhai Thakar (ed.). Ahmedabad: Gurjar Grantharatna Karyalaya, 1983.

Steele, Arthur. *The Hindu Castes: Their Law, Religion and Customs* Delhi: K.M. Mittal, 1986.

Rast Goftar, (20th August 1854): 268. [translation from the Bombay Telegraph].

Rast Goftar, (20 January 1856): 23.

Gujarat Vernacular Societyno Itihas. Ahmedabad: Gujarat Vidyasabha, 18-25.

Notes on Contributors

Makrand Mehta

Makrand Mehta is Emeritus Professor of History, Gujarat University, Visiting Professor, University of Sunderland, U. K. and former president, Indian History Congress — Modern India Section. He has published *The Ahmedabad Cotton Textile Industry: Genesis and Growth* (1982), *Indian Merchants and Entrepreneurs in Historical Perspective 17th to 19th Centuries* (1991), and edited *Regional Roots of Indian Nationalism* (1990), and co-authored *Business Houses in Western India : A Study in Entrepreneurial Response,* 1850-1956 (1990).

Achyut Yagnik

Achyut Yagnik, journalist and human rights activist, is honorary secretary of SETU: Centre for Social Knowledge and Action (Ahmedabad), a social organisation working among vulnerable communities in Western India. He was the Gujarat coordinator of the Lokayan Project of the Centre for the Study of Developing Societies and General Secretary of the People's Union for Civil Liberties in the State. He was consultant and Fellow of the United Nations University, Tokyo (1986-87) and the Founder Editor of the Gujarati research journal *Arhat* of the Centre for Social Studies. He is the Gujarat correspondent of the *Economic and Political Weekly,* he has published extensively in Gujarati and English and has co-authored with Ashis Nandy, *Creating a Nationality: Ramjanmabhoomi and Fear of the Self* (OUP, Delhi, 1995).

N. R. Sheth

N. R. Sheth has an M. A. and a Ph.D. from M. S. University, Baroda. He taught at the Universities of Baroda, Manchester and Delhi; He was Assistant Director, Shri Ram Centre, New Delhi; Professor, Indian Institute of Management, Ahmedabad; Hon. Senior Fellow, Gujarat Institute of Development Research. He has research interest and publications in industrial relations, trade unions, human values and related sociological themes.

Takashi Shinoda

Takashi Shinoda, Ph.D. (Kanagawa University), is Professor of Economics at Daito Bunka University, Japan. The major areas of his interest are institutional change and caste mobility; entrepreneurial development among the weaker sections; slum development programmes and slum dwellers' organizations; livestock development and environment; and issues on water users' associations. He has conducted field surveys on the above themes in India (particularly Gujarat), Nepal and Pakistan. He is the author of *A Study on the Status of Sweepers in India* (in Japanese; Shunjusha (1995), and has edited *Entrepreneurial Development in Developing Countries* (in Japanese; Miraisya, 1997) and has co-edited *A Comparative Study on Irrigation Systems in Asia* (in Japanese; Shinhyoron, 1996).

Ghanshyam Shah

Ghanshyam Shah is Professor at JNU, New Delhi. He was Director of Centre For Social Studies, Surat. He has published twelve books, including: *Politics of Scheduled Castes and Scheduled Tribes* (1974), *Caste Association and Political Process in Gujarat* (1975), *Economic Differentiations and Tribal Identity* (1984), *Public Health and Urban Development* (1998) and *Social Movements* (1990).

Sudarshan Iyengar

Sudarshan Iyengar, Ph.D. (MSU, Baroda), is Professor at the Gujarat Institute of Development Research, Ahmedabad. He has worked with an NGO, ARCH-Vahini, in Gujarat during 1989-94 and was involved in planning and implementing resettlement and rehabilitation of families displaced by the Sardar Sarovar Project on the Narmada river. His main areas of interest include rural development and natural resource management.

Anil Gumber

Anil Gumber is a Senior Research Fellow at the Centre for Health Services Studies, Warwick, UK. He was awarded Ph.D. from Gujarat University, Ahmedabad and Post-Doctoral Takemi Fellowship from Harvard School of Public Health, Boston. Dr. Gumber's research papers have focused on issues relating to human development including migration, resettlement, poverty, employment, education, health and nutrition. He is the author of *Displaced by Development: Oustees of an Irrigation Project* (Spellbound Publications, Rohtak) and co-author of *Inter-Village Differences in Social Overheads and Their Correlates in Matar Taluka* (ICSSR, New Delhi).

Sujata Patel

Sujata Patel is a historical sociologist who has done research on issues such as class and class conflict; caste, reservation and communalism; gender and history and social movements and collective violence in contemporary India. She is the author of *The Making of Industrial Relations: Class and Class Conflict in Ahmedabad Textile Industry* (OUP, Delhi) and has co-edited two books, *Bombay: Metaphor for Modern India and Bombay: Mosaic of Modern India.* (OUP, Bombay and Delhi). She is presently affiliated to the Department of Sociology, University of Pune as Professor and Head. She is in the editorial advisory committee of Current Sociology and Contemporary Sociology.

Junko Kiso

Junko Kiso is currently an Associate Professor of Economics at the Kumamoto Gakuen University, Japan. Prior to joining the University in 1991, she worked at the Embassy of Japan in Dhaka as a special analyst of Bangladesh Economy. Thereafter, she often visited India and Bangladesh to undertake field survey on the related issues. Her major interests include Economic Development, Labour Problems and Gender Issues in South Asia. She has published a number of research papers, among them being: 'Organisation of Workers and Changes in Their Condition' in Nishiguchi, A. and T. Hamaguchi (eds.), *Indian Economy: Devaluation and Transformation,* Sekaishisosha, 1986, 'Rural Non-Farm Economy in Asia: Realities and Prospects in Bangladesh' in Honda, K. and Y. Ogawa (eds.), *Economic Structures in Contemporary Asia,* Sekaishisosha, 1994, 'Feminisation of Labour in India: Changes and Reality of Working Women' in F. Oshikawa (ed.), *Social Transformation and Women in South Asia, Institute of Developing Economies,* 1997.

Mario Rutten

Mario Rutten studied sociology at Erasmus University in Rotterdam. He obtained his Ph.D. in 1991 at the University of Amsterdam with a study on the economic behaviour and lifestyle of rural entrepreneurs in West India, published as *Farms and Factories; Social Profile of Large Farmers and Rural Industrialists in West India* (1995). Since 1991 he has been Research Manager of the Centre for Asian Studies, Amsterdam (CASA) of the Amsterdam School for Social Science Research, University of Amsterdam. He obtained a post doctoral fellowship from the Royal Netherlands Academy of Arts and Sciences to undertake a comparative study on the class of rural capitalists in South and Southeast Asia, based on fieldwork conducted in central Gujarat (India), central Java (Indonesia) and Kedah state (Malaysia). Mario Rutten is co-editor of *Economic Growth and Social Welfare; Managing Development in New Order Indonesia* (1993) and author of *Asian Capitalists in the European Mirror* (1994).

Tsuguo Nakasato

Tsuguo Nakasato is Professor of Geography at Fukuoka University of Education, Japan. He obtained his Ph. D (Literature) at Hiroshima University with a study entitled 'A Geographical Study on the Economic Diversification in India Villages: On the Basis of the Agricultural Development from the Green Revolution to the White Revolution' (unpublished Ph.D. thesis in Japanese). His areas of interest include rural developement and economic diversification; women's participation in cooperative movements; and various issues on livestock sector such as white revolution, goat development, and slaughter problems. He has published many papers and reports on these issues based on his intensive field survey in Japan, India and Indonesia.

Amita Shah

Amita Shah, Ph.D. (Gujarat University), is an economist with the Gujarat Institute of Development Research, Ahmedabad. She has undertaken research on rural and small-scale industries, agricultural development and environment with special references to dryland regions. Her areas of interest include development of micro-enterprises and employment in rural economies and she has worked closely with several government, non-government and international agencies in the field of rural development.

Indira Hirway

Indira Hirway is Director and Professor of Economics at the Centre For Development Alternatives, Ahmedabad, India. She has done her Masters in Economics and also her Ph.D. in Economics. The major areas of her specialization are labour, employment and labour market analysis; poverty and human development; environment and development; gender and development and development alternatives. She has written several books and published articles in these areas. She has also chaired and worked in several committees and task forces set up by national and state governments in India.

Darshini Mahadevia

Darshini Mahadevia is a faculty member at School of Planning, Centre for Environment Planning and Technology, Ahmedabad. After obtaining a Ph.D. from Jawaharlal Nehru University, New Delhi, she is teaching housing and environment courses and guiding a number of students for their Masters dissertation at the Centre. She is engaged in research relating to housing and urban development, environment, gender studies and human development. She has contributed a number of research and popular articles in these areas. She works actively and in close collaboration with local non-government organisations on development issues of immediate concern.

Jeemol Unni

Jeemol Unni, Associate Professor at the Gujarat Institute of Development Research, Ahmedabad, did her M. Phil in Applied Economics at the Centre for Development Studies, Trivandrum and her Doctorate at the Sardar Patel Institute of Economics and Social Research, Ahmedabad, India. She was a Visiting Fellow at the Economic Growth Center, Yale University, USA and a Senior Research Fellow at the Institute of Social Studies, The Hague, The Netherlands. She has worked as a Consultant to the World Bank, International Labour Organisation, International Development Research Center, Canada and to the NABARD and SIDBT. Her research interests are on the themes of informal sector, rural labour markets, non-farm employment, national income and social sectors, particularly education and social security. She has published three books and many articles in reputed journals. She has been a member of many National and International Expert Groups on the Informal Sector. She has been actively involved with addressing issues related to women in the informal sector in close association with the Self Employed Women's Association (SEWA), Ahmedabad.

Varsha Bhagat Ganguly

Varsha Bhagat Ganguly is associated with SETU: Centre for Social Knowledge and Action, Ahmedabad, a non-government agency supporting backward and marginalised communities in their struggles and social justice. While actively participating in all activities of SETU, her work focuses on women's issues in Gujarat — the situation of Bhangi (untouchable) women, domestic violence, status of widows, women's access to natural resources, etc. She has a number of publications on these issues. She is currently working on a source book on Women in 19th Century Gujarat; and also studying the effects of displacement caused by large development projects and problems of rehabilitated people in Gujarat.

Amrita Shodhan

Amrita Shodhan is a freelance researcher, concerned with women's studies and contemporary women's issue. She obtained Ph.D. in South Asian Studies from the University of Chicago on the subject of colonial legal transformation of religious collectives. Her published papers include 'Rakhmabai: A Woman Centered Perspective' in *Stree Jivan Vishayak Sthityantar: Mumbai Parisar*, Mumbai: SNDT University, 1992; *'Framing the idea of community'*, *Social Action*, Delhi: ISI, 1994; 'Women in Maharaj Libel Case', *Journal of Gender Studies*, June-Dec. 1997.